Artful Experiments

Edinburgh Critical Studies in Victorian Culture
Series Editor: Julian Wolfreys

For a complete list of titles published visit the Edinburgh Critical Studies in Victorian Culture web page at www.edinburghuniversitypress.com/series/ECVC

Also Available:
Victoriographies – A Journal of Nineteenth-Century Writing, 1790–1914, edited by Diane Piccitto and Patricia Pulham
ISSN: 2044-2416
www.eupjournals.com/vic

Artful Experiments

Ways of Knowing in Victorian Literature and Science

Philipp Erchinger

EDINBURGH
University Press

Edinburgh University Press is one of the leading university presses in the UK. We publish academic books and journals in our selected subject areas across the humanities and social sciences, combining cutting-edge scholarship with high editorial and production values to produce academic works of lasting importance. For more information visit our website: edinburghuniversitypress.com

Edinburgh University Press Ltd
The Tun – Holyrood Road,
12(2f) Jackson's Entry,
Edinburgh EH8 8PJ

Typeset in 11/13 Adobe Sabon by
IDSUK (DataConnection) Ltd, and
printed and bound in Great Britain.

A CIP record for this book is available from the British Library

ISBN 978 1 4744 3895 7 (hardback)
ISBN 978 1 4744 3897 1 (webready PDF)
ISBN 978 1 4744 3898 8 (epub)

Contents

Series Editor's Preface

'Victorian' is a term, at once indicative of a strongly determined concept and an often notoriously vague notion, emptied of all meaningful content by the many journalistic misconceptions that persist about the inhabitants and cultures of the British Isles and Victoria's Empire in the nineteenth century. As such, it has become a by-word for the assumption of various, often contradictory habits of thought, belief, behaviour and perceptions. Victorian studies and studies in nineteenth-century literature and culture have, from their institutional inception, questioned narrowness of presumption, pushed at the limits of the nominal definition, and have sought to question the very grounds on which the unreflective perception of the so-called Victorian has been built; and so they continue to do. Victorian and nineteenth-century studies of literature and culture maintain a breadth and diversity of interest, of focus and inquiry, in an interrogative and intellectually open-minded and challenging manner, which are equal to the exploration and inquisitiveness of its subjects. Many of the questions asked by scholars and researchers of the innumerable productions of nineteenth-century society actively put into suspension the clichés and stereotypes of 'Victorianism', whether the approach has been sustained by historical, scientific, philosophical, empirical, ideological or theoretical concerns; indeed, it would be incorrect to assume that each of these approaches to the idea of the Victorian has been, or has remained, in the main exclusive, sealed off from the interests and engagements of other approaches. A vital interdisciplinarity has been pursued and embraced, for the most part, even as there has been contest and debate amongst Victorianists, pursued with as much fervour as the affirmative exploration between different disciplines and differing epistemologies put to work in the service of reading the nineteenth century.

Edinburgh Critical Studies in Victorian Culture aims to take up both the debates and the inventive approaches and departures from convention that studies in the nineteenth century have witnessed for the last half century at least. Aiming to maintain a 'Victorian' (in the most positive sense of that motif) spirit of inquiry, the series' purpose is to continue and augment the cross-fertilisation of interdisciplinary approaches, and to offer, in addition, a number of timely and untimely revisions of Victorian literature, culture, history and identity. At the same time, the series will ask questions concerning what has been missed or improperly received, misread, or not read at all, in order to present a multi-faceted and heterogeneous kaleidoscope of representations. Drawing on the most provocative, thoughtful and original research, the series will seek to prod at the notion of the 'Victorian', and in so doing, principally through theoretically and epistemologically sophisticated close readings of the historicity of literature and culture in the nineteenth century, to offer the reader provocative insights into a world that is at once overly familiar, and irreducibly different, other and strange. Working from original sources, primary documents and recent interdisciplinary theoretical models, Edinburgh Critical Studies in Victorian Culture seeks not simply to push at the boundaries of research in the nineteenth century, but also to inaugurate the persistent erasure and provisional, strategic redrawing of those borders.

Julian Wolfreys

Acknowledgements

I wish to thank the German Research Foundation (DFG) for the financial support that this project received at various stages during its long gestation. Most of the work was conducted with the help of a research fellowship (ER 644/1–1) that enabled me to spend more than two years at the University of Exeter's Centre for Victorian Studies. I am especially grateful to the following colleagues, friends and interlocutors for their warm hospitality and support during this formative time: Will Abberley, Andy Brown, Sally Flint, Regenia Gagnier, Jason Hall, Vike Plock, John Plunkett, Jude Piesse, Angelique Richardson, Corinna Wagner, Paul Williams, Peggy Yoon and Paul Young. Moreover, I would like to acknowledge the DFG graduate school Cultural Hermeneutics at the University of Erlangen-Nürnberg, by which I was employed as a postdoctoral fellow before I went to Exeter, its follow-up institution Presence and Tacit Knowledge, to which I was briefly affiliated after my return, and, finally, the Erlangen Centre for Literature and Natural Science. At all three associations, I have been inspired by many kind and generous companions, but I am particularly indebted to Doris Feldmann, who has provided helpful criticisms of an earlier version of this book. Ingo Berensmeyer, Dirk Kretzschmar, Roger Lüdeke and Anne-Julia Zwierlein have also kindly read and commented on the first draft, offering invaluable suggestions. During the final phases of writing and editing this book, my colleagues at the University of Düsseldorf, notably Michael C. Frank, Sonja Frenzel, Thomas Gurke, Alex Zimbulov and the members of colloquia and reading groups (especially the media and cultural studies circle), have been as much a source of motivation and joy as the students with whom I had the pleasure to learn. While I was preparing the book for publication, I benefited from observations and commentaries by Noah Heringman, Nicola Wood and two anonymous readers at Edinburgh University Press. Ersev Ersoy, Michelle Houston and Julian Wolfreys, finally, have been very kind and supportive editors.

I first began to explore issues of this book in two independent articles, in which small fragments of primary material from Chapters 1, 3 and 7 have already been used, though in different ways and to different ends. These are: '"Moving Things into Certain Places": Nature, Culture and Art as Practice in Victorian Writing', *Literature Compass* 9.11 (2012), 786–800, and 'Transport, Wayfaring and Ways of Knowing in Victorian Writing', *REAL: Yearbook of Research in English and American Literature* 28 (2012), 285–311. Moreover, a small portion of Chapter 3 has, in a preliminary version, appeared in 'Mobility, Movement, Method and Life in G. H. Lewes', in Ingo Berensmeyer and Christoph Ehland (eds), *Perspectives on Mobility*, Amsterdam: Rodopi, 2013, 151–75. Earlier drafts of parts from Chapters 1, 7 and 8 have been published as 'Art as Process and Skill: On the Work of Literature in Wilkie Collins and Robert Browning', in Andrea von Hülsen-Esch (ed.), *Materie – Material – Materialität: Disziplinäre Annäherungen*, Düsseldorf: dup, 2016, 59–77.

Introduction: Experiment and the Art of Writing

Experience, as we know, has ways of *boiling over*, and making us correct our present formulas.[1]

Empiricism is conceived of as tied up to what has been, or is, 'given'. But experience in its vital form is experimental, an effort to change the given.[2]

This is not a book about Victorian knowledge, but about the activities through which knowledge is brought into being, sustained, debated, modified, adapted, corrected, used, reimagined, extended and made subject to continuous transformation and change. In fact, all that follows is premised on the assumption that there is no knowledge without (or outside of) practices and processes that assemble and disassemble it, or that put it to work, thus exposing it to the possibility of becoming otherwise. '[I]f there is a sun around which all else revolves, it is performance, not knowledge,' as Andrew Pickering puts it, 'knowledge is a planet or maybe a comet that sometimes participates in the dynamics of practice and sometimes does not'.[3] Building on this assumption, my title promises a work about *ways* of knowing,[4] about pursuits of what is not yet (not quite) or no longer known, rather than about the ideas and theories in which such pursuits may be taken to originate or terminate. In short, this book is concerned with what takes place in the midst of ongoing knowledge formation, on the way towards goals and insights that are yet to be (more precisely) defined. It examines what I call the experimental field, the scene of emergent meaning, in which people's experiences of the material world come to be gradually translated, by means of actions, instruments, controversies and skills, into forms of generally readable, but not necessarily finished text.

Being a literary scholar, I will specifically explore how these 'processes of finding out and making sense' are debated and carried out in writing,[5] by means of literature in the most general sense of 'everything written with letters or printed in a book', as Matthew Arnold has it.[6] Yet, much of the methodical approach that informs my readings has been suggested by historical and sociological studies of 'science in action'.[7] What all of these studies have in common is that they do not view science merely as a body of established ('objective') knowledge, or as a self-contained system of abstract models and theories. Rather, scientific knowledge is taken to be inseparable from the interplay of 'human and material agency' through which it is constructed and extended in practice.[8] Concomitantly, knowing, on this practice-based view, is seen as a way of attending to, and learning from, a field of sentience and activity, in the composing and recomposing of which scientific observers participate alongside various sources of movement and action. These may include other humans as well as animals, plants, minerals, technical devices, machines, institutional regulations, social conventions and the forces and energies of physical nature. Indeed, one reason why historians and sociologists have increasingly turned their attention to the study of 'experience in the making' is that they took it to constitute the site in which the human and the non-human, the cultural and the natural as well as the material and the ideal components of science can be seen to intersect with, and become translated into each other.[9] Surely, if the 'central paradox of science' is that it is both a product of human culture, a man-made construct, *and* a supposedly true account of (non-human) nature, then the 'dirty' work of practical research must be the medium in which these 'two sides' are brought together and made to correspond.[10] As Bruno Latour, David Gooding, Hans-Jörg Rheinberger and others have abundantly shown, scientific facts are not either fabricated or true to what is real. They are both at the same time, at least as long as they are (accepted as) well made, that is: as long as they (are taken to) agree with acknowledged standards defining what is exact, useful and right. In practice, the artificial (cultural) and the natural, or the constructed and the real have never been divided in the first place. This, among other things, is what scholars discovered when they began to follow the convoluted pathways by which scientific facts come into existence. 'Facts were facts – meaning exact – *because* they were fabricated – meaning that they emerged out of artificial situations.'[11]

Knowledgeable Practice

Broadly speaking, what the study of scientific practice and 'laboratory life' has brought out is that true justified knowledge is the mostly provisional result of artful, often messy, laborious, multifarious, ineffective and time-consuming work that has a logic and structure worthy of being examined in its own right.[12] Therefore, one aim of historical enquiries into workshops, laboratories and building sites was to reconcile the social discourses of science with the material activities, the dexterous practices that are instrumental to the production, reconfiguration and application of knowledge but tend to be largely cleared out of its official representation. More precisely, practice-based studies of knowing, such as David Gooding's meticulous examinations of Michael Faraday's experimental techniques, tried to close the gap between the texts representing science to the public eye and the material processes through which they come to be written and rewritten.[13] In this way, such studies made apparent that the activities of bringing knowledge to matter cannot entirely be contained in the terms and figures to which they give rise or on which they are based. They showed that processes of meaning-making are much more encompassing than what is known as their products and premises. In short, these investigations made evident that the 'making' continuously overtakes and outgrows the made, being 'always bigger' than it.[14]

One key insight to be derived from what has been called 'the practice turn in contemporary theory', then, is that activities of knowing tend to be ahead and in excess of the ideas and theories by which they are supposed to be directed or grasped.[15] Actions, on this view, can express an intelligence that exists only by virtue of being enacted, not (yet) having the abstract form of a theory. It is this type of practical knowledge that the Victorian anthropologist Edward Tylor had in mind when he described the earliest ancestors of mankind as incipient scientists. 'In a rude way,' Tylor said about primitive man,

> he is a physicist in making fire, a chemist in cooking, a surgeon in binding up wounds, a geographer in knowing his rivers and mountains, a mathematician in counting on his fingers. All this is knowledge, and it was on these foundations that science proper began to be built up, when the art of writing had come in and society had entered on the civilized stage.[16]

In practice, Tylor's statement suggests, one can have knowledge without being aware of it, or rather, without possessing theoretical terms for it. More than eighty years later, the general premise of this claim has been made explicit in Michael Polanyi's now famous argument 'that *we can know more than we can tell*'.[17] It would, however, be more precise to say that we can know more than we can articulate in propositional terms because the central characteristic of the excess of knowledge that inheres in practical action is not that it is necessarily silent. It can show itself, for instance, through the action of telling stories.[18] While stories are obviously modes of saying something, they do not specifically explicate their meanings, remaining sufficiently open to be adapted to different circumstances, and to be varied and reinterpreted in multiple ways. The point, therefore, about practical or 'personal knowledge' (as Polanyi called it) is not that it is tacit,[19] but that it is malleable and adaptable, always capable of becoming different, rather than arrested in determinate theories, images and ideas.[20] To use the terminology that I will introduce in the first chapter: practical knowledge is typically expressed through the *arts*, such as storytelling, scribbling, drawing,[21] building, mending, which, as Tylor's statement suggests, are part of all 'proper' *sciences*.

In the nineteenth century, as Tylor's sentences indicate too, the 'faculty of saying or writing anything well', as John Ruskin called it, was one such 'art' or way of knowing among others.[22] Much Victorian writing does not just represent facts, ideas or stories that have been assembled without, and can therefore just as well be abstracted from, it. Rather, Victorian practices of writing actively contributed to the production of the subject-matters that they sought to depict or understand. This applies not only to what is usually called 'creative writing', such as poetry or fiction, but also to works of philosophy and science. When scientists discovered or engendered yet unfamiliar phenomena, they simultaneously had to find ways of extracting conceptual terms from them. The use of verbal language was just as central to this endeavour as other material practices, including drawing, mapping, model-making and later photography. 'Writing up is part of the discovery process', rather than a secondary operation that started only when the results had already been fixed.[23] Often researchers could not even begin to explore the significance of their observations until they had found ways and means of transforming them into readable texts through which they could be circulated, debated, adopted and rewritten. As Latour puts it: 'Scientists start seeing something once they stop looking at nature and look exclusively and obsessively at prints and flat inscriptions.'[24] For example, when in 1820 the Danish chemist Hans Christian Oersted accidentally noticed that the forces of magnetism and electricity seemed to influence each other, no one could yet construe the meaning of this observation, even though many immediately sensed its importance.[25] In England, Michael Faraday was one of those who did most to draw out the wider implications of the new discovery in symbolic terms. Among other things, 'he adapted the existing discourse of "lines" and "curves"' to this end, 'developing it into a powerful visual language for his electromagnetic theory'.[26]

Experimental Writing

Likewise, in the field of nineteenth-century geology, as Noah Heringman, Ralph O'Connor and Adelene Buckland have shown, writing was a 'scientific practice' by itself, a way of knowing without which the new discipline could never have become what it now is.[27] Deeply 'embroiled in literary debate, geology was *written* into existence in the nineteenth century as much as it was found, discovered, collected, mapped, or modeled'.[28] While the writing of geology grew out of 'a confluence of disparate genres', including poetry, drama, pageants, and prose fiction, it had special affinities to the narrative forms of epic and romance.[29] Both of them seemed particularly well suited to tell the vast and spectacular history of an earth that had existed millions of years longer than the human race, and that once used to be inhabited by wondrous creatures resembling the dragons of romantic fantasy and ancient mythology. To be sure, the use of narrative and fiction, as much as it 'helped geology to win cultural authority',[30] was also frequently attacked for being speculative and deceptive. Yet, geologists such as Charles Lyell were more than willing to respond to these critiques, as Buckland has argued, because, far from being 'mere' popularisers, they were deeply concerned with the search for literary forms that are true to the form of the earth and its history.[31] Literature, in the sense of writing, was part of their scientific work because much of their scientific work was carried out through writing. 'Geologists were keen to experiment with the ways in which different forms of writing could help them see the "truth" better, and to delimit those kinds of writing [. . .] that they felt encouraged excessive speculation.'[32]

Drawing on the work of Robert Mitchell and Michael Gamper, this book proceeds from the supposition that such references to writing as a mode of experimentation, of which there are many, are by no means just metaphorical.[33] For while writing is frequently referred to as a way of performing experiments, experiments have also been described as activities of writing. According to Rheinberger, for example, experiments are designed to make scientific objects 'traceable' in the form of inscriptions or signs to be read.[34] By virtue of the experimental configuration, that which is to be known, the 'epistemic thing',[35] is transformed into a matter of signification, an entity of potential significance that can then be viewed and manipulated as part of an assemblage of 'graphemes', as he calls them. 'The arrangement of these graphemes composes the experimental writing.'[36] Thus viewed, scientific experiments, far from being no more than standardised devices for the testing of preconceived hypotheses, are 'machines for making the future', or initiators of surprising events.[37] They are ways of opening up 'spaces of representation' in which novel experiences, or experiences of novelty, can be both provoked and marked as traces of meaning, capable of being followed along an emergent trail.[38] In other words, experiments do not just execute predefined hypotheses or give answers to questions that are already known. They rather operate as 'vehicles' through which indefinite problems are made to take the form of 'material signs', the pursuit of which may lead to (provisional) solutions at some point.[39] To be sure, isolated, local experiments may serve to confirm or refute hypothetical assumptions. However, according to Rheinberger, such single experiments tend to be regarded as successful only if they turn out to be productive within a larger 'system' of research, the 'driving force' of which is 'the generation of the unknown'.[40] One might therefore say that experiments, as part of 'experimental systems', recreate questions as traces of answers that are yet to be found.[41] They enable the making of new or future knowledge without fully anticipating or controlling it, because the 'signifiers' produced through experimental configurations, like all others, can be inserted into multiple contexts and therefore read and reproduced in more than one way.[42] As Jacques Derrida put it: 'To write is to produce a mark that will constitute a kind of machine that is in turn productive, that my future disappearance in principle will not prevent from functioning and from yielding, and yielding itself to, reading and rewriting.'[43]

If experiments are, in a general sense, practices of writing, then it should be justifiable to call practices of writing experiments too. As nineteenth-century writers such as T. H. Huxley and Claude Bernard have already suggested, what the terms 'writing' and 'experimenting' certainly have in common is that they refer to ways of translating modes of personal experience into forms of generally readable text. They designate ways of knowing that mediate between the subjective and the objective, between inside and outside or between the modes of the first person and that of the third person. There is no doubting that all comparisons of writing and experimenting are premised on a very general understanding of both of these terms. But if one defines 'writing' broadly as a process of producing marks or traces and 'experimenting' as a way of provoking observations,[44] then one can see these activities are mutually included in each other: by inscribing traces, one provokes observations and by provoking observations one inscribes traces. This view explains not only why comparisons between writing and experimenting intuitively seem to make sense; more importantly, it allows for a process-based approach to the exploration of Victorian literature and science that does not take the arts of writing and experimenting to belong, by definition, to separate discourses or social domains.

Thus, rather than placing 'writing' and 'experiment' in different epistemological containers labelled 'literature' and 'science' respectively, this study seeks to reintegrate them into a single, though internally multifarious, site of artful practices. As I hope to show, in this 'plenum' of activities,[45] multiple works of making 'literature' and 'science' can be seen to develop together with, rather than being opposed to, each other. In the following chapters, I have therefore consistently avoided speaking of 'literature' and 'science' as if these terms designated macro-level discourses that, by definition, precede the micro-level practices of composition and recomposition through which they are, in multiple instances, brought into existence, maintained, debated, made to evolve and transformed. Instead, I have chosen to proceed by a performative approach that follows the ways of writing, many of them highly controversial, through which 'science' and 'literature' take form as various types of text. This approach is, of course, not meant to abandon any sense of a difference between the public documents by which people have come to recognise 'literature' and 'science' as works of discrete kinds. There is no doubt, for example, that the self-proclaimed experiments George Eliot and Wilkie Collins conducted at their desks gave rise to fictional forms of invention that are quite unlike the non-fictional texts produced by the experiments people like Michael Faraday performed in their laboratories. But if one takes account of the artful activities through which these works *become* different in the Victorian period, then one will be able to learn that writing and creative imagination are often just as integral to the experiments that constitute science as experimentation and rational calculation are integral to the writing that constitutes (fictional) literature.

In what follows, I shall therefore examine all texts not only as seemingly finished products, as containers of stories or arguments, but also as acts of writing in the process of taking shape. One goal of this method is to elucidate the collective making of 'science', the very category of which was, throughout the nineteenth century, still deeply immersed in processes of self-demarcation and self-justification. As a result, the composition of science repeatedly became entangled with what it was supposed not to be, such as the writing of poetry or literary fiction. Perhaps the most famous case in point is the first edition of Charles Darwin's *On the Origin of Species* (1859) in which the theory of evolution by natural selection is illustrated with the help of so many surmises and imaginary scenarios that the first reviewers of the book regularly questioned its claim to represent science. For example, Darwin describes it as 'conceivable that flying-fish, which now glide far through the air, slightly rising and turning by the aid of their fluttering fins, might have been modified into perfectly winged animals'.[46] Likewise, he declares it to be 'possible that the membrane-connected fingers and fore-arm of the Galeopithecus', a peculiar kind of lemur, 'might be greatly lengthened by natural selection' in a way that 'would convert it into a bat'.[47] And even 'so extreme a case' as the gradual transformation of a 'race of bears' into a creature 'as monstrous as a whale' is presented as a possible development.[48] This technique of seeing one type of animal as another is so obviously metaphorical that many early critics of *The Origin* considered Darwin's '*may be* philosophy' or 'argument from metaphor'[49] to be more suggestive of poetry than of science.[50] 'With such a range and plasticity as Mr Darwin pleads for we know not where to stop,' one reviewer writes, 'centaurs, dryads, and hamadryads, and all those remarkable forms we enjoyed so much as schoolboys to read about, but were taught to look upon as mere poetic fancy, may have been really our old progenitors in a transition state to improvement.'[51] To be sure, such critiques were highly exaggerated, ideologically skewed polemics using rhetorical ploys that had been commonplace for a long time. But at the same time, they were sufficiently pointed to incite Darwin to revise parts of his text in response to them, and to cut out some of the most 'poetic' passages, such as the one about the bear and the whale, in subsequent editions. What this example shows, then, is not only that writing was part and parcel of, rather than extraneous to science, but also that the practices of making science readable were subject to continual debate.[52] More precisely, the controversies swirling around the publication of *The Origin of Species* indicate that it was not so much the idea of science that was at stake as the activity of bodying it forth, of transforming it into text. In short, these debates draw attention to the practice of making forms of literature that are justifiable as science. In this way, they are apt to make evident that science was a highly volatile notion, a concept in formation that had to be continuously defined and redefined in relation to what it was supposed not to be.[53]

Like science, nineteenth-century literature, too, could not be placed without, but was immersed within, the activities of writing through which it was continuously recreated in all manner of varieties and shapes. As we shall see, the art of producing literature, in which the writing of science was implicated as one kind among others, was perpetually inventing novel and creative forms to define itself. The result was a 'reckless diversity of writing' that often tended to overspill whatever boundaries of genre or discourse were supposed to contain it.[54] According to Philip Davis, this 'anxious, voracious, and unwieldy experimentation'[55] is the symptom of a self-styled 'epoch of transition in the very foundations of belief and conduct', 'an age of disquietude and doubt' that was often wanting categories and frameworks to understand its own cultural productions.[56] The sensational writing of the 1860s, for example, was itself part of the critical endeavour to make sense of the enormous excitement that it produced. As I will argue, sensation fiction was a genre in search of its meaning and function within a culture of serial text production that was increasingly driven by economic concerns. Similarly, much Victorian verse writing can be described as the result of 'experiments with language';[57] and this phrase, again, is more than a metaphor, not only because a considerable amount of Victorian poetry, even that of the Pre-Raphaelites, has been shown to be 'a mode of scientific enquiry',[58] but also because many scientists, conversely, experimented with poetry.[59] As the Victorian critic Edward Dowden argued, what poetic and scientific practices have in common is an interest in versions of 'truth': in the making of forms that are true – albeit not necessarily in the same way – to experiences of being in the world.[60]

Perhaps 'the most important poetic experiment' of what has been said to be an 'unusually experimentalist' period is the dramatic monologue,[61] a genre that, as we shall see in Chapter 7, has often been described as a literary form of empiricism. More precisely, the dramatic monologue represents a way of investigating a certain subject from the inside, by inhabiting it, rather than by gazing at it from a detached point of view. Take Robert Browning's 'Childe Roland to the Dark Tower Came',[62] which has been called 'the quintessential

Victorian experiment'.[63] Representing a process of moving towards an indefinite 'end' (18), the speaker's utterances do not take the form of a story about past experiences. Rather, they make up a future-bound search for meaning and direction that is characterised by tentativeness, uncertainty, conjecture and trial. Surrounded by 'Nothing but plain to the horizon's bound', the speaker is shown to grope his way forward through a 'starved ignoble' landscape that presents itself as eminently difficult to read (53, 56). 'What made those holes and rents / In the dock's harsh swarth leaves, bruised as to baulk / All hope of greenness?' (69–71) Or: 'Whose savage trample thus could pad the dank / Soil to a plash?' (130–1). In this manner, all signs of meaningful structures faced by the speaker are subject to interpretation: 'a furlong on – why there! / What bad use was that engine for, that wheel, / Or brake, not wheel – that harrow fit to reel / Men's bodies out like silk?' (139–42). Until the end, the poem never reaches a position outside of this mode of being in question and under scrutiny. Instead of telling us what the speaker knows, his text shows us how he proceeds along a path that only takes shape as he struggles through a world of grotesque phenomena, always apprehensive about what he will find next: 'I feared / To set my foot upon a dead man's cheek, / Each step, or feel the spear I thrust to seek / For hollows, tangled in his hair or beard!' (121–4). In short, the poem enacts an experimental process while simultaneously inviting its readers to reflect upon it. One might say that Browning's monologue examines a process of experimentation by performing it.

Outline and Goals

Dramatic poems such as 'Childe Roland to the Dark Tower Came' exemplify a commitment to forms of experience-based enquiry and participant observation that is at the centre of all the chapters of this book. It can not only be found in the writing of poetry and sensation fiction (Chapters 4, 7 and 8), but also in the multifarious debates about the relationship between the arts and the sciences (Chapters 1 and 6), in Thomas Henry Huxley's lectures and essays on science education (Chapter 2), as well as in George Eliot's and George Henry Lewes's fictional and non-fictional studies in life and mind and the environment that surrounds and sustains them (Chapters 3 and 4). Even the enquiries of Victorian anthropologists and scientists of language, such as Friedrich Max Müller and Edward B. Tylor, with their ambitious project of understanding the form and evolution of the very speech that they used to do so, can be seen to enact a way of 'knowing from the inside',[64] even though some philologists actually 'imagined their scholarly discourse as existing "outside" of the language they described' (chapter 5).[65] What certainly ties all of these experiments and investigations, both fictional and non-fictional, together is a concern with ontology, with the fact that observers 'owe' their 'very being' to the world that they study and seek to understand.[66] While the Victorian period is often associated with the rise of 'the modern scientific method' of detached registration and self-denial, 'embodied' practice, as Tiffany Watt Smith has shown, 'remained at the heart of experimental life'.[67]

One ideology, after all, that came thoroughly under stress as the nineteenth century progressed, is the idealist belief in a disembodied mind or reason that stands above the material world, rather than being deeply involved within and made to grow by means of it.[68] As a result, Victorian psychology was generally physiological psychology, and the mind of the human could not be thought of without the animal body with which it was taken to be entwined. What is more, the matter of Victorian thought and exploration was subject to a widespread experience of contingency and change that tended to override whatever concepts of reason and design were traditionally used to domesticate it. Nature, on an evolutionary view, was conducting experiments of her own, thus making her own future infinitely variable and difficult to predict. The material world was regarded as changeable and incomplete rather than accomplished and ready-made.

By highlighting the experimental or performative quality of Victorian writing, the subsequent chapters tie in with, and build upon, the work of such scholars as Rick Rylance, Christopher Herbert and Peter Garratt.[69] They have shown that epistemological views premised upon dynamic relations, rather than pre-positioned entities, were not an invention of the modernists but a staple of much Victorian thought. According to Herbert, for instance, the world that Victorian science and literature investigated and sought to understand was both 'indivisible', with all things 'bound up together' in a 'single' continuum, and 'uncontrollably multiple'.[70] As a result, he argues, nothing could be conceived or perceived as one thing 'just by itself', but only in comparison with all the other things – its opposite among them – that were taken to be part of its existence.[71] 'Everything known to us is known in connexion with something else,' as the influential Victorian philosopher Alexander Bain puts this, 'light implies darkness; heat supposes cold. Knowledge, like consciousness, in the last resort, is a transition from one state to another; and both states are included in the act of knowing either'.[72] In accordance with this claim, my own way of knowing, as acted out in the following pages, ought to be seen as an attempt to see Victorian literature and science as continuous with contemporary concerns, rather than as closed off from them in a historical 'box'.[73] What we contemporaries may learn from the Victorians, I argue, is that the sciences and the arts are made up of practices and procedures that are not essentially confined to separate places and domains. The notion of experiment, for example, has never been owned by the sciences, as I shall show in Chapters 2, 3 and 4, but has long been part and parcel of artful genres like the essay, the study and the sketch. Rather than being only of historical value, the explorations carried out in this book might therefore suggest that the sciences and the arts are caught up in and dependent upon each other in ways that the current structure of our academy, with its seemingly insurmountable institutional barriers, has made us tend to forget. The mesh of works composed by nineteenth-century writing, whether philosophical, scientific, poetic or fictional, is much messier and more volatile than is suggested by the neat conceptions and categorical distinctions – subject vs object, culture vs nature, human vs non-human etc. – by means of which we moderns have become accustomed to think.

As I wish to bring out, then, 'science' and 'literature' were, in the nineteenth century, not confined to separate social spheres, with ideas and images travelling back and forth across a permeable boundary between them, as the widely used metaphor of the 'two-way' 'traffic' suggests.[74] Rather, they were made through practical works which often participated in one and the same venture of drawing general forms out of experiences of living in the world. In this common endeavour, both scientific and literary practitioners had to make use of language, which brings the making of science into the remit of literary criticism. However, by drawing attention to the art of writing that both associates and distinguishes science and literature, I do not mean to say that science is 'merely writing' or 'merely fiction'.[75] Nor do I want to suggest that literature can be reduced to the making of science in the sense of knowledge. All I want to claim is that *what* science and literature are (taken to be) cannot be abstracted from *how* they are figured forth as text. 'Science,' like literature, 'cannot be conducted without language, and language is not a neutral tool,' as Charlotte Sleigh puts it. 'It actively shapes knowledge just as much as does the decision to dissect this animal, use that microscope, perform this test, and so on.'[76] Without the use of language, in short, literature and science (as we have come to know them) could not exist as separate realms. One could say that I view writing not only as a practice of boundary-crossing, but also of what Karen Barad has called 'boundary-making'.[77]

With these preliminaries in mind, the subsequent chapters follow a representative, though diverse, group of Victorian writers in their attempts to come to terms with a world in formation and motion, of which they often took their own art to be one activity among others. More precisely, my work has three closely interrelated aims. Firstly, it seeks to elucidate the role of experimentation and skilful practice as key themes in debates on epistemology, science education, natural history, language and aesthetics. Secondly, it examines the forms in which much Victorian writing can itself be seen to engage in what Tim Ingold has called an 'art of inquiry', a practice of learning with, and attuning to, certain subject-matters, of coming to know them from the inside, rather than from a predefined vantage point outside of them.[78] In this mode of investigation, 'every work is an experiment', as Ingold explains, 'not in the natural scientific sense of testing a preconceived hypothesis, or of engineering a confrontation between ideas "in the head" and facts "on the ground", but in the sense of prising an opening and following where it leads'.[79] As I hope to show, what such texts as, among others, G. H. Lewes's studies in life and mind, George Eliot's *The Mill on the Floss*, Robert Browning's *The Ring and the Book* and Wilkie Collins's *Armadale* represent are not so much structures of knowledge as ways of knowing in this sense: experimental enquiries that are conducted through the writing of texts. Last but not least, the book aims to open up avenues for thought and research that allow scholars of Victorian culture to steer clear of what Barbara Herrnstein Smith has termed 'the *ideology* of "the two cultures"'.[80] Epistemologically, scientific and literary practices may be taken to exist in separate spheres, but ontologically, as many Victorians knew as well as contemporary theorists, they operate from within an experience of a material world that enables and sustains them both.

Notes

1. James, *The Meaning of Truth*, p. vii.
2. Dewey, 'The Need for a Recovery', p. 7.
3. Pickering, *The Cybernetic Brain*, p. 381.
4. Referring either to processes of knowledge making or to modes of knowledge in the making, the term 'ways of knowing' sometimes turns up in anthropology and in the history and philosophy of science, but it is less common in literary studies. A broad survey, written for a wide

audience and ranging from the Renaissance up to the twenty-first century, is offered by Pickstone, *Ways of Knowing*. For an anthropological view see Mark Harris (ed.), *Ways of Knowing*.

5. Pickering, 'Living', p. 275.
6. Arnold, 'Literature and Science', p. 58. Arnold adds that 'Euclid's *Elements* and Newton's *Principia* are thus literature' (p. 58).
7. Latour, *Science in Action*; see also Rouse, 'Understanding'.
8. Pickering, *Mangle*, p. 19.
9. Gooding, *Experiment*, p. 135.
10. Bhaskar, *A Realist Theory*, p. 21. For an extensive discussion of this apparent paradox from a literary critical point of view see Koschorke, *Wahrheit und Erfindung*, pp. 341–3.
11. Latour, *Reassembling*, p. 90. See also Latour, 'One more turn'.
12. Latour and Woolgar, *Laboratory Life*.
13. See Gooding, 'Putting Agency Back', pp. 65–112.
14. Massumi, 'Prelude', p. xi.
15. Schatzki et al. (eds), *The Practice Turn*; Lüdeke, 'The Eigensinn'; Bode, 'Theorietheorie'; Reckwitz, 'Grundelemente'; Rouse, 'Practice Theory'; Bertram, 'Praktiken'; Certeau, *Practice*; Bourdieu, *The Logic of Practice*.
16. Tylor, *Anthropology*, p. 309.
17. Polanyi, *The Tacit Dimension*, p. 4.
18. Ingold, *Making*, pp. 109–11.
19. Polanyi, *Personal Knowledge*. For further commentary on this kind of knowledge see Kogge, 'Empeirìa'; Ernst und Paul (eds), *Präsenz*.
20. Personal knowledge, as Tim Ingold puts it, is what 'streams around and amidst the fixed points' of reference that articulate knowledge 'joins up' (*The Life of Lines*, p. 148).
21. On the importance of drawing in the making of science, especially astronomy, see Nasim, *Observing by Hand*.
22. Ruskin, *The Eagle's Nest*, p. 125.
23. Gooding, *Experiment*, p. 6.
24. Latour, 'Drawing Things Together', p. 39.
25. Gooding, 'Magnetic Curves'.
26. Gooding, 'Envisioning Explanations', p. 3.
27. Buckland, *Novel Science*, p. 15; cf. O'Connor, *The Earth*, pp. 1–27; Heringman, *Romantic Rocks*, pp. 19–29.
28. Buckland, *Novel Science*, p. 4.
29. O'Connor, *The Earth*, p. 23.
30. O'Connor, 'From the Epic of Earth History to the Evolutionary Epic', p. 214.
31. Buckland, *Novel Science*, pp. 18–22.
32. Ibid., p. 18.
33. Mitchell, *Experimental Vitalism*, pp. 14–42; Gamper, 'Experimentierkunst'.
34. Rheinberger, *Toward a History*, p. 111.

35. Ibid., p. 8 and generally.
36. Ibid., p. 111.
37. Francois Jacob, qtd in Rheinberger, *Toward a History*, p. 28.
38. Rheinberger, *Toward a History*, pp. 102–13.
39. Ibid., pp. 28, 111.
40. Rheinberger, 'Experimental Systems', p. 419.
41. Ibid., p. 417.
42. Rheinberger, *Toward a History*, pp. 28, 110.
43. Derrida, 'Signature, Context, Event', p. 316. This definition of writing has of course been criticised for being too general (see Kogge, 'Erschriebene Denkräume'). But while generality may obliterate nuances, it can also help to bring into view correspondences that would otherwise remain obscured.
44. Gamper, 'Einleitung', p. 11.
45. Schatzki, 'Praxistheorie', p. 32.
46. Darwin, *Origin*, p. 182.
47. Ibid., p. 181.
48. Ibid., p. 184.
49. Unsigned Review, 'Mr Darwin's Recent Inductions', p. 352.
50. Hopkins, 'Physical Theories', p. 80.
51. [Jardine], '[Review]', p. 282.
52. The debates about Darwin's theory are extensively analysed in Ellegård, *Darwin*.
53. Böhm-Schnitker and Erchinger, 'Scientific Cultures', p. 3.
54. Davis, *The Victorians*, p. 7.
55. Ibid., p. 7.
56. Morley, *On Compromise*, p. 28; Bulwer-Lytton, *England*, p. 166.
57. Armstrong, *Victorian Poetry*, p. 8.
58. Holmes, 'Poetry on Pre-Raphaelite Principles', p. 16.
59. See Brown, *The Poetry of Victorian Scientists*.
60. Dowden, 'The Scientific Movement', p. 86.
61. Plunkett et al. (eds), 'Introduction', p. 14; Mason, 'Browning', p. 231.
62. Browning, *Robert Browning's Poetry*, pp. 181–8. I shall quote by lines, using this edition.
63. Slinn, 'Experimental Form', p. 48.
64. Ingold, *Making*, pp. 1–15.
65. Abberley, *English Fiction*, p. 4.
66. Ingold, *Making*, p. 5.
67. Watt Smith, *On Flinching*, p. 38.
68. See Staten, *Spirit*, pp. 1–30; Zwierlein, *Der physiologische Bildungsroman*, pp. 1–17.
69. Rylance, *Victorian Psychology*; Herbert, *Victorian Relativity*; Garratt, *Victorian Empiricism*.
70. Herbert, *Victorian Relativity*, p. 50.
71. Ibid., pp. 5, 61.

72. Bain, *The Senses and the Intellect*, 3rd edn, p. 565.
73. Felski, 'Context Stinks!', p. 574; cf. Lüdeke, 'Die Gesellschaft', pp. 361–6.
74. Beer, *Darwin's Plots*, p. 5.
75. For critiques of the view (possibly never really held by anyone) that science can be identified with literature in the sense of literary fiction see Levine, *Realism, Ethics*, pp. 165–81 and Norris, *Against Relativism*, esp. pp. 265–324. While I have learned much from Norris's work, his argument for 'realism' and against 'cultural relativism' is premised on a polemic opposition between these two terms that I find difficult to sustain.
76. Sleigh, *Literature and Science*, p. 6. This is not meant as a critique of what has been called 'the rhetoric of science'. On this issue see Vanderbeke, *Theoretische Welten*, pp. 57–132.
77. Barad, *Meeting the Universe*, p. 149.
78. Ingold, *Making*, p. 6.
79. Ibid., p. 7.
80. Herrnstein Smith, *Scandalous Knowledge*, p. 115.

Chapter 1

The Art of Science: Nineteenth-Century Theory and the Logic of Practice

Regularity and Dexterity

The English word 'art', like the German 'Kunst', can still be used in various senses, each of which includes traces of all the others. While 'art' can mean 'any kind of skill',[1] it may also refer, slightly more narrowly, only to the exercise of such a skill. 'Art' can, moreover, denote the (more or less finished) product of skilful action, and, finally, it has now come to stand specifically for the more recent concept of 'fine art', the manifestations of which, although representing relatively free and open forms of play, are typically shown in museums and art galleries or otherwise marked as distinct from ordinary experience and goal-directed work.[2] Throughout the nineteenth century, all of these meanings were still commonly used alongside each other, even though 'fine art' was increasingly taken to be informed by an idea of the aesthetic, closely allied with the notion of genius, that allegedly distinguished it from art as ('mere') technical skill.[3] Yet, even without the specifically 'fine' aspect, to which I will return, the task of defining 'art' posed a considerable challenge to critics, as the respective article in the ninth (or scholars') edition of the *Encyclopaedia Britannica* indicates.[4] 'Art, whether used of all arts at once or of one at a time,' the author points out, 'is a name not only for the power of doing something, but for the exercise of the power; and not only for the exercise of the power, but for the rules according to which it is exercised; and not only for the rules, but for the result' (*EB* 636).

As this shows, the meaning of art was taken to stretch across a continuum that could encompass the (individual) ability to 'do something' as well as the (social) 'rules' that enable and constrain it and the process of performing an action as well as its 'result'. 'Painting, for instance, is an art, and the idea includes not only the power to paint, but the act of painting; and not only the act, but the laws for performing the act rightly; and not only all these, but the material consequences of the act or the thing painted' (*EB* 636). In an attempt to register all of these nuances of meaning inherent in 'art', 'leaving room for every accepted usage of the word' (*EB* 637), the article eventually suggests a definition that is as firm and precise as it is adjustable and soft. 'Art', on this conception, may refer to: '*Every regulated operation or dexterity by which organised beings pursue ends which they know beforehand, together with the rules and the result of every such operation or dexterity*' (*EB* 637).

On the one hand, then, the '*regulated operation*' called art was supposed to be governed by rules and directed at ends which the 'organised beings' performing the operation know 'beforehand'. On the other hand, however, the author tempers this emphasis on the priority of rules and ends by the insertion of an element of '*dexterity*', ambiguously placed next to the '*regulated operation*', only separated from it by an indiscriminate '*or*'. In this way, the definition mingles the rule-governed 'regularity' of art with a more flexible and dynamic mode of 'dexterity', capable of showing itself in multiple ways and moves which, arguably, cannot all be contained in, or controlled by, predefined ideas. One can therefore say that the above definition comprises two different modes of practice, each of which implies a particular type of intelligence. The first one is a 'regulated' way of acting which is premised on the abstract knowledge of which rules have to be observed in order to attain certain ends, rather than others. The second mode of practice implied in the definition manifests itself in the capability to modify and adjust one's principles and goals according to circumstantial variations not wholly foreseeable in advance. Art as a regulated practice, in short, is premised on a type of 'knowing *that*' an action has to be performed in a particular way in order for it to have certain effects, whereas art as a dexterous practice involves a mode of 'knowing *how*' it has to be carried out in relation to the changeable material conditions provided at a particular time and in a particular place.[5]

The definition of art, as it is proposed here, then, combines a form of theoretical knowledge based on impersonal rules with a type of practical intelligence based on personal experience. As John S. Mill, whose writings are one of the main reference points for the *Encyclopaedia* article, explains in his *System of Logic* (first published 1843), theoretical knowledge is what is typically taught in the form of 'maxims handed down to us by books or tradition'.[6] Practical knowledge is what is typically learned by doing, as one repeatedly moves through a field of trial and error, 'much oftener' reasoning 'from particulars to particulars directly, than through the intermediate agency of any general proposition' (*SL* I, 215). In this way, Mill argues, adroit practitioners have learned to fine-tune their perceptions to their actions in a way that they often cannot spell out fully in abstract, impersonal terms. In order to illustrate this 'tacit' logic of practical 'skill' and 'manual dexterity' (*SL* I, 216, 217), Mill provides a series of examples, one of which involves 'a working dyer, famous for producing very fine colours' whom a Scots manufacturer once 'procured from England, at a high rate of wages', so as to make him teach 'to his other workmen the same skill', as Mill recounts in a short narrative worth quoting in full (*SL* I, 217).

> The workman came; but his mode of proportioning the ingredients, in which lay the secret of the effects he produced, was by taking them up in handfuls, while the common method was to weigh them. The manufacturer sought to make him turn his handling system into an equivalent weighing system, that the general principle of his peculiar mode of proceeding might be ascertained. This, however, the man found himself quite unable to do, and therefore could impart his skill to nobody. He had, from the individual cases of his own experience, established a connexion in his mind between fine effects of colour, and tactual perceptions in handling his dyeing materials; and from these perceptions he could, in any particular case, infer the means to be employed, and the effects which would be produced, but could not put others in possession of the grounds on which he proceeded, from having never generalized them in his own mind, or expressed them in language. (*SL* I, 217)

The point of this example is that the 'tactual perceptions' and the material actions ('handling his dyeing materials') of the workman have become so intimately entwined 'in his mind' that he is incapable of separating them analytically in order to determine the 'grounds' of their relation, the 'general principle' upon which he proceeds. The 'system' on which he relies has been incrementally formed through, but never been abstracted from, the 'peculiar mode' of his 'handling' of the 'dyeing materials'. As a result, his wisdom is of an entirely practical or embodied kind. He can only enact what he knows while failing to capture it in theoretical terms through which it could be transmitted to others. The personal knowledge exemplified by his very own 'handling system' remains disconnected from the general knowledge that is represented by the 'weighing system'. What is wanting in this case, then, is a method of translating the practical into the theoretical and the individual into the social mode. The craftsman lacks a means by which he can represent his rule-of-thumb 'dexterity' as a 'regulated operation' based on general rules.

Science and Art

As I wish to argue, the 'history of the name' art (*EB* 637), parts of which are also sketched out in the *Encyclopaedia* article is above all a history of the shifting and disputed relations between these aspects of the dexterous and the regulated, as well as of the personal and the general. For instance, while the Greek *techné*, as referring to the skilled practice of the artisan, was still largely separated from the theoretical and contemplative knowledge of the philosopher named *episteme*, the Latin word *ars* comprehended both of these meanings in a single term. 'Scientia', by contrast, like its derivative 'science', was for a long time used only as a very broad term for various types of 'knowledge', while the kind of systematic examination of a specific subject that we nowadays tend to ascribe to 'science' was subsumed under the term 'art'. In fact, one can even say that until the eighteenth century, 'most sciences were arts'.[7] One example of this identification of science with art are the *artes liberales* or liberal arts, which constituted the medieval and early modern canon of general knowledge as it was taught at universities across Europe. Made up of the *trivium* (grammar, logic and rhetoric) and the *quadrivium* (geometry, astronomy, music and arithmetic), these liberal arts encompassed the propositions and ideas that constituted specific fields of knowledge as well as the techniques of establishing and implementing these ideas. Subsequently, to keep these two aspects apart, 'science' and 'art' were often associated with 'theory' and 'practice' respectively, as in Kant's assertion in the *Third Critique*: 'Art regarded as human skill differs from science (as *can* from *know*) as a practical faculty does from a theoretical, as technique does from theory (as mensuration from geometry).'[8] Yet, as Raymond Williams suggests, 'the modern distinction between science and art, as contrasted areas of human skill and effort, with fundamentally different methods and purposes' is mainly the product of controversies which took place in the nineteenth century.[9]

The *Britannica* article not only participates in this discussion on the relationship between art and science but also puts forth a provisional conclusion to it, which is summed up as follows. 'Science consists in knowing, Art consists in doing. What I must do in order to know, is Art subordinate to or concerned in Science. What I must know in order to do, is Science subordinate to or concerned in Art' (*EB* 638). Thus conceived, science and art, knowing and doing, or genesis and structure are neither strictly distinct from each other nor can they be conflated into a single term. Instead, they are said to be 'concerned in' each other in a mutually inclusive way. Although art is taken to be different from science, it is still claimed to fulfil an 'instrumental' function within it, every science having its 'practical discipline' (*EB* 637). This means that the art or skill ('know-how') by which 'the scientist solves any given problem in his science' is both conditional for and excessive of the propositional knowledge ('knowing that') represented by science (*EB* 637). Art is that by virtue of which science is productive and inventive rather than consummated and closed.[10]

While this way of conceiving the relationship between science and art establishes a contrast between the two terms, it conspicuously avoids privileging one of them over the other. It therefore deviates from an influential way of thinking, deeply ingrained in the history of Western thought, according to which practice is what follows theory. In this view, the theoretical conception or the abstract design is supposed to precede the process of executing it, or of putting it into practice.[11] This implies that whatever is to be done needs to be known in advance. One of the most influential elaborations of this idealist, or 'theory-first view'[12] is represented by William Paley's widely read *Natural Theology*.[13] On Paley's account, the whole world of human and non-human nature is an artefact made by God whom he variously addresses as either an 'artist', an 'artificer' or a 'workman' (*NT* 8, 19, 45 and generally), evidently taking all of these terms to be interchangeable with each other.[14] In Paley's usage, they refer to a creative producer who is capable of shaping a given material according to an ideal form. Correspondingly, he regards the finished artwork as a secondary function of a predesigned purpose that it is supposed to fulfil.

Paley therefore does not view the material components of God's artwork, nature, as variable parts of an open-ended process of evolution, but as operators of a predefined form.[15] The 'feet, wings, and fins' of birds and fish are '*instruments of motion*', he says (*NT* 124). The eye 'is an optical instrument', made 'for vision' like a 'telescope' (*NT* 137, 16), and the animal organism as a whole is taken to function like 'an automatic statue' assembled in a manner that enables it to live and move on its own (*NT* 17). As is well known, the paradigmatic model for all of these examples is the mechanism of a watch, a close inspection of which, Paley argues, will invariably lead to the conclusion that there must have been 'an artificer or artificers who formed it for the purpose which we find it actually to answer; who comprehended its construction, and designed its use' (*NT* 8). The point Paley seeks to make, then, is that the appearances of nature, just as the mechanism of a watch, can only have been made by an intentional agency who knows, and lets others see, the plan and motivation behind its art.

Focusing almost solely on what the subtitle of *Natural Theology* describes as the 'appearances of nature', the visible effects of God's 'art and skill' (*NT* 15), Paley does not usually consider the generative processes through which God's theoretical plan was translated into the materials supposed to reveal it or, conversely, through which these materials were made into the purposeful forms he claims them to be. And yet there are several instances in his book in which this art of making re-enters Paley's writing in a way that inadvertently nudges his argument away from the theory-first view and towards a rather different way of conceiving the relationship between practice and theory, or art and science. Symptomatically, one of these instances follows upon Paley's extended description of the enormously complex architecture of the animal eye. This architecture strikes him as so extraordinary that it prompts him to reflect at length on the question of why God as a totally wise and powerful being actually had to build such a highly complicated apparatus only to endow his creatures with the benefit of eyesight. 'Why should not the Deity have given to the animal the faculty of vision *at once*?', he asks (*NT* 26):

> Why this circuitous perception; the ministry of so many means? an element provided for the purpose; reflected from opaque; substances, refracted through transparent ones; and both according to precise laws: then, a complex organ, an intricate and artificial apparatus, in order, by the operation of this element, and in conformity with the restrictions of these laws, to produce an image upon a membrane communicating with the brain? Wherefore all this? Why make the difficulty in order only to surmount it? If to perceive objects by some other mode than that of touch, or objects which lay out of the reach of the sense, were the thing purposed, could not a simple volition of the Creator have communicated the capacity? Why resort to contrivance, where power is omnipotent? (*NT* 26)

What Paley's question exposes here is the extravagant, almost lavish use of 'substances' and materials in the making of the eye – materials which appear to be luxurious and superfluous, in excess of, and therefore contingent upon, the purpose they are supposed to fulfil. More precisely, Paley foregrounds that the very deployment of material instruments or media constitutes a difference between the composing activity and the composed product, a field of practical work, through which one would not have to pass if creation were an instantaneous event, a single stroke of genius, not dependent on 'so many means'.

As Paley suggests, the fact that it is God, said to be the most accomplished being, who had to proceed by such 'circuitous' ways of production is apt to make the eye look even stranger. After all: 'Contrivance, by its very definition and nature, is the refuge of imperfection,' as he puts it. 'To have recourse to expedients, implies difficulty, impediment, restraint, defect of power' (*NT* 26). To regard the eye as a work of art, it seems, can make the great artist appear as someone who met with difficulties and obstructions in the course of his work, compelling him to correct and adapt his original design as he went along. In fact, the multi-layered composition of the eye could even be taken to expose God's procedure as a way of tinkering and *bricolage*, the work of someone who assembled his work in an incremental or piecemeal fashion, not quite knowing what it would look like until it was finished. In short, what Paley's question inadvertently suggests is that the art which is instrumental to the execution of a predefined conception may emancipate itself from it, generating unforeseen outcomes and opening up multiple paths. In this view, the results of God's artful work might even have come, at least partly, as a surprise to their creator. This would align Paley's God with Mary Shelley's *Frankenstein*, published only sixteen years after *Natural Theology*, in which the creator is not only stunned and 'overcome',[16] but horrified and shocked by what he thinks of as the 'accomplishment' of his plan.[17]

If Paley had allowed such 'monstrous' considerations to flourish, he would of course have done serious damage to his argument that the 'appearances' of nature bespeak an intelligent maker in full control of his acts. He therefore goes on to provide an answer to his sceptical question by which he hopes to put the whole issue to rest. 'It is only by the display of contrivance, that the existence, the agency, the wisdom of the Deity, *could* be testified to his rational creatures,' he argues (*NT* 27). 'Whatever is done, God could have done, without the intervention of instruments or means: but it is in the construction of instruments, in the choice and adaptation of means, that a creative intelligence is seen' (*NT* 27). While this is a cunning move, it also prompts Paley to substantiate his proposition by inspecting more closely the manner of construction through which he takes God's intelligence to have been acted out. God, Paley argues, had deliberately chosen to restrict his power by self-imposed obstacles so as to provide himself with an opportunity to show how well he is able to surmount them. As Paley explains, 'God prescribes limits to his power, that he may let in the exercise, and thereby exhibit demonstrations, of his wisdom' (*NT* 27).

> For then, i.e. such laws and limitations being laid down, it is as though one Being should have fixed certain rules; and, if we may so speak, provided certain materials; and, afterwards, have committed to another Being, out of these materials, and in subordination to these rules, the task of drawing forth a creation: a supposition which evidently leaves room, and induces indeed a necessity, for contrivance. Nay, there may be many such agents, and many ranks of these. (*NT* 27)

Paley's idea, then, is one of deliberate self-limitation: God, he suggests, established certain natural laws and constraints in the materials he used, before he set out to bring the ideal form of his work in tune with these constraints. In this way, Paley not only divides the activity of creation into a theoretical (or conceptual) and a practical (or executive) phase, into 'one Being' and 'another Being'. More importantly, he draws attention to the 'room' of 'contrivance', the space of practical work in which the conceptual mode of 'Being' is transfigured into the material one. He foregrounds the process of working out or 'drawing forth a creation', in the course of which one and the same ideal form may come to matter in multiple ways. In fact, Paley even suggests that this 'room' or passage between before and after 'may' be inhabited by 'many' different 'agents' all of whom contribute to the inventive process, perhaps even causing it to proliferate or develop a life of its own. Thus conceived, the source of a constructed object, the agency that brings it about, could no longer be located in a self-contained subject. Instead, it would have to be seen as distributed across a dynamic network of agents ('many [. . .] agents, and many ranks of these'), all participating in the composition of a piece of art.[18]

Practice First

To sum up, Paley's 'supposition' inadvertently makes 'room' for an incalculable element of variability which cannot be fully contained in, or anticipated by, preconceived patterns or plans. His answer to the 'question which may possibly have dwelt in the reader's mind' (*NT* 26) makes him divide the artful work of divine creation into that of an intellectual and an executive 'Being'. In this way, he clears a space in which the relationship between theory and practice, or science and art could subsequently be renegotiated under the aspect of evolution in time.[19] More specifically, Paley's theory-first view of artful work came to be supplemented with what one might call a practice-first view. In this perspective, forms and patterns are the products of slow and long-winded activities of 'accumulative selection', as Charles Darwin termed them, which need not necessarily follow preconceived theories or designs.[20] In Darwin's writing, these activities are typically represented by the arts of breeding and gardening which famously served him as a model for his theory of evolution by means of 'natural selection' (*OS* 82).[21] Crucially, the work of breeders and gardeners, as described by Darwin, is not only, and not even predominantly, based on the propositional knowledge of predefined rules and laws. It also presupposes a supple capacity to respond to the observation of variations in circumstances, either by preserving and reproducing or by disregarding them. It follows that the skill of breeders or horticulturalists shows itself in the ability to know how and when to select those of the modifications they encounter which best suit their 'use or fancy' at a particular time (*OS* 30).

Thus conceived, novel breeds or desirable forms are built up gradually and cumulatively, by means of a continuous process of giving and taking, through which human goals and needs are worked into non-human environments, as Darwin suggests: 'nature gives successive variations; man adds them up in certain directions useful to him' (*OS* 30). While 'the strawberry', for instance, 'had always varied since it was cultivated', it could not be altered significantly in kind as long as minor variations in its qualities were neglected (*OS* 41).

> As soon, however, as gardeners picked out individual plants with slightly larger, earlier, or better fruit, and raised seedlings from them, and again picked out the best seedlings and bred from them, then, there appeared (aided by some crossing with distinct species) those many admirable varieties of the strawberry which have been raised during the last thirty or forty years. (*OS* 41–2)

As Darwin points out, 'the principle of selection' which informs such practices of breeding from the 'best seedlings' has for a long time been transmitted in terms of 'explicit rules' and general propositions (*OS* 34). At the same time, however, this science- or theory-based way of cultivating the animate world has always been accompanied, he emphasises, by a mode of operation which involves no conscious knowledge of its own premises, or its underlying rationale.

In his remarks on the techniques of breeding and gardening, Darwin therefore distinguishes sharply between two types of selection which he calls 'methodical' and '[u]nconscious' (*OS* 34). Having first introduced these terms in the introductory chapter of the *Origin of Species*, he continues to employ them in later texts such as *The Variation of Plants and Animals under Domestication*, in which their meaning is defined most clearly:

> *Methodical selection* is that which guides a man who systematically endeavours to modify a breed according to some predetermined standard. *Unconscious selection* is that which follows from men naturally preserving the most valued and destroying the less valued individuals, without any thought of altering the breed; and undoubtedly this process slowly works great changes.[22]

This division relates a methodical, 'theory-first' way of acting 'according to some predetermined standard' to a non-methodical way of operating according to tacit or 'unconscious' principles of which one is not, or not fully, aware. Both, for Darwin, are forms of art, or of exercising a skill. Yet, whereas the first kind of art is, by virtue of being methodical, evidently at a remove from the natural, the second one, following 'from men naturally preserving' what they like best, is claimed to be continuous with it. Indeed, there is little doubt that Darwin considers the mode of operation called 'unconscious' to be premised on what he terms a 'natural' way of proceeding. What he means by this is a kind of practice in which the decision of what is the best choice is not guided by an abstract set of propositional rules or a predetermined purpose but by the ability to respond, and adapt, as best as possible to individual situations. 'Thus, a man who intends on keeping pointers naturally tries to get as good dogs as he can, and afterwards breeds from his own best dogs, but he has no wish or expectation of permanently altering the breed' (*OS* 34).

The key argument here is that this 'man' does not adhere to a conscious, fully-fledged strategy, or a long-term intention to create an entirely new breed. All that motivates his decisions is the 'natural' desire to do his work as well as he can if only to maintain a status quo, to 'keep' his pointers as before. To say, as Darwin does, that this motive of always choosing what, to a given practitioner, seems to be the best of all available options is often acted out 'unconsciously' is of course not to say that it presupposes a state of being without consciousness, as in a dream. Nor does this phrase imply that acts of unconscious selection will necessarily always pick out what a more methodical way of operation would deem, on the basis of a 'predetermined standard', to be the best possible choice. What Darwin does refer to by the term 'unconscious selection' is a way of making decisions and performing actions whose logic cannot be explained in terms of a conscious method, a set of principles or norms existing outside of the process of putting them to work. If a method is unconscious, this is to say, then it never achieves the form of a general theory but remains inherent in the personal practice that has given rise to it in the first place. Not unlike the *Britannica* article, then, Darwin describes the art of breeding and gardening both in terms of a regularity based on theoretical knowledge and in terms of a dexterous flexibility that outruns this knowledge. At the same time, he suggests, again like the *Encyclopaedia*, that both aspects – the regular and the flexible – are essential to art as skilled practice. In fact, he goes so far as to say that they can only be separated in theory while they are almost always interlaced in practice. 'Unconscious selection graduates into methodical, and only extreme cases can be distinctly separated'; or yet again: 'Unconscious selection so blends into methodical that it is scarcely possible to separate them.'[23]

To review the argument so far, let me highlight two related points which will be elaborated in the remainder of the chapter. Firstly, Darwin made the arts of breeding and gardening continuous with, and part and parcel of, physical processes. This enabled him to justify his claim that natural selection works, albeit on an immeasurably larger scale, like the unconscious selection of men who keep pointers or cultivate strawberries. Secondly, Darwin introduced an unconscious element into skilled practice for which one cannot fully account in terms of conceptions and intentions. He thus acknowledged what Paley only inadvertently discovered when he took his reluctant glimpse into the workshop of his ideal artisan: that the causes and consequences of (human) actions often far exceed the conscious ideas on which they may be based. More pointedly still, what Darwin's concept of unconscious selection registers is that doing tends to precede and run ahead of knowing, or, most briefly, that art cannot be reduced to science. For example: 'When a fancier long ago first happened to notice a pigeon with an unusually short beak,' to use one of Darwin's cases, 'or one with the tail-feathers unusually developed, although he bred from these birds with the distinct intention of propagating the variety, yet he could not have intended to make a short-faced tumbler or a fantail, and was far from knowing that he had made the first step towards this end'.[24] Darwin's point is that this 'fancier' was 'far from knowing' what would eventually become of the work he had begun by choosing to breed from a pigeon with an unusually short beak, rather than from another. He may have had the 'distinct intention of propagating' this particular short-beaked variety, but most likely, Darwin argues, he was entirely unaware of the fact that he contributed to the making of what would become the tumbler or the fantail. On this view, the design of the maker cannot contain and control what he makes.

In sum, Darwin and Paley not only stand for cosmological views which are hard to reconcile; they also argue from different notions of art or skilful work. Paley's artist or workman is taken to execute a theoretical plan that encapsulates and anticipates the results of his actions. The practice of Darwin's breeders, by contrast, can engender designs and proliferate into forms of which they had no idea when they began with their work. Paley presupposes that an artist knows, and is in control of, what he does, whereas Darwin assumes that he may not even be entirely conscious of it. In short, in Paley's case, the use of art is designed to minimise or even exclude unpredictable occurrences and contingent variations, whereas the art of Darwin's gardeners and pigeon fanciers is capable of integrating, and even playing with them. Moreover, it is instructive to note that the two theories conceive rather differently of the relationship between art and nature. Paley's divine, though quasi-human, artist stands above, and apart from nature, imposing his ideal form on it. Darwin's skilled practitioners, by contrast, inhabit, and are sustained by, the very evolving nature that they manipulate by means of their craft. They cannot step outside of it, so as to view it as a finished whole.

The Art and Science of Logic

As I wish to show, the relationship between these two views of art – art as guided by knowledge and different from nature on the one hand; art as productive of knowledge and continuous with nature on the other – is central to the epistemological controversies of the Victorian period, especially to a debate between John S. Mill and William Whewell that was carried out between 1840 and 1872.[25] One of Mill's major contributions to these controversies was his widely read *A System of Logic, Ratiocinative and Inductive* which, according to the subtitle, seeks to present 'a connected view of the principles of evidence, and the methods of scientific investigation'.[26] As this phrase suggests, Mill's system is supposed to consist of a more theoretical ('principles') as well as of a more practical ('methods') component. In his introduction, Mill therefore emphasises that the term 'logic', as he wants it to be defined, 'comprises the science of reasoning, as well as an art, founded on that science', with reasoning meaning 'simply to infer any assertion, from assertions already admitted' (*SL* I, 3). While this definition may seem to give precedence to science, to the 'principles' on which the practice of reasoning is supposed to be 'founded', Mill insists that art can, by definition, not be subsumed under or equated with science. On the one hand, he therefore claims that 'art, in any but its infant state, presupposes scientific knowledge' (*SL* I, 2). But on the other hand he stresses that there is no one science which is capable of containing the art concomitant to it, 'because several sciences are often necessary to form the groundwork of a single art', as he avers (*SL* I, 2). 'So complicated are the conditions which govern our practical agency, that to enable one thing to be *done*, it is often requisite to *know* the nature and properties of many things' (*SL* I, 2).

In his *An Examination of Sir William Hamilton's Philosophy*,[27] Mill adduces 'the art of navigation' to illustrate this view of the relationship between the practical and the theoretical (*HP* 377). More specifically, he contends that no 'single science' could encompass the whole range of knowledge that informs the art of navigating a ship (*HP* 377). Rather: 'Navigation is an art dependent on nearly the whole circle of the physical sciences,' as he explains (*HP* 377):

> on astronomy, for the marks by which it determines the ship's place on the ocean; on optics, for the construction and use of its instruments; on abstract mechanics, to understand and regulate the ship's movements; on pneumatics, for the laws of winds; on hydrostatics, for the tides and currents, and the waves as influenced by winds; on meteorology, for the weather; on electricity, for thunderstorms; on magnetism, for the use of the compass; on physical geography, and so on nearly to the end of the list. Not only has each one of all these sciences furnished its contingent towards the rules composing the one art of navigation, but many single rules could only have been framed by the union of considerations drawn from several different sciences. For the purposes of the art, the rules by themselves are sufficient, wherever it has been found practicable to make them sufficiently precise. But if the learner [. . .] wishes to understand their reasons, and so possess science as well as art, he finds no one science, corresponding in its object-matter with the art. (*HP* 377–8)

Mill's point is that it is impossible to capture in the form of a particular science all of the multifarious wisdom that makes it possible for humans to travel the seas by ship. Nor is it necessary to have theoretical expertise in the many different branches of knowledge listed above in order to master the art of navigation. Arts, in short, are typically grounded in a multiplicity of sciences, Mill says, which refuse to be held together as a single, self-contained whole. For Mill, this shows that theory and practice, science and art, 'systems of truths' and 'systems of precepts' have to be regarded as different, even though they inevitably come to depend on each other as soon as they are put to any use (*HP* 377). Indeed, as Mill sees it, all disciplines with an evidently practical or application-oriented bent, such as 'Ethics' and 'Politics' are 'like Logic, both sciences and arts' (*HP* 376).

What Mill has in mind, and seeks to promote, then, are practical theories and theoretically aided practices in which the two components, science and art, interact in a way that he specifies at the end of his *System of Logic*. Here, in a final chapter on 'the Logic of Practice or Art; including Morality and Policy', he imagines the relationship between science and art as a collaborative venture which, in his view, is usually initiated by the need for something to be done, for a step to be taken or a goal to be reached. 'The art proposes to itself an end to be attained, defines the end, and hands it over to the science,' he writes.

> The science receives it, considers it as a phenomenon or effect to be studied, and having investigated its causes and conditions, sends it back to art with a theorem of the combination of circumstances by which it could be produced. Art then examines these combinations of circumstances, and according as any of them are or are not in human power, pronounces the end attainable or not. The only one of the premises, therefore, which Art supplies, is the original major premise, which asserts that the attainment of the given end is desirable. Science then lends to Art the proposition (obtained by a series of inductions or of deductions) that the performance of certain actions will attain the end. From these premises Art concludes that the performance of these ends is desirable, and finding it also practicable, converts the theorem into a rule or precept. (*SL* II, 547–8)

Inadvertently reminiscent of Paley's twofold 'Being', this passage conceives of science and art as complementary instances, one of which supplies 'theorems' and 'propositions' (science) while the other one decides whether they are 'desirable' and 'practicable' (art). As Mill suggests, moreover, the definition of an 'object' that is asserted to be desirable belongs 'exclusively' to the domain of art (*SL* II, 552). As a consequence, 'the original major premise' that motivates the exchange described above has to issue from a practice that cannot (yet) rely on a theory. 'Every art has one first principle, or general major premise, not borrowed from science; that which enunciates the object aimed at, and affirms it to be a desirable object' (*SL* II, 552). Two of Mill's examples are 'the medical arts' which assume that it is good to cure diseases, and 'the builder's art' which is premised on the desire 'to have buildings' (*SL* II, 552). In conjunction with other considerations, they lead him to the conclusion that the arts are characteristically concerned with what '*ought* or *should be*' whereas science is constituted of propositions which assert what '*is, or will be*' (*SL* II, 553).

Mill is certainly attracted to the idea of placing the whole circle of arts and sciences on an ethical footing which would enable all decisions about what is good or desirable to be justified on general (scientific) grounds. At the same time, however, he is thoroughly aware that this would presuppose a mastery of nothing less than what he calls 'the Art of Life, in its three departments, Morality, Prudence or Policy, and Aesthetics; the Right, the Expedient, and the Beautiful or Noble, in human conduct and works' (*SL* II, 553). And while Mill takes 'all other arts' to be 'subordinate' to this comprehensive art of human conduct and social interaction, he also concedes that it, 'in the main, is unfortunately still to be created' (*SL* II, 553). In this way, Mill uncovers an unsettled ethical and aesthetic foundation at the bottom of all the sciences and arts, including his own logic, which sustains them in a way that can, as he frankly admits, not or not yet be fully defined in general terms. As a result, he reveals both the making and the using of theoretical knowledge to be dependent on what he calls 'principles of Practical Reason' by virtue of which the scientific pursuit of general truths is deeply entangled with considerations of 'the Right, the Expedient, and the Beautiful or Noble, in human conduct and works' – considerations which 'determine whether the special aim of any particular art is worthy and desirable, and what is its place in the scale of desirable things' (*SL* II, 553). As Mill points out, the knowledge which enables us to decide what, in any situation, is the most worthy and desirable action to take must remain susceptible to be continuously adjusted and revised in relation to the 'counteracting contingencies' and 'combinations of circumstances' specific to each individual case (*SL* II, 549). 'By a wise practitioner, therefore, rules of conduct will only be considered as provisional,' as he puts it, indicating that he takes the foundation of the arts to be essentially caught up in the flux of an open-ended process (*SL* II, 549).

By including the logic of practice or art in his methodological system, to sum this up, Mill could not help building a dynamic and contingent element into it, a tendency towards extension and supplementation that prevented its closure. To be sure, Mill's introduction suggests that he wanted his 'connected view' of logic to serve as a 'common judge and arbiter of all particular investigations', an authoritative apparatus of methods and terms that would help his readers to justify their own individual observations and beliefs in general terms as well as to determine whether the claims of others could stand the proof of systematic thought (*SL* I, 9). Yet, it is telling that the judge, as Mill's writing presents this figure, personifies not only the scientific decision-maker and keeper of theoretical laws but also 'the practical inquirer, who is endeavouring to ascertain facts not for the purposes of science but for those of business' (*SL* I, 328). This metaphorical slippage seems to be a direct consequence of the double-bind of Mill's logic which, as we have seen, is supposed to be a science as well as an art. Logic, thus viewed, represents not only the theoretical knowledge of what justifies science as science, but also the skilled practice of using, adapting and revising this knowledge so as to make it fit to be applied to particular contexts and changeable demands. The *persona* of the judge embodies both of these aspects, which can be described as 'knowing how' and 'knowing that' respectively. In one capacity, the judge represents and protects unshakeable norms and rules, but in another capacity, he or she is also the one who has to interpret them in accordance with variable circumstances which cannot all be contained in the book of the law as it is already laid down. In practice, by way of reading the law, judges therefore always contribute to the process of rewriting, adding to and correcting it, frequently creating precedents that inform the way legal propositions are defined afterwards. In Mill's terms one can say that their activity is equally aligned with the scientific mode of *what is* as with the political and ethical mode of *what ought to be* right. They need to have a foot in both science and art.

As the example of the judge brings out, Mill's conception of logic as the science and art of reasoning remains capable of being adapted and renegotiated in response to unexpected exceptions and particular cases. His system, its intellectual rigour notwithstanding, testifies to a respect for the singular and contingent, for the always impending possibility of occurrences and events which may cause any pre-established structure to be rectified and considered anew. As I wish to argue, this 'pragmatic openness of mind', singled out by William James as Mill's most appealing quality,[28] is a consequence of what Laura Snyder called his 'ultra-empiricism' which committed him to the view that there is strictly no other source of knowledge apart from experience.[29] Concomitantly, Mill's thoroughgoing empiricism led him to repudiate any kind of metaphysical belief in final truths or sense-transcendent laws of thought which cannot, by definition, be affected by the experience of surprising or recalcitrant phenomena. 'There is no proposition of which it can be asserted that every human mind must eternally and irrevocably believe it' (*SL* II, 98), as he puts this. 'In matters of evidence, as in all other human things, we neither require, nor can attain, the absolute. We must hold even our strongest convictions with an opening left in our minds for the reception of facts which contradict them' (*SL* II, 107–8).

On Mill's account, even such seemingly irrefutable mathematical or geometrical truths as the proposition that two straight lines cannot meet twice, or that two plus two makes four must therefore not be regarded as ideal certainties which cannot be otherwise, but as 'experimental truths', or contingent 'generalizations from experience', subject, in principle, to be modified or abandoned, if – at some point, in some place – experience refuses to confirm them (*SL* I, 291, 296).[30] Mill is far from denying that geometrical and mathematical conclusions can *follow* necessarily from certain predefined axioms or first principles, but he does hold that these first principles themselves never afford any evidence 'independent of and superior to observation and experience' (*SL* I, 290). Rather, he takes 'axioms' to be 'but a class, the most universal class, of inductions from experience' (*SL* I, 290). As a consequence, he strictly refuses to endorse the view that they are any more certain than other inductions from experience, such as the proposition that snow is white.[31] These, however, Mill regards as contingently certain at best, because, like David Hume, he believed that experience, being 'flat' and open-ended, can never yield forms of knowledge that are absolutely, necessarily true. 'I may have seen snow a hundred times, and may have seen that it was white, but this cannot give me entire assurance even that all snow is white, much less that snow *must* be white' (*SL* I, 273). This, to be sure, is a point to which even Mill's staunchest opponents, such as William Whewell or Stanley Jevons, would have subscribed.[32] Yet, what they rejected is Mill's attendant submission that the same argument has to be extended to mathematical and geometrical axioms which, on his account, are not only derived from experience but also point back to it, rather than being true or false '*à priori*', regardless of any information received by the senses (*SL* I, 291).

According to Mill, then, 'the foundation of all sciences, even deductive or demonstrative sciences, is Induction' (*SL* I, 258). This being his central conviction, he concludes 'that Deductive or Demonstrative Sciences are all, without exception, Inductive Sciences; that their evidence is that of experience' and that the 'character of necessity' often ascribed to them is nothing short of 'an illusion' (*SL* I, 291, 290, 258).

Effectively, this is tantamount to a reconception of the very science of logic which was thus divested of the 'special hardness', traditionally taken to be definitive of it.[33] As Elijah Millgram has shown, by making the point that there is 'no such thing as deductive inference', Mill attempted to remove the 'logical *must*' which was (and still is) typically considered to be what separates mathematical reasoning from other, softer modes of drawing inferences.[34]

As Millgram argues, Mill, aspiring towards what Auguste Comte described as the 'mature positive stage' of the sciences, endeavoured to dissociate logic from the transcendental (or metaphysical) laws of the mind in which its claims to absolute necessity were often taken to be anchored.[35] Instead, he tried to place logic, typically taken to be deductive by definition, on a par with the inductive sciences which are based on nothing but open-ended experience. In fact, on Mill's account 'a theory of induction *is* a full-featured theory of logic'.[36] This means that Mill's logic, despite the somewhat forbidding complexity and terminological edge of his system, is relatively 'soft', less apodictic and exclusive than one might expect, because it is capable of including the experience-based practices through which all general theories are applied (or related) to, and potentially modified by, particular contexts. As a result, his writing both represents and enacts 'science', including the science of logic, as a kind of knowledge that is in progress, subject to become otherwise, rather than grounded in an idea of necessary, unchangeable truth.

As it turned out, however, this attempt to remove the notion of necessity from the very logic that was supposed to justify and define science became a key site of contention in Mill's dispute with Whewell, 'one of the leading men of science in the Victorian age'.[37] For Whewell not only disagreed with Mill's concept of induction but, as a result of this, also worked from a rather different view of what constitutes a logical argument or proof that is sufficiently sound to qualify as scientific. In his *Philosophy of Discovery*, which represents his latest and most comprehensive engagement with Mill's thought, Whewell himself cogently identifies the nub of the debate: 'To me it appears that there are *two* distinct elements in our knowledge, Experience, without, and the Mind, within. Mr Mill derives all our knowledge from Experience *alone*.'[38] As this reveals, Whewell's epistemology, unlike Mill's, is built upon the assumption of a 'Fundamental Antithesis', as he calls it (*PD* 315), a principal ontological distinction between 'Experience, without, and the Mind, within', the parameters of which he defines by means of a host of corresponding oppositions: things and thoughts, facts and theories, sensations and ideas, objects and subjects, matter and form.

While Whewell emphasises that both of these ingredients are necessary for the inductive generation of true justified knowledge, he clearly privileges theoretical forms over material facts, suggesting that the source of truth is the world of thoughts or ideas, rather than that of sensations or things. Hence his (Kant-like) account of induction as a way of interpreting sensual data by means of intellectual schemata which synthesise and clarify them, transforming 'their apparent confusion into order, their seeming chance into certainty, their perplexing variety into simplicity' (*PIS* II, 49). The key point to note here is that inductive knowledge, thus conceived, effectively issues from a theorem or conception which is not built up from experience, but passed down from the mind. 'Thus in each inference made by Induction, there is introduced some General Conception, which is given not by the phenomena, but by the mind' (*PIS* II, 49). For example, when Johannes Kepler discovered that Mars moves in the shape of an ellipse, 'he bound together particular observations of separate places of Mars by the notion, or, as I have called it, the *conception*, of an *ellipse*, which was supplied by his own mind' (*PD* 253). In contrast to Mill, Whewell is convinced that an ideal (mathematical or geometrical) conception which is found to correspond with certain perceptual givens necessarily constitutes their true form of representation.[39] The shape of Mars's motion, he holds, cannot be anything but an ellipse. It *must* be an ellipse, otherwise it would be inconceivable as an empirical fact.

On these grounds, Whewell describes the 'Progress of Science' as an increasingly expansive '*Idealization of Facts*', or 'a perpetual reduction of Facts to Ideas', to use his own words (*PD* 301–2). 'Portions are perpetually transferred from one side to another of the Fundamental Antithesis: namely, from the Objective to the Subjective Side' (*PD* 302). Unlike Mill (but rather like Kant), moreover, Whewell took the subjective element of the antithesis to be made up of necessary mental laws, exemplified by the axioms of mathematics and geometry (such as 'two straight lines cannot meet twice'), that are sharply distinguished from the contingent insights derived from experience (such as 'snow is white'). For him, therefore, science proceeds by a continuous attempt to translate sensory perceptions into mathematical conceptions that allow us to see them in terms of 'hard' laws transcending the changeable qualities of experience. It follows that, for Whewell, induction is a way of domesticating the contingent information received by the senses, or of transferring it upwards, into an enclosed sphere of theory that is separated from the messy and changeable environment in and through which human lives unfold in practice. In fact, he even limits the very meaning of the term 'induction' to methodically refined ways of reasoning that, being informed by a theoretical grasp of their premises, operate at a remove from the practical experience of individual things. 'Induction is experience or observation *consciously* looked at in a *general* form' (*PD* 245). On this view, neither a child, whose experience has taught it that fire is hot, nor a skilled billiard player, who knows how to make a ball move at a particular speed, can be said to have learned this by induction; for both usually reason unconsciously, as Darwin would say, having no specific idea of the general principles of heat and velocity on which their practical decisions may be based. According to Whewell, this distinction between theory-guided methods and experience-based activities bears directly on the very 'nature of Science, and of the mental process by which Sciences come into being' (*PD* 244). For science, as he sees it, ought to be confined to 'necessary truths contemplated by the intellect' while excluding such varieties of practical reason as habits, skills and what he calls 'instincts and the like', all of which, as he stresses, 'appear in action, and in action only', often lacking any theoretical knowledge of the laws and premises underlying them (*PD* 243–4).

Unlike Mill, Whewell therefore makes a point of insisting on 'a rigorous separation of the Practical from the Theoretical', or of 'art' from 'science', two terms which he takes to refer to entirely separate domains, namely the 'merely empirical' and the 'purely intellectual' respectively (*PIS* II, 113, 112, 106–13). He even opposes the suggestion, as put forth by the *Britannica* article, to see the arts as instruments or applied forms of the sciences, arguing that they each pursue different ends. 'The object of Science is *Knowledge*; the object of Art are *Works*' (*PIS* II, 108), as he puts this, trying to associate science firmly with 'intelligible principles' and art with a mode of relative ignorance. 'The truths on which the success of art depends, lurk in the artist's mind in an undeveloped state; guiding his hand, stimulating his invention, balancing his judgement, but not appearing in the form of enunciated propositions' (*PIS* II, 109, 111). In an attempt to underline this distinction between practices of unconsciously operating on certain principles and states of being knowingly acquainted with them, Whewell repeatedly compares the *modus operandi* of the arts with what he describes as instinctive behaviour. At the same time, he accuses Mill of having recklessly blurred this distinction between '*Instinct*' and '*Insight*' (*PIS* II, 109–10), as well as between the conscious and the unconscious, not only by merging the sciences with the arts but also by extending such terms as 'induction' and 'knowledge' to everyday practices. In one case commented on by Whewell, Mill uses the example of digging to put the case that the ideas in our minds are deeply rooted in the experience of a material world that surrounds and sustains us. 'I cannot dig the ground unless I have the idea of the ground, and of a spade, and of all the other things I am operating upon, and unless I put those ideas together,' he writes:

> But it would be a very ridiculous description of digging the ground to say that it is putting one idea into another. Digging is an operation which is performed upon the things themselves, though it cannot be performed unless I have in my mind the ideas of them. (*SL* I, 97–8)

Mill's point here is that ideas cannot be separated from the matter upon which they operate and which, conversely, operates on them. Whewell, by contrast, seeks to keep the material as much distinct from the ideal as he wants to keep the unconscious mode of what he describes as 'mere practical instinct' apart from the conscious mode of 'rational thought' (*PD* 245). He therefore embarks on a harsh criticism of Mill's 'use of words which', he thinks, 'can only tend to confuse our idea of knowledge by obliterating all that is distinctive in *human* knowledge', as he puts it (*PD* 241).

> It seems to me quite false to say that I cannot dig the ground, unless I have an idea of the ground and of my spade. Are we to say that we cannot *walk* the ground, unless we have an idea of the ground, and of our feet, and of our shoes, and of the muscles of our legs? Are we to say that a mole cannot dig the ground, unless he has an idea of the ground and of the snout and paws with which he digs it? Are we to say that a pholas cannot perforate a rock, unless he have an idea of the rock, and of the acid with which he corrodes it? (*PD* 242)

The seamless way in which Whewell here moves from human to animal activities indicates that what he objects to is Mill's suggestion that such activities as ordinary as walking or digging the ground involve ideas or even knowledge. To Whewell's mind, this suggestion is 'quite false' because he takes a human being who digs or walks the ground to be engaged in the same kind of unthinking behaviour as a mole who burrows into the ground or a pholas (a kind of mollusc) who perforates a rock by means of a self-produced acid. While this repeated equation of practical experience with instincts may seem oddly overstated, it allowed Whewell, in keeping with his antithetical logic, to map the difference between art and science onto a set of other oppositions that were already in place, such as the mind and the body, the physical and the intellectual, or, indeed, the animal and the human.

A Tightrope Dance

In summary, it emerges that Mill and Whewell disagreed not only about the meaning of key terms such as 'science' 'knowledge' and 'induction', but also about the function of logic and, consequently, about the very question of what counts as a valid argument.[40] Whewell's epistemology is premised on a structure of oppositions that, by definition, exclude each other. Mill's epistemology, by contrast, is built upon the experience of flexible relations, provisional patterns that may become different. As a result, Whewell often argues by means of an 'either-or rhetoric' that clashes with Mill's more inclusive use of central terms. The above example of digging is a case in point. Whereas Whewell insists that practical habits and skills must not be taken to be informed by ideas or knowledge (but at best by 'instincts'), Mill sees no reason why the meaning of 'idea' and 'knowledge' should not be seen to cut across a continuum that ranges from the practical to the theoretical. In fact, it seems as if Mill had been entirely unable or unwilling to take Whewell's point. Thus his response to Whewell's critique, first published in a footnote to the third edition of his *Logic* (1851), is no more than a curt refusal to acknowledge that the problem outlined by his opponent even exists. He knew neither what passed in a mole's mind, Mill writes in a provocatively unfazed manner, nor whether his 'instinctive actions' were accompanied by a degree of 'mental apprehension'. 'But a human being does not use a spade by instinct; and he certainly could not use it unless he had knowledge of a spade, and of the earth which he uses it upon' (*SL* I, 98). Apparently, the concept of instinct, so important for Whewell, is just not one of Mill's concerns because he considered it to be gratuitous to distinguish as sharply between practical and theoretical knowledge as his antagonist did. Whewell, by contrast, used the notion of instinct to cut a chasm between these two domains that he did not want to see crossed. At best, Whewell concedes, artful thinking may on occasion 'lead to science', but by no means must it be taken to be a part of it (*PD* 244). 'This distinction is essential to the philosophy of science,' he asserts emphatically, before once again using his comparison with animals (*PD* 244).

> The rope-dancer may, by his performances, suggest, to himself or to others, properties of the center of gravity; but this is so, because man has a tendency to speculate and to think of general truths, as well as a tendency to dance on a rope on special occasions, and to acquire skill in such dancing by practice. The rope-dancer does not dance by Induction, any more

than the dancing dog does. To apply the terms Science and Induction to such cases, carries us into the regions of metaphor; as when we call birds of passage 'wise meteorologists', or the bee 'a natural chemist, who turns the flower dust into honey'. This is very well in poetry: but for our purposes we must avoid recognizing these cases as really belonging to the sciences of meteorology and chemistry,– as really cases of Induction. Induction for us is general propositions, *contemplated as such*, derived from particulars. (*PD* 244–5)

According to Whewell, then, science, along with the inductive method taken to define it, needs to be placed on a firm footing of 'general propositions' so as to be separated from all manner of skilled practices such as rope-dancing which properly belong to art. Mill's science, by contrast, is sufficiently flexible and open to include, or remain in dialogue with, the arts of using, adapting, rearranging and correcting it. Not unlike a tightrope dance, the work of science, in Mill's view, is dependent on, and involved in, an open-ended process of adjusting it to the experience of changeable materials and unforeseen events.[41] In this way, knowledge is made subject to perpetual renewal and variation, however minute, even if it seems to remain the same.

Mill is keen to stress that the methods of investigation that correspond to this process-based notion of knowledge are all, in one way or another, centred on observation and experiment. Both of these actions involve a movement of introducing a qualitative modification into a material environment, or, as Mill calls it, of '*varying the circumstances*' (*SL* I, 440). The only difference between them is that observation denotes the more or less accidental *finding* of such variations whereas experiment refers to a way of *making* them by means of 'an artificial arrangement of circumstances' (*SL* I, 440). Yet, while experiment and observation may not differ 'in kind', there are a number of 'practical distinctions' between them, Mill points out, the most notable of which is the fact that experimentation is 'an immense extension' of observation (*SL* I, 440). As he argues, 'it enables us to obtain innumerable circumstances which are not to be found in nature, and so add to nature's experiments a multitude of experiments of our own' (*SL* I, 441). On this view, nature is not an inert, inactive substance, experimented on by human agents who stand apart from or look down upon her, but an agent in and of herself, just as much engaged in experiments as the people investigating her. Nature, Mill suggests, is caught up in a process of becoming, continuously transforming the components which constitute her being. Man, in his turn, participates in this process by repeatedly varying some of the conditions that surround him and, in this way, 'adding to nature's experiments a multitude of experiments of his own'. By this account, nature does not exclude, but include the various ways in which it is manipulated, modelled, or marked by human practices and works. It refers to an evolving environment in which human beings work as one power among others. 'Nature,' as Mill puts it in an essay specifically dedicated to this term, 'is a collective name for all facts, actual and possible: or (to speak more accurately) a name for the mode, partly known to us and partly unknown, in which all things take place'.[42]

As Mill emphasises, this inclusive conception of nature affects the distinction between the natural and the artificial (or man-made) because it 'entirely conflicts with the common form of speech by which Nature is opposed to Art', to quote him again.[43]

> For in the sense of the word Nature which has just been defined, and which is the true scientific sense, Art is as much Nature as anything else; and everything which is artificial is natural – Art has no independent powers of its own: Art is but the employment of the powers of Nature for an end. Phenomena produced by human agency, no less than those which as far as we are concerned are spontaneous, depend on the properties of the elementary forces, or of the elementary substances and their compounds. The united powers of the whole human race could not create a new property of matter in general, or of any one of its species. We can only take advantage for our purposes of the properties which we find.[44]

All the artificial (or cultural) objects humans make (out) of their environment, remain dependent 'on the properties' and 'substances' that constitute it. 'The corn which men raise for food,' for example, 'grows and produces its grain by the same laws of vegetation by which the wild rose and the mountain strawberry bring forth their flowers and fruit.'[45] Likewise, 'a steam engine works by the natural expansive force of steam'.[46] According to this conception, human activities and technologies are not to be seen as modes of separation, setting the world of culture neatly apart from the world of nature. They are rather to be seen as modes of extension and supplementation, drawing out possibilities that are inherent in nature in order to appropriate them for human wants and ends. Hence Mill's claim that 'Art has no independent powers of its own: Art is but the employment of the powers of Nature for an end.'

This view of art converges with Darwin's account of the techniques of breeding and gardening which he takes to have been part of the natural world for a very long time. 'From a remote period, in all parts of the world, man has subjected many animals and plants to domestication or culture.'[47] This is not meant to say that man has been imposing some kind of non-natural culture on his fellow beings, depriving them of everything natural. Darwin's point is rather that man has long been interfering with the 'generative currents' in and through which the animate world unfolds,[48] putting natural actions to work for human ends. As long as human beings have existed, one might phrase it, they have inscribed their operations into the ongoing processes of the non-human world. 'Man, therefore, may be said to have been trying an experiment on a gigantic scale; and it is an experiment which nature during the long lapse of time has incessantly tried.'[49]

For both Mill and Darwin, then, the experimental method is a means of reproducing natural activities in a way that can be measured and controlled in artificial forms accessible to human minds. On this view, experiments work as mediators between the natural and the artificial as well as between the non-human and the human, the possible and the actual, the unknown and the known. As Mill puts it: 'When we can produce a phenomenon artificially, we can take it, as it were, home with us, and observe it in the midst of circumstances with which in all other respects we are accurately acquainted' (*SL* I, 441). One of his examples is 'the electric machine', by means of which (as by means of the Leyden jar and the voltaic battery), the natural forces manifesting themselves in lightning and thunder have been made reproducible (and readable) in artificial forms allowing people to know far more about them than they could ever have found out by mere observation (*SL* I, 441). Briefly, then, the method of experiment, as defined by Mill, is made up of a twofold operation: the activity of engendering yet unknown phenomena, of provoking new experiences by varying existing circumstances on the one hand, and the activity of drawing inferences from the phenomena so produced on the other. The first process renders experience doubtful or strange while the second process 'takes it home' to interpret it in the context of what is already known, thus modifying this context, if only slightly, or making it appear in a different light.

One key point, moreover, is that induction by experiment and observation, as Mill conceives it, is a way of investigating nature from the inside of the evolutionary process that constitutes it, rather than from a point outside of it. By contrast, Whewell's notion of induction is premised on a conception of scientists as detached spectators importing inert facts into a mental apparatus which identifies and synthesises, but is not itself part of, them. On his account, scientists extract facts from or project ideas onto a material world that is taken to be situated apart from or outside of their minds. Whewell's view of induction as a kind of upward transport is therefore rather different from Mill's concept of observation and experiment as ways of interfering with the material forces of a world with which scientific practitioners, by virtue of being products of nature, are themselves enmeshed. More specifically, Whewell not only thinks of induction as a kind of jump across the gap between antithetical terms that cuts through his whole argument. He also claims, unlike Mill, that induction could not be scientific if it were not always accompanied by deduction. 'Deduction is a necessary part of Induction,' as he puts this, comparing the two actions to a rapid upward- and a slower downward-movement respectively (*PIS* II, 93). 'Induction mounts by a leap which is out of the reach of method,' he says. 'She bounds to the top of the stair at once; and then it is the business of Deduction, by trying each step in order, to establish the solidity of her companion's footing' (*PIS* II, 92). While this instantaneous leap or single stroke of genius is described as a 'happy thought, of which we cannot trace the origin' and 'some fortunate cast of intellect, rising above all rules' (*PIS* II, 20), the crucial operation is the deductive process of determining, on the basis of the necessary laws of the mind, whether the insights found by induction are sound. In Whewell's model, deduction is a way of moving gradually down from the top, testing the 'solidity' of steps whose existence is presupposed. What is conspicuously missing in this model, therefore, is the often slow and long-winded activity of *building* these steps in the first place, of constructing a ground on which one can proceed. Instead, Whewell hides this activity behind a conjectural leap which he takes to be 'out of the reach of method'. It follows that Whewell has no way of accounting for the temporally extended arts of learning something new, of finding the way to forms of thought that have not yet appeared in the mind. As we have seen, on his account, these practices – Darwin and Mill refer to them by the term 'experiment' – belong to the domain of the unconscious and instinctive which is of no avail to a theory of science.

As several commentators, starting with John Herschel in 1841, have remarked, there are good reasons to argue that the process Whewell terms induction is better described as a version of deduction, induced by a 'happy thought' or a hypothetical idea.[50] The logician John Venn, for instance, claims that it is 'scarcely an exaggeration of Whewell's account of the inductive process to say of it, as has been said, that it simply resolves itself into making guesses, and then justifying these guesses by subsequent deduction'.[51] As Venn's summary indicates, it seems as if, towards the close of the century, more and more scholars became critical of the idealist approach represented by Whewell. This suggests that the notion of induction as a leap across a gap between subjects and objects, or ideas and sensations was increasingly supplemented with, if not supplanted by, an experimentalist view which does not presuppose this antithesis but regards it as an effect of practices of comparing, contrasting, combining, separating and moving about things. As a result, the methodology of science began to include the particular activities of applying, adapting and transforming the general structures that were supposed to represent the forms of logical thought. Venn, for example, introduces his *Principles of Empirical or Inductive Logic* (1889) by asserting 'that the complete attainment of the ideal position of the mere observer is nowhere to be secured even in Physics'.[52] This means that the logic of science lacks an abstract theoretical vantage above the matter to which it is supposed to refer in practice. 'No one of us can be spared to occupy the ideal logician's seat,' as he explains, "and if he try to do so he would find that he was perpetually leaving it, and mixing himself up in some way or other in the course of what should have been to him a wholly external world.'[53] On this view, one can no longer presuppose a clear-cut distinction between the mind inside and 'a wholly external world'. Human beings, scientists included, can, as a rule, never stand outside of whatever they may want to examine, Venn suggests, but only move in relation to it. To take up one position is to slip out of another and vice versa, but there is no one standpoint in which this relational motion could ever be brought to a halt. 'Each one of us has his own position amongst the objects which compose the world,' as he puts it; 'he has his own little sphere of activity which he may change only by taking up some other'.[54] It follows, Venn argues, that the position of a mere spectator must be regarded as a 'fictitious post' because no one can avoid mixing themselves up, to some degree, with the matter they seek to examine.[55] Even the astronomer, being subject to the same laws of gravitation as the stars, cannot help perturbing their course, however slightly, by the sheer 'fact of observing them', as Venn points out. 'Every motion to or from his instrument, nay the very calculations he writes down on paper or the words he utters by his voice, are motions of matter, and therefore react on the motions of every other material thing in the universe, including the planets themselves.'[56]

As we shall see in the next chapter, the more this entanglement of the observer and the observed was acknowledged as a logical insight in its own right, the more science came to be seen as inseparable from the experience-based arts of making and remaking it. In fact, by the turn of the century, the experimental method could already be identified as nothing less than the defining characteristic of 'Science, in its widest significance', as the corresponding entry in Chambers's popular *Encyclopaedia* has it. 'The gardener and the breeder led the way in a form of experimentation which Darwin made scientific; while such branches of the subject as Embryology and Bacteriology are as truly experimental as Chemistry itself.'[57]

Notes

1. Williams, *Keywords*, p. 40.
2. See the entry on 'art' in Williams, *Keywords*, as well as the *OED* article 'art, n.1'.
3. Ingold, 'Beyond Art', pp. 17–20. See also Staten, 'Wrong Turn'.
4. Unsigned Article, 'Art', *The Encyclopaedia Britannica*, vol. 2. All references to this article (abbreviated as *EB*) will be given in the text.
5. Ryle, 'Knowing How', pp. 212–26.
6. Mill, *A System*, I, p. 215. All references to this edition (*SL*), published one year before Mill's death, will be given in the main text by volume and page number.
7. Williams, *Keywords*, p. 42.
8. Kant, *Critique of Judgement*, p. 146 (B 175).
9. Williams, *Keywords*, p. 42.
10. As Klancher has pointed out, this view of the relationship between art and science came to prominence in the latter decades of the eighteenth century (*Transfiguring*, p. 14). It unsettles an earlier view, underpinning the quarrel between the Ancients and the Moderns, according to which the sciences are progressive whereas the arts are static (p. 15). Klancher's book, which is focused on the Romantic age, provides a specifically institutional history of the complicated relationship between the arts and the sciences.
11. Cf. Ingold, *Being Alive*, pp. 210–11.
12. Gooding, 'Mapping Experiment', p. 167.
13. Paley, *Natural Theology*. All references to this edition (*NT*) will be given in the text.
14. To use these terms interchangeably was not unusual in the first half of the nineteenth century. Cf. Norton Wise and Smith, 'Work and Waste (II)', p. 420.
15. Paley's use of such terms as 'design' and 'mechanism' are all informed by the Industrial Revolution, as Gillespie ('Divine Design') has shown.

16. Latour, *Pandora's Hope*, p. 283.
17. Shelley, *Frankenstein*, p. 35.
18. Cf. Latour, *Reassembling*, p. 46.
19. An all-encompassing consciousness of time has often been identified as a hallmark of the later nineteenth century; see Middeke, *Kunst*, pp. 43–60.
20. Darwin, *Origin*, p. 30. References to this edition (*OS*) are given in the text.
21. Rheinberger and McLaughlin, 'Darwin's Experimental Natural History', p. 349. Elsewhere, I have written in more detail, and provided further research literature, on the debate that ensued from Darwin's choice of modelling natural on artificial selection. Cf. Erchinger, 'Nature, Culture'.
22. Darwin, *The Variation*, II, p. 193.
23. Ibid., pp. 193, 211.
24. Ibid., p. 211.
25. My discussion of Mill and Whewell leaves out most of the wider social, political, institutional and media historical setting of their work because this has been extensively covered by Snyder, *Reforming Philosophy*, esp. pp. 204–66 and 267–334 and, with a focus on Whewell, Yeo, *Defining Science*.
26. Mill, *A System*, title page. At Oxford, Mill's *Logic* was used as 'the standard textbook on logic' for several decades, and at Cambridge, too, it was part of the canon of 'widely read' texts (Snyder, *Reforming Philosophy*, p. 99).
27. Mill, *An Examination*. All references to this edition (*HP*) are given by page numbers.
28. James, *Pragmatism*, dedication.
29. Snyder, *Reforming Philosophy*, p. 163. Mill's *Logic* was written with the self-avowed intention to reform the method of philosophy, so as to free it from 'intuitionist epistemology' and its belief in *a priori* truths or laws, an approach that Mill took to foster 'political and social conservatism' (p. 96).
30. 'A mode of concluding from experience must be pronounced untrustworthy, when subsequent experience refuses to confirm it' (*SL* II, p. 101). 'The proposition, Two straight lines cannot inclose a space – or, in other words, Two straight lines which have once met, do not meet again, but continue to diverge – is an induction from the evidence of our senses' (*SL* I, p. 266).
31. Balaguer evaluates Mill's philosophy of mathematics from a contemporary point of view: 'Mill and the Philosophy of Mathematics'. More generally, Mecke offers a physicist's view of the function of numbers in the making of knowledge ('Zahl und Erzählung').
32. The critique of the economist and logician Jevons is an attempt to reveal what he calls 'the inextricable difficulties and self-contradictions' of Mill's 'so-called "Empirical Philosophy"': 'John Stuart Mill's Philosophy', p. 182. While Jevons considered himself to be an empiricist, too, he refused to share Mill's inductive account of mathematics.

33. Millgram, 'John Stuart Mill', p. 190.
34. Ibid., p. 190.
35. Ibid., p. 190.
36. Millgram, 'Mill's and Whewell's Competing Visions', p. 104.
37. Yeo, *Defining Science*, p. 5.
38. Whewell, *Philosophy of Discovery*, p. 286. All page references to this book (*PD*) are given in the text. Likewise, all references to William Whewell, *The Philosophy of the Inductive Sciences*, vols 1 and 2, are provided as *PIS* I and *PIS* II.
39. Mill also provided an account of Kepler's discovery which is, needless to say, quite different. For details see Snyder, *Reforming Philosophy*, pp. 101–6.
40. Millgram, 'Mill's and Whewell's Competing Visions', p. 109.
41. De Certeau also refers to tightrope dancing as a metaphor for the 'art of operating' (*Practice*, p. 73).
42. Mill, 'Nature', p. 374.
43. Ibid., p. 375.
44. Ibid., p. 375.
45. Ibid., p. 375.
46. Ibid., p. 375.
47. Darwin, *The Variation*, I, p. 2.
48. Ingold, *Being Alive*, p. 214.
49. Darwin, *The Variation*, I, p. 3.
50. [Herschel], '[Review]'. For a more recent interpretation of Whewell's induction as hypothetico-deduction see, for instance, Laudan, 'William Whewell'. Contesting this view, Snyder has come to Whewell's defence by expounding his approach as 'Discoverer's Induction'; see also Snyder, *Reforming Philosophy*, pp. 51–66.
51. Venn, *Principles*, p. 355.
52. Ibid., p. 20.
53. Ibid., p. 21.
54. Ibid., p. 21.
55. Ibid., p. 21.
56. Ibid., p. 20.
57. 'Science', *Chambers's Encyclopaedia*, p. 230.

Chapter 2

Learning by Experiment: T. H. Huxley and the Aesthetic Nature of Education

The Subject of Science

The debate between Mill and Whewell is not so much a scientific controversy as a controversy about the very idea of science and its operative supplement, namely art. It is about how science is to be defined in relation to the art of making, extending and applying it. On Whewell's account, to repeat, 'science' refers to a theoretical sphere that ought to be kept neatly apart from all modes of experience-based reasoning and embodied thought. For Mill, by contrast, the practical domain of life, along with the moral and political issues inherent in it, must be acknowledged as continuous with scientific ideas. While this may appear like a mere quarrel over the meaning of words, it draws attention to an unsettled relationship between people's theoretical knowledge *about* the world and their practical experience of being engaged *with* it.

This interplay between being and knowing, as I shall argue in this chapter, between sensual involvement and intellectual detachment and, for that matter, between ontology and epistemology, was of central concern to many Victorians and has remained relevant ever since. It is best explored by way of another influential definition of 'science' that was originally proposed by John Herschel in 1830. 'Science,' Herschel writes in his *Preliminary Discourse on the Study of Natural History*, 'is the knowledge of many, orderly and methodically digested and arranged, so as to become attainable by one.'[1] On this conception, science represents a general mode of knowledge that is abstracted from individual circumstances, interests and points of view. Science, thus defined, is what has been purified of the multiple ways in which it may be perceived so as to be contained in an ideal, often mathematical form 'attainable by one'. As Peter Galison and Lorraine Daston have argued, this notion of 'science' as justified general knowledge, which conforms with Whewell's, is both premised on and productive of an ethos of disengagement and self-restraint that, towards the end of the nineteenth century, came to define what is now usually conceived of as a professional culture of scientific pursuit.[2] Fostered by new technologies of mechanical representation, such as the photograph, this professional approach, Daston and Galison argue, turned the scientific method into a way of extracting abstract figures from what is given to the senses, or of translating personal perceptions into impersonal forms. Subjective experience was to disappear in favour of allegedly objective modes of recording and reproducing it. It was therefore believed, they claim, that the researcher's personal feelings, tastes, prejudices and desires had to be disciplined in a way that disentangled them from the matter to be understood. As a human being, the scientist had to be, to invoke George Levine's pithy twist of a well-known proverb, 'dying to know'.[3]

One consequence of this widespread belief in self-renunciation as a prerequisite of gaining justified knowledge was that the scientific stance became heavily charged with moral demands. The pursuit of objectivity was taken to be inseparable from the cultivation of a particular kind of subjectivity. 'Science was a moral discipline, its success depending on the "courage, patience and self-denial" of the practitioner.'[4] There is indeed no shortage of Victorian intellectuals who recommended a version of such self-denial as the only path towards certain belief. Samuel Smiles, for example, never tires of advertising qualities like 'patience', diligence, 'steady perseverance' and 'painstaking industry' as key virtues of a sound and prosperous character.[5] Likewise, Karl Pearson identifies 'self-elimination', or the ability to form 'judgements independent of the idiosyncrasies of the individual mind' as central to the work of the scientist.[6] At the same time, however, this trust in the epistemological virtue of self-effacement was often underpinned by an understanding that the investigator and the investigated are, in reality, closely entwined rather than neatly distinct. George H. Lewes, for instance, repeatedly underscores this point: 'The Subject is inseparable from the Object, in any real sense; is only separable ideally.' Or yet again: 'The object is always object-subject; the thing is always the thing felt. We may distinguish the aspects by marks, we cannot isolate the factors.'[7]

This presupposition that the personal and the general, or the felt and the known, are deeply interwoven often resulted in a concern with the ways and means of drawing the (feeling) subject out of the (known) object, or vice versa, and, in this way, to separate the mode of the scientific from all that which was not supposed to be part of it. In the nineteenth century, as the controversy examined in the first chapter has made evident, it could not be taken for granted what 'science' is, where it begins and ends, and how exactly it is related to other ways of making sense of experience, such as the painting of pictures or the writing of poetry. What had to be attended to, therefore, was the way science was to be made in order to count as such. Hence, for example, Karl Pearson's insistent claim that it was the method that defined science, not its subject matter. '*The unity of all science consists alone in its method, not in its material.*'[8] For Pearson too, as Levine has shown, the purpose of this method was to eliminate all traces of 'individual fancy' and personal bias from the knowledge represented by science.[9] This methodically induced 'death' of the scientist was to ensure that science captures an impartial, context-independent truth on which everyone could rely, irrespective of their personal views. Moreover, Pearson considers the use of the scientific method to have an ethical value. By means of this method, he argues, one learns to subordinate one's personal prejudices to an ideal goal, 'the complete interpretation of the universe', that is larger than anything a single person could ever achieve on their own.[10] In fact, Pearson regards the capacity to free one's judgements from 'blind emotional excitement' and 'individual bias' as no less than a precondition 'of ideally good citizenship'.[11] In order for this capacity to be trained, he thinks, it is less important what someone learns than how they learn it. 'It does not indeed matter for the purpose we have in view whether he seek to make himself proficient in geology, or biology, or geometry, or mechanics, or even history or folklore, if these be studied scientifically.'[12] Or, in short: 'The scientific method is one and the same in all branches, and that method is the method of all logically trained minds.'[13]

Again, however, my point is that this emphasis on the boundary-making function of the scientific method was informed by a widely shared belief that propositional and personal (or theoretical and practical) knowledge have never been distinguished in the first place. Writers as different as J. S. Mill and Friedrich Max Müller both highlighted that all sciences were 'originally' meant to answer 'practical requirements', rather than discover general laws.[14] 'Such,' for instance, 'was medical investigation, before physiology and natural history began to be cultivated as branches of general knowledge', as Mill points out (*SL* II, 465). 'The only questions examined were, what diet is wholesome, or what medicine will cure some given disease; without any previous systematic inquiry into the laws of nutrition' and organic life (*SL* II, 465). To be sure, the scientific method, as described by Pearson, was meant to define the sciences as something distinctly other than the skilful practices they may once have been. This explains why Müller finds it necessary to stress, like Whewell, that a science in its practical stage 'is hardly a science yet: that measuring a field is not geometry, that growing cabbages is very far from botany, and that a butcher has no claim to the title of comparative anatomist'.[15] Yet even he insists, like Mill, that 'historically we are justified in saying that the first geometrician was a ploughman, the first botanist a gardener, the first mineralogist a miner'.[16]

The Common Sense of Science

It is this awareness of what Müller calls the 'more humble beginnings' of all sciences that many Victorian writers share with the practice-based approach in contemporary science studies.[17] David Gooding, for instance, opens his book on experimental meaning-making by announcing that he would drop the now widely held 'article of faith' according to which 'scientists', having 'special methods', 'do not also need the same ways of interacting with the world as the rest of us do'.[18] In this way, Gooding abandons a distinction between 'scientists' and 'the rest of us' that the (often blind) trust in the ideal of scientific method helps to maintain. Instead, he re-establishes a connection between scientific and everyday work that is still presupposed in many Victorian texts. One of its best-known instances is T. H. Huxley's famous dictum, first voiced in 1854 and then variously repeated, that science, including its method, is 'nothing but *trained and organised common sense*, differing from the latter only as a veteran may differ from a raw recruit'.[19] In theory, scientists may certainly know more and otherwise than many other people; in fact, they may even know commonsense reasoning to be false. But Huxley's point is that, in practice, their specialist wisdom must issue from, and remain in tune with, the same 'primary power', the same experience of being alive, that informs, often inarticulately, all human ways of coming to terms with the world.[20] In the last instance, the knowledge of scientists must be made of, and apply to, the same world as the practical experience of everyone else. For Huxley, therefore, the scientific method is continuous with common sense. 'So, the vast results obtained by Science are won by no mystical faculties, by no mental processes, other than those which are practised by every one of us, in the humblest and meanest affairs of life.'[21] When a lady, to quote one of his few gender-sensitive examples, on finding 'a stain of a peculiar kind upon her dress', decides that some-one must have spilled ink over it, she essentially engages in the same process of induction and deduction by means of which astronomers discover new planets, even though she may not be conscious of this at all.[22] 'The man of science,' as Huxley concludes, 'simply uses with scrupulous exactness the methods which we all, habitually and at every moment, use carelessly; and the man of business must as much avail himself of the scientific method – must be as truly a man of science – as the veriest bookworm of us all'.[23] All human beings, then, draw on 'the scientific method', whether they are aware of it or not; for one can very well carry out processes of induction and deduction without having even heard of these terms, just as one may know how to talk prose without knowing that one talks 'prose'. In short, as Huxley stresses in a lecture series for a working-class audience, 'scientific investigation is not, as many people seem to suppose, some kind of modern black art'.[24] For the much-vaunted 'principles of the "Baconian philosophy"' to be seen in operation, for example, one has to look no further than an ordinary 'fruiterer's shop' where they will unconsciously guide the action of whoever seeks to ascertain, by taste and inference, which apples taste sour and which sweet.[25] The 'methods of modern scientific inquiry' did not originate with Bacon or his age, Huxley insists; 'they originated with the first man, whoever he was; and indeed existed long before him, for many of the essential processes of reasoning are exerted by the higher order of brutes as completely and effectively as by ourselves'.[26]

In summary, this view of the scientific method as refined common-sense entails that all human beings, whatever they do, are nascent scientists. Even the most refined theoretical and methodological knowledge takes its rise, according to Huxley, in everyday practice. This primacy of the practical, which both precedes and overtakes whatever theory one may seek to abstract from or impose upon it, is further emphasised by the French physiologist Claude Bernard. 'Man can do,' Bernard declares in his influential book *Experimental Medicine*, 'more than he knows', which explains, to his mind, why 'great experimenters appeared before all precepts of experimentation, as great orators preceded all treatises on rhetoric'.[27] If all learning comes into being by doing, moreover, then whatever knowledge is generally regarded as new must emerge from a mode of personal intelligence, from what Bernard calls 'a feeling for relations' that does not yet have an articulate conceptual form.[28] This feeling for what might be true, he argues, engenders the designs upon which experimental investigations can proceed. 'Feeling gives rise to the experimental idea or hypothesis, i.e., the previsioned interpretation of natural phenomena.'[29] It 'releases an act', giving 'a motive' to the experimental process that arises from it. 'Feeling alone guides the mind and constitutes the *primum movens* of science.'[30]

Bernard never defines 'feeling' in more definite terms, but what is clear from his account is that he uses it, along with intuition and imagination, to refer to a category of the first person as opposed to justification or proof, which are categories of the third person. Equally allied with both of these sides, the experimental method, as described by Bernard, is the process through which relatively inchoate surmises, made up of both sense-perception and experience-based intimation, are converted into justified true belief. There can be no experiment without an idea based on feeling, he argues. 'But the object of the experimental method is to transform this *a priori* conception, based on an intuition or a vague feeling about the nature of things, into an *a posteriori* interpretation founded on the experimental study of phenomena.'[31] If '"Art is myself"' and '"science is ourselves"', as Bernard suggests (quoting an unnamed poet), then the experimental method is the temporally extended work that integrates these two sides.[32] 'Experiment,' in short, 'becomes the one mediator between the objective and the subjective, that is to say, between the man of science and the phenomena which surround him.'[33]

The logic of what Bernard calls 'experimental reasoning', therefore, does not exist before or after the process of experimentation through which it is constituted and maintained.[34] It subsists only *in* this process, in a provisional, flexible form that may, at any moment, become surpassed by a slightly different one. Whereas the scholastic or mathematician, as Bernard explains, 'must always have a fixed and indubitable starting point',[35] the premise of the experimenter is never 'immutable', but always 'dubitative', subject to be modified in response to (unexpected) events that occur, as it were, on the way.[36] In other words, the reasoning of the experimenter, for Bernard, turns not on permanence and certainty, but on fluidity and uncertainty. 'Experimenters, then, always doubt even their starting point; of necessity they keep a supple and modest mind and accept contradiction, on the condition that it be proved.'[37] As a result, 'experimental truths' can only ever be 'unconscious and relative', as Bernard stresses, 'because the real conditions on which they exist are unconscious and can be known by us only in their relation to the present state of our science'.[38] This is another way of saying that experimental knowledge, by definition, resists finality. It depends upon changeable circumstances which means that it must remain sufficiently open to become adjusted or redefined as they demand. Indeed, the greatest flaw of an experimenter, for Bernard, 'consists in thinking that he knows what he does not know, and in taking for absolute, truths that are only relative'.[39]

In one of his most illuminating metaphors, Bernard compares the use of the experimental method with a walk along 'a winding road in the dark and over unknown hilly ground'. For in such conditions the wanderer is compelled to move slowly and cautiously, pausing after each step.[40] 'Before taking a second step, he must make sure that he has placed his first foot on a spot that is firm, then go forward in the same way verifying experimentally, moment by moment, the solidity of the ground, and always changing the direction of his advance according to what he encounters.'[41] Like walkers in mountaineous terrain, then, experimenters are exposed to the ups and downs and turns of a path that is never wholly in view. Taking one stride after the other, Bernard suggests, they have to join their actions with the flows and currents of their surroundings, following the clues and impressions that they gather as they thread their itinerary through an environment. On this view, experimenters, like walkers unfamiliar with the area, do not know the course upon which they proceed. It is not predefined for them. They rather come to know their way by virtue of the physical movement that runs their thinking along the composite of materials and tangled lines making up the phenomenal world in which they are immersed.[42]

As the following passage from Huxley's essays suggests once more, this 'pedestrian' conception of the experimental method as a refinement of ordinary activities such as walking in the hills was still commonplace in the Victorian age.

> How did Harvey determine the nature of the circulation, except by experiment? How did Sir Charles Bell determine the functions of the roots of the spinal nerves, save by experiment? How do we know the use of a nerve at all, except by experiment? Nay, how do you know even that your eye is your seeing apparatus, unless you make the experiment of shutting it; or that your ear is your hearing apparatus, unless you close it up and thereby discover that you become deaf?[43]

Huxley's juxtaposition of the relatively sophisticated procedures of the physicians William Harvey and Charles Bell with the opening and shutting of one's eye reinforces the point that I have been making so far: the experimental method, as understood by many Victorians, is not exclusive to the sciences that it is nowadays often taken to define. Rather, it is common to everyone who is faced with the task of having to 'feel' their 'way forward' through intractable grounds.[44] As one can gather from Bernard's exposition, some of the elementary operations constituting this experimental movement are variation, repetition, comparison and reintegration, all of which, as it happens, are integral components of children's play too.[45]

The Experimental Field

Far from being only of historical value, to study these Victorian accounts of scientific methodology as 'refined commonsense' may allow researchers in the arts and humanities to reappropriate the notion of experiment for their very own concerns. The method of performing experiments, Huxley and Bernard can teach us, has never been owned by the sciences, but is part and parcel of all knowledge-making processes that constitute the world of human affairs. The philosopher and journalist Grant Allen, in a late essay worthy of a closer look, even described experimentation in anthropological terms, as an enabling mechanism at the very 'origin of cultivation'.[46] The only way in which 'primitive man' could have come to know 'that plants grew from seeds', he argues, is 'by the experimental process of sowing and growing them'.[47] However, as man 'is not likely ever to have tried deliberate experiments on the properties of plants, as if he were a Fellow of the Royal Society', the essay continues, there must have been some other motive that led him to start cultivating fields.[48] Allen's theory is that such a motive was provided by the 'primitive burial system' which involved the custom of offering food and drink at the tombstone of the deceased, including 'fruits, seeds', 'berries' and some 'rich grains'.[49] According to Allen's account, these seeds probably thrived 'exceedingly in the newly-turned and well-manured soil of a grave or barrow; and producing there a quantity of rich and edible grain, would certainly attract the attention of that practical and observant man, the savage'.[50]

What is described here is what Bernard and Mill would have called a 'disturbance of the phenomena',[51] or a variation of the circumstances. Although this variation, in Allen's narrative, was brought about by accident rather than design, it still motivated his 'observant' 'savage' to compare the situation thus produced with the one that had preceded it and to infer, in this manner, 'that cereals and other seeds only throve exceptionally upon newly-made graves, not on graves in general'.[52] One can say, then, that Allen imagines these primitive people to have used the same method that is described by Bernard who characterised an 'experiment' as a 'variation or disturbance brought into a phenomenon' in order to compare its disturbed condition with its undisturbed one.[53]

Allen concedes that his early men, being superstitious people, are likely to have ascribed the exceptional harvest to 'the powerful ghost in the barrow', rather than the physicochemical condition of the soil.[54] But this could hardly have prevented them, he argues, from producing the favourable modification themselves. 'Hence might gradually arise a habit of making a new grave annually, at the most favourable sowing time.'[55] And the conclusion of Allen's story is that this habit eventually evolved into controlled agriculture. 'Thus slowly there would develop the cultivated field, the wider clearing, dug up or laboured by hand, and finally the ploughed field, which yet remains a grave in theory and in all essentials.'[56] While Allen speaks exclusively about the rise of agriculture, as well as its seed in the custom of paying tribute to the dead, one may read his argument as one about the experimental roots of culture more generally. The very term 'culture', after all, was first used to refer specifically to the field of gardening and planting, and it was not until much later that it generally designated the whole realm of man-made artefacts and constructions. In its earlier meaning, which remained in use throughout the nineteenth century,[57] culture denotes the skilful process through which experiences of natural phenomena are made to grow into man-made patterns and designs.[58] Culture, thus conceived, is worked out of and inscribed into nature, rather than being in any way separate from it. While culture refers to an artificial process, it is carried out from the inside of a natural environment on which it depends.

What Allen's essay sketches out may therefore serve as a general paradigm for the experimental field, as I have called it, or the 'developmental niche', in which the cultural and the natural, as well as the customary and the novel, are continuously translated into each other by means of artful work.[59] As Allen's account indicates, this field is not primarily composed of facts or objects that are known but of relations that are not quite or not yet known. In his case, for example, the experimental field is made up of spiritual (the primitive belief in ghosts), ritual (the custom of burying the dead), physicochemical (the condition of the 'newly-turned and well-manured soil') and climate-related factors ('the most favourable sowing time'). But how exactly, on the basis of which laws, these factors interact in order to produce 'a quantity of rich and edible grain' was not yet clear to the people Allen describes. The only way through which the rules of this interaction could be made out, he suggests, is by 'half-conscious experiment and observation'.[60] It follows that the medium of cultivation and, by implication, of culture at large, as it is described here, is not articulate knowledge, but 'the experimental', to use E. Warwick Slinn's term, 'that which is based on experience only – on direct acquaintance or personal knowledge, not on separate or agreed authority'.[61] Bernard's 'experimental reason' is a form of reason that is 'based on experience only' in this sense: 'on direct acquaintance or personal knowledge', not on a set of acknowledged standards or mathematical laws.

It should have become evident that the emphasis of many Victorians lay at least as much on science as a body of established knowledge as on the practical skills of perception and experimentation by means of which such knowledge was to be attained. This interest in the art of knowing, in the process of connecting the individual with the general, explains, for instance, why Huxley always insisted on how crucial it is for students of science to be trained in what he calls their 'aesthetic' capacities, meaning those of their 'faculties' which operate primarily through felt perception rather than conscious reflection.[62] In one of his lectures on education, Huxley claims 'that all the subjects of our thoughts' can be said to come either within 'the province of the intellect', which involves what 'can be put into propositions and affirmed or denied', or within 'the province of feeling', 'the aesthetic side of our nature', as he calls it, which includes what can be known only affectively, by feeling (or unconsciously, as Darwin and Bernard might say), rather than proved or disproved in rational terms.[63] Yet even though Huxley thus divides all human thinking into two distinct domains, he is far from asserting that a useful education is to be concerned with the intellectual one only. To be sure, Huxley does, in what appears to be a dualist vein, align 'the reasoning faculty' with the field of 'science' while committing 'all things feelable, all things which stir our emotions' to 'the term of art, in the sense of the subject-matter of the aesthetic faculty'.[64] But nowhere does he adduce this binary 'classification' in order to privilege the rational over the aesthetic or 'matters of science' over 'matters of art', with 'art' here being used specifically in what he calls 'the narrow and technical' meaning of fine art.[65] Rather, he explicitly draws attention to the 'very remarkable fact', as he puts it, 'that there is hardly anything one-sided, or of one nature'.[66] In fact, he points out, it is not even 'immediately obvious what of the things that interest us may be regarded as pure science, and what may be regarded as pure art'.[67]

Huxley concedes that in theory mathematics may be seen as the ideal type of 'pure science' while music may be taken for the ideal type of 'pure art'.[68] Yet, in practice, he argues, music is just as much informed by the intellectual faculty as mathematics is informed by aesthetic feeling. Thus, 'mathematicians' (he says) regularly 'speak of solutions and problems as "elegant"' or describe a pattern of abstract symbols as '"beautiful, quite lovely"'.[69] For Huxley, such formulations are not just metaphors, but expressions of an aesthetic perception that is part and parcel of the supposedly 'pure' mathematical *logos*, even though the uninitiated may be unable to see anything beautiful in numbers or geometrical forms. Mathematicians, by contrast: 'They do see it, because the intellectual process, the process of comprehending the reasons symbolised by these figures and these signs, confers upon them a sort of pleasure, such as an artist has in visual symmetry.'[70] What this suggests is that the rational logic 'symbolised' by mathematical figures and equations is inextricably entangled with the 'process of comprehending' it. Such a process of giving shape and meaning to the symbols of which science is composed, Huxley argues, can yield aesthetic pleasure whenever it results in the perception of some kind of 'unity in variety', as he calls it.[71]

> I cannot give you any example of a thorough aesthetic pleasure more intensely real than a pleasure of this kind – the pleasure which arises in one's mind when a whole mass of different structures run into one harmony as the expression of a central law. That is where the province of art overlays and embraces the province of intellect.[72]

The point of intersection between 'the province of art' and 'the province of intellect', then, is the experience of 'unity' in multiplicity. This description of 'aesthetic pleasure' as one that is motivated by a perception of 'harmony' in diversity and that activates different faculties at the same time, creating a form of dynamic accordance and reconciliation among them, harks back to eighteenth-century theories of aesthetic judgement. According to Kant, for instance, the perception of beauty not only refuses to be judged on the basis of definite concepts, but also hovers between subjective taste and universal consent.[73] Yet, one does not even have to review once more the whole history of aesthetics in order to notice the relevance of this conception for Victorian theories of education and scientific methodology. As we have seen, what both Huxley and Bernard argue is that forms of knowledge can be perceived aesthetically – as a vague intimation of unity in variety – before they are grasped conceptually. Hence Bernard's argument that hypotheses are built upon 'a feeling for relations' – relations which might contain some truth, but whose meaning cannot (yet) be made out in propositional terms.

What all of this shows is, once again, that science and art, just as the personal ('myself') and the general ('ourselves'), were often taken to be caught up in each other because the mental faculties with which these domains were typically associated had to be seen as mutually interactive too. In theory, one may try to classify aesthetic feeling and intellectual thought under two separate heads. But in practice, Huxley and Bernard suggest, they can only work in conjunction. Indeed, for Huxley, 'pure science' is an equally unreal phantasm as 'pure art' because aesthetic feeling is just as much tied up with intellectual thought as intellectual thought is informed by aesthetic feeling. Thus, while the felt harmony of mathematical or morphological patterns tends to instigate aesthetic pleasure, he argues, the reception of music ('Bach') or poetry ('of Shakespeare or of Goethe'), conversely, often produces what he calls 'unconscious excitement of the intellect'.[74] As he puts it, 'the great mass of the literature we esteem is valued, not merely because of having artistic form, but because of its intellectual content'.[75]

The Nature of Education

To sum up, just as science, on Huxley's account, can be aesthetically pleasing, so literature and music can be intellectually invigorating. In practice, there is (to his mind) no gap between the aesthetic and the intellectual since both are abstractions from one and the same dynamic continuum of capabilities and faculties, all of which together, in continual interaction, make up what Huxley variously terms 'reason' or intelligence.[76] Education, for him, is the process whereby one learns to use this capacious and malleable, both practical and theoretical, intelligence in accordance with what he calls 'laws of Nature',[77] a purposely broad and indefinite notion that he takes to 'include not merely things and their forces, but men and their ways'.[78] Rather than being confined to institutions of learning, education, thus conceived, is a passage of excursions and recursions that, for each human being, begins as soon as it is first exposed to the challenges of being alive. Strictly speaking, in fact, there is 'no such thing as an uneducated man', Huxley avows, because from the moment humans enter the world they cannot avoid being receptive to sensations and perceptions that teach them how and how not to react to them. 'Take an extreme case,' as he exemplifies this:

> Suppose that an adult man, in the full vigour of his faculties, could be suddenly placed in the world, as Adam is said to have been, and then left to do as he best might. How long would he be left uneducated? Not five minutes. Nature would begin to teach him, through the eye, the ear, the touch, the properties of objects. Pain and pleasure would be at his elbow telling him to do that and avoid that; and by slow degrees the man would receive an education which, if narrow, would be thorough, real, and adequate to his circumstances, though there would be no extras and very few accomplishments.
>
> And if to this solitary man entered a second Adam, or, better still, an Eve, a new and greater world, that of social and moral phenomena, would be revealed. Joys and woes, compared with which all others might seem but faint shadows, would spring from the new relations.[79]

Although this example presupposes an 'adult man' to learn 'in the full vigour of his faculties' what human beings usually learn when these faculties are still in a nascent state of development, it is meant to illustrate Huxley's point that the natural culture of intelligence begins long before humans start going to school. Moreover, it is supposed to buttress his case that the methods of institutional education ought to be continuous with the ways in which 'Nature', having a physical as well as a social and moral force, has been acting on people's senses long before they even become aware of it. For Huxley, then, the 'Nature' to be included in the culture of education stands for an openness towards that which has always been making people reach out of themselves and become attentive to what is, at any moment, beyond their understanding and control.[80] Hence his insistence that education, as a process of being exposed to the new, of being moved out of one's position, can never be complete. 'For every man the world is as fresh as it was at the first day, and as full of untold novelties for him who has the eyes to see them.'[81] In fact, 'Nature is still continuing her patient education of us in that great university, the universe, of which we are all members.'[82] However much someone may know, this is to say, there is still an abundance of matters that they do not (yet) know. The human mind, by this account, exists in a mode of suspension and extension, rather than closure and self-containment. It remains susceptible to be surprised, to be pushed out of its familiar grooves. Therefore, the 'university', as Huxley imagines it, should leave its doors open to the 'universe' that 'naturally', as he would say, teaches its lessons to all of us.

As Huxley's image of capitalised Nature as a benign teacher indicates, his views on education resonate with a Romantic legacy that comprises Coleridge's 'primary IMAGINATION', 'the prime agent of all human perception',[83] as well as Wordsworth's intimation 'that there are powers, / Which of themselves our minds impress'.[84] Moreover, Huxley's emphasis on the child in the adult man, on the primitive in the cultivated, or on that which remains uneducated in whoever is conceived to be educated harks back to Wordsworth's emblematic claim that 'The Child is the Father of the Man', uttered by an adult speaker admiring the appearance of 'a rainbow in the sky', as the corresponding poem has it:

> My heart leaps up when I behold
>   A Rainbow in the sky:
> So was it when my life began;
> So is it now I am a Man;
> So be it when I shall grow old,
>   Or let me die!
> The Child is Father of the Man;
> And I could wish my days to be
> Bound each to each by natural piety.[85]

What Wordsworth's speaker contemplates and, indeed, venerates here is precisely what Huxley's 'adult man in the full vigour of his faculties' has not lost either: the childlike capacity and readiness to be affected and instructed by the appearance of whatever has not yet been contained in, and subdued by, pre-existing ideas. Just as the lyrical 'I' of the poem hopes to preserve this capacity through all stages of his life, so Huxley wants everyone, and especially all aspiring scholars and scientists, to remain responsive to a phenomenal world that is 'full of untold novelties' and 'as fresh as it was at the first day'. In his 1802 Preface to *Lyrical Ballads* Wordsworth, in fact, proposes that this ability to perceive the world as novel and unfamiliar as it is to the child is integral to poetry. At the same time, he suggests that, in representing the world in this 'impassioned' way, poetry constitutes a kind of universal knowledge that encompasses science.[86] 'Poetry,' Wordsworth famously argues, 'is the breath and finer spirit of all knowledge; it is the impassioned expression which is in the countenance of all Science.'[87] Furthermore, 'the Poet binds together by passion and knowledge the vast empire of human society, as it is spread over the whole earth, and over all time'.[88] And finally: 'Poetry is the first and last of all knowledge – it is as immortal as the heart of man.'[89] While poetry is here explicitly said to be capable of producing knowledge, what Wordsworth seems to have in mind specifically is an 'impassioned' knowledge, or a knowledge of the passions that impresses the mind, making it active in turn. This is not to say that poetry 'resists knowledge' per se, as Andrew Bennett has argued,[90] but only that it is opposed to the sort of *dispassionate*, increasingly specialised and disciplined knowledge of 'the Chemist', 'Mathematician', 'Anatomist', 'Botanist' or 'Mineralogist' that Wordsworth seems to have associated with the term 'science'.[91] Thus, whereas the poet is characterised as someone who 'converses with general nature', the 'Man of Science' is claimed to take as the 'objects of his studies' only 'particular parts of nature'.[92] To be sure, both share a sense of pleasure in what they do, an aesthetic feeling that 'accompanies' them through their 'studies'. 'The knowledge both of the Poet and the Man of Science is pleasure,' in Wordsworth's words,

> but the knowledge of the one cleaves to us as a necessary part of our existence, our natural and unalienable inheritance; the other is a personal and individual acquisition, slow to come to us, and by no habitual and direct sympathy connecting us with our fellow-beings. The Man of Science seeks truth as a remote and unknown benefactor; he cherishes and loves it in his solitude: the Poet, singing a song in which all human beings join with him, rejoices in the presence of truth as our visible friend and hourly companion.[93]

What can be gathered from this exposition is that the 'knowledge' of the poet is a 'necessary', 'natural' and 'unalienable' part of human 'existence' connecting 'all human beings' 'in the presence of' a universal 'truth'. By contrast, the knowledge of the scientist is described as a 'remote' abstraction from the nature of (human) existence, an 'individual acquisition' gained by a movement towards specialisation and particularisation that effectively divides the members of human society ('solitude') rather than tying them together. As Amanda Jo Goldstein has suggested, however, Wordsworth's aim in contrasting the poetic and the scientific is not primarily to privilege the former over the latter but to keep them in touch with each other as well as with the material world.[94] Wordsworth worries that without the work of the poet, 'carrying sensation into the midst of the objects of the Science',[95] disciplined ways of knowing might become inadequate to human and non-human nature alike. 'The professionalizing habitus of the "Man of Science"', in Goldstein's words, 'needs poetic "transfiguration" for the sake of full and accurate knowledge'.[96]

Even more explicitly than Wordsworth, Huxley, too, is keen to situate the perceptual or aesthetic in the midst of the rational, identifying it as that which enables 'the adult man' to see the familiar world as singular and uncommon: 'as fresh' as it appears to a child. While the aesthetic faculty, he argues, enables human minds to remain hospitable to what they perceive as strange or indeterminate, the intellect is what allows them to translate the unknown into what is considered to be already known. Thus, in Huxley's view, 'the foundations of all natural knowledge were laid', as he notes, 'when the savage first learned that the fingers on one hand are fewer than those of both', or 'that if he struck his fellow savage a blow he would make him angry, and perhaps get a blow in return'.[97] As this suggests, what, according to Huxley, enabled our ancestors to come to know their world, including the ways of their fellow-inhabitants, and, as a result, to emancipate themselves from their 'savage' condition, is the ability to develop a feeling for what, in the long run, was and was not conducive to their pleasure and well-being. According to Huxley, this aesthetic feeling corresponded to a rough intellectual understanding of recurring patterns and relatively stable relations. In this way, a 'rude' outline of science and systematic thought began to take form on which all future activities could be built.

Everything Huxley had to say about science education – and he was one of the most prolific Victorian propagators and reformers of education – is premised on this belief in the interrelation of feeling and thought.[98] Hence, for example, his conviction, repeatedly put forth in his texts, that facts ought not to be taught in the form of finished results, readily prepared for students to pick them up. Instead, he held that one should motivate young people to enact for themselves the whole passage from sensation to conception, so as to activate both the aesthetic and the intellectual 'side' of their being at once. The teaching, in short, must 'be made practical', as Huxley puts it himself.

> That is to say, in explaining to a child the general phenomena of Nature, you must, as far as possible, give reality to your teaching by object-lessons; in teaching him botany, he must handle the plants and dissect the flowers for himself; in teaching him physics and chemistry, you must not be solicitous to fill him with information, but you must be careful that what he learns he knows of his own knowledge. Don't be satisfied with telling him that a magnet attracts iron. Let him see that it does; let him feel the pull of the one upon the other for himself. And, especially, tell him that it is his duty to doubt until he is compelled, by the absolute authority of Nature, to believe that which is written in books.[99]

The gaining of new insights, this suggests, is a process of converting theoretical propositions ('a magnet attracts iron') into aesthetic feelings ('the pull of the one upon the other') and vice versa. Concomitantly, knowledge, rather than a body of abstract 'information', is what students make out of their own perception. Its foundation can therefore never be that which, at any time, is 'written in books', but only 'the absolute authority of Nature'. As this phrase implies, what Huxley (here and elsewhere) calls 'Nature' represents an order of being that is both open and closed. While it seems to embody 'absolute' truths, it can only be known through human forms that are contingent and provisional, subject to be supplemented and revised. Nature, signifying what has not (yet) been fully converted into human terms, is, by definition, different from any text, formula or image that is supposed to speak for her. What makes her authority 'absolute' is that her mode of existence can always be found to be otherwise than what the human forms that represent it may want to make one believe.

Arguably, then, what Huxley calls 'Nature' fulfils a similar function as what, in less secularised periods and contexts, would have been called God. She embodies a mode of being that, in its totality or as a whole, is (still) partly foreign to the provisional human constructions that purport to model it. One might even say that nature, for Huxley, is the only 'God' (the only 'absolute authority') in which people are to put their trust. But whereas the way from the human mind to 'the theological world' traditionally led, as Huxley puts it, through the 'Scriptures, the traditions of the Fathers, and the authority of the Church', the way from the mind to 'Nature' can only pass through the experience of sensible matter.[100] It follows that the medium between man and God (says Huxley) is a text that has already been written, whereas the medium between man and nature must be one that is still in the making. One had to learn about nature through the experimental, not through the scriptural because, in contrast to people's belief in God, their experience of nature did not yet have an authoritative discourse on which it could rely. Hence Huxley's insistence that students of the 'phenomena of Nature' should be taught that it was their 'duty' to 'doubt [. . .] that which is written in books', rather than to believe it.

For Huxley, in short, the only acceptable instrument for the accumulation of knowledge about nature is, in the last instance, not 'that which is written in books', but that which is experienced. Yet, he is more than aware that experience is an inherently uncertain and untrustworthy basis of knowledge. As Huxley argues, expressly taking his cue from Hume,[101] what is, at any point in time, experienced to be true can, at a later point, always be found to be untrue since we have no 'reason to believe that our present knowledge of the nature of things exhausts the possibilities of nature'.[102] Just because our actual experience of the world may tell us, to use Huxley's own examples, that it is 'extremely improbable' for a man to walk on water or for water to be turned into wine, we are anything but justified in concluding that the accomplishment of these feats is generally impossible.[103] 'There are impossibilities logical, but none natural.'[104] Thus, on Huxley's account, one can say that it is impossible that a square is round or that two parallel lines intersect. 'But walking on water, or turning water into wine, or procreation without male intervention, or raising the dead, are plainly not "impossibilities" in this sense.'[105] Rather, such events must be viewed as possibilities (Huxley claims) because human beings have no way of excluding that at some point in the (distant) future the world will be in a state in which they have become realities.

> We have knowledge of what is happening and of what has happened; of what will happen we have and can have no more than expectation, grounded on our more or less correct reading of past experience and prompted by the faith, begotten of that experience, that the order of nature in the future will resemble its order in the past.[106]

This is a reformulation of what has become famous, after Hume, as the notorious 'problem of induction': the proposition that people's experience of the present and the past can never be a sufficient basis for the inference of certain knowledge about the future. But it is testament to Huxley's, as well as Bernard's and Mill's, pragmatism that he does not see much of a problem in this state of affairs. Instead, he regards it as evidence of 'the limitations of our faculties' which he takes to be 'such that we never can be in a position to set bounds to the possibilities of nature'.[107]

The attitude concomitant to this insight is one of modesty and caution. It is an attitude that is prepared to acknowledge that nature is a vast, unfathomable resource of developments and forms, infinitely greater and far less calculable than anyone's current knowledge of it may suggest. Thus conceived, nature, by definition, exceeds the contrivances of order that human beings make out of it. For instance, 'laws of nature', viewed in this modest way, are not fixed causes forever determining the motions of the world in exactly the same way.[108] Rather, for Huxley, a law of nature is 'a mere record of experience', or a human 'product of a mental operation upon the facts of nature which come under our observation'.[109] It 'has no more existence outside the mind than colour has', he says, having been made to exist only through practices of working recognisable forms out of experience.[110] Although the results of such practices, registrations of regular occurrences, are called 'laws of nature', Huxley points out, nobody 'knows whether they bind nature or not'.[111] Naturalists certainly had to, and did, assume that nature is, to some degree, constant and consistent in the way she works; otherwise it would have been impossible to make general statements about her. But such 'uniformity' was regarded as a methodological premise, rather than an ontological fact.[112] For Huxley at least, nature cannot be said to be confined by the rules and patterns that human beings extract from their experience of it. In his view, nature rather includes the possibility to be (and remain) not what it seems to be. One could perhaps say that Huxley took the laws and properties of nature to evolve co-extensively with the (ever more refined and exact) human perception and description of them. Nature, thus viewed, is essentially emergent. It exists in transition, neither its end nor its origin having been fully fathomed to date.

Texts and Facts

In sum, the concept of nature, as Huxley uses it, encompasses both that which is known about the material world, including its inhabitants, and that which is not (yet) known but might be learned about it at a future point. Hence his emphasis on the 'duty to doubt' whatever is presented as an established fact, an emphasis that he shares with Bernard. Both men sought to underline that all human ways of knowing must remain adaptable and open because the structure of nature might be so too. People's thinking about nature, they argued, must remain free to question 'that which is written in books' if their own experience contradicts it. It is this commitment to a (temporary) suspension of belief as the linchpin of all scientific research which made Bernard dub the experimental method 'the free thinker's method' and which instigated Huxley to speak of his model of education as 'liberal'.[113] For both writers, the best starting point of all scientific enquiries is the phenomena as they appear themselves, rather than the formulae and propositions that have been abstracted from them.

The process of learning, as Huxley described it, should therefore not begin with articulated ideas written up as texts, but with what he calls 'sense-images'.[114] He uses this term to refer to the patterns of perception produced by means of practical experiments, as one can learn from his essay 'On the Study of Biology' which includes a detailed report of what he and his students 'do in the biological laboratory'.[115] Although his 'class have, of course, their text-books', Huxley writes, the 'essential part of the whole teaching' is that in which the students are encouraged to 'work through the structure of a certain number of animals and plants', as he puts it.[116]

> We dissect a star-fish, an earth-worm, a snail, a squid, and a fresh-water mussel. We examine a lobster and a cray-fish, and a black beetle. We go on to a common skate, a cod-fish, a frog, a tortoise, a pigeon, and a rabbit, and that takes us about all the time we have to give. The purpose of this course is not to make skilled dissectors, but to give every student a clear and definite conception, by means of sense-images, of the characteristic structure of each of the leading modifications of the animal kingdom; and that is perfectly possible, by going no further than the length of that list of forms which I have enumerated.[117]

What Huxley calls 'sense-images', then, is the result of practical operations which are supposed to help students gain 'a clear and definite conception' of the most common forms to be found in the animal world. Pupils should see, feel and 'work through' particular organisms, before trying to understand the typical structures that these creatures can be seen to represent. In this practical way, Huxley believes, the student is enabled to build up a mental 'apprehension' of 'the essential features' constituting the 'kingdom' of animate forms.[118] More to the point, such an apprehension will make it easier and more beneficial for the student to peruse symbolic accounts of biological life:

> And it then becomes possible for him to read with profit; because every time he meets with the name of a structure, he has a definite image in his mind of what the name means in the particular creature he is reading about, and therefore the reading is not mere reading. It is not mere repetition of words; but every term employed in the description, we will say, of a horse, or of an elephant, will call up the image of the things he had seen in the rabbit, and he is able to form a distinct conception of that which he has not seen, as a modification of that which he has seen.[119]

As this implies, the activity of reading, or of connecting words with concepts is made more profitable and effective, Huxley thinks, if one can already draw on at least a limited reservoir of what he calls 'images'. These are 'apprehensions' of ideal patterns that have been formed on the basis of sensual perception and practical experience. The image of what the student 'has seen' (for example a rabbit) will then enable him to construe more quickly and distinctly the referent of what 'he has not seen' (for example an elephant or a horse). Thus, what Huxley terms 'image' or 'sense-image' functions as a translator between individual, local perception and more general, global conception. By way of extending and transforming the images of what one has experienced for oneself, it is possible to infer that which one has not experienced for oneself. One might therefore say that the formation of 'distinct conceptions' and propositions is here premised on an activity of making, modifying and remaking images. Conception is closely allied with transformative imagination. Indeed, for Huxley, as Virginia Richter has shown, imagination is by no means alien to science or scientific education.[120] Nor is it a power that is exclusively aligned with either the experimental or the scriptural. Rather, it is the process that connects, and mediates between, the two, allowing for the one to be prolonged and woven into the other.

As Huxley's laboratory report suggests, imagination, the formation and transformation of mental images, begins with the process of experimenting on sensual matter and is continued in and through the reading of written texts. Thus, even though Huxley advocates an education that begins with the material and experimental, rather than the textual and ideal, he is far from wanting to uncouple the one from the other. While he is sometimes represented as a die-hard materialist with a strong aversion to everything literary, he is in fact the last one who would have been opposed to the reading of texts. Even the students in the laboratory, after all, still have their textbooks too. Moreover, Huxley indicates that the process of dissection is from the start aided and accompanied by a number of 'diagrams and preparations illustrating the structure of all the other forms of life we examine', to quote him once more.[121]

> Thus the student has before him, first, a picture of the structure he ought to see; secondly, the structure itself worked out; and if with these aids, and such needful explanations and practical hints as a demonstrator can supply, he cannot make out the facts for himself in the materials supplied to him, he had better take to some other pursuit than that of biological science.[122]

In order to make out 'facts', then, students have to compare and contrast their relatively immediate experience of a 'structure worked out' with a more mediated model of this structure that has been provided before. What they have to learn, says Huxley, is to recognise what they actually perceive in terms of pictures and texts that represent what they ideally 'ought to' perceive.

One might therefore say that education is here centred on activities of converting one thing into another, or of drawing lines of connection between seemingly different domains: the particular and the general, the material and the ideal, the sensual and the intellectual, the pictorial and the scriptural and so on. For Huxley, the only way to arrive at scientific knowledge is through processes of continuous translation and trial (often erroneous) in which 'time is of the essence', to use Latour's phrase.[123] 'Work done in a laboratory involves a good deal of expenditure of time without always an obvious result, because we do not see anything of that quiet process of soaking the facts into the mind, which takes place through the organs of the senses.'[124] This emphasis on processes rather than products and on experimental practices rather than abstract concepts explains, moreover, why Huxley considered it 'absolutely necessary for everybody, for a longer or shorter period, to learn to draw', a skill that he takes all people to be able to acquire.[125] In fact, for him, the ability to draw is such an important part of education because he regards it as a basic practice of making lines of connection and distinction that even encompasses writing. 'Writing is a form of drawing; therefore if you give the same attention and trouble to drawing as you do to writing, depend upon it, there is nobody who cannot be made to draw, more or less well.'[126]

An instructive counterpoint to Huxley's experimental, process-based concept of learning and education has been famously ridiculed by Charles Dickens in *Hard Times*.[127] In this novel, the schoolmaster Thomas Gradgrind – 'A man of realities. A man of facts and calculations. A man who proceeds upon the principle that two and two are four, and nothing over' – represents the sort of rigid, inflexible, and idealist (or theory-based) concept of human and non-human nature to which Huxley's model is opposed.[128] Gradgrind is the epitome of what Bernard called 'scholasticism' and Huxley the 'dilettante "paper-philosopher" way':[129] 'With a rule and a pair of scales, and the multiplication table always in his pocket, sir, ready to weigh and measure any parcel of human nature, and tell you exactly what it comes to'.[130] The medium through which Gradgrind perceives the world is not so much the experimental as the theoretical. For what he takes to be the empirical world has already been converted into a set of standardised units and self-contained 'parcels' that can be 'weighed and measured' in abstract terms. The world by which he wants people's experience to be regulated and governed is composed of mathematical figures and pre-comprehended 'facts', such as the ones making up the concept of a horse that is presented in the second chapter.

> 'Bitzer', said Gradgrind. 'Your definition of a horse.'
> 'Quadruped. Graminivorous. Forty teeth, namely twenty-four grinders, four eye-teeth, and twelve incisive. Sheds coat in the spring; in marshy countries, sheds hoofs, too. Hoofs hard, but requiring to be shod with iron. Age known by marks in mouth.' Thus (and much more) Bitzer.[131]

This is an account of an ideal or general horse, a text-book horse that has been dissociated from the particular phenomena and (sense) images through which a horse is perceived when one actually sees, hears, smells, draws or imagines one. Indeed, what is here said to define a horse is precisely what Huxley would have called a 'mere repetition of words' and phrases, each isolated from the other, as the elliptic, staccato style suggests. In this way, Bitzer's horse is purified of the practical, experimental movement of translation and association that, on Huxley's model, is supposed to integrate sensation, perception, imagination and conception into a single (temporally extended) continuum. Instead, the horse is turned into a 'dead' array of disjointed terms and arrested in a formulaic (spatial) order that allows for it to be conveniently conserved and reproduced as if it were a matter of impersonal facts.

One might say that all Bitzer knows about the horse is what Huxley calls its 'grammar'.[132] But while Dickens's Gradgrind wants everybody to teach and learn nothing but the grammar of reality – the abstract laws and facts of which he takes this reality to be composed – Huxley considers this grammar to be 'science in a very bad form'.[133] What he seeks to teach and wants his students to learn is to integrate facts into their experience by means of drawing them out of it. In Huxley's view, the grammatical and theoretical can only be properly known by means of the experimental. People should therefore be instructed in the skill of working their way through the experimental field. 'If there is any good at all in scientific education it is that men should be trained, as I said before, to know things for themselves at first hand, and that they should understand every step of the reason of that which they do.'[134] Once again, it is the art of drawing lines of inference that is at the centre of his educational model, not the knowledge of what is 'written in books'.

Indeed, the only reason for Huxley's opposition to literary education as it was still current when he wrote is that it is almost entirely focused on grammatical structures, an emphasis that he finds 'scandalously insufficient and almost worthless'.[135] 'It is taught just as you would teach the rules of chess or draughts.'[136] This emphasis on presupposed orders and rules may be representative of what Daston and Galison have called 'mechanical objectivity' and 'Noninterventionist objectivity', terms that they, somewhat too sweepingly, claim to capture the standard notion of objectivity in the later nineteenth century.[137] For Huxley, however, this ethos of mechanical self-abandonment represents exactly the kind of 'bad' scientific practice that his reform of education intended to replace with a more open-minded and dynamic approach. Huxley stresses that he wished 'to speak with the utmost respect of that science – philology – of which grammar is a part and parcel'.[138] But he remains firm on his conviction 'that grammar, as it is usually learned at school, affords no scientific training'.[139] What is more, he leaves no doubt about why he takes this to be so: 'There is nothing that appeals to the aesthetic faculty in that operation; and I ask multitudes of men of my own age, who went through this process, whether they ever had a conception of art or literature until they obtained it for themselves after leaving school?'[140] As such statements indicate, Huxley would have been the last one to question the general value of literature and the fine arts. All he was opposed to was a particular way of studying written texts as if they were containers of abstract facts. In his view, texts, like dissected animals, should not be seen as representative of a scholastic grammar of knowledge that has already been set down. Rather, they ought to be used as component parts of an activity of drawing the lines of meaning through which the subjective and the objective as well as the material and the ideal, or the particular and the general come to be both separated and associated in the medium of the experimental. It is this activity of setting up links between the aesthetic and the intellectual faculties that is at the core of Huxley's educational programme, not a specific subject-matter.[141]

To be sure, Huxley cautiously submits that, in his opinion, 'the use of physical science as an instrument of education [. . .] exercises young minds in the appreciation of inductive evidence better than any other study'.[142] But the popular image of him as a fiercely scientific 'bulldog', with no interest in the arts and letters whatsoever, does not do justice to his writing and lecturing at all. G. K. Chesterton even went so far as to declare that 'Huxley, especially, was much more a literary man than a scientific man,'[143] a view that was perpetuated by Huxley's son Leonard and his grandson Aldous, both well-known writers themselves.[144] What one can certainly say is that the role of the 'man of science', as interpreted by Huxley, was entirely incompatible with the kind of narrow specialism that later came to be associated with the professional 'scientist', a term that was coined by Whewell in the 1830s.[145] In fact, Huxley always resented this denomination because it clashed with his view of himself as a man 'of wide learning'.[146] Even his notorious public skirmish with Matthew Arnold in the early 1880s does not turn him into a champion of an exclusively scientific training.[147] For Huxley's 'claim', as Paul White and Bernard Lightman have demonstrated, 'was not that science was superior to, or independent of, literature, but that each was dependent on the other'.[148]

To sum up, then, the experimental method, as propagated by Huxley, had the capacity to interweave scientific, aesthetic and literary components, drawing them together in a practice-based approach that is central to his thought. His model of education was therefore not primarily focused on the transmission of *what* is generally known about, say, a horse or a rabbit. Rather, he wanted to enable his students to learn *how* they can come to know this (and more) through their own experience. In short, what Huxley proposed is a way of 'knowing from the inside', to repeat Tim Ingold's term. As he sees it, to teach people is not to transport pre-established facts from one side to another, but to enable students to make these facts out for themselves: from within the experimental field, rather than from a vantage point that has been predefined for them. To learn something, conversely, is not to consume what has already been written, but to practise the art of writing in the general sense outlined in the Introduction. Broadly conceived, writing, which can never be entirely separated from reading, may therefore be seen as a common medium of scientific and literary work: it refers to the process of leaving marks, following traces, drawing lines and mapping out relations through which people come to make meaningful structures out of their experience of being in the world.

Notes

1. Herschel, *Preliminary Discourse*, p. 18.
2. Daston and Galison, 'The Image', p. 122; see also Daston and Galison, *Objectivity*, pp. 191–252.
3. Levine, *Dying*, p. 2.
4. White, 'Ministers of Culture', p. 118.
5. Smiles, *Self-Help*, pp. 158, 109.
6. Pearson, *The Grammar of Science*, p. 7.
7. Lewes, *Problems: First Series*, vol. I, p. 174; vol. II, p. 13. For an extensive analysis of Lewes's *Problems* see Chap. 4.
8. Pearson, *The Grammar of Science*, p. 15.
9. Ibid., p. 12; Levine, *Dying*, pp. 220–67.

10. Pearson, *The Grammar of Science*, p. 17.
11. Ibid., pp. 11, 14.
12. Ibid., p. 14.
13. Ibid., p. 13.
14. Müller, *Lectures on the Science of Language*, I, p. 8.
15. Ibid., p. 8.
16. Ibid., p. 8.
17. Ibid., p. 8.
18. Gooding, *Experiment*, p. 4.
19. Huxley, 'On the Educational Value', p. 45.
20. Ibid., p. 45.
21. Ibid., p. 45.
22. Ibid., p. 45.
23. Ibid., p. 46.
24. Huxley, 'Six Lectures to Working Men', p. 361.
25. Ibid., pp. 361, 365.
26. Ibid., p. 363. As such lectures indicate, Huxley regarded the public promulgation of science as an integral part of it. Yet, he was never just a populariser but always saw himself as a practitioner as well. Cf. Lightman, *Victorian Popularizers*, pp. 353–421.
27. Bernard, *Experimental Medicine*, p. 50. The French original of this book was published in 1865, but earlier versions of Bernard's experimental theory circulated and were read in England as early as 1856.
28. Ibid., p. 45.
29. Ibid., p. 32.
30. Ibid., p. 43.
31. Ibid., p. 27.
32. Ibid., p. 43.
33. Ibid., p. 31. Bernard here quotes Goethe's essay 'Der Versuch als Vermittler'.
34. Ibid., p. 21.
35. Ibid., p. 49.
36. Ibid., p. 49.
37. Ibid., p. 50.
38. Ibid., p. 53.
39. Ibid., p. 49.
40. Ibid., p. 47.
41. Ibid., p. 47.
42. A recent take on the relationship between walking and knowing that resonates with Bernard's account can be found in Ingold, *The Life of Lines*, pp. 46–9, to which I am indebted, and Masschelein, 'E-ducating'.
43. Huxley, 'On the Educational Value', pp. 49–50.
44. Polanyi, *Personal Knowledge*, p. 62.
45. Sennett, *The Craftsman*, pp. 270–3.
46. Allen, 'The Origin of Cultivation'.
47. Ibid., p. 580.

48. Ibid., p. 581.
49. Ibid., pp. 582, 583.
50. Ibid., p. 584.
51. Bernard, *Experimental Medicine*, p. 9.
52. Allen, 'The Origin of Cultivation', p. 584.
53. Bernard, *Experimental Medicine*, p. 10.
54. Allen, 'The Origin of Cultivation', p. 584.
55. Ibid., p. 584.
56. Ibid., p. 584.
57. According to Raymond Williams's influential account, the genera-
    tive sense of culture, 'which had usually been a culture *of* something,
    was changed, in the nineteenth century, to *culture* as such, a thing in
    itself' (*Culture and Society*, 16). Amigoni has revised this argument in
    Colonies, Cults, pp. 1–30, arguing that culture remained a '"hothouse"
    of spiritual and intellectual productivity' (p. 23), rather than becoming
    what Williams called 'a court of human appeal' (*Culture and Society*,
    p. 17). For a text that preserves the older meaning of culture see, for
    example, Addington Symonds, 'Culture'. Taking his departure from the
    'etymology of the word', according to which 'culture [. . .] implies till-
    age of the soil, artificial improvement of qualities supplied by nature',
    Symonds goes on to describe culture as an activity of self-improvement
    that brings together nature and art (p. 196).
58. Cf. Williams, *Keywords*, p. 87.
59. Gagnier, 'Ecosystems', 'title'.
60. Allen, 'Origin of Cultivation', p. 584.
61. Slinn, 'Experimental Form', p. 47.
62. Huxley, 'Science and Morals', p. 121.
63. Huxley, 'Science and Art in Relation to Education', p. 175.
64. Ibid., p. 175.
65. Ibid., p. 175.
66. Ibid., p. 176.
67. Ibid., p. 176.
68. Ibid., p. 176.
69. Ibid., p. 176.
70. Ibid., pp. 176–7.
71. Ibid., p. 177.
72. Ibid., p. 177.
73. Cf. Kant, *Kritik der Urteilskraft*, pp. 95–9 (B 64–B 68).
74. Huxley, 'Science and Art in Relation to Education', pp. 177, 179.
75. Ibid., p. 179.
76. Cf. Huxley, 'Science and Morals', p. 126.
77. Huxley, 'Liberal Education', p. 83.
78. Ibid., p. 83.
79. Ibid., pp. 83–4.
80. Cf. Masschelein, 'Experimentum Scholae'.
81. Huxley, 'Liberal Education', p. 84.

82. Ibid., p. 84.
83. Coleridge, *Biographia Literaria*, p. 304. For further details see Lobsien, *Zeit der Imagination*, pp. 63–94.
84. Wordsworth, *Selected Poetry*, p. 55 ('Expostulation and Reply').
85. Ibid., p. 122.
86. Wordsworth, 'Preface', p. 168
87. Ibid., p. 168.
88. Ibid., p. 168.
89. Ibid., p. 168.
90. Bennett, 'Poetic Ignorance', p. 20.
91. Wordsworth, 'Preface', pp. 167–8.
92. Ibid., pp. 167, 167–8.
93. Ibid., p. 168.
94. Goldstein, *Sweet Science*, pp. 11–13.
95. Wordsworth, 'Preface', p. 168.
96. Goldstein, *Sweet Science*, pp. 12–13.
97. Huxley, 'Improving Natural Knowledge', p. 32.
98. On Huxley as a reformer of education see White, *Thomas Huxley*, pp. 67–99; Desmond, *Huxley*, pp. 339–79; and Bibby, *T. H. Huxley*, pp. 123–93.
99. Huxley, 'Scientific Education', p. 127.
100. Huxley, 'Scientific and Pseudo-Scientific Realism', p. 65.
101. The wider reception of Hume's work in Victorian philosophy is treated in Garratt, *Victorian Empiricism*, pp. 43–70.
102. Huxley, 'Possibilities and Impossibilities', p. 198.
103. Ibid., p. 198.
104. Ibid., p. 197.
105. Ibid., p. 197.
106. Ibid., p. 198.
107. Ibid., p. 198.
108. Huxley, 'Scientific and Pseudo-Scientific Realism', p. 80.
109. Ibid., pp. 77, 76.
110. Ibid., p. 76.
111. Huxley, 'Scientific and Pseudo-Scientific Realism', p. 81.
112. Stanley, 'Naturalism and Theism', p. 243.
113. Bernard, *Experimental Medicine*, p. 43; Huxley, 'Liberal Education'.
114. Huxley, 'Study of Biology', p. 285.
115. Ibid., p. 284.
116. Ibid., p. 284.
117. Ibid., pp. 284–5.
118. Ibid., p. 285.
119. Ibid., p. 285.
120. Richter, 'Anschauung', pp. 373–7.
121. Huxley, 'Study of Biology', p. 286.
122. Ibid., p. 286.
123. Latour, 'A Text-Book Case', p. 88.

124. Huxley, 'Science and Art in Relation to Education', p. 172.
125. Ibid., p. 183.
126. Ibid., p. 183.
127. On the cultural history of Victorian education more generally see Birch, 'Education'.
128. Dickens, *Hard Times*, p. 4.
129. Huxley, 'Study of Biology', p. 282.
130. Dickens, *Hard Times*, p. 4.
131. Ibid., p. 5.
132. Huxley, 'Science and Art in Relation to Education', p. 181.
133. Ibid., p. 181.
134. Ibid., p. 181.
135. Ibid., p. 180.
136. Ibid., p. 181.
137. Daston and Galison, 'The Image of Objectivity', pp. 83, 122.
138. Huxley, 'Science and Art in Relation to Education', p. 181.
139. Ibid., p. 181.
140. Ibid., p. 181.
141. Huxley, 'Science and Morals', p. 126.
142. Ibid., p. 126.
143. Chesterton, *The Victorian Age*, p. 39.
144. White, *Huxley*, p. 68.
145. Yeo, *Defining Science*, p. 3.
146. Porter, 'Scientific Naturalism', p. 276. As Porter brings out, historically speaking, the distinction between amateur and professional is much more complicated than it is often taken to be because it intersects with other faultlines, such as that between religion and natural science, gentleman scientist and bourgeois careerist as well as 'scholarly inquiry and unreasoning orthodoxy' (p. 268). See also Turner, 'The Victorian Conflict'.
147. See Huxley, 'Science and Culture', to which Arnold responded with his 'Literature and Science'. As White ('Ministers', p. 118) has emphasised, the two men, despite their slightly divergent views on the importance of classical studies, were not only friends during most of their careers but 'working allies', pursuing a 'shared agenda' of educational 'reform' that was supposed to integrate science and literature within a universal understanding of 'culture'. While their exchange has often been taken to foreshadow the twentieth-century idea of 'the two cultures', it is more likely that they would have been astonished at the suggestion that they represented 'two polar groups', each divided from the other by a 'gulf of mutual incomprehension', to quote C. P. Snow's famous phrase (*The Two Cultures*, p. 4).
148. White, *Huxley*, p. 80.

Chapter 3

Following the Actors: G. H. Lewes's and George Eliot's Studies in Life

Moving Knowledge

Huxley's lectures, as the last chapter has shown, were not primarily concerned with closed structures of knowledge, but with open-ended processes of learning. More precisely, Huxley sought to give advice on how one is supposed to draw noticeable and reproducible 'sense images' out of a field of practical intervention and trial. He saw these images as apprehensions of meaningful relations which would allow students to translate their (first person) perception into, or recognise it as, a form of (social) communication, such as a diagram or a written text. As we have seen, for Huxley, this activity of extending and converting modes of sensual perception into structures of ideal conception is not to be seen as a division of the aesthetic from the scientific. Rather, it is seen as a way of prolonging the perceptual (or personal) into the intellectual (or impersonal) and, conversely, of checking the intellectual by means of the perceptual. In short, what Huxley had in mind is a mutual interplay of what he called the 'aesthetic' and the 'intellectual' faculties, each informing the other.

Thus, Huxley's writings register a concern with experimentation and the scientific method that variously resonates with other texts of the period, both fictional and non-fictional. For example, the many half-mad scientists and maladroit scholars peopling the Victorian novel may be taken to show that there was a widespread awareness of the danger of wrongheadedly taking leave of one's senses, a danger which was seen to be inherent in the progress from the personal towards the general. One of these scientists on the verge of going mad is Dr Benjulia in Wilkie Collins's late novel *Heart and Science* in which,[1] as the title indicates, the relationship between the 'hard' and the 'soft' takes centre stage.[2] For Benjulia, the scientific method is no more than a vehicle for attaining an ideal end, namely knowledge, for the sake of which he is willing to sacrifice his very ability to be affected by whatever might interfere with his predetermined course. 'Have I no feeling, as you call it?', he asks his brother (as much as himself) at one point.

> My last experiments on a monkey horrified me. His cries of suffering, his gestures of entreaty, were like the cries and gestures of a child. I would have given the world to put him out of his misery. But I went on. In the glorious cause I went on. My hands turned cold – my heart ached – I thought of a child I sometimes play with – I suffered – I resisted – I went on. All for Knowledge! all for Knowledge! (*HS* 191)

This is a caricature of precisely the kind of 'ethos of restraint' and 'moral self-discipline' that Daston and Galison took to define the method of Victorian science.[3] Totally focused on knowledge as an object that he considers to be separate from himself, Benjulia deliberately suppresses most of his feelings and propensities, so as to avoid an intermixture of the personal and the general.[4] He is, one might say in a phrase compounding Huxley and Levine, dying so much to know that he is willing to annihilate the aesthetic side of his being, along with the moral sensibility and emotional responsiveness that is inherent in it. As a result, Benjulia's 'grand problem' (*HS* 190) possesses his existence, nags away at his body ('his enemies spoke of him as "the living skeleton"', *HS* 95) and takes him out of his senses, such that the mode of dying to know becomes, for him, tantamount to a process of being consumed by a phantasm of complete knowledge to which he has ceded all control. 'I labour at it all day. I think of it, I dream of it, all night. It will kill me. Strong as I am, it will kill me' (*HS* 190).

Benjulia's problem, then, is that he believes in a pseudo-Platonic idea of pure knowledge that is, by definition, independent from the information received by the senses. As a result, knowledge, for him, becomes a 'sacred cause' that is to be held apart from the worldly matter of personal affairs (*HS* 190). Yet, to hold knowledge 'sacred' implies not only that something can only be known if it is enshrined in a safeguarded place distinct from the multiplicity of subjective modes of experience and points of view. To declare knowledge 'sacred' also means that knowledge is dissociated from the collective practices through which it is acquired, applied, extended and continuously transformed. Instead, it turns into an end in itself, as Benjulia points out. 'Knowledge for its own sake, is the one god I worship. Knowledge is its own justification and its own reward. The roaring mob follows us with its cry of Cruelty. We pity their ignorance. Knowledge

sanctifies cruelty' (*HS* 190). In order to attain knowledge, as this
suggests, Benjulia is prepared to emancipate himself not only from
the moral and aesthetic part of his existence, but also from his fellow
humans, scornfully degraded to 'a roaring mob', whose sentiment he
is no longer able (or willing) to share. Small wonder that, apparently
estranged from society, he lives in a house 'in the middle of a barren
little field' – 'not even an attempt at flower-garden or kitchen-garden
was visible' – inhabiting a palpable emptiness that parallels the intellectual purity of his (ideal) world (*HS* 129). In contrast to 'the land of
his neighbour', where 'the trees rose again', there is nothing to please
or even stimulate the senses in Benjulia's infertile place (*HS* 129).
Instead, the sheer vacuity and desolation of his dwelling excludes
all sources of potential distraction. This is supposed to ensure that
his mind remains fixated on the idea of knowledge with which he is
obsessed. But at the same time, it places him in a void, depriving his
aesthetic perception of any nourishment from which new intellectual insights could grow. There is even 'something unnatural' in the
scientist's abode because it appears to have been artificially cut off
from the environment that vitalises and sustains it (*HS* 129). What
is left is so 'bleak', 'drab', empty and without embellishment that
it conjures up an entirely abstract, purely intellectual world from
which all traces of sensuous enjoyment and aesthetic experience have
been banned (*HS* 131). All that pierces through the 'impenetrable
composure' that divides Benjulia from the surrounding world are the
'paroxysm[s] of pain', caused by his 'tortured gouty foot' (*HS* 245,
131, 130). While the feelings of pleasure and pain suggest that the
moral part of the scientist's person might still be alive, they are also
marked as diseased.

   This image of an experimenter who is dying so much to know that
his sheer existence as a human being has become painful to him can
be read as a distorted version of the kind of detached and constrained
ethos that was (and still is) often taken to define the ideal scientist.
Benjulia seems to work under the illusion that knowledge must, by
definition, refer to objects that are distinct from those gazing at them,
supposedly from a different plane. Yet, the very fact that, in Collins's
novel, this idealist or objectivist notion of knowledge is embodied
by an unhealthily eccentric, slightly deranged and ultimately suicidal
character indicates that it had already been on the wane when Collins's
novel appeared. More fundamentally, it seems to have been supplemented with a view of science as process-based. According to this latter conception, knowledge is not acquired by subjects who have to
jump across a gap in order to capture the matters of fact, by definition

outside of them, that they seek to grasp.[5] Rather, knowledge, on this view, takes the form of a movement in the course of which one travels along, and grows in accordance with, the experiences one undergoes.[6] Knowing, thus conceived, is a way of following the motions of that which one seeks to understand. In this process, as Herbert Spencer suggested, subjects and objects are mutually constituted without ever becoming entirely completed or distinct.[7]

Nothing could better exemplify this notion of knowledge as emergent than the prolific work of George Eliot's partner George Henry Lewes as it is documented in, and carried out through, writings such as *Sea-Side Studies*, *Studies in Animal Life* and his five-volume fragment *Problems of Life and Mind*. All of these texts, as their titles imply, are best regarded as portions of an unfinished project that was, at the time of its publication, still in progress. They present themselves as practical studies, that is, as sketches, exercises or tentative investigations of (yet) unresolved problems, rather than as representations of scientific facts or records of certain results that had already been found before the process of writing and publishing began.[8] Especially in the *Sea-Side Studies*, a rich and variegated series of essays on the popular outdoor activity of hunting, collecting and examining 'marine animals of simple organization', knowledge is throughout pursued and described as something that is not fixed, but continually coming into being in conjunction with the movements of the naturalist explorer.[9] Concomitantly, the position of the researcher is not that of a sovereign spectator, dispassionately dissecting and classifying what he has before him. Instead, his position is closer to that of Wordsworth's child in the man or Huxley's adult in view of a world appearing 'as fresh as it was at the first day'. As Lewes himself puts it:

> The delight of getting new animals is like the delight of childhood in any novelty, an impulse that moves the soul through the intricate paths of knowledge, – knowledge, which is but broken wonder; and this delight the naturalist has constantly awaiting him. Satiety is not possible, for Nature is inexhaustible. Knowledge unfolds vista after vista, for ever stretching illimitably distant, the horizon moving as we move. New facts connect themselves with new forms; the most casual observation often becomes a spark of inextinguishable thought running along trains of inflammable suggestion. (1857: June, 680)

Knowledge is here described as both an effect and a source of astonishment and 'delight', rather than as a result of self-elimination and studious restraint. Concomitantly, the perceived objects, 'new animals', are not referred to as arrested in an abstract form, dissociated from their environment. Rather, they are productive of experiences that 'move' the researcher along a track whose end is not in view. In fact, it is telling that 'the soul' of the investigator can here be seen to be 'moved' in both a metaphorical and a literal way. It can be regarded as affected and excited ('moved') by an 'epistemic thing', a 'mixture of hard and soft', half-object, half-signifier, that represents 'what one does not yet know'.[10] Or the 'soul' (and body) of the investigator can be taken, more literally, to be motivated ('moved') to follow the 'paths' of examination, the ways of knowing that are opened up by such an unknown thing. Yet, for Lewes, as his designation of 'knowledge' as 'broken wonder' – an oblique reference to Bacon – suggests,[11] these two kinds of motion, being affected and being made to act, seem to be conjoined in a single, seamless trajectory that connects the experience of being moved emotionally with the attempt to scrutinise and understand the sources of this affection intellectually. Lewes's notion of knowledge, then, similar to Huxley's, is premised on a continuity of the aesthetic and the intellectual, with the aesthetic experience of an ill-understood 'delight' acting as an incentive, 'a spark of inextinguishable thought', releasing 'trains of inflammable suggestion' along which the process of learning can proceed. In short, the referent of knowledge, as it is described here, does not stand still, waiting to be grasped as a distinct object cut off from the knowing subject.[12] Rather, knowledge is (yet) 'multiple in space and mobile in time', as Michel Serres puts it in congenial terms, 'unstable and fluctuating like a flame, relational'.[13] What is to be known is not (yet) determined, but 'unfolds vista after vista, for ever stretching illimitably distant', compelling the investigator to go along with it, to follow the trail pointed up by it.

Lewes's *Sea-Side Studies* can therefore be seen to enact a movement that is inherent in the very concept of method, composed of the Greek words *hodos*, meaning 'path' or 'track', and *meta*, meaning 'after' or 'with'.[14] This etymology suggests that the 'method' of investigation refers to the way of following a thing or topic, or to the process of accompanying it on its course, rather than to the act of enclosing it in a predetermined frame of ideas.[15] In agreement with this notion of method, Lewes's investigations are set in motion, as he indicates at the beginning of the first instalment of the *Sea-Side Studies*, by a migratory impulse to leave his familiar environment and become 'acquainted' with what is yet unknown to him. He compares this impulse to what the birds 'must feel when certain dim but imperious influences of atmosphere and temperature urge them' to leave their regular habitat for a warmer place. 'I too was impatient to take wing' (1856: Aug., 184).

Yet, rather than flying above a flat surface and looking down upon it from the elevated point of view of a bird, Lewes soon finds himself in the position of a pedestrian, immersed in the moving terrain around Ilfracombe. This is a landscape that compels his eye to wander along with its qualities and outlines while resisting all attempts to be seen as a whole. Thus, what Lewes presents to his readers is not a 'picture' held in place by a frame but a world in progress that continually impinges on the observer, affecting and informing his representation with its 'manifold' 'charms', as Lewes's writing makes clear (1856: Aug., 185).

> The country all round is billowy with hills, which rarely seem to descend into valleys. The paradox may move your scepticism; you may bring excellent reasons, physical, geological, and geographical, to prove that wherever there are hills there must be valleys. Nevertheless, the abstract force of *what must be* vanishes before the concrete force of *what is*; and at Ilfracombe you will find hills abounding, hills rising upon hills, but not always making valleys. What the French picturesquely call the *mouvement du terrain*, which suggests hills in motion like the waves, is here seen on every side; and these waving slopes are in springtime pale with primroses, or flaming with furze. If you get sight of a bit of earth to vary the verdure, it is of that rich red-brown marl which warms the whole landscape. If you climb one of those hills, the chances are that you come upon a rugged precipice sheer over the sea, unless a green slope leads gently down to it. (1856: Aug., 185)

The environment, the 'country all round', in the midst of which the walker is situated presents him with a spectacle of 'motion' that refuses to conform to predictable patterns or pictures of what 'must be' expected to be seen in such a scenery. Instead, what he perceives is a rolling, billowing landscape, 'hills rising upon hills' but rarely seeming 'to descend into valleys', in which terrestrial matters behave 'like the waves' of the sea while they are simultaneously 'flaming with furze'. This is a landscape in formation, a moving world that *does things* (rather than containing them), with hills rising and descending, slopes waving and flaming and the earth warming the whole terrain. As a result, the experience of being *with* the world, or 'the concrete force of *what is*', tends to overtake what is known *about* it, or the 'abstract force of *what must be*'. The countryside does not lie before the observer as if it were fully mapped out, but unfolds in relation to him, moving as he moves.

Emergent Matters

As this already indicates, one can venture to say that Lewes's studies are premised on an emergent ontology, or an ontology of an 'open world', a world of 'comings and goings' and 'productive movements', rather than of bounded units and self-contained spheres.[16] 'Such productive movements may generate formations, swellings, growths, protuberances and occurrences, but not objects,' as Tim Ingold explains.[17] This means that in an open or emergent world nothing exists without the motions and actions that make it appear in one way or another. 'Fires burn,' for instance, 'pebbles grate', stars shine, 'hills rise up' and 'clouds billow'. In fact, according to Ingold, all the modifications of the empirical world, whether they are fires, pebbles, clouds, stars or hills, are defined solely by the activities through which they come into their specific mode and shape of being. They are composed of 'formative and transformative *processes*', rather than of material essences.[18] Stars and clouds '*are*, respectively, their shining and billowing, just as the hills *are* their rising, the fire *is* its burning and the pebbles *are* their grating'.[19] For Ingold, such generative processes can be matters of perception only if they are also 'of the essence of what is perceived'.[20]

In accordance with such an ontology of emergence, what one reads about in Lewes's *Sea-Side Studies*, first published in eight instalments in *Blackwood's Edinburgh Magazine*, is not a world 'furnished'[21] with fully-fledged objects or subjects that are abstracted from the formative activities through which they become such definite beings in the first place. Rather, large parts of Lewes's texts are composed of the paths along which the subject-matters of his studies take shape. For example, Lewes refrains from representing the town of Ilfracombe, in and around which the first sequence of Sea-Side Studies is performed, as if it were a completed whole. Instead, his writing traverses through Ilfracombe in the mode of a walker on his way to the shore, directing the reader's attention to whatever the writer considers to be worthy of a closer look. 'To the shore, then! and as we pass, we can take a glimpse at the town' (1856: Aug., 185).

In this pedestrian manner, Lewes's writing proceeds on a slow, winding course to the beach, climbing up and down a 'steep hill', passing beside a babbling 'stream' and through 'a tunnel, dark, indeed, but with a light at the end', before we are finally allowed to take in the first view of the sea: 'and oh! what a *thrill* runs along the sentient paths to our souls as the blue of the sea bursts upon us. We lean upon a parapet of rock, and see the waves running up the rugged face of the cliffs, and falling back in spray' (1856: Aug., 186). Such formulations are representative of the emergent environment in and through which Lewes's studies are acted out: the view of an exterior motion, 'the waves running up the rugged face of the cliffs, and falling back in spray' is mirrored in the expression of an interior emotion, the 'thrill' which 'runs along the sentient paths to our souls'. And the result of both, taken together, is an interactive 'run' of events which suggests that the two kinds of movement, the exterior and the interior one, do not exist separately, but are part of one and the same world-in-progress.

Lewes's studies, then, take place in a world in flux, in which the naturalist's activity and perception is one motivating factor among others. Thus, when Lewes's writing, having passed through '[a]nother tunnel' and 'leaned upon another parapet', has eventually brought the reader to the shore, it does not arrive at a resting place or a definite position from which a set of distinctive objects could be observed (1856: Aug., 186). Rather, the writing is once again drawn into a shifting landscape compelling the reader's viewpoint to follow the 'wild and rugged' lines which mark out the contours of the scene: the shore. 'And what a shore!', Lewes cries out (1856: Aug., 186).

> Precipitous walls and battlements of rock rise on each side, making a bay; before us, sharply-cut fragments of dark rock start out of the water for some distance. Every yard of ground here is a picture. The whole coast-line is twisted and waved about into a series of bays and creeks, each having a character of its own; and whether you stand on the Tors, and look along the coast – or on the shore, and look up at the rocks, it is always some new aspect, something charming for the eye to rest upon [. . .] Look at that reef round and along which the stealthy tide is crawling; see how the back of it is ridged with sharp sudden lines cutting against the sky – and cutting you when you stumble on them; or look at that sombre precipice over which the gull is floating broad-winged, uttering its piteous cry, or startling you with its strange mocking laugh. Follow it a little further and the eye rests on a purple tinted wall of rock, from the sides of which jut ledges covered with vegetation. The soil here is so generous that Nature seems to be bursting into life through every crevice and on every inch. (1856: Aug., 186–7)

As before, what is described here denies the viewer the comfort of a stable vantage point from which it could be inspected and taken hold of in an accomplished form. The observed scenery does not stand still, but performs 'twisting', 'waving', 'starting', 'crawling', 'cutting' and 'jutting' movements, continuously impelling 'you' to go along with these movements and to adjust your position and perspective in response to them. Consequently, the land- and seascape that Lewes sees is made up of multiple pictures ('Every yard of ground here is a picture'), but refuses to be captured in the form of a single one. Whatever bay or creek he looks upon does not just act, whether it twists, waves, cuts or starts forth. It also acts on him by making him follow its outlines or look at it from various angles ('Look at that reef [. . .] or look at that [. . .] Follow it a little further') as well as by influencing his feelings, or impressing him with its multiple 'characters'. As a result, the coast-line around Ilfracombe is not represented as objectively given, as if it existed separately from the observer who looks at it. Rather, it is readable as an effect of a 'turbulent interlacing of self and world', or as a 'pre-positional movement' from, towards, with and around the cliffs that does not correspond to an abstract or general idea of predefined geographical space.[22] This mutual entwining of self and world also means that the emotions and moods of the observer become just as much part of the countryside as the appearance and 'character' of the countryside becomes part of him, impacting on his movements and directing his vision. In this passage, for instance, the 'precipice over which the gull is floating' is made 'sombre', the tide 'stealthy' and the cry of the bird 'piteous' while, conversely, the observer is attracted by 'a purple tinted wall of rock' inviting his eye to rest on it, and deterred by 'cutting' ridges, which threaten to bruise him.

As these passages indicate, Lewes as a researcher does not try to disentangle himself from the subject-matter of his investigations. Rather, his personal motions (such as his walks) and emotions are presented as an integral part of the exploratory processes that make up his *Studies*. What is more, it is quite representative of these texts that, up to this point, Lewes's writing has not even arrived at any of the 'marine animals' that it has set out to study. What we have read instead is a circuitous ramble towards, around and across the place where these animals are supposed to be found. In fact, large parts of Lewes's *Studies* do not even deal with the act of examining something that has already been caught and identified, to say nothing of the results of such acts. Instead, one is provided with vivid descriptions of what Lewes calls 'hunting', along with detailed information on the equipment that is needed for this 'sport' (1856: Aug., 189), including 'a geologist's hammer', 'a *cold* chisel [. . .], an oyster-knife, a paper-knife, a landing-net, and, if your intentions are serious, a small crow-bar' (1856: Aug., 187). These instruments are 'necessary', as Lewes warns his readers, for no one should be under the illusion that all a naturalist has to do is pick up, or gaze at, what is spread out, readily prepared, before him. On the contrary: 'hunting among the rocks is not easy nor always safe, nor certain to be successful', as he writes (1856: Aug., 187). 'You must make up your mind to lacerated hands, even if you escape bruises, to utter soakings, to unusual gymnastics in wriggling yourself into impossible places' (1856: Aug., 187). As this shows, what the naturalist has to learn is to adjust his movements to those of his subject-matters, to act in tune with the character and constitution of the marine animals with which he wants to become acquainted, even if this means that he must be prepared to share the same medium with them ('make up your mind [. . .] to utter soakings'), or even perform similar actions ('wriggling yourself into impossible places').

The method of study that Lewes recommends, then, is an activity whereby the investigator attempts to adapt to the investigated material, to become like it, or at least to enter into a relationship of interplay and mutual resonance with it: into a 'dance of agency', to use Pickering's phrase.[23] Accordingly, the relationship between the researcher and his living materials is not represented, as it often used to be, in terms of warfare, with the scientist seen as a courageous, self-denying fighter for knowledge who seeks to conquer and possess what he takes to be foreign to himself. Much to the contrary, Lewes's language is dominated by metaphors of courtship, 'intimacy' and love (1857: Aug., 222) which make the (male) naturalist appear like an eager suitor, attracted, enchanted and occasionally bewildered by a coy and evasive (female) counterpart. According to Isobel Armstrong, Lewes even 'vulgarly sexualizes knowledge'.[24] The *Eolis*, for example, is described as 'one of the loveliest of sea-charmers' (1856: Aug., 193) while the 'Daisy (*Actinia bellis*)' is said to be a 'coquette', who 'draws adventurous seekers after her', as Lewes puts it (1856: Aug., 188).

> What a coquette is the Daisy (*Actinia bellis*), who displays her cinq-spotted bosom, beautiful as Imogen's, in the crystal pool. You are on your knees at once; but no sooner is your hand stretched towards her, than at the first touch she disappears in a hole. Nothing but chiselling out the piece of rock will secure her; and after all, your labour is the price paid for the capture, and the captive is priced accordingly [. . .] (1856: Aug., 188)

Here, the behaviour and appearance of the sea-anemone is made legible by being likened not only to that of a human being, a coquettish woman, but also to that of a literary figure, Shakespeare's Imogen.

The 'chiselling' actions of the naturalist, in turn, are represented as those of a desperate lover falling 'on his knees' to win the affections of the woman he adores. Yet, no matter how many times more lovely and high-'priced' the Daisy may be made through the hard labour invested into the pursuit and 'capture' of her, Lewes leaves no doubt that the joy of hunting, just as the joy of love, comes, in fact, from a fleeting 'thrill' of which one can never quite take hold: 'There is something sad in the fugitive keenness of pleasure. I shall never feel again the delight of getting my first actinia,' as he writes, claiming that the same is true for the delight of one's first love (1856: Aug., 188). 'There is a bloom on the cheek which the first kiss carries away, and which never again meets the same lips' (1856: Aug., 188). As Lewes suggests, the only way of coming to terms with this experience of transience is to measure neither love nor knowledge by some (Romantic) idea of originality, finality and completion that is very unlikely to be realised for more than a short, transitory moment. Both love and knowledge should, on his account, rather be seen as works in progress, a final end of which is not (yet) in view, even though their structures become ever more steady and reliable the longer one continues to engage in constructing and maintaining them. On this account, the fading of the '*first* thrills' of novelty is amply compensated by 'the new vistas which open with increasing knowledge' of the other, as Lewes remarks, continuing to use the analogy with a love affair: 'Knowledge widens and changes its horizon; and as we travel we pass under newer skies lighted by serener stars' (1856: Aug., 189).

My point, then, is that Lewes conceives of knowledge as he does of love: namely in terms of ongoing practices, rather than in terms of ideal structures that reside (as they do for Collins's Benjulia) in some 'sacred' realm outside of such activities. More precisely, for Lewes, such processes of knowing (loving), as the above quotation indicates, should be seen as ways of 'travelling' along with an object – meaning both subject-matter and goal – that gradually 'widens and changes its horizon', becoming less exciting, but more trustworthy and reliable as one continues to follow its trail. This suggests that Lewes's theoretical concept of science is substantially informed by his practical experience as a naturalist since, for the practitioner, knowledge is not attached to a final destination but takes shape step by step, along an open-ended track. 'Practitioners,' as Tim Ingold puts this, 'are wanderers, wayfarers, whose skill lies in their ability to find the grain of the world's becoming and to follow its course while bending it to their evolving purpose.'[25] This explains, for example, Lewes's keen emphasis on a point he makes at the beginning of the second instalment: that 'the naturalist, and especially the physiologist, has a Morrow to his pleasure, when all other hunters have but a fine To-day' (1856: Sept., 312).

Whereas the actions of the ordinary hunter are finite and purpose-bound, this is to say, with their pleasing effects terminating as soon as the kill has been eaten, the pleasure of the naturalist has what Lewes calls the 'savour of the infinite, which all true and great pleasures must possess' (1856: Sept., 312). Therefore, Lewes says, the 'finale' of the dinner table is 'an anticlimax for a hunter' because, albeit 'vigorous in sensation [. . .] it is circumscribed; it throws out no feelers into other, wider regions; it generates no thoughts; it leads nowhither; it is terminal' (1856: Sept., 313). By contrast, the 'finale' of 'the dissecting table', the 'scene on which my captures made a last appearance', as he describes it, 'was not, strictly speaking, a *finis*', at which the explorations of the naturalist regularly came to a conclusion:

> for when the last shred of delicate tissue had been examined under the microscope, when various parts of the animal had been made into 'preparations' for after-study, when everything to the physical eye may have seemed concluded, no *end* was reached, no dead wall of terminal blankness; on the contrary, the metaphysical eye followed the devious paths of speculation into which new facts conducted; and thus the feast of reason and the flow of physiology generated pleasures superior to the pleasures of the ordinary hunter by quite transcendent degrees. (1856: Sept., 313)

What makes the 'pleasures' of the naturalist 'superior to the pleasures of the ordinary hunter', then, is precisely that his activities do not yield something like consummate results, well-cooked morsels of knowledge, ready to be consumed. Even when everything may seem finished and concluded, the 'facts' thus established do not, in Lewes's view, typically constitute a 'wall of terminal blankness'. Rather, they frequently engender new possibilities, 'conducting' 'the metaphysical eye' into 'devious paths of speculation' to be 'followed' in practice. 'The facts are the least of the attractions in this study, although they are the bricks with which you build', as he points out a few paragraphs later (1856: Sept., 318).

'Something Zoological and Strange'

Lewes's *Sea-Side Studies* as a whole are best described as an account of his various attempts to build reliable structures of knowledge out of the facts (or 'bricks') of marine biology that he assembled during two separate trips to Ilfracombe, Tenby, the Isles of Scilly and Jersey, both undertaken, in 1856 and 1857, together with George Eliot.[26] What these texts represent, that is to say, is a learning process, motivated by not much more than the 'desire' to become familiar with something, namely the sea, that, albeit 'an old playfellow', was 'in respect of its inhabitants', as Lewes notes in the first instalment, 'a perfectly new acquaintance to make' (1856: Aug., 184). Typically, therefore, Lewes's *Sea-Side Studies* present themselves as investigative movements in pursuit of an ill-defined, largely unknown theme. 'Another day, in idler mood, we ramble along the shore in receipt of windfalls,' Lewes, for example, writes at one point (1857: June, 679). 'A bottle is always ready in the pocket, and something is certain to turn up' (1857: June, 679). This can either be read as a report of Lewes on the prowl or as an ironic self-portrait of his writing which, in such instances, does precisely what it speaks about: it proceeds in the style of idling or rambling, with the matter of examination yet to be found.

As Lewes's *Studies* are expressly premised on what he calls 'ignorance', on a condition of being unfamiliar with one's subject-matter (1856: Aug., 184), it is not surprising that this unfocused, 'rambling' mode is the predominant one. When everything is potentially interesting 'something is certain to turn up', suggesting new lines of enquiry for both the naturalist and the text that describes his activities.[27] 'The stem and root of that oar-weed, for example, is worth an investigating glance, certain as it is of being a colony of life' (1857: June, 679). In this case, the thing of interest, the epistemic thing, turns out, upon closer inspection, to yield 'a pink-and-white feathery creature' that Lewes recognises, from 'hazy descriptions and inadequate engravings', to be a specific one: 'By heavens! it is a *Comatula*, "the romance of the sea",' as he cries out fondly, putting it into one of his jars (1857: June, 679). Here and elsewhere, Lewes's writing presents its subject-matter as a 'world of wonders' and curiosities that exists in excess of any attempt to impose an intellectual order upon it (1857: July, 7). 'Singular, is it not?' (1856: Sept., 321); 'Did you ever see anything more exquisite?'; 'Really this pool is enchanting!' (1856: Aug., 192). Such exclamations testify to a kind of first-person experience that remains subject to be overwhelmed by the 'singularity' of what it encounters. 'We walk amid surprises,' as Lewes himself puts this, suggesting, once more, that his studies develop from the inside ('amid') of an aesthetic perception, a volatile mode of affect, rather than being premised on an ideal point of view (1857: July, 7).

In fact, if Lewes is firm on anything, then it is his conviction that people should always expect their subject matter to take them by surprise. Therefore, the perspective of the naturalist has to remain as open to modification as the living forms that he seeks to know. 'We should as much as possible keep the mind in a state of loose moorings,' as he puts this,

> not firmly anchoring on any ground, unless our charts are full of explicit detail; not *believing* (but simply acquiescing, and that in a provisional way) in any fact which is not clear in the light of its own evidence, or which, in default of our having verified it for ourselves, has the trustworthy verification of another. (1856: Oct., 480)

It is this floating, flexible non-position of being in an incipient 'state of loose moorings' that enables the naturalist to remain alive to the element of unpredictability and variability that, in the wake of evolutionary theory, was increasingly taken to be part of the productive processes constituting the natural sphere. 'We never know all that we have captured until some day afterwards' (1857: Sept., 348), Lewes writes at one point, indicating that his work always calculated on the possibility that the performance of an operation may bring about unexpected results. 'Repeated examinations of our vases and bottles with a lens, enable us to detect many a curious novelty which was unsuspected among the weed, and has now emerged' (1857: Sept., 348). Repetition, this suggests, frequently engenders variation which, in the course of time, may cause 'unsuspected' novelties to arise. Therefore, Lewes argues, one should not be afraid to count on the unaccountable, or to exploit the creative potential of chance events. 'It is,' in other words, 'a good plan always to bring home some "chance-weed", especially if it have a root, the red weeds being the most advantageous' (1857: Sept., 348).

Lewes, then, worked through and along with contingency or 'the adjacent possible',[28] rather than seeking to ward it off. He acknowledged that, in practice, all plans are made subject to the vicissitudes of a process that may cause them to become corrected and adapted in accordance with unforeseen events. Rather than trying to root out this incalculable component of scientific action in favour of a perfect design, he integrated it into his studies, accepting, even welcoming, the very fact that seeking is always in part, as he says, '"chance-seeking"' (1857: Sept., 348). Lewes's *Studies*, in sum, represent an exploratory practice that is always prone to drift into 'chance-seeking' since neither its motivation nor its object is sufficiently robust to commit it to a straight course of actions or a definite focus and place. As a result, everything that Lewes says about his avowed subject-matter, 'marine animals of simple organization', remains open-ended and loosely moored, offering material for further study rather than conclusive results.

To be sure, Lewes exposes his readers to several lengthy descriptions of the various experiments he performed while he was staying by the sea, sometimes claiming that he had disproved certain details that his text-books represented as established facts or even that he had found out something no one had noticed before. Yet, in the context of the state of the art of Victorian marine biology, none of these allegations, as they are put forth by Lewes's texts, is sufficiently indubitable to be regarded as justified general knowledge, even though they often do call common beliefs into question or indicate possible tracks for further enquiry (cf. 1857: July, 14–17). This lack of conclusions is typical, for Lewes's *Studies* never aim to be more than steps towards a destination whose appearance is likely to change as one advances towards it. As the reader is told from the start, these steps are not based on a firm ground of expert knowledge, but on the unsettled passion of the amateur whom the attraction of the unknown lures into novel terrain. Moreover, throughout the *Sea-Side Studies*, it is the sea itself which, like nothing else, epitomises this ill-known subject in the making, the boundaries of which are (yet) to be made out. Crucially, however, the sea, thus conceived, does not exist outside of the investigator, but partakes of his very self, influencing his actions. 'The fact is, the sea is a passion,' as Lewes puts this (1856: Oct., 477). 'Its fascination, like all true fascination, makes us reckless of consequences' (1856: Oct., 477).

In Lewes's writing the sea therefore figures as a kind of seductive power that drives and draws his studies forwards, forgetful of their directions and aims. 'The sea is like a woman: she lures us, and we run madly after her; she ill-uses us, and we adore her; beautiful, capricious, tender, and terrible!' (1856: Oct., 477). In fact, what is so alluring about the sea, it seems, is precisely what resists being integrated into an intellectual frame. Profoundly 'mysterious', 'life-abounding' and endlessly suggestive of possible stories, as Lewes describes her at another point, the 'peculiar charm' of the sea is that her contents are unfathomable and inexhaustible, continuously tempting the naturalist to look at them once more (1856: Aug., 193). 'There is no satiety in this love; *can* there be in true affection?' (1856: Oct., 477).

One might say, then, that Lewes's *Sea-Side Studies* represent a love affair with an elusive subject, instigated by a powerful passion that seems beyond rational control because it keeps throwing up ever fresh aspects of maritime life for the naturalist to pick up and examine, like the sea itself, flinging her creatures onto the shore. 'I go out on the sands, and at my feet the sea throws a Calamary (*Loligo*) with which I rush back to my lodgings in great glee' (1856: Oct., 478). According to Lewes, the 'true affection', which allegedly governs the loving relationship between the investigator and his capricious subject-matter, works in two ways. Having once been affected *by* the sea, the naturalist subsequently tends to feel an affection *for* it. Or as Lewes says: 'The direction of his thoughts is constantly seawards' (1857: June, 669). 'At least it was thus with me', he writes at the beginning of the second series, before setting off for the Isles of Scilly (1857: June, 669):

> The iodine of the sea-breezes had entered me. I felt that I had 'suffered a sea change' into something zoological and strange. Men came to look like molluscs; and their ways the ways of creatures in a larger rock-pool. When forced to endure the conversation of some friend of the family, with well-waxed whiskers and imperturbable shirt-front, I caught myself speculating as to what sort of figure *he* would make in the vivarium – *not* always to his glorification. In a word, it was painfully evident that London wearied me, and that I was troubled in my mind. I had tasted of a new delight; and the hungry soul of man leaps on a new passion to master, or be mastered by it. (1857: June, 670)

The actuating force that lies at the bottom of Lewes's travels and studies is notably double-faced. While it emanates from the speaker's mind, causing him to spot aspects of his own vision of life wherever he looks, it is also disturbingly beyond his control, inciting him to view his familiar world in odd and unfamiliar ways. The cause of Lewes's affection, that which moves him along the lines of his studies, cannot be clearly located. It is both inside and outside of him. Leaping on a 'new passion' is the speaker's deliberate action, but it is also a chemical reaction to a substance ('iodine') that has 'entered' his reason from elsewhere, making him feel as if he had turned into an uncouth frame.

As indicated by the quotation from Shakespeare's *Tempest*, which is partly transferred to the rich world of the 'zoological and strange', Lewes's *Sea-Side Studies* is a thoroughly hybrid series of texts. In fact, in the context of Lewes's career as a writer, their appearance marks a point of transition from philosophy and literary criticism, about which he had mainly been publishing thus far, to natural history and biology,

which thenceforth became a main centre of his interests.[29] But while
the appearance of the *Sea-Side Studies* can be seen as a symptom of
Lewes's own 'sea-change' from literary critic to marine zoologist, they
are transitional in more than just a biographical respect. For what
they represent is not science as such, but the practical paths, the ways
of knowing through which science comes into being in the first place.
Writing, as Lewes himself indicates, is an integral part of the art of
paving these paths. It is not a performance that only begins after certain facts have already been established; rather, it is one of the enabling
operations through which such facts are constituted and made into
recognisable forms. 'To this intent,' he points out,

> the naturalist should always have pencil and note-book on his working-
> table in which to record every new fact, no matter how trifling it may
> seem at the moment; the time will come when that and other facts will
> be the keys to unlock many a casket. (1857: June, 680)

Writing, thus conceived, is an activity of inscribing traces, of transforming ideas and observations into material marks which 'record'
them as possible 'keys to unlock many a casket', or as parts of a
larger pattern that is yet to appear. Lewes's *Sea-Side Studies*, both
the articles and the book, have never been thoroughly purified of
this kind of provisional writing. For they do not represent a coherent
argument, but episodes of the generative processes by way of which
such an argument may be composed. Their intention, as Lewes makes
very clear, was not so much to teach their readers *that* this and that
is the case as to show them *how* they might go about finding things
out for themselves. 'If these Papers have amused him, and been of
the slightest assistance,' Lewes tells his reader at the end of the first
series, 'either in awakening a desire for sea-side studies, or in giving
practical hints for their prosecution, their object is attained' (1856:
Oct., 484).

For the student of Victorian literary and cultural history, Lewes's
'Papers' are certainly instructive, not least because they provide
us with glimpses of the process through which professional science
emerged from the amateur pursuit of natural history. As the success
of popularising books by Philip Henry Gosse, Charles Kingsley and
others demonstrates, there was a considerable interest, at times
amounting to a regular craze, in combing the beaches, dipping into
ponds and ransacking tide-pools for all kinds of animals.[30] Lewes, too,
catered to this interest, but at the same time, he seems eager to make
a step beyond natural history in its established form. 'You may hunt
for animals, keep them in glass tanks and vases, watch their habits,

and make pets of them,' he writes in the first instalment, 'but with the Scalpel and the Microscope these pleasures are converted into august studies, carrying the mind into those arcana where the early Beginnings are revealed' (1856: Aug., 185). As this suggests, Lewes's studies straddle the threshold between the method of the natural historian who merely acts as a passive spectator, content with naming and classifying the world around him, and the work of the experimental scientist who actively engages his environment, changing the conditions under which he acts in order to provoke new experiences and to extend what is already known.[31] What appealed to Lewes about the study of natural history, it seems, was precisely that it was not (yet) a specialised discourse, but enabled forms of writing that were flexible enough to mix what Philip Henry Gosse called the 'aesthetic aspect' and 'poetic interest'[32] of animal life with what came increasingly to be defined as 'severe science' (1856: Aug., 185). Thus viewed, Lewes's texts are not just studies in a particular subject-matter, but also in a new style of writing, as he suggests in the last paragraph of the series. 'The naturalist may be anything, everything,' Lewes concludes.

> He may yield to the charm of simple observation; he may study the habits and habitats of animals, and moralise on their ways; he may use them as starting-points of laborious research; he may carry his newly-observed facts into the highest region of speculation; and whether roaming amid the lovely nooks of Nature in quest of varied specimens, or fleeting the quiet hour in observation of his pets – whether he make Natural History an amusement, or both amusement and serious work – it will always offer him exquisite delight. (1857: Oct., 423)

What all these modes of exploration, from the 'laborious research' at the desk to the 'roaming' search for 'varied specimens' have in common, it seems, is not that they produce reliable knowledge, but that they offer 'exquisite delight'. This encapsulates once more that Lewes's studies constitute an experimental field in which the intellectual pursuit of science has not yet been separated from the aesthetic apprehension of beautiful forms.

Eliot's Animals

As I wish to show, it is this field of the experimental that Lewes cultivated and inhabited together with George Eliot, who not only accompanied him on his journeys to the coast, but also used similar methods to perform her own (novelistic) studies in rural life. How closely Lewes and Eliot worked together can be gleaned from Eliot's own *Ilfracombe Journal*, which contains many of the same observations and formulations also to be found in Lewes's writing. For example, in one passage that reappears in almost exactly the same form in the first instalment of the *Sea-Side Studies*, Eliot reflects on 'the strong family likeness between ourselves and all other building, burrowing[,] house-appropriating and shell-secreting animals', to quote her own words.[33]

> The difference between a man with his house and a mollusc with its shell lies in the number of steps or phenomena interposed between the fact of individual existence and the completion of the building. Whatever other advantages we may have over molluscs and insects in our habitations, it is clear that their architecture has the advantage of ours in beauty – at least considered as the architecture of the species. Look at man in the light of a shell-fish and it must be admitted that his shell is generally ugly, and it is only after a great many more 'steps or phenomena' that he secretes here and there a wonderful shell in the shape of a temple or a palace.[34]

This observation draws attention to the successive actions, the 'steps or phenomena' that, in the life of human beings, are inevitably 'interposed' between the naked 'fact' of their 'individual existence' and the completed 'building' or 'habitations' that they make a part of it. To molluscs and insects, Eliot suggests, the secreting of shells or the building of nests is a natural process, an activity that they instinctively or unconsciously know how to complete in a way that suits their needs. In fact, the 'beauty' that Eliot admired in the mollusc's shell is its perfect 'utility', as Lewes adds in his version of the idea (1856: Aug., 195). More precisely, what Eliot and Lewes perceived as beautiful is the way in which the architecture of the animal dwelling seems to be seamlessly assimilated, made 'subservient' to the life of the organism (1856: Aug., 195). By contrast, they suggest, human beings cannot rely on an unconscious instinct telling them how they are to make themselves a(t) home in the world. For the houses and habitations of man are not forms of natural adaptation, but products of artificial construction. Animals know by nature how to make dwellings that are 'beautifully' fit for them, Eliot intimates, whereas human beings have to acquire this skill as part of an education or culture. This process of learning how – in what 'shells' and by what means – to inhabit the world not only takes time; it also requires a conscious effort, a temporally extended activity made up of several 'steps', each of which could be taken otherwise since there is no single, natural way for humans to live their lives.

As Sally Shuttleworth has shown, this process of niche-building by which humans come to settle into and seek to maintain a mutually sustaining relationship with their physical and social environment is at the heart of most, if not all, of Eliot's novels.[35] In fact, according to Anne-Julia Zwierlein, the very notion of human self-formation or personal development, as it is represented or enacted in many fictional texts of the nineteenth century, those of Eliot among them, is informed by, and modelled on, physiological ideas about the reciprocal exchange between an organism and its medium.[36] Just as the organism was taken to be nourished and made to grow by means of a continuous interaction with the (food) materials supplied by its environment, Zwierlein argues, so the formation of the human individual was often described as a process of responding to, and receiving insights from, the constitution of the surrounding world.[37] In short, what the self had to learn, according to Victorians such as Lewes, Comte and others, was to build up a dynamic relationship with its social and physical environment by way of which it is able to fulfil both its own needs and the demands of its fellow (human) beings. According to Shuttleworth, Eliot's novels can be seen as enquiries into the moral conflicts between 'self-fulfilment' and 'social duty' that arise from this very process of searching for a way of life suitable both to one's own being and to the others that, as Lewes repeatedly points out, are a part of it.[38] 'Man is by his constitution forced to live for others and in others.'[39]

Eliot's novels, then, as the subtitle of *Middlemarch* ('A Study of Provincial Life') indicates, seem to be designed as studies of human sociability and interaction, or as contributions to 'the Natural History of social bodies', in her own terms.[40] Indeed, it is telling how frequently Eliot makes her readers look at human beings, as she does in the above quotation, 'in the light of' animals. For example, in *The Mill on the Floss*, which was begun shortly after Eliot's and Lewes's sojourn by the sea,[41] Maggie Tulliver, 'shaking the water from her black locks as she ran', is made to appear 'like a Skye terrier' (*MF* 28) while the friend of her brother Tom, Bob Jakins, 'as he shuffled along, keeping his blue eyes fixed on the river', is compared to 'an amphibious animal who foresaw occasion for darting in' (*MF* 48). Likewise, when Mrs Stelling seeks to make Philip Wakem 'feel that she behaved exceedingly well to him', he meets 'her advances towards a good understanding very much as a caressed mollusc meets an invitation to show himself out of his shell' (*MF* 174). And after Tom and Maggie have quarrelled early in the novel, while they are still children, they become reconciled by way of feeding each other 'just for company' and by rubbing 'each other's cheeks and brows and noses together, while they ate, with a humiliating resemblance to two friendly ponies' (*MF* 39). Thus described, Eliot's characters are well suited to their environment, the country town of St Ogg's which is itself 'a continuation and outgrowth of nature, as much as the nests of the bower-birds or the winding galleries of the white ants' (*MF* 115).

To be sure, such analogies may be regarded as no more than ordinary rhetorical devices, deployed for illustration or comic effects. Conspicuously, however, in *The Mill on the Floss* these devices are often used to represent an innocent or unthinking way of maintaining a relationship between one's self and its medium, a way that is characteristic either of children or of adults who have become so blind to their habits that they have ceased to reflect their contingency. An example for the second kind of unthinking behaviour is the teaching of Tom's tutor Mr Stelling who conducts his lessons 'with that uniformity of method and independence of circumstances, which distinguish the actions of animals understood to be under the immediate teaching of nature' (*MF* 138). Having stopped (or never even started) to consider that his customary fashion of interacting with the social world is not the only possible one, he continues in this fashion as if it were natural. In this respect, he resembles Tom and Maggie in their childhood when their behaviour towards the exterior world is still of a relatively unconscious kind, 'very much like young animals' (*MF* 39). While Stelling seems *no longer* aware of the non-necessary 'steps' through which he makes connections between himself and his social environment, Tom and Maggie are, as children, *not yet* aware of them. In both instances, what takes place between inside and outside or organism and environment is not reflected or even perceived as a mediated activity of 'steps' that could be otherwise. Rather, it is (said to be) akin to the 'actions of animals' whose relationship to the outside world is not organised according to the contingent forms and norms of an acquired culture, but according to the 'immediate teaching' of (their) nature.

As these examples show, the (animal) 'nature' that is here said to prompt and direct the behaviour of the (human) characters is anything but a reliable source of knowledge about the grounds and motives of human action. Rather, it is presented as a highly ambiguous force, capable of instigating various, sometimes contradictory ways of relating to the environment. Thus, in the case of Maggie and Tom, the unconscious property which is said to make them behave 'like young animals' is presented as a source of loving mutuality and agreement saving them from the kind of 'dignified alienation' characteristic of much social intercourse among adults (*MF* 39). By contrast, the unconscious obedience to the 'teaching' of quasi-natural habits that can be seen in Mr Stelling and most of the townsfolk of St Ogg's results in a stubborn and inflexible mindset closing one character off from the other. The point to be noted, then, is that sociability and implicit understanding can just as much be seen as part of man's animal nature as the kind of irrational tenaciousness and mutual incomprehension that comes out, for example, in the conflict between Mr Wakem and Mr Tulliver: 'To suppose that Wakem had the same sort of inveterate hatred towards Tulliver, that Tulliver had towards him, would be like supposing that a pike and a roach can look at each other from a similar point of view' (*MF* 251).

While all of these analogies suggest that *The Mill* can be read as a study of human life which, in principle, is comparable to Lewes's studies in the life of animals, they have a peculiar effect worthy of special emphasis: by presenting human actions in analogy to those of animals, that is, in zoological terms, Eliot's writing makes these actions into something unfamiliar that, paradoxically, is *not* as 'natural' as it is made to appear.[42] Indeed, if 'to naturalize' something means to make 'the strange or deviant [. . .] seem natural' by bringing it 'into relation with a type of discourse or model which is already, in some sense, natural or legible', then one can say that Eliot's analogies have rather a de-naturalising effect.[43] They make the agency of humans appear like something, the behaviour of animals, which – despite the biological kinship between humans and other mammals – could and can immediately be perceived as unlike it. After all, the very construction of an analogy, in contrast to that of a metaphor, is predicated on the assumption of a difference between the two fields that are to be compared. They prompt the reader to see human habits and actions as something other that it is not or not only: instinctive animal behaviour. By the use of analogy, then, Eliot's writing exposes the nature of human agency as strange and uncommon, as something that is yet to be naturalised, yet to be translated into a legible text.

One might therefore say that the (yet) unknown or ill-known subject of Eliot's studies, the problem explored by her writing, is the strange nature of human agency, inextricably entangled as it is with the social cultures (or ways of life) through which it is educated and expressed. For example, the clash between a 'sense of self founded on memory, and past social experience, and the direct promptings of passion', which is set in play in Maggie's relationship with Stephen,[44] can be read as an enquiry into the question of what would, in this situation, be the most natural decision for her to take. Is it 'natural', as Stephen argues, to follow the urge of one's love for someone, even if this means that one has to inflict pain on others to whom one had been committed before? 'It is come upon us without our seeking: it is natural – it has taken hold of me in spite of every effort I have made to resist it' (*MF* 448). For Stephen, the arrival of this 'natural' force, which he takes to be necessary and irresistible, justifies the undoing of existing social bonds, which he regards as arbitrary shackles, perverting the essence of love. 'It is unnatural – it is horrible [. . .] We should break all these mistaken ties that were made in blindness, and determine to marry each other' (*MF* 448). According to Stephen, then, the choice is between the personal and natural, which he takes to define the morally right, and the social and artificial, which he considers to be morally wrong because it commits humans to cultural ties that go against 'the immediate teachings' of their (animal) nature. '"The pledge *can't* be fulfilled," he said, with impetuous insistence. "It is unnatural: we can only pretend to give ourselves to any one else. There is wrong in that too – there may be misery in it for *them* as well as for us"' (*MF* 449). Maggie, as Eliot's text indicates by the use of another telling analogy, which has the heroine react 'like a lovely wild animal timid and struggling under caresses', is by no means immune to the kinds of animal feeling and (sex) drive that underpin Stephen's argument (*MF* 449). All the same, she confesses herself unable, in her moral choices, to pit the natural as clearly against the social as her (potential) lover. 'It seems right to me sometimes that we should follow our strongest feeling,' Maggie points out (*MF* 449).

> But I see – I feel it is not so now: there are things we must renounce in life; some of us must resign love. Many things are difficult and dark to me; but I see one thing quite clearly – that I must not, cannot, seek my own happiness by sacrificing others. Love is natural; but surely pity and faithfulness and memory are natural too. And they would live in me still, and punish me if I did not obey them. (*MF* 449–50)

Some critics have pointed to Maggie's self-denial, her final decision to subject herself to internalised social contracts, in order to corroborate their view of her as a weak woman, a failing character, or 'a heroine of renunciation',[45] restrained by 'crippling norms' from which she is unable to break free.[46] Implicitly, they have thus taken the side of Stephen who similarly emphasises the disempowering effects of social rules, casting them as 'unnatural' constraints against what he believes to be more fulfilling (and indeed 'natural') for Maggie to do.

Other critics, by contrast, have praised Maggie's loyalty to pre-determined commitments as a token of her moral strength and reso-lution.[47] On this view, the story of Maggie is that of a successful process of *Bildung* through which the heroine learns to forsake the short-lived temptations of individual desire in favour of a more last-ing ideal of selfless sympathy and social good. Finally, a third strand of criticism might be identified that seeks to steer clear of the alter-native between self-surrender and self-fulfilment, focusing instead on the 'competition of narratives' that is carried out by Eliot's text.[48] As Susan Fraiman has put it, 'perhaps the novel of development should be thought of less as the apprenticeship of its central figure than as a drama of dissonant ideas about just what formation is or should be'.[49] Seen in this light, Eliot's writing is founded nei-ther upon a particular idea of *Bildung* or intellectual and emotional growth, nor on the negation of such an idea. Rather, it is itself an investigation into the question of what it means to become a fully formed human being capable of living in tune with one's physical and social circumstances. *The Mill*, one might say, is concerned with the 'steps' that are 'interposed' between one's existence and what-ever moral life one makes out of it.

As criticism has shown, habits and customs, in Victorian physi-ological psychology, were conceived of as ways of organising these 'steps' that constitute the relationship between a human being and the social and material medium in and through which it develops.[50] But even though such customary modes of action may help one 'to make the world habitable',[51] they are never as necessary as they may sometimes appear because, for human beings, as Eliot knew and Maggie learns, there is not just one, natural way of inhabiting the world. The appeal to nature, as Maggie suggests in her discussion with Stephen, can therefore never serve as a moral guideline. Indeed, the voice of nature, as it is invoked in this discussion, remains palpa-bly silent, because what is right and wrong refuses to be derived from the fact of human existence.[52] Sometimes it seems right to 'follow our strongest feeling', as Maggie argues, but this does not mean that it is 'natural' to do this at all events. For sometimes socially moulded cus-toms define tacit contracts, the breaking of which would be wrong: 'Love is natural; but surely pity and faithfulness and memory are natural too.' In short, if the nature of human agency is the subject of Eliot's study, then this nature is never converted into a form of reliable knowledge. Instead, it figures as the unsettled site of activities and controversies that are played out between one's experience of being in the world and the (cultural, ideal) habitations and institutions by means of which it comes to be formed. Human nature, on this conception, includes what is not yet known. It remains emergent, open to respond to, and be influenced by, changing social environments.[53] In this particular situation, it seemed right to Maggie to resist her attraction to Stephen, but neither she nor the novel as a whole suggests that such self-restraint is generally (always, for everyone) the best way to deal with one's passions.[54] As a reader, one cannot even tell whether it was the right choice for her not to marry Stephen. Instead, all answers to such questions are, in the end, drowned in a torrential flood that submerges the very possibility of narrative resolution in a dizzying flux.

'Experiments in Life'

This inconclusive termination of Eliot's work not only resonates with the open-ended 'state of loose moorings' that underpins Lewes's *Sea-Side Studies*. It also corresponds with Eliot's own characterisation of her fictions as 'experiments in life'.[55] All of these experiments, as she indicates in a famous letter to Dr Frank Joseph Payne, contribute to an investigation into the moral condition of human existence. They make up 'an endeavour to see what our thought and emotion may be capable of – what stores of motive, actual or hinted as possible, give promise of a better after which we may strive'.[56] The vagueness of this formulation is inevitable, for Eliot's 'endeavour' is expressly described as a search for a pre- or non-logical wisdom, for 'something more sure than shifting theory'.[57] As this suggests, what she hoped to make readable was something that cannot (yet) be captured in the form of theories or propositional statements. Consequently, the knowledge (if any) that Eliot attempts to outline through her writing must be a non-propositional or practical wisdom, a kind of quasi-instinctive know-how of living that cannot be detached from the particular situations and actions in and through which it is made to manifest itself. Indeed, if there is any kind of general insight to be gained from a text like *The Mill*, then it is 'the truth, that moral judgements must remain false and hollow, unless they are checked and enlightened by a perpetual reference to the special circumstances that mark the individual lot', as the narrator says in one of the last chapters (*MF* 498): 'The great problem of the shifting relation between passion and duty' cannot be resolved with a 'masterkey that will fit all cases' (*MF* 497).

Therefore, the one reading position that is not borne out by the text is that of 'the man of maxims', as the narrator calls him, 'the popular representative of the minds that are guided in their moral judgement solely by general rules' (*MF* 498).[58] This means that Eliot's description of her writing as 'experiments in life' can be regarded as a kind of excuse that this writing can, as it is, never be more than that. It is an expression of modesty and diffidence, pointing out to her readers that her work represents a search for moral wisdom, but nothing beyond that search: no context-independent insight could be lifted out of it and taught in the terms of a commonplace book. This does not mean that one can learn nothing from the reading of Eliot's novels. But it does mean that whatever one may learn from them is, like the incipient structure of an experiment, still variable and disputable, open to be contested, modified and supplemented by experiences which have not yet been recognised in or drawn out of the text. What is experimental about Eliot's novels, one might say, is that by virtue of which they are not settled and closed.[59]

The point, then, is that Eliot's writing never leaves the experimental space, which it opens up, for a vantage point outside of it. Rather, whatever her text represents remains poised in the transitional field of process and trial, the 'developmental niche' in which human life is lived and meaning worked out in time. Therefore, to say that for George Eliot 'the novel was an instrument of knowledge' like a scientific experiment is misleading,[60] unless one adds that the kind of knowledge that her writing exemplifies is not the assertive knowledge that Whewell associated with science. Instead, it is more the non-assertive knowledge of practical reason that Mill associated with practice or art. Thus qualified, Eliot's view of her novels as 'experiments in life' corresponds roughly with Emile Zola's concept of the experimental novel, one of the most ambitious attempts to redefine the writing of (naturalist) novels in terms of the making of scientific knowledge. According to Zola, the experimental method is an expression of the modern insight that scientific practice produces phenomena as often as it registers them. In fact, Zola's whole theory of the experimental novel is self-avowedly inspired by Bernard's claim that 'experiment is but provoked observation', as he paraphrases it. 'The idea of experiment carries with it the idea of modification.'[61] But while neither the experimental scientist nor the experimental novelist can, on Zola's account, be 'solely photographers' of what already exists, they cannot be fantasists or romancers either. Their aim, he says, is neither to invent purely imaginative realms, nor to copy a static nature that is taken to exist, in a completed form, outside of the observer. It is rather a way of manipulating the phenomena of personal experience by creative intervention. 'We start, indeed, from the true facts,' he notes, 'but to show the mechanism of these facts it is necessary for us to produce and direct the phenomena; this is our share of invention.'[62] In short, what the performance of scientific experiments and the writing of novels have in common is that 'share of invention' by which they seek to discover what has not, in the same way, been discovered before.

Yet, while Zola wanted novelists to use the same method as scientists such as Bernard he also insisted that they use it to a different end. The purpose of the experimental novel, he argued, is not, like a medical or chemical experiment, to provide the reader with binding insights into the laws of 'physical life'. Rather, it is supposed to yield a 'knowledge of the passionate and intellectual life' which cannot be reduced to physical conditions because it is influenced by social circumstances that may vary from case to case.[63] 'Man is not alone; he lives in society, in a social condition; and consequently, for us novelists, this social condition unceasingly modifies the phenomena.'[64] What the experimental novelist – in contrast to the experimental scientist – seeks to investigate, then, is not so much the relation between man and his physical environment as that between man and his social environment. 'Indeed our great study is just there, in the reciprocal effect of society on the individual and the individual on society.'[65] Zola is far from purporting that man's social life is independent from his physical life, but he does insist that this social life cannot yet be explained in physical terms: 'We are not yet able to prove that the social condition is also physical and chemical.'[66] In order to investigate this 'social condition', the novelist, Zola argues, has to conduct experiments of his own. He has to continue the work of 'the physicist and the chemist' by adopting his method for a different end.[67] 'We are, in a word, experimental moralists, showing by experiment in what way a passion acts in a certain social condition.'[68]

It is this idea of the novelist as an 'experimental moralist' that links Zola's theory with the work of George Eliot, not least because it suggests that the knowledge produced by the novelist is not the same as the knowledge produced by the physicist or chemist. 'Lewes and Eliot understood,' Richard Menke has argued, 'that even as fiction emulated experimental physiology it should also exceed it.'[69] Surely, what Eliot's novels examine are the laws of man's moral life which are different from, although they may interact with, the laws of his physical life. Her writing demonstrates 'in what way a passion acts in a certain social condition', but it refuses to tell the reader whether this implies a general truth that is valid beyond that particular condition.[70] Thus, while there are chapter headings in *The Mill on the Floss* such as 'Illustrating the Laws of Attraction' (*MF* 399) or 'Showing that Old

Acquaintances are Capable of Surprising Us' (*MF* 498), the concomitant episodes make no claims to the representation of justified general knowledge. All they provide are provisional, experimental models of social life at large, episodic sketches or studies of a theory of human sociability that, at best, is yet to be worked out.

The argument that Eliot's novels are experiments can be substantiated by pointing out that, in the first chapter of *The Mill*, the narrator introduces herself as a participant in the action that is going on around Dorlcote Mill, at no remove from the unfolding events. 'And this is Dorlcote Mill. I must stand a minute or two here on the bridge and look at it, though the clouds are threatening, and it is far on in the afternoon' (*MF* 7). This beginning seems to be subsequently justified as a daydream, from which the narrator awakes in order to embark on the narrative proper. 'I have been pressing my elbows on the arms of my chair, and dreaming that I was standing on the bridge in front of Dorlcote Mill' (*MF* 8–9). But I would like to suggest that the opening scene is more than a prologue of 'Proust-like submergence into the world of unconscious memory' that is sharply contrasted 'with the start of the linear, conscious narration of the story'.[71] More precisely, I wish to argue that the narrator's initial immersion into the world of her own narrative draws attention to the immediacy of an activity that can only be registered from the inside of an unfolding experiment, and not represented from a vantage point outside of a completed story.

The function of the first chapter, thus viewed, is to represent the becoming conscious of the narrator as a participating actor in the very arrangement that she is about to compose. After all, the narrator not only begins the narrative by telling the reader 'what Mr and Mrs Tulliver were talking about [. . .] on that very afternoon I have been dreaming of' (*MF* 9); she also never withdraws entirely from the scene of events, but indicates her presence at various points, either by drawing her own actions and perceptions into the setting ('The wood I walk in on this mild May day, with the young yellow-brown foliage of the oaks between me and the blue sky [. . .] what [. . .] could ever thrill such deep and delicate fibres within me as this home-scene?', *MF* 41), or by giving directions to the reader ('You may see her now, as she walks down the favourite turning, and enters the Deeps by a narrow path through a group of Scotch firs –', *MF* 299). In this way, the reader is made to go along with the narrator ('In order to see Mr and Mrs Glegg at home, we must enter the town of St Ogg's', *MF* 115) and to follow her through an experimental arrangement in which she takes part as one actor among others. As we shall see, such a reading of *The Mill* as an experimental study in human (social) life – a reading which emphasises what is middling and in motion, still in the process of being investigated – comes closest, perhaps, not only to Eliot's own view of her novels as experiments, but also to the philosophical work of her partner, which found an even more congenial expression in her later texts.

Notes

1. All page references marked *HS* are to Collins, *Heart and Science*.
2. This novel is often read as a response to the vivisection debate during the latter decades of the nineteenth century; see Bourne-Taylor, 'Later Novels', pp. 89–91, and French, *Antivivisection*.
3. Daston and Galison, 'The Image', p. 122. The phrase 'moral self-discipline' is from Levine, *Dying to Know*, p. 27.
4. As White has pointed out, vivisectionists considered this capacity to master their sentiments and sympathy as a central prerequisite of their work on domestic animals such as dogs on which Benjulia chiefly seems to work ('Experimental Animal', p. 74).
5. Latour, 'Text-Book Case', pp. 87–8.
6. Hence the title of this chapter, which is a reference to Latour's methodical slogan 'follow the actors' (*Reassembling*, p. 12).
7. Spencer, *First Principles*, p. 85.
8. The *OED* entry for the noun 'study' lists, among others, the following two definitions: 'An artistic production executed for the sake of acquiring skill or knowledge, or to serve as a preparation for future work'; and 'A discourse or literary composition devoted to the detailed consideration of some question, or the minute description of some object; a literary work executed as an exercise or as an experiment in some particular style or mode of treatment.' The first usage was not common until the middle of the eighteenth century, the second not even until the middle of the nineteenth century ('study, n.' *OED Online*).
9. 1856: Aug., 184. Lewes's *Sea-Side Studies* first appeared in two series in *Blackwood's Edinburgh Magazine*. The first series was published in three successive instalments from August to October 1856. The second series consisted of five more instalments that came out under the title *New Sea-Side Studies* from June to October 1857. I shall quote these texts by year, month and page number. One year later (1858), both series were republished, with some alterations and additions, in book form. My reason for quoting from the journal texts is that I am interested in the relative immediacy of Lewes's writing.
10. Rheinberger, *Epistemic Things*, pp. 28–9.
11. Lewes seems to remember a passage from the first book of *The Advancement* in which Bacon notes that 'the contemplation of God's creatures and works produceth (having regard to the works and creatures themselves) knowledge; but having regard to God, no perfect knowledge, but wonder, which is broken knowledge' (*Major Works*, p. 125).

12. Cf. Ingold, *Being Alive*, p. 212.
13. Serres, *Genesis*, p. 91.
14. Schulz, 'Wandern', p. 110.
15. Ibid., p. 110.
16. Ingold, *Being Alive*, p. 117.
17. Ibid., p. 117.
18. Ibid., p. 117.
19. Ibid., p. 117.
20. Ibid., p. 117.
21. Ibid., p. 117.
22. Merriman, 'Unpicking', pp. 187, 185.
23. Pickering, *Mangle*, p. 22 and generally. Cf. Deleuze and Guattari, *Thousand Plateaus*, p. 342.
24. Armstrong, *Victorian Glassworlds*, p. 333; see also Stott, 'Darwin's Barnacles', pp. 172–3.
25. Ingold, *Being Alive*, p. 211.
26. Cf. Ashton, *Lewes*, pp. 169–94.
27. The claim that 'something is certain to turn up' is a reference to Dickens's Wilkins Micawber from *David Copperfield*, showing to what extent Lewes's writing is steeped in the literary culture of his age.
28. Johnson, *Good Ideas*, p. 23.
29. Lewes's decision to start exploring this (to him) relatively new field may also have been motivated by the fact that, in 1854, his *Comte's Philosophy of the Sciences* had been criticised by T.H. Huxley in the *Westminster Review*. Huxley accused Lewes of errors resulting from a lack of practical training and experience in the scientific investigation of nature, as Paul White and Bernard Lightman have pointed out (White, *Huxley*, pp. 72–3; Lightman, *Popularizers*, p. 360). The *Sea-Side Studies* may be seen as Lewes's attempt at countering this criticism in the mode of the self-professed amateur trying to become specialist. Lewes's work plays no further role in White's and Lightman's books, though.
30. Merrill, *Romance*, pp. 29–50.
31. Shuttleworth, *George Eliot*, p. 143; cf. Gamper, 'Einleitung'.
32. Gosse, *Romance*, pp. v, vi.
33. Eliot, 'The Ilfracombe Journal', p. 219.
34. Ibid., p. 219.
35. Shuttleworth, *George Eliot*.
36. Zwierlein, *Der physiologische Bildungsroman*.
37. Ibid., p. 392.
38. Shuttleworth, *George Eliot*, p. 9.
39. Lewes, *Problems: Third Series*, vol. 1, p. 41.
40. Eliot, 'Natural History', p. 131.
41. All page numbers marked *MF* refer to Eliot, *The Mill on the Floss*.
42. My reading here complements and updates, with a special focus on *The Mill*, a number of studies on the 'rhetoric' of George Eliot's fiction. See, for instance, Hillis Miller, 'The Two Rhetorics', and Mann, 'George

Eliot's Language'. The precarious relationship between technical and figural language is analysed in Duncan, 'George Eliot's Science Fiction'.

43. Culler, *Structuralist Poetics*, pp. 137, 138.
44. Shuttleworth, *George Eliot*, p. 57.
45. Showalter, *A Literature*, p. 112.
46. Ermarth, 'Maggie Tulliver's Long Suicide', p. 587. Cf. also Zwierlein, *Der physiologische Bildungsroman*, pp. 53–6.
47. Levine, *Realism, Ethics*, pp. 25–50.
48. Fraiman, 'The Mill', p. 146.
49. Ibid., p. 146.
50. O'Toole, *Habit*, pp. 1–32; Allen, 'Habit'.
51. O'Toole, *Habit*, p. 5.
52. This is of course an insight that goes at least as far back as the Enlightenment.
53. In this sense, one can, in answer to Gillian Beer's question, say that 'nature' *does* have a future. See Beer, 'Has Nature a Future?'
54. Staten has shown that, in Eliot, the Christian values of self-denial and love for the other, which, in a secular version, remained central to her work, are tightly interwoven, and always in conflict with, a physiological paradigm of energies and instinctive drives. (*Spirit*, pp. 76–131).
55. Eliot, *Letters*, p. 466.
56. Ibid., p. 466.
57. Ibid., p. 466.
58. Anger refers to this passage to illustrate what she calls Eliot's method of 'ethical intuitionism' ('George Eliot', p. 81). On the potential 'modernity' of Eliot's moral philosophy see Newton, *Modernizing*, esp. pp. 41–51.
59. Derrida, 'Genesis', p. 201.
60. Paris, *Experiments*, p. 116.
61. Zola, 'The Experimental Novel', pp. 53, 56.
62. Ibid., p. 56.
63. Ibid., p. 53.
64. Ibid., p. 58.
65. Ibid., p. 58.
66. Ibid., p. 59.
67. Ibid., p. 58; cf. Bender, 'Novel Knowledge', p. 132.
68. Zola, 'The Experimental Novel', p. 60.
69. Menke, 'Fiction as Vivisection', pp. 618–19.
70. This corresponds to what Deeds Ermarth says about Eliot's concept of culture. 'Culture exists only in the sum of the diverse array of particulars, uniquely arranged and selected in each individual case' (*George Eliot*, p. 55).
71. Shuttleworth, *George Eliot*, pp. 52–3.

Chapter 4

Steps Towards an Ecology of Experience: Empiricism, Pragmatism and George Eliot's *The Spanish Gypsy*

Making Sense of Experience

It should have become clear that the notion of knowledge that can be extracted from the earlier writings of Lewes and Eliot is deeply entwined with the practical 'steps' that mediate between perceiving and conceiving as well as being and thinking. As a result, their studies do not have the form of a theoretical system or a completed structure of ideas. They ought rather to be viewed as activities that remain subject to being affected and redirected by experiences, or events, that cannot (yet) qualify as knowledge. As I hope to show in this chapter, one may therefore say that the work of Eliot and especially Lewes exemplifies or foreshadows an experimentalist or pragmatist understanding of knowledge that is centred on what Richard Sennett has called the 'idea of experience as a craft'.[1]

While this active meaning of 'experience' as a mode of being engaged in and by productive work may seem uncommon today, it is worth noting that 'in one main sense', as Raymond Williams has pointed out, experience was for a long time 'interchangeable with *experiment*'.[2] To experience anything was to make sense of it by some kind of tentative operation.[3] Around the end of the eighteenth century, this view of experience as an activity began to separate itself from the insights produced by it. As a result, 'experience' came to refer mainly to the wisdom derived from personal observation and practical exercise while 'experiment' was increasingly confined to the more specific meaning of controlled intervention and examination that became particularly salient in an increasingly professionalised context of laboratory science. In a related development, moreover, 'experience' was, by the end of the eighteenth century, also often used to denote an intense and open state of consciousness, a condition of heightened aesthetic sensibility and awareness that, unlike the other meanings of both 'experience' and 'experiment', was sometimes seen as decidedly opposed to justified knowledge and logical thought.[4]

Summing this up, one can isolate at least two senses of experience from the history of the term, namely 'practical wisdom' and 'intense awareness', each of which came to be associated with a specific temporality or tense. Whereas the first meaning generally refers to 'lessons' learned from events in the *past*, the second is usually taken to constitute a feeling of living in the *present*, or of being alive to the present moment.[5] Therefore, these seemingly separate modes of experience are sometimes designated by the German words *Erfahrung* and *Erlebnis* which serve as technical terms in the Anglophone world as well. As Sennett suggests, to think of experience as a craft means to focus on the interaction between these two modes of being sentient in time. More precisely, the notion of experience as a craft foregrounds the practical process through which present experience (*Erlebnis*) is translated into past experience (*Erfahrung*) while, conversely, the knowledge based on past experience, is confirmed or modified by each *Erlebnis* that had, in its present form, not yet been part of it.[6] Experience, thus conceived, is sustained and (re)assembled through a continuous process of resolving tensions within a life that would otherwise be felt (*erlebt*) as disparate or dissonant. According to Brian Massumi, this process informs the most basic perceptual operations. For instance, even the seemingly simple vision of self-contained objects presupposes an activity of translating into a 'singular image' the 'disjunctive plurality built into the human body' in the shape of 'our two offset eyes'.[7] By this account, the very experience of a three-dimensional world is enabled by a work of skill, a corporeal technique involving both biological and social (historical) determinants. Or, in Massumi's terms: 'The life of the body is naturally crafty.'[8]

As I wish to show, it is in a remarkably similar way that G. H. Lewes, in his *Problems of Life and Mind*, describes 'Experience' as 'the registration of feelings', with a 'feeling' being specified as 'the reaction of the sentient Organism under stimulus' (*P* I, 92, 193).[9] As Lewes emphasises, this means that both feelings and experiences by definition involve a responsive action of the whole human organism, mind and body together, rather than solely of one of its parts. An isolated physiological reflex like the 'secretion of a gland', for instance, is not a feeling (by his account), even though it may contribute to the formation of one (*P* I, 193). Nor can any feeling be called 'an *experience*, unless it be *registered* in a modification of structure, and thus be *revivable*'. Feelings, that is to say, which leave no 'permanent' traces in one's physical and psychical make-up are not experiences in Lewes's sense (*P* I, 194). 'A feeling passed away, and incapable of revival, would never be called an experience by any strict writer' (*P* I, 194).

Thus conceived, experience can be seen as one of the foundational notions of Lewes's epistemological thought – which, in turn, is deeply informed by his experimental practice – because it not only functions as the medium through which human organisms make sense of their being in the world; it also defines the limits of what one can possibly know, for while experience or 'the empirical', in Lewes's view, includes both 'the *positive* or known' and the '*speculative* or unknown' it strictly excludes 'the *unknowable*' or 'metempirical' – that which exceeds the boundaries of 'possible Experience', as he puts it (*P* I, 26, 16). 'The metempirical region is the void where Speculation roams unchecked, where Sense has no footing, where Experiment can exercise no control' (*P* I, 16). Whatever refers to this 'metempirical region' can therefore, on Lewes's account, not be called knowledge in the proper sense of the term because, for him, one can only come to know anything, however speculative it may be, by means of 'reproductions of analogical experiences', as he repeatedly stresses.

> Our mental vision is a reproduction of the past and application to the present. It is Experience – our own or that of others – on which we rest. We are not at liberty to *invent* Experience, nor to infer anything *contrary* to it, only to extend it analogically. Speculation to be valid must simply be the extension of Experience by the analogies of experiences. (*P* I, 29)

Such formulations reveal that experience, as Lewes conceives it, mediates between *Erfahrung* and *Erlebnis*, past experience and present experience. Anticipating John Dewey's experimental theory of knowledge, Lewes takes all 'mental vision' to be formed in the interstices in which present experiences are recognised by way of reviving past ones, or, conversely, through which experiences of the past are extended into the present.[10] In his view, then, empirical knowledge, or knowledge inferred by way of experience, is premised on an activity of seeing one experience in the form of (as if it were) another. It presupposes a creative practice, a craft of 'making *like*', as Lewes puts it. 'All knowledge is reproduction of experiences, the direct or indirect assimilation (making *like*) of the new phenomena to phenomena resembling them, formerly experimented on' (*P* I, 31).

Similar to the notion of self-formation considered in the last chapter, Lewes's conception of how experience is built up through 'reproduction' and 'assimilation' is here based on physiological theories about the interaction between an organism and the medium in relation to which it lives. 'What Growth is, in the physical sense, that is Experience in the psychical sense, namely, *organic registration of assimilated material*' (*P* I, 110). On this conception, the constructive or experimental activity of 'making like' corresponds to 'an intermediate stage' of the organic process in which 'the inorganic, unvitalized material' becomes, as Lewes puts it, 'transformed into organizable, vitalized material' (*P* I, 107). One can say, then, that the experimental craft shows itself in a capability of converting the encounter with what is unfamiliar or unexpected (*Erlebnis*) into patterns of experience (*Erfahrung*) that have already been installed. For Lewes, just as for Huxley, this activity of conversion begins on the level of ordinary perception which Lewes describes as 'the assimilation of the Object by the Subject, in the same way that Nutrition is the assimilation of the Medium by the Organism' (*P* I, 173). As this indicates, Lewes's thinking – unlike that of the 'philosophic realist' with which he contrasts it – is not premised on the belief in an ontological difference between subject and object, mind and matter or inside and outside (*P* I, 173). Instead, he considers all of these terms to be extractions from what he calls 'the general web of Existence' in which they are inextricably intertwined (*P* I, 173). 'Subject' and 'object', thus conceived, do not *really* exist in any distinct and self-contained way; they only exist so *ideally*, as we have already seen. Indeed, for Lewes, all that really exists is a continuum of experiences that is 'interposed', as he writes, 'between the Cosmos and the Consciousness' (*P* I, 114). Small wonder, therefore, that the one single point that he never stops repeating is that the real world exists only as it is experienced, not as it is conceived to exist independently of experience. 'The Real is that which is felt,' as he puts it (*P* I, 157). It is not a world of ideal substances or essences or things in themselves that are placed outside of the multiple ways in which they can be perceived and acted upon.

More precisely, one of Lewes's central claims is that all real things are relative to the activities, both human and non-human, through which they are formed and made subject to continuous, incremental change. 'Things are groups of Relations, – conjunctures of events. Take a stone, for instance, and ask, What is it? You can only answer by describing its properties, qualities, history' (*P* II, 22), as he puts this. This is to say that there is nothing apart from the multiplicity of modes in which each thing moves and changes in relation to an equally active and changeable environment. 'Ask a man what anything is, and he will describe all the characteristics which it is known (or supposed) to combine, all the ways in which it acts on him and on other things. Ask him, What more is it? and he will be silent, unless he is a metaphysician' (*P* II, 391). As such pronouncements show, the one position to which Lewes's writing is consistently opposed is that of the metaphysician who believes that above or below the changeable play of empirical 'phenomena' and material powers there is a world of ideal substances, or 'Noumena', which define each thing in a wholly objective way (*P* II, 386). For Lewes, this belief in things as immutable, self-enclosed objects is no more than a 'logical fiction' engendered by the need for a stable basis at the bottom of the 'fountain of possible appearances' as which humans perceive the material world (*P* II, 394).

Being grounded in experience as a 'paradoxically foundationless foundation' of an extending world that is partly known and partly unknown,[11] but always knowable (never unknowable),[12] Lewes's thought can be seen to anticipate, I wish to argue, the sort of pragmatism or radical empiricism that is now mainly associated with the names of William James and John Dewey. As is well known, both of these authors drew heavily on British empiricists and evolutionists from J. S. Mill to Herbert Spencer and Charles Darwin, to name but a few.[13] Lewes, however, is hardly ever included in the list of forebears of Pragmatism. In fact, even though his work has received more and more attention among scholars of Victorian literature and culture in recent years,[14] its position within the wider history of empiricist and pragmatist philosophy is rarely commented on. One way of compensating for this deficiency is to compare Lewes's thinking with the kind of empiricist 'mosaic philosophy' as which William James later characterised his own approach.[15] 'In actual mosaics the pieces are held together by their bedding, for which bedding the Substances, transcendental Egos, or Absolutes of other philosophies may be taken to stand,' James writes in what is perhaps one of the most concise summaries of his thought.[16] 'In radical empiricism there is no bedding; it is as if the pieces clung together by their edges, the transitions experienced between them forming their cement.'[17] As this indicates, the 'radical' component in James's version of empiricism is the claim that what one experiences are not only disaggregated 'pieces' or atoms of a world but also the relational 'cement' that both separates and holds them together.

In this way, James insists, more radically than Locke and Hume, with whom he takes issue, that the advancing movement of experience is the only source of whatever recurrent patterns may be derived from it. Hume, for instance, had still postulated 'three principles of connexion among ideas, namely, *Resemblance*, *Contiguity* in time or place, and *Cause or Effect*', by means of which the fleeting and disaggregate multiplicity of successive perceptions is supposed to be brought into general forms persisting, in a relatively stable manner, through time.[18] James, by contrast, holds that continuity and coherence are themselves effects of experience, rather than of ideal principles that are added to or imposed upon it. Thus, what makes James's engagement with the tradition of early empiricism radical is that he eradicated from it the pre- or 'metempirical' root which would later grow into the notion of a transcendental reason developed by Kant and other idealists. For James, experience, which he takes to be made up, in a mingled manner, of both 'percepts' and 'concepts',[19] does not require such metaphysical guidance in order to yield structures that are sufficiently continuous to be lived by. 'The directly apprehended universe needs, in short, no extraneous trans-empirical connective support, but possesses in its own right a concatenated or continuous structure.'[20] Hence his claim that the 'cement' that equally associates and divides the component parts of what is perceived by the senses is itself a product of experience, not of an autonomous consciousness or mind standing before or hovering above it. James concedes that the somewhat static imagery of mosaic pieces glued together may not be quite adequate to illustrate the notion of a dynamic experience in which 'the more substantive and the more transitive parts run into each other continuously'.[21] But what the metaphor can underline, he argues, is the idea of an emergent pattern, or one to which ever further particles can be added, each stabilising but also modifying the organisation of the whole. 'Knowledge of sensible realities,' in this view, 'comes to life inside the tissue of experience. It is *made*; and made by relations that unroll themselves in time.'[22] Knowledge is not founded on an ideal ground outside of experience. 'Experience itself,' however, 'taken at large, can grow by its edges,'[23] or along 'the thin line of flame advancing across the dry autumnal field which the farmer proceeds to burn', as James puts it in a well-known passage. 'In this line we live prospectively as well as retrospectively', it being the 'continuation' of the past into the future.[24]

Mind in Life

Like James's radical empiricism, I am suggesting, Lewes's philosophy takes knowledge to grow and be sustained 'inside the tissue' of an experience that is not founded on a safe (substantial or transcendental) 'bedding' outside of it. That is to say, experience or experimental knowledge, as Lewes conceives it, is constituted in the passage between the past and the future, in 'the thin line of flame', or the process of 'making like', of becoming both similar and otherwise, through which connections and distinctions are made. Consequently, what Lewes calls 'mind' is subject to a 'life' that takes place, quite emphatically, in transitions and through relations: in an advancing middle, as he suggests in a statement that resonates strongly with James's approach.

> In life, it is the present moment, the present fact, which is important; the moment which preceded, the facts which went before it, borrow all their interest from their relation to it. The mind, indeed, must 'look before and after,' but it stands upon the now and the 'fact' with which it has to deal. (*P* II, 377)

As Lewes points out, the mindset that corresponds to this kind of incipient experience that 'grows by the edges' is what he calls the 'practical intellect' that 'deals with the *now* and *here*, and cannot determine its present action by what *has been*, or *may be there*' (*P* II, 390). Therefore, it neither can nor seeks to see the whole at once, from a point before or after the actions through which it expresses and sustains itself. Instead, the practical intellect builds up its underpinnings from within an evolving order of which it is one active part among others. 'This is the working spirit of the world. We call it Common Sense in the ordinary affairs of life; Experimental Science in affairs of intelligence' (*P* II, 390). To be sure, Lewes repeatedly stresses that the aim of scientific practice is to advance beyond common sense: to translate the experimental into the general and, in this way, to engender ideal patterns that are more reliable than the shifting grounds of personal experience out of which they have to be drawn. 'Science everywhere aims at transforming isolated perceptions into connected conceptions, – facts into laws', as he notes. 'Out of the manifold irregularities presented to Sense it abstracts an ideal regularity; out of the chaos, order' (*P* I, 397). Yet, despite this emphasis on the idealising tendency of scientific activity, Lewes's own work is testament to his concomitant insight that science could never make any progress if it did not return its accomplished patterns, again and again, to the turbulent mode of the experimental from which they have to be extracted by means of various technologies and techniques.

For example, in the first chapter of what is probably Lewes's most openly didactic work, his *Studies in Animal Life* – first published in the *Cornhill Magazine* in 1860 and then as a book in 1862 – Lewes presents his readers with a 'dead frog that [. . .] has already been made the subject of experiments' and that he now proposes to use 'as a text from which profitable lessons may be drawn'.[25] The frog, in this instance, appears as an object of past experience, as a predefined 'text' to be consulted for the 'lessons' that may be derived from it. One of the lessons Lewes seeks to impart to his readers is that the 'liquid' in the frog's 'digestive tube', if placed under a microscope, can be found to contain other forms of life, such as a small 'animalcule' which the reader is asked to 'watch' closely.[26] 'What is it? It is one of the largest of the Infusoria, and is named *Opalina*.'[27] As the rhetorical question suggests, Lewes's writing here performs the role of an instructor guiding his students through a pattern of teachable knowledge that is already assumed to be complete. Yet, in the very process of expounding to the reader the supposed fact that the object under inspection is 'one of the largest of the Infusoria', this same object seems to start assuming a slightly different aspect, instigating Lewes to adapt his teaching accordingly. 'When I call this an Infusorium I am using the language of text-books; but there seems to be a growing belief among zoologists that the Opalina is not an Infusorium, but the infantile condition of some worm (*Distoma?*).'[28] By way of using the 'language of text-books' to describe the Opalina, then, Lewes draws this very language out of the text-books and, as he does so, finds it to clash, to some extent, with what his personal experience tells him about the thing at hand. The present experience (*Erlebnis*) of the animalcule refuses to be seamlessly assimilated to the legible knowledge that has been made out of experience past (*Erfahrung*). As a result, the seemingly closed structure of bookish knowledge is subjected to the possibility of becoming otherwise: of being altered or revised. The very act of defining the observed microorganism as an infusorium 'named *Opalina*' seems to open it up to a virtual reality of other possible definitions among which the most widely accepted one (infusorium named Opalina) is no longer necessarily the right choice. It is as if Lewes's attempt to translate the knowledge of the text-books into his personal perception of the thing in the frog's digestive tube unexpectedly engenders 'the infantile condition of some worm (*Distoma?*)' which threatens to undermine the reliability of the acknowledged definition while simultaneously suggesting a new or nascent one. The Opalina, in short, is made contingent, exposed as something that might not be what it seems.

In this way, Lewes's writing reintegrates the discourse of the text-books into the slipperiness of the experimental field that it is supposed to have left behind. The act of reading the 'text' of the dissected frog for the 'profitable lessons' that are supposed to be contained in it begins to veer into a process of rewriting it in different terms.[29] To be sure, Lewes immediately seeks to restore the order from which he has digressed by assuring his readers that the nascent worm, if it is one, 'will not grow into a mature worm as long as it inhabits the frog; it waits until some pike, or bird, has devoured the frog, and then, in the stomach of its new captor, it will develop into its mature form: then and not till then'.[30] But this concession, whatever else it is supposed to achieve, certainly does not make the phenomenon in question any less strange than it already is, as Lewes himself admits. 'This surprises you? And well it may; but thereby hangs a tale, which to unfold–for the present, however, it must be postponed, because the Opalina itself needs all our notice.'[31] By way of demonstrating that the thing in the cut-up frog is 'one of the largest of the infusoria', in sum, Lewes's writing has produced a puzzlingly ambiguous epistemic thing, half infusorium, half worm, that agitates the relation between the knowing person and the object he claims to know.[32] The connection between perception and conception, or the observed thing and its name, loses its self-evidence and the transition from the one to the other is shown to presuppose a constructive act that can be performed in more than one way.

Even when Lewes is at his most didactic, then, the established knowledge gained from past experience (*Erfahrung*) remains always susceptible to be reinterpreted by way of a present experience (*Erlebnis*) that extends towards an infinite future, harbouring novel findings and untold tales. In the *Problems* Lewes stresses that this infinite extension, in which he takes experience (and, for that matter, knowledge) to be embedded, is not to be confused with an indefinite one. For 'the Infinite', as he sees it, must not be taken as a quantity, not even as a negative one, but as 'the sign of that continuity of Existence which has been ideally divided into discrete parts in the affixing of limits' (*P* II, 384). This idea of an existential continuity that surrounds and outruns whatever definitions and limitations one may extract from or inscribe into it is central to Lewes's experimentalism. It means that experience, for him, will always include a degree of what is yet unmeasured and open-ended, a tendency towards infinite extension and transformation, by virtue of which it resists closure.[33] As a result, the concomitant conception of 'Mind' as 'movement' foreshadows what William James would later call 'the stream of thought' or 'the stream of consciousness', as Lewes's choice of words makes clear.[34] 'Now, because Feeling is in a constant flux,' he writes, 'one feeling succeeding and blending with another, and

Thought is ever moving into new forms, shifting its limits, Mind, as the symbol of all Feeling and Thought, is the very type of that ceaseless flow which is designated by the Infinite' (*P* II, 384).

As Rick Rylance has argued, the very form of Lewes's writing, with its unfinished, 'ramshackle appearance' and its kaleidoscopic display of mutable images,[35] can be seen as an exemplification of the kind of 'mobile', unsettled and 'energy-filled system' that it examines.[36] By this account, the 'calculated diversity' of Lewes's imagery is the formal expression of an experimental mind, a mind in the making that resists being pictured as a stable and abstract structure outside of the processes through which it lives and grows.[37] It can only be represented through a series of interlaced figures of speech, each of which potentially supplements or corrects the one which went before it. For example, while there are many metaphors which draw on the register of energy physics with its immaterial waves, currents, flows, forces, charges and discharges, the formless mobility suggested by these terms is often qualified, Rylance shows, by a set of images taken from architecture or economics which suggest a less fluid and more palpably material order or mode.[38] Seen as components of Lewes's practice of writing, all of these metaphors, in their interaction, nevertheless sketch out an emphatically dynamic relation of 'life and mind' that privileges unpredictable processes over predesigned structures. The loose, tentative and somewhat messy composition of the *Problems* can therefore be seen to enact the very movement of testing and probing which is constitutive of what Lewes calls 'Psychogenesis', the evolution of mental structures through the experimental (*P* I, 208).

The conditions that influence or determine this psychogenetic process, as well as the motivating factors which participate in it, make up one of the central concerns of Lewes's work. Briefly, Lewes identifies two main 'sources' of human mental life which he calls 'the animal organism' and 'the social organism' (*P* I, 115). Each of these two organisms, moreover, is taken to correspond to a specific type of medium, namely the physical and the social one respectively. As Shuttleworth, Zwierlein and Rylance have pointed out, it is especially Lewes's emphasis on the formative impact of the 'Social Medium', defined as 'the collective accumulations of centuries, condensed in knowledge, beliefs, prejudices, institutions, and tendencies', that constitutes one of his most original contributions to the field of Victorian psychology (*P* I, 114).[39] According to Lewes, there is no way of studying the physiological make-up of the human frame in isolation from the 'social conditions', under which it is conceived and formed (*P* I, 118). Indeed, for Lewes, the physical medium is, in its very essence, intermixed with the social. 'We breathe the social air,' as he puts it in a telling phrase, since 'the Organism brings with it inherited Experience, i.e. a mode of reaction antecedent to all direct relation with external influences, which necessarily determines the results of individual Experience' (*P* I, 160, 149). For Lewes, therefore, all actions and perceptions seemingly based on the experience of individuals are simultaneously, at a deeper level, reactions to the experiences that have been accumulated by their ancestors. Human experiences have 'a history at their back', for they take place in an environment that has been pre-organised by one's ancestral kin (*P* I, 150). In short: 'The sensitive subject is no *tabula rasa*; it is not a blank sheet of paper, but a palimpsest,' as Lewes stresses in opposition to what he calls 'the sensational school'. 'What the Senses inscribe on it, are not merely the changes of the external world; but these characters are commingled with the characters of preceding inscriptions' (*P* I, 149).

Embodied Inheritance

This view of the human organism as a 'palimpsest', with present 'inscriptions' made by the senses meeting and mingling with layers of past ones, enables Lewes to propose a specific conception of instinct as 'organized Experience: i.e. *undiscursive* Intelligence' (*P* I, 208) that contributed to a wider discussion on heredity and what Herbert Spencer called 'unconscious or organic memory'.[40] According to Lewes, even instincts, such as the preference of a particular type of food, are, at least in the case of humans, not simply natural, but must be seen as mediated, all the way down, by an experience that is inherently social. Human experience, on this view, has always included influences of both the biological (animal, organic) and the social (cultural, historical) medium. In the empirical world, the world that can be registered by experience – and this is the only world with which Lewes is concerned – there is no level at which these two aspects of what it means to be human can be kept strictly apart.

To be sure, this conception was neither the only nor the final word on the formative factors of experimental psychogenesis. Rather, it is part of a general concern with personal agency, family lineage and the question to what extent one's present experiences and choices can still be influenced, or even determined, by those of one's ancestral kin. One of George Eliot's later works in which she engages most thoroughly with these questions is her 'conspicuously neglected' dramatic epic *The Spanish Gypsy* (1868),[41] a text that Lewes quotes in one of the passages of his *Problems* in which he makes the general case that: 'Like the body, the Mind is shaped through its history' (*P* I, 202). This reference could hardly be more apt because the history shaping both the body and the mind of man is indeed announced, within the first few lines, as a central concern of both Eliot's verse narrative and the historical moment, fifteenth-century Spain, in which it is set:

> The soul of man is widening towards the past:
> No longer hanging at the breast of life
> Feeding in blindness to his parentage –
> Quenching all wonder with Omnipotence,
> Praising a name with indolent piety –
> He spells the record of his long descent,
> More largely conscious of the life that was.
> And from the height that shows where morning shone
> On far-off summits pale and gloomy now,
> The horizon widens round him, and the west
> Looks vast with untracked waves whereon his gaze
> Follows the flight of the swift-vanished bird
> That like the sunken sun is mirrored still
> Upon the yearning soul within the eye. (*SG* I.103–16)[42]

In the world introduced here, the (conspicuously indefinite) 'soul of man' is 'no longer' seen as a pre-given essence, an emanation of divine 'Omnipotence' in which one can believe 'in blindness' and indolence – like a child snuggling into the 'breast' of a 'life' whose grounds and sources it has not yet started to question. Rather, the text opens up a context in which man increasingly regards his soul as a product of history, of a 'long descent' whose 'record' he seeks to 'spell'. Concomitantly, the 'far-off summits' and the 'untracked waves' to the west are transformed into projective spaces of a curious, or 'yearning soul' that finds its own unconsummated condition 'mirrored' in the gloomy vastness around it. This theme of a soul that 'widens towards the past', becoming 'conscious' of its descent and therefore uncertain about its future is then played out through the identity transformation of the beautiful Fedalma, who is engaged to be married to Don Silva, the Spanish Duke of Bedmar, among whose people she has grown up. Towards the end of the first (and longest) book Fedalma learns that she is (probably) not, as she believed, a Christian Spaniard by birth, but a Gypsy of the Zíncali tribe, alleged daughter of the nomad king Zarca, who has now come to restore her to her true identity by acquainting her with her ethnic roots.

Yet, even though the scene in which Zarca reveals himself to his (putative) daughter – first announcing his appearance through a message written 'with blood' – marks an obvious turning point in the narrative (*SG* I.2656), indications of a latent component in Fedalma's biography are given much earlier. In one central scene, for instance, Fedalma, 'swayed by impulse passionate' (*SG* I.1315), performs an involuntary dance in public which is observed by Prior Isidor who then, in the passage partly quoted by Lewes, warns her betrothed husband that he had seen something in her that cannot be, as he says, 'read' on the surface.

> I read a record deeper than the skin.
> What! Shall the trick of nostrils and of lips
> Descend through generations, and the soul
> That moves within our frame like God in worlds –
> Convulsing, urging, melting, withering –
> Imprint no record, leave no documents,
> Of her great history? Shall men bequeath
> The fancies of their palate to their sons,
> And shall the shudder of restraining awe,
> The slow-wept tears of contrite memory,
> Faith's prayerful labour, and the food divine
> Of fasts ecstatic – shall these pass away
> Like wind upon the waters, tracklessly?
> Shall the mere curl of eyelashes remain,
> And god-enshrining symbols leave no trace
> Of tremors reverent? – That maiden's blood
> Is as unchristian as the leopard's. (*SG* I.1700–16)

The 'record' that the Prior claims to have 'read' in Fedalma is that of a 'soul' which cannot be equated with strictly material, physiognomic conditions ('the trick of nostrils and of lips'), but which 'moves within our frame' in an immaterial way, 'like God in worlds'. At the same time, however, the 'documents' that these motions 'leave' in or on the human 'frame' testify to a 'great history' that is inextricably entwined with our corporeal life. Tellingly, the 'frame' invoked by the Prior is indeterminate enough to include both the material and the ideal, or the physical and the mental, suggesting that the soul which 'moves within' it encompasses the body as well as the mind.[43] Indeed, according to the Prior, the 'traces' of what he considers to be the soul's history manifest themselves in gestures of

an inherited belief in certain 'god-enshrining symbols', a belief that
has become incorporated into the way one behaves under particular
conditions. Hence Lewes's approving quotation of the Prior's speech:
for thus conceived Fedalma's 'shudders' of 'awe', 'tremors reverent'
and 'slow-wept tears of contrite memory' are not just involuntary
reflexes of her body, but also performative interpretations of a cultural 'imprint' that has become part of her very 'blood'. The soul,
by this account, is both a passive recipient of social customs and an
active shaper and (re-)inventor of them, just as her 'Convulsing, urg-
ing, melting, withering' action can equally be seen as self-induced or
as instigated by foreign stimuli.

Gregory Tate, quoting the same passage, has pointed out that
Eliot's way of using 'the word "soul"' in *The Spanish Gypsy* 'questions and resists the reduction of human psychology to material
conditions, restoring a transcendent dimension to the workings of
the mind'.[44] It should be emphasised, however, that this 'transcendent dimension', which is undoubtedly part of the meaning of 'soul'
as it occurs in Eliot's text, is not typically represented as something
apart from, or even opposed to, the 'material conditions' through
which it has to be expressed. Rather, what the text foregrounds are
the motions and emotions that integrate body and soul, making the
one fold into the other. One example of this interaction of the material and the ideal is the description of Fedalma's dance during which
'The spirit in her gravely glowing face / With sweet community
informs her limbs' (I. 1330–1) while everything about her, 'Even
the pliant folds that cling transverse', responds to 'a soft undertone
/ And resonance exquisite from the grand chord / Of her harmoni-
ously bodied soul' (*SG* I. 1337, 1340–2). Through Fedalma's dance,
then, – through her action on, and reaction to, particular musical
'strains' (*SG* I.1281) – the 'soul' of a yet indefinite 'community'
seems to be given (a) body.[45] Further traces hinting at the activity
of this 'bodied soul', the soul which is bodied forth through the
dance, appear when Fedalma exchanges looks with a passing gypsy
prisoner (who turns out to be her father), wondering what it is that
fascinates her about him and him about her. 'His deep-knit brow, /
Inflated nostril, scornful lip compressed, / Seem a dark hieroglyph of
coming fate / Written before her' (*SG* I. 1471–4).

Symptomatically, the preposition 'before' that defines the relation
between Fedalma and the cryptic text seeming to be contained in the
prisoner's physiognomic features can be read both spatially and temporally. What is written 'before' Fedalma appears to be a 'fate' that
makes her look to the past and faces her in the present, waiting to

be understood. As Herbert Tucker has argued, all that follows after the early scenes of Eliot's work can be read as 'a set of variations on' a single 'theme' that is already announced in them: 'Heredity Equals Destiny.'[46] To some extent, this claim is confirmed by Eliot herself who, in her 'Notes on the Spanish Gypsy and Tragedy in General', asserts that she took the subject of her work to be 'the part which is played in the general human lot by hereditary conditions in the largest sense', along with 'the fact that what we call duty is entirely made up of such conditions'.[47] Yet, it needs stressing that in Eliot's epic these 'hereditary conditions' – that which is handed down from one generation to the next – are not composed of some kind of biological or racial essence. Instead, they make up a record of 'organized Experience', as Lewes would say, that is always open to be (in some measure) re- or overwritten, as Fedalma herself points out in response to her father's claim that it was her destiny to become a Gypsy queen. 'Father, my soul is not too base to ring / At touch of your great thoughts; nay in my blood / There streams the sense unspeakable of kind,' Fedalma concedes, before going on to qualify this statement in a crucial way (*SG* I.2960–2):

> Look at these hands! You say when they were little
> They played about the gold upon your neck.
> I do believe it, for their tiny pulse
> Made record of it in the inmost coil
> Of growing memory. But see them now!
> Oh, they have made fresh record; twined themselves
> With other throbbing hands whose pulses feed
> Not memories only but a blended life –
> Life that will bleed to death if it be severed. (*SG* I. 2964–72)

The 'record' that Fedalma's little hands have, during her early childhood, made 'in the inmost coil' of her 'growing memory' is that of an experience (*Erfahrung*) which, though formative, does not determine her character in an inescapable way. Rather, her hands have always kept making 'fresh record', accumulating novel experiences (*Erlebnisse*) that mixed themselves with the ones that had already been stored in her 'soul', altering and reconfiguring them in life-changing ways.

What Fedalma has inherited from the race of her father, in short, is not determinate (or 'hard') enough to stay the same. One can therefore say that one problem that is explored by *The Spanish Gypsy* is the question of whether 'duty' can be 'made up', as Eliot suggested, of 'conditions' which are likely to become different in the course of one's life. Why, after all, should Fedalma be more strongly committed to a father whom she had not known for most of her conscious life than to her fiancé whom she loves dearly? What, moreover, constitutes that 'sense unspeakable of kind' which allegedly still 'streams' in Fedalma's 'blood'? In the nineteenth century, as Laura Otis and others have shown, one of the most widely accepted answers to these questions was provided by the theory of 'organic memory' which held that 'just as people remembered some of their own experiences consciously, they remembered their racial and ancestral experiences unconsciously, through their instincts'.[48]

One of the most noteworthy aspects of this definition of organic memory as a kind of unconscious wisdom, made up of embodied habits and 'instinctive' tendencies, is that it affected not only the concept of personal identity, but also that of science as a mode of conscious knowledge. Samuel Butler, for instance, one of the oft-quoted contributors to the discourse on organic memory, begins his *Life and Habit* by turning the very concept of knowledge thoroughly on its head.[49] 'Certain it is that we know best what we are least conscious of knowing,' he writes.[50]

> Indeed, it is not too much to say that we have no really profound knowledge upon any subject – no knowledge on the strength of which we are ready to act at all moments unhesitatingly without either preparation or after-thought – till we have left off feeling conscious of the possession of such knowledge, and of the grounds on which it rests.[51]

Such reasoning entails that in order for something to be fully and unquestionably known, it must not be understood as such. All 'profound knowledge', Butler suggests, is tacit or unreflecting, for as soon as one's thoughts are made conscious or explicit, they are instantly laid open to doubt. One of Butler's examples is the fact of man's 'own existence' which, on his account, was rendered dubious at the very moment in which man started to think he knew anything about it.[52]

The consequence that Butler draws from such examples is that consciousness of knowledge gives rise to consciousness of ignorance; for as soon as people become aware of what they know, they will also become (or be made) aware of what they do not (yet) know. 'Whenever we find people knowing that they know this or that, we have the same story over and over again. They do not yet know it perfectly.'[53] What Butler's epistemological intervention amounts to, then, is the argument that all avowed knowledge is, by definition, imperfect. In fact, for him, the only way to know anything completely is not to know that one knows it. 'It is only those who are ignorant and uncultivated who can know anything at all in a proper sense of the words.'[54] Conversely, all knowledge that is not of the 'ignorant and uncultivated' kind must include a sense of its own instability and insufficiency, as Butler maintains. 'Cultivation will breed in any man a certainty of the uncertainty even of his most assured convictions.'[55] Hence his claim that all expressions or propositions that explicitly claim to represent knowledge must remain suspended in what he calls 'an inchoate state' or a period 'of twilight between the thick darkness of ignorance and the brilliancy of perfect knowledge'.[56] Another way of putting this is to say that 'perfect knowledge' and perfect 'ignorance' are ideal conditions which, in Butler's words, are 'alike unselfconscious' while all forms of either conscious knowledge or conscious ignorance are produced in an experimental field in which the known and the unknown are (still) intermixed.[57] In short, what Butler advocates is an anti-idealist theory of knowledge that has much in common with both Lewes's experimentalism and the radical empiricism of Pragmatists like Dewey and James. For it takes all propositional statements to be premised on the experience of an uncertain and unpredictable world: a world that includes the possibility of being and becoming otherwise than one knows (or takes) it to be.

This little detour through the concept of knowledge with which Butler prefaces his investigation into organic memory may help to elucidate the way Eliot engages with this latter notion in *The Spanish Gypsy*. More precisely, it enables me to clarify that Eliot's epic is not so much motivated by the proposition *that* 'Heredity Equals Destiny', to come back to Tucker's phrase, but by the question *if* (to what extent, with what consequences, for what reason) this equation holds good in the first place. Whatever knowledge about organic memory is represented or created by *The Spanish Gypsy* is doubtful knowledge in Butler's sense: knowledge that knows about the shiftiness of its base. In tune with Butler's argument, this hesitant knowledge that, as he puts it, 'dwells upon the confines of uncertainty' most prominently enters the epic through Fedalma's becoming conscious that she is not only who she had thought she was.[58] When Fedalma learns that she is 'more' than a Spaniard, but not necessarily 'less than a true Zíncala' (*SG* III.519–20), she simultaneously loses the self-assurance 'on the strength of which', to repeat Butler's terms, she is 'ready to act at all moments unhesitatingly without either preparation or after-thought'. As a result, her knowledge of who she is ceases to be self-evident and becomes corroded by at least one other possibility of who she might be. 'At stake for Fedalma,' as Deborah E. Nord puts it, 'is the very nature of her femininity: what kind of woman will she be allowed, or forced, to be?'[59] Indeed, the figure of the gypsy, as Nord argues, often helped nineteenth-century writers to explore such questions.

Eliot's *The Spanish Gypsy* is a good case in point because in the aftermath of the first meeting with Zarca, Fedalma neither renounces the bond with her father by remaining, against his will, on the road towards conventional marriage, nor does she, after recognising who she 'really' seems to be, simply turn into the Zíncala that she has been all along. She does not just replace one state of being with another, even though the reader next meets her among the 'little swarthy tents' of the Gypsy camp (*SG* III.34), wearing '*a Moorish dress*' and '*a while turban on her head*' and carrying '*a dagger by her side*' (*SG* 178). Rather, despite this external transformation, Fedalma, by joining Zarca's people, enters a field of insecurity and vacillation, in which her whole sense of self and belonging have to be negotiated afresh. This is most clearly brought out in a monologue, explicitly spoken '*alone*' (*SG* 196), in which Fedalma contrasts the instability of her condition with that of her new fellow Hinda who 'has the strength I lack', as Fedalma begins:

> Within her world
> The dial has not stirred since first she woke:
> No changing light has made the shadows die,
> And taught her trusting soul sad difference.
> For her, good, right, and law are all summed up
> In what is possible: life is one web
> Where love, joy, kindred, and obedience,
> Lie fast and even, in one warp and woof
> With thirst and drinking, hunger, food, and sleep.
> She knows no struggles, sees no double path:
> Her fate is freedom, for her will is one
> With her own people's law, the only law
> She ever knew. (*SG* III.750–62)

The first point to be noted here is that Hinda's world is premised on what Butler would call that 'perfect', but naive knowledge that rests content 'within' the confines of an inherited 'law' circumscribing 'what is possible' in moral, ethical and legal terms. Secondly, readers familiar with Eliot's work will instantly recognise the metaphor of 'life' as a 'web' which occurs variously across her writings, most famously in the inconclusive 'Finale' of *Middlemarch*. This begins with the narrator's declaration that 'the fragment of a life, however typical, is not the sample of an even web: promises may not be kept, and an ardent outset may be followed by declension; latent powers may find their long-waited opportunity; a past error may urge a grand retrieval'.[60] What causes the web of a life to be uneven, on this view, is the possibility of unexpected turns and incalculable occurrences which may disrupt any 'promise' of a steady continuity connecting one's experience of the present with that of one's past.

Against this backdrop, the life of Hinda appears as the epitome of a regular and unbroken web in which all possible feelings (of 'love, joy, kindred, and obedience') are safely contained, 'lie fast and even', in 'one warp and woof', or in 'a unified design'.[61] As a result, in her case, these feelings are never raised to a level of abstract thought that would enable her to experience them as signs that can be interpreted in different ways. Fedalma's 'thoughts', by contrast, are like 'flakes' of 'chilling snow' to her that freeze her will to move forward, making her hesitate and 'totter', as she suggests in the following lines:

> For me – I have fire within,
> But on my will there falls the chilling snow
> Of thoughts that come as subtly as soft flakes,
> Yet press at last with hard and icy weight.
> I could be firm, could give myself the wrench
> And walk erect, hiding my life-long wound,
> If I but saw the fruit of all my pain
> With that strong vision which commands the soul,
> And makes great awe the monarch of desire.
> But now I totter, seeing no far goal:
> I tread the rocky pass, and pause and grasp,
> Guided by flashes. (*SG* III.762–73)

Fedalma's 'life-long wound' is caused by a dissonance between 'fire' and 'snow', which may be taken to stand for what Lewes called 'the Logic of Feeling' and 'the Logic of Signs' (*P* I, 125–6 and generally). She suffers from a sense of discontinuity between perception and conception that leaves her unable to maintain a 'strong vision' of what 'far goal' she wants to attain. 'Guided by flashes' and hesitant steps her experimentalist character presents a stark contrast, not only to Hinda's simple-minded trust, but also to the resolute idealism of her purported father.

In a subtle way, however, even Zarca's strength of will seems to be underwritten by a sense of uncertainty that is present, if only minutely, in his unwavering call to 'never falter', as his own words indicate:

> Nay, never falter: no great deed is done
> By falterers who ask for certainty.
> No good is certain, but the steadfast mind,
> The undivided will to seek the good:
> 'Tis that compels the elements, and wrings
> A human music from the indifferent air.
> The greatest gift the hero leaves his race
> Is to have been a hero. Say we fail! –
> We feed the high tradition of the world,
> And leave our spirit in our children's breasts. (*SG* I.3145–54)

On the face of it, Zarca seems to argue that 'the steadfast mind' or 'the undivided will', being the only thing that is 'certain', must determine what is and is not (a) good. While this is supposed to say that no good can be certain by and of itself, it also implies that the certainty of the will is dependent upon the good that it is there 'to seek'. Apparently, one cannot be certain what is (a) good, unless one is willing to seek it out. But if the will is that which wants a good to be certain, then the will cannot be certain by and of itself either. Hence Zarca's ambiguous use of the word 'good' which refers both to 'the steadfast mind, / The undivided will' and to that which it has to seek. My point, therefore, is that Zarca's appeal that one 'never falter' includes the concession that the mind's 'certainty' is premised on an activity of searching for and maintaining it which is subject to drifting into uncertainty. That Zarca's speech seems to concede this in spite of his apparent intention to say something quite different makes it of course even more evident: Zarca's 'steadfast mind' cannot be as self-determined as he may will it to be.[62] It exists for a good that it does not (yet or quite) possess, even if it is certain that it wants to attain it. Implicitly, the passage therefore includes an insight that William James has made explicit in the 'Will' chapter of his *Principles of Psychology*, in which he points out that *'we reach the heart of our inquiry into volition when we ask by what process it is that the thought of any given object comes to prevail stably in the mind'*.[63]

The Ecology of Experience

My point is that this very process by which an 'object', both the referent of a 'thought' and the goal of an action, 'comes to prevail stably in the mind' is at the centre of *The Spanish Gypsy*. More specifically,

Eliot's text is about the conditions and consequences of personal choice: about coming to know one's object or oneself through one's object. On the face of it, one extreme view on this theme seems to be represented by Zarca who expressly professes to 'choose not', but to follow the path prescribed by an absolute idea of heredity and tribal belonging which, in turn, determines what he wills to be his good. Zarca claims to do only what he considers to be in accordance with what he believes to be the essence of who he is ('I choose not – I *am* Zarca', *SG* I.2817), a belief that, on his interpretation, precludes the necessity of making decisions: 'Is there a choice for strong souls to be weak [. . .],? Let him choose / Who halts and wavers' (*SG* I.2815, 2817–18). As Eliot's writing suggests, the flipside of Zarca's mental steadfastness is that he is, both literally and metaphorically, a fettered person, a captive, enchained by an ideology of race and heredity that admits of no escape. Consequently, for Fedalma, to do as Zarca wants her to – that is, to help in the liberation of him and his companions ('you will ope that door, / And fly with us', *SG* I. 2955–56) – would not only mean to renounce all chances of re-aligning herself with Don Silva ('You cannot free us and come back to him', *SG* I.2999). It would mean to give up her very freedom of choice, as Zarca asserts upon Fedalma's request whether he would compel her to proceed on the course he takes to be appointed for her: 'Yes, for I'd have you choose; / Though, being of the blood you are – my blood – / You have no right to choose' (*SG* I.3001–3). By this logic, Fedalma's decision to acknowledge her kinship with her father would be tantamount to submitting herself to a mindset that holds the very act of choice to be no more than a function of what Zarca calls 'a compulsion of a higher sort' (*SG* I.3006). For Fedalma, to free her kin from their physical fetters is to become bound by their ideological ones.

If Zarca represents one extreme view on the concept of volition and choice, then Don Silva, Fedalma's designated husband, stands for the other extreme. While Zarca believes that one's life is governed by an inherited fate which forestalls the need for choice, Don Silva regards even one's ethnical affiliation as something that can be freely changed. Hence his offer to leave his current social standing and religion behind and 'adopt' the identity of 'a true Zíncalo' (*SG* III.1127, 1139) instead (a name he later disowns). In his case, the readiness to replace one culture with another seems to correspond to an insouciant attitude towards associations and commitments which makes one suspect that his character, 'a self / That is not one', is just as fleeting and insubstantial as the 'waves' of the sea with which he compares his condition (*SG* II.218–19). 'I shall be no more missed / Than waves are missed that leaping on the rock / Find there a bed and rest' (*SG* III.1149–51). In relation to Zarca's unflinching dogmatism and Silva's nonchalant opportunism, Fedalma herself is left to occupy a middle position, an experience in search of a place, made up of compromises and flexible decisions. This means that she comes to represent an identity in transition that resembles that of the Zíncali, but is not subsumed by it. Indeed, the suggestion of Eliot's text is not that Fedalma is and has always been a Zíncala, but that she makes herself like one. She becomes anew, in a different way, what she may once have been. She joins her past and present experience as a Christian Spaniard with that of a group of rootless, but not indefinite

> wanderers whom no God took knowledge of
> To give them laws, to fight for them, or blight
> Another race to make them ampler room;
> Who have no Whence or Whither in their souls,
> No dimmest lore of glorious ancestors
> To make a common hearth for piety. (*SG* I.2742–7)

The community of the Zíncali, on this account, is not built upon a theistic creed ('no God'), a political constitution ('laws'), a patch of land, or even 'some dimmest lore of glorious ancestors'. What holds them together as a group seems to be nothing fixed, but a flexible mode of interrelation that remains in circulation, moving between options and directions. Having no permanent abode, they are compelled, and have learned, to adapt to various environments, becoming flavoured by each of them. Their sense of personal identity is therefore composed of what Zarca calls 'multitudes', of a plurality of places and social relations, rather than a substantial ground (*SG* III.625). What they represent is an open way of life, or a way of living in the open that is most explicitly described by another outsider, Juan, a 'minstrel' or 'troubadour' (*SG* III.316, 321) who 'is not a living man all by himself: / His life is breathed in him by other men. / And they speak out of him. He is their voice', as he puts it. 'We old, old poets, if we keep our hearts, / Should hardly know them from another man's. / They shrink to make room for the many more / We keep within us' (*SG* I.2458–60, 2463–6).

Juan's characterisation of himself as a ventriloquist that speaks through different voices partaking just as much of him as he partakes of them evokes a theory of the poet as a person characterised by what E. S. Dallas describes as a 'capacity for varying the mood indefinitely, rather than for retaining and keeping up one moral gesture or resolution through all moods'.[64] Yet, one may say that the ascription of these properties to particular types, such as 'the poet' or 'the Gypsy' is symptomatic of a much more fundamental 'vanishing' of the human subject as a moral centre or source of agency.[65] Thus, in *Life and Habit*, Samuel Butler emphatically stresses that 'personality' is not 'a simple, definite whole', but 'a nebulous and indefinable aggregation of many component parts which war not a little among themselves', as he writes.[66]

> Moreover, as the component parts of our identity change from moment to moment, our personality becomes a thing dependent upon time present, which has no logical existence, but lives only upon the sufferance of times past and future, slipping out of our hands into the domain of one or other of these two claimants the moment we try to apprehend it.[67]

Personal identity, thus conceived, is subject to a time-bound experience which continuously recedes into the past or extends into the future. What it is needs to be defined in relation to what it has been or will become. The experience of being a person can therefore only be had in the mode of an ongoing process, 'slipping out of our hands' as soon as we try to grasp it as something self-contained. More fundamentally still, it is not only the fleetingness of human experience which calls the notion of selfhood into doubt. In addition, 'the parts which compose it', as Butler continues, 'blend some of them so imperceptibly into, and are so inextricably linked on to, outside things which clearly form no part of our personality, that when we try to [. . .] determine wherein we consist, or draw a line where we begin or end, we find ourselves baffled'.[68]

Both temporally and spatially, then, persons exist only in and through entanglements with what seems to be different from them. Just as the future and the past are intermixed with what one perceives as present, so the 'outside things' which appear to 'form no part of our personality' are 'inextricably linked on to' 'the parts which compose it'. 'Wherein' people consist can only be determined by attending to the historical and material environment out of which their distinctive selves are assembled. Indeed, Butler's examples of things which 'link us on, and fetter us down, to the organic and inorganic world about us' include not only 'the food we eat' and 'the air we breathe', but also a 'man's clothes'.[69] As he sees it, even such seemingly objective technologies and devices are not extraneous to those who use them, but become entwined with the very substance of their being. 'Thus we find that we melt away into outside things and are rooted in them, as plants into the soil in which they grow, nor can any man say he consists absolutely in this or that, nor define himself so certainly as to include neither more nor less than himself'.[70] Such formulations bespeak what has been called an '*environmental mode of awareness*':[71] an awareness that is 'rooted in', or at least related to, things outside of the subject while still seeming to issue from its inside. More precisely, it is an awareness through which the distinction between inside and outside, subject and object or human and non-human is dissolved in favour of their 'co-composition' in an emergent 'field of experience', as Massumi and Erin Manning have put it in a related context.[72] This ecological view of experience is characteristic of much Victorian poetry and fiction. For example, it can be found, to indicate just one famous instance, in Catherine Earnshaw's assertion that she was Heathcliff ('Nelly, I *am* Heathcliff – he's always, always in my mind [. . .] as my own being'), especially since Heathcliff is just as much another human individual as he is the epitome of the non-human earth on and with which he lives: 'Heathcliff is – an unreclaimed creature, without refinement, without cultivation; an arid wilderness of furze and whinstone.'[73] Being 'a dark-skinned gypsy in aspect',[74] Heathcliff represents the (human and non-human) otherness that is a part of Cathy, just as Zarca represents the otherness that is a part of Fedalma.

In sum, one can say that what one witnesses in *Wuthering Heights*, as well as in Butler, Lewes, William James and in Eliot's *The Spanish Gypsy* is a movement of opening the subject to an outside which interacts with it, involving the conscious human body in a process that casts doubt on its self-sufficiency. After all, the key consequence of Butler's claim that no one can define themselves 'so certainly as to include neither more nor less than' themselves is that everyone is both more *and* less than what they may take themselves to be. 'Not only are we infinite as regards time, but we are so also as regards extension, being so linked on to the external world that we cannot say where we either begin or end.'[75] Arguably, one result of such observations was that experience could no longer be ascribed to an autonomous subject but spread itself out across an unbounded field in which no one was seen as more than one participant among others. As Lewes repeatedly points out, the experience of an individual does not begin and end with what he or she may think of as their own feelings and sensations. It is not confined to a single body, but ranges over the whole, open-ended environment in which one lives and works. 'Not only the individual experiences, slowly acquired, but the accumulated Experience of the race, organized in Language, condensed in Instruments and Axioms, and in what may be called the *inherited Intuitions*, – these form the multiple unity which is expressed in the abstract term Experience' (*P* I, 26). In short, experience (thus viewed) makes up a 'multiple unity' that traverses (or rather, breaks down) the boundary between the individual and the collective, the material and the ideal as well as passive perception through the senses and active construction through instruments and artefacts. While experience needs the feeling of an individual (*Erlebnis*) to be activated, it also rests on, and is mediated through, an inherited complex of 'instruments', 'symbols', 'thoughts' and 'machines' in which the experiences (*Erfahrungen*) of preceding actors are 'condensed' in general forms (*P* II, 215, 216). As Lewes suggests in one of his many metaphors, neither the heritage of 'organized tendencies' into which someone is born nor their individual sensations are sufficient to constitute 'experience', just as it takes more than an acorn to make an oak. 'The oak is quite as much in the atmosphere and soil; it really is in neither, but will be evolved from both' (*P* I, 219, 220).

Becoming Epic

The point, then, is that experience is here conceived of as a process whose seeds are 'quite as much' in the body as they are in its environment. At all events, experience, for Lewes as well as for his Pragmatist successors, was taken to involve both a feeling (human) actor and something other which could affect and influence it in multiple ways. '*Experience means experience of something foreign supposed to impress us*, whether spontaneously or in consequence of our own exertions and acts,' as William James puts it.[76] James, accordingly, called experience 'double-barrelled', a term that John Dewey picked up as well.[77] Both argued that experience straddles the supposed divide between 'thing' and 'thought' because it can 'figure in both groups simultaneously', giving us 'every right to speak of it as subjective and objective both at once'.[78] It is clear by now that this integrative conception of experience can neither be reconciled with the notion of a strong human subject made self-sufficient by his will, nor with a deterministic view of heredity and racial community. Indeed, as Martin Jay has shown, it is in the work of James and Dewey that some of the first and most clearly delineated traces of 'the paradoxical ideal of experience without a subject' can be found.[79] To be sure, the later writings of Eliot and Lewes represent anything but a wholehearted embrace of this ideal, but neither do they suggest a straightforward rejection of it, or an argument in favour of the belief that experience presupposes a conscious, independent and undivided self who bears, and benefits from, it.[80] Rather, they interrogate the experience-based processes through which selves, communities, beliefs, relationships and objects (goals) come into being and are sustained.

The Spanish Gypsy can perhaps be seen as Eliot's most conspicuously experimental attempt to come to terms with these generative activities by tackling them in a different genre. As several commentators have remarked, when Eliot embarked on *The Spanish Gypsy*, she was under no pressure to try her hand at new generic forms. On the contrary, she had every good reason to stick to her usual trade, being as she was a well-respected author of prose fiction who had already published four novels to widespread critical acclaim.[81] The fact that she made her writing venture nevertheless into what for her and her readers must have been rather unfamiliar terrain, suggests a sense of 'disquiet', a reluctance to settle into established patterns that, though typical for the experimentalist attitude as it is exemplified by Lewes's *Problems*, clashes with the view of Eliot's work as that of a consummate and '*sanguine*' artist, in full control of her art.[82] Some critics, reluctant to register fully the experimental quality of the work, have therefore tended to see the *The Spanish Gypsy* as a rare failure or oddity, sticking out in an otherwise relatively homogeneous oeuvre.[83] There is, to be sure, nothing specifically odd about the themes that dominate *The Spanish Gypsy*, many of which must have been recognisable to Eliot's readers by that point in her career. Yet, the decision to translate these themes into a slightly different medium is not only a 'retreat from' the 'fame' she enjoyed among these readers, a retreat that is mirrored in Fedalma's renunciation of Don Silva's wealth and rank.[84] Eliot's decision to try out a new style of writing can also be seen as symptomatic of a lingering uncertainty about the use of the form in which she had so far conducted her self-proclaimed 'experiments in life'.

As critics have remarked, when Eliot first started to write *The Spanish Gypsy* in 1864 she seems to have intended it as a play, working on it in the dramatic mode for about six months until health issues and other projects made her abandon the piece. When she returned to it in October 1866, she decided to recompose it in the form of a verse narrative, before eventually publishing it in 1868. Unsurprisingly perhaps, the result of this comparatively long-winded and uneven evolution is not a homogeneous epic form, but a mixed kind in which long passages of omniscient narration in majestic blank verse alternate with play-script dialogues, lengthy stage directions in prose, and pieces of lyrical song in italics.[85] The text as a seemingly finished product, in short, displays manifest traces of the generative process through which it has been made to appear. It is not an epic which – as the epic genre is typically said to do – 'gives form to a totality of life that is rounded from within'.[86] Rather, it includes the inconsistencies and disruptions, repeatedly represented by the '*clanking noise*' or the 'jarring cruel sound' of the Gypsy prisoner's chains, which such an organic form would have to edit out (*SG* 76, I.2120). One can therefore say that Eliot's text presents itself as a formal analogue of the kind of mobile and unsettled (nomad) identity, most conspicuously represented by the Zíncali, with which it is concerned. Like the writing of *The Spanish Gypsy*, they are an assemblage of parts that refuse to be contained in, or defined by, a generic place or ground. Instead, the Zíncali make up a movement-based identity. Similar to Eliot's text, their being remains open to the integration of outsides, or other sites, which may, at any time, bring about variations, extensions or interruptions of each of its present states.

As a reader of *The Spanish Gypsy*, then, one is constantly faced with a form of epic narration in the process of becoming a play, or, conversely, with a play on the verge of turning into an epic. On the story level, this formal conflict between epic unity and playful dialogue can be seen to be repeated in the relationship between Zarca and the nomad people over whom he presides. More specifically, while Zarca is made to appear as an epic hero, a character who is 'rounded from within', the Gypsies, whom he is supposed to guide 'forth to their new land', represent a tendency towards variation and proliferation that continuously overspills such an ideal place (*SG* I.2828). As the ending of the text suggests, this tendency fully manifests itself only when Zarca is dead and Fedalma has stepped into his shoes. For, even though her father's people 'were not unfaithful' to his successor, as the text assures us, 'their natures' soon 'missed the constant stress / Of his command, that, while it fired, restrained / By urgency supreme, and left no play / To fickle impulse scattering desire' (*SG* V.76, 79–82). No doubt:

> They loved their Queen, trusted in Zarca's child,
> Would bear her o'er the desert on their arms
> And think the weight a gladsome victory;
> But that great force which knit them into one,
> The invisible passion of her father's soul,
> That wrought them visibly into its will,
> And would have bound their lives with permanence,
> Was gone. (*SG* V.83–90)

The unity and 'permanence' of life associated with the epic, then, is premised on an activity of 'restraining' the 'play of fickle impulse scattering desire' which runs counter to it. A state of being, just as a form of verse, which lacks 'the constant stress' reaffirming its identity again and again is likely to be carried away by the tendency to change inherent in the very current of time, as the narrator has Fedalma think.

> In a little while, the tribe
> That was to be the ensign of the race,
> And draw it into conscious union,
> Itself would break in small and scattered bands
> That, living on scant prey, would still disperse
> And propagate forgetfulness. Brief years,
> And that great purpose fed with vital fire
> That might have glowed for half a century,
> Subduing, quickening, shaping, like a sun –
> Would be a faint tradition, flickering low
> In dying memories, fringing with dim light
> The nearer dark. (*SG* V.100–11)

This suggests that it will only take a short space of time ('a little while'; 'Brief years') for the open-ended process represented by the Gypsy people to 'propagate forgetfulness' and, in this way, to emancipate itself from the 'great purpose' intended for them by their late chief. Evidently, Fedalma, unlike her father, lacks the 'vital fire' or will power which is necessary to keep the heritage left to her 'glowing' in the future now lying ahead. 'Far, far the future stretched / Beyond that busy present on the quay, / Far her straight path beyond it' (*SG* V.112–14). In what follows, the claim that Fedalma's path is 'straight', slightly disavowed by the triple emphasis on how 'far' beyond her it extends, is further called into doubt by a 'dream / Alternate', the possibility of 'another track' on which Fedalma follows not the will of her father but the figure of an unnamed 'wanderer' (*SG* V.114–17). This may well be Don Silva who quickly reappears at the very end, but the reunion between the two lovers remains a virtual road not taken by the text. Instead, the narrative ends, tellingly, on the shore, in a twilight zone between 'The land that bred' Fedalma and the 'Fresh Night emergent' into which she and 'the last strong band / Of Zíncali' finally sail (*SG* V.403, 406, 384–5).

Where they sail and whether they ever arrive at anything like a final destination or a homeland is not made known by the text. Eliot's writing, it seems, is unable to contain, or arrest the open-ended movement of the Gypsy band. Rather, I would argue, it enacts an experience of being on the threshold, 'in the thin line of flame' between the past and the future in which associations and distinctions have to be continually remade if they are supposed to be sustained. This transformative experience without 'a bedding' or resting place is the experience of a contingent world, a world which could be, or become, otherwise than it is, at any moment, taken to be. One reason, arguably, why Eliot's later work seems to be so centrally concerned with unsettled or diasporic peoples such as the Zíncali or the Jews (in *Daniel Deronda*) is that they represented a mobile state of being which resonated with the restless mode in which many Victorians saw themselves and, by extension, the whole of mankind to be living, too. According to Lewes, for instance, the life of man is forever suspended between what he calls 'the world of Feeling and the world of Thought': between the experience of being on the earth and the meanings which can be made of it (*P* II, 108). 'The Present is to him a complex web, with threads of the Past and threads of the Future inextricably interwoven' (*P* II, 108). How commitments, social relationships and systems of reliable knowledge are to be created out of, and maintained throughout, the experience of being involved in such an unpredictable, or 'uneven' net is the (unresolved) question with which much of Eliot's later work is concerned.

Notes

1. Sennett, *The Craftsman*, p. 289.
2. Williams, *Keywords*, p. 116.
3. Cf. 'Experience, n.', *OED Online*.
4. Cf. Williams, *Keywords*, pp. 126–7.
5. Williams, *Keywords*, p. 127. Cf. also Kambartel, 'Erfahrung' and Maag, 'Erfahrung'.
6. Cf. Sennett, *The Craftsman*, pp. 286–96.
7. Massumi, 'Envisioning', p. 63.
8. Ibid., p. 64.
9. All quotations marked as *P* are from: Lewes, *Problems, First Series*, 2 vols. Lewes's *Problems* appeared in three series, which altogether consist of five volumes because the first and the third series are split into two parts. The first two volumes (first series) are subtitled *The Foundations of a Creed*; the third volume (second series) is about *The Physical Basis of Mind*; the fourth volume addresses *The Study of Psychology*; while the fifth volume, published posthumously by George Eliot, remains untitled (third series). Epistemological questions are mainly treated in the first and third series.

10. Cf. Dewey, 'The Experimental Theory'.
11. Jay, *Songs*, p. 276.
12. This is what distinguishes Lewes's philosophy from that of Spencer who insisted that all that is 'knowable' (*First Principles*, part I) must be related to a realm of the 'unknowable' (*First Principles*, part II). The latter concept points to a quasi-religious or transcendental remnant in Spencer's philosophy that Lewes does away with. If we cannot know the unknowable, Lewes argues, then we do not have to assume that it exists. Instead, we might as well keep to that which is knowable.
13. Cf. Stachowiak (ed.), *Der Aufstieg*; Jay, *Songs*, pp. 261–311 and Roth, *British Empiricism*, pp. 1–28.
14. Cf. Rylance, *Victorian Psychology*, pp. 251–330; Garratt, *Victorian Empiricism*, pp. 102–26; Dale, 'Scientific Aesthetic'.
15. James, *Radical Empiricism*, p. 212.
16. Ibid., p. 212.
17. Ibid., p. 212.
18. Hume, *Enquiry*, p. 101.
19. James, *Radical Empiricism*, p. 233 and generally.
20. James, *The Meaning of Truth*, p. xiii.
21. James, *Radical Empiricism*, p. 212.
22. Ibid., p. 201.
23. Ibid., p. 212.
24. Ibid., p. 213. For an engagement with the literary theoretical implications of James's concept of experience see my 'Reading Experience'.
25. Lewes, *Animal Life*, pp. 8–9.
26. Ibid., p. 9.
27. Ibid., pp. 9–10.
28. Ibid., p. 10.
29. Referencing Barthes one could also say that, here, science (knowledge) becomes literature (writing): 'From Science to Literature', p. 10.
30. Lewes, *Animal Life*, p. 10.
31. Ibid., p. 10.
32. Connor, 'A Short Stirring', p. 199.
33. Derrida, 'Genesis', p. 201.
34. James, *Principles of Psychology*, I, p. 269. For the similarities between Lewes and James see especially Chapter IX of James's work ('The Stream of Thought'), I, pp. 224–401. Large parts of this chapter had already appeared, in 1884, in the journal *Mind*. Lewes is repeatedly referenced in *The Principles of Psychology*, so there is no doubt that James was influenced by his work.
35. Rylance, *Victorian Psychology*, p. 255.
36. Ibid., p. 306.
37. Ibid., p. 306.
38. Ibid., pp. 307–10.
39. Ibid., pp. 251–330; Shuttleworth, *George Eliot*, pp. 19–20; Zwierlein, *Der physiologische Bildungsroman*, p. 212.

40. Spencer, *Principles of Psychology*, p. 452.

41. Tucker, *Epic*, p. 414.

42. All quotations marked as *SG* refer to: Eliot, *The Spanish Gypsy*. Quotations are located by book and line numbers, unless I quote from the prose directions frequently accompanying the dialogue scenes. These are not counted as part of the verse lines, for which reason they shall be cited by page numbers. For the formal peculiarities of *The Spanish Gypsy* see my comments in the last section of this chapter.

43. Tucker makes the same point with regard to a different passage (*Epic*, p. 421).

44. Tate, *The Poet's Mind*, p. 145.

45. As Tate shows in *The Poet's Mind*, Eliot is, in fact, far from using the concept of the 'soul' in an unequivocal manner in *The Spanish Gypsy*. Rather, the word assumes a score of different meanings ranging from 'racial memory' (p. 148) and 'moral lessons learned from experience' (p. 149) to 'a more conventionally metaphysical sense' (p. 148). On Tate's reading, Eliot's ambiguous usage of 'soul' suggests that *The Spanish Gypsy* 'maintains a "twofold mind" over its approach to psychology', trying but perhaps never quite managing, to integrate 'metaphysical intuition with the observational evidence of psychological science' (p. 148).

46. Tucker, *Epic*, p. 416.

47. Eliot, 'Appendix A', *The Spanish Gypsy*, p. 274. For an attempt to 'grasp' the 'intention' that is behind *The Spanish Gypsy* by means of a close reading of Eliot's 'Note' see Fleishman, *Intellectual Life*, p. 129.

48. Otis, *Organic Memory*, p. 3; Zwierlein, *Der physiologische Bildungsroman*, pp. 211–17, 232–8.

49. For an overview of the criticism on Butler see Paradis, ed. *Samuel Butler*.

50. Butler, *Life and Habit*, p. 17.

51. Ibid., p. 18.

52. Ibid., p. 18.

53. Ibid., p. 35.

54. Ibid., p. 24.

55. Ibid., p. 24.

56. Ibid., pp. 25, 6.

57. Ibid., p. 6, cf. p. 15.

58. Butler, *Unconscious Memory*, p. 22.

59. Nord, 'Marks', p. 203. Cf. also Nord, *Gypsies*, pp. 99–124.

60. Eliot, *Middlemarch*, p. 779.

61. Hillis Miller, 'Conclusion', p. 135. Lewes, too, speaks of 'the web of Experience', likewise using the metaphor of the 'warp and woof' (*P* I, 33).

62. No doubt, the portrayal of Zarca, with his unfaltering belief in the duty to 'feed the high tradition of the world' through acts of selfless leadership gestures at a discourse of heroism as it can be extracted, for example, from the work of Thomas Carlyle, especially from *Heroes*, pp. 233–87

(Lecture VI: 'The Hero as King'). Yet, whereas Carlyle tends to see the resolute will of man as an instrument for the unfolding of a great idea, 'the magnitude which Nature has made him of' (p. 266), Zarca's will, I am arguing, conspicuously (although against his intention) wants this basis in a transcendental ideal. For the reference to, and role of, Carlyle see Campbell, *Rhythm*, pp. 15–63.
63. James, *The Principles of Psychology*, II, p. 1166.
64. Dallas, *Gay Science*, II, p. 200.
65. Ryan, *The Vanishing Subject*, pp. 6–22.
66. Butler, *Life and Habit*, p. 64.
67. Ibid., p. 64.
68. Ibid., p. 64.
69. Ibid., pp. 65, 66.
70. Ibid., pp. 65–6.
71. Manning and Massumi, *Thought*, p. 6 and generally.
72. Ibid., pp. 68, 8.
73. Brontë, *Wuthering Heights*, pp. 64, 80.
74. Ibid., p. 5.
75. Butler, *Life and Habit*, p. 85.
76. James, *The Principles of Psychology*, II, p. 1217.
77. James, *Radical Empiricism*, p. 172.
78. Ibid., p. 172; Dewey, *Experience and Nature*, p. 8.
79. Jay, *Songs*, p. 265.
80. Cf. Jay, *Songs*, p. 264.
81. Cf. Baker, 'Preface', pp. ix–xxv; Tucker, *Epic*, pp. 414–15; Kurnick, 'Unspeakable'.
82. Kurnick, 'Unspeakable', p. 490.
83. Reynolds, for instance, saw it as an 'example of the strange things that can happen when people who are not poets set themselves to writing poetry' (*Realms*, p. 192).
84. Krasner. '"Where no man praised"', 'title'.
85. Cf. Kurnick, 'Unspeakable', pp. 492–3.
86. Lukács, *Theory*, p. 60.

Chapter 5

Speech in Action: Victorian Philology and the Uprooting of Language

Language and Reason

As we have seen, 'experience', according to the (proto-)pragmatist conception, could no longer be confined to the thoughts and feelings of a single, clearly defined body, but was taken to ramify across the unbounded historical and spatial field in relation to which individual lives unfold. As a result, the distinctions between inside and outside, the past and the present, the conscious and the unconscious, the voluntary and the involuntary, as well as the 'animal organism' and the 'social organism', inevitably started to blur. 'Who shall draw the line,' Samuel Butler asks, between that which is and that which is not part of the human self.[1] 'There is no line possible. Everything melts away into everything else; there are no hard edges; it is only from a little distance that we see the effect as of individual features and existences.'[2] It barely needs saying that this general blurring of boundaries responded to, and was influenced by, the rise of evolutionary theory, with the most hotly debated of all dividing lines being that between the human and the animal.[3] Yet, one of the most noteworthy aspects of this debate was that it compelled even some of the most stalwart defenders of the development hypothesis to reconsider their own kind of being anew, 'from a little distance', so as to work out what, in spite of all similarities, might still render the animal other than themselves.

A welcome way to answer this question, to be unpacked in this chapter, was suggested by the emergent science of language. For it was the use of words and symbols that was widely considered to make the difference between the physical world of feelings and sensations, and the ideal world of representations and thoughts. While humans were taken to share the material world with their animal kin, it was the ideal sphere in which 'man' was considered to shape 'the programme' peculiar to his very own human 'existence', as Lewes puts it in a representative statement. 'Language is the creator and sustainer of that Ideal World in which the noblest part of human activity finds a theatre, the world of Thought and Spiritual Insight, of Knowledge and Duty, loftily elevated above that of Sense and Appetite' (*P* I, 154). As Lewes's choice of words betrays, language, by this account, is much more than a means of symbolic abstraction; it is the path to moral 'elevation' and 'Spiritual Insight', through the use of which man is automatically raised 'above' the animal state. This suggests that even for some of the most committed evolutionists such as Lewes and Huxley, or perhaps especially for them, the reference to language offered a welcome opportunity to rebuild the very barrier between the animal and the human sphere that they had just begun to demolish. In fact, there seems to have been considerable comfort in the observation that no animal, despite its close relationship with the human race, has ever been heard to voice anything other than cries, whistles or roars. For example, in T. H. Huxley's long essay on 'Man's Place in Nature' (1863), which goes to great lengths to make the case that the animal has to be acknowledged as a part of mankind, one also comes across the assertion that this very insight, 'the knowledge that Man is, in substance and in structure, one with the brutes', could still not lessen 'Our reverence for the nobility of manhood', as Huxley puts it in an almost defiant way;

> for, he alone possesses the marvellous endowment of intelligible and rational speech, whereby, in the secular period of his existence, he has slowly accumulated and organised the experience which is almost wholly lost with the cessation of every individual life in other animals; so that, now he stands raised upon it as on a mountain top, far above the level of his humble fellows, and transfigured from his grosser nature by reflecting, here and there, a ray from the infinite source of truth.[4]

What asks for an explanation in such statements is not so much the emphasis on 'intelligible and rational speech' as the distinctive quality of the human as the enthusiastic way in which the possession of this 'endowment' is praised. One effect, after all, of Huxley's and Lewes's way of using the 'marvellous' capacity to speak is a concomitant definition (and degradation) of 'the animal' as that which remains 'far' below man, unable to recognise and organise its experience in abstract forms and therefore unable to partake of the human world. There is, however, no need for such exclusive rhetoric because the difference between man and his animal kin is, by Huxley's own logic, inevitably reaffirmed with every 'intelligible' word or sentence that is pronounced. 'To speak of our animal heritage is at once to disavow it,' as Christine Ferguson has it.[5] One suspects, therefore, that there are other reasons why, in Huxley's (and Lewes's) view, the use of language does not just separate humans from their animal kin, but 'transfigures' their 'grosser nature' and lifts them 'far above' their 'humble fellows', into a region where they can catch the rays from 'the infinite source of truth'.

As I wish to argue, one way of accounting for this imagery is to see it as the remainder of an idealist (or theistic) concept of language, which, though foremost in Victorian philology, jars with the (proto-pragmatist) emphasis on process and activity otherwise character-istic of Huxley's and Lewes's work. For, according to this idealist theory, language is not (as Huxley in fact seems to suggest in the above statement) the product of a slow evolution of communica-tive practices which involves an arbitrary component. Instead, on the idealist model, language, or the capacity to interact through words which is common to most human beings, is the expression of an absolute, divinely made reason essentially devoid of contingency and time. Thus, according to Richard C. Trench, initiator of the *Oxford English Dictionary* and author of the popular book *On the Study of Words* (1851), language is the receptacle of 'a thousand precious and subtle thoughts', or the container of 'ten thousand lightning flashes of genius', co-emergent with human reason itself.[6] 'God gave man language, just as He gave him reason, and just because He gave him reason (for what is man's word but his reason coming forth, so that it may behold itself?).'[7] The text that was most often adduced to justify this idealist account of linguistic meaning as an expression of divinely ordained reason, instituted by a set of instantaneous 'light-ning flashes', is the biblical narrative of creation at the beginning of Genesis. The decisive passage occurs in the second chapter when God, having already made a man, 'did not think it good that the man should be alone', as the text has it.

> So out of the ground the Lord God formed every animal of the field and every bird of the air, and brought them to the man to see what he would call them; and whatever the man called every living creature, that was its name. The man gave names to all cattle, and to the birds of the air, and to every animal of the field.[8]

For Trench, this passage is nothing less than 'the clearest intimation of the origin at once divine and human, of speech; while yet neither is so brought forward as to exclude or obscure the other'.[9] More precisely, he regards the '*power of naming*' or the 'capacity' to speak as the medium which connects human existence with the reason of God.[10] Thus, on Trench's reading of the biblical text, Adam did not act completely of his own accord when he gave the animals their names, but 'at the direct suggestion of his Creator'.[11] Trench seeks to corroborate this interpretation by emphasising that the activity of naming was not initiated by Adam but by God's bringing the nameless creatures 'to the man to see what he would call them'. Yet, it is noteworthy that this formulation, as Derrida has argued in his reading of the same passage, does not expressly indicate that God is in control of the action that he has prepared.[12] On the contrary, there seems to be something conspicuously unobtrusive and detached in how God is said to behave. He does, it seems, not so much oversee what he has arranged to happen as he observes it: like a scientific spectator who is ready to 'abandon himself to his curiosity, even allow himself to be surprised and outflanked by the radical novelty of what was going to occur'.[13] In this way, Derrida suggests, the text of Genesis introduces an element of difference and deferral (*différance*) into the relationship between the name and its referent as well as between God's idea and man's practical execution of it. If God is indeed curious 'to see' what Adam 'would call' the other creatures, after all, then he cannot have known it in advance. In short, whereas Derrida reads Adam's act of naming the animals as part of an experimental arrangement which, although prepared by God, involves an element of unpredictability and contingency, Trench regards it as a way of extending divine reason into human terms. When Adam called the creatures by their names, Trench claims, he was effectively making a verbal expression out of an ideal meaning represented by God. 'It was not merely the possible, but the necessary, emanation of the spirit with which he had been endowed.'[14] According to this reading, then, the key point to be noted about the biblical narrative is that the capacity to speak which defines man as human is also what connects him with the capitalised Word, the 'infinite source of truth' associated with the divine. When man gave names to his fellow creatures, Trench suggests, he simultaneously gave voice to the spirit or *logos* 'breathed' into him by God.

Symptomatically, what Trench says little about is the role of the animals in this first use of speech as it is described in Genesis. Yet, it is suggestive that humans could only come to know themselves as humans – as speaking creatures endowed with a higher reason – by defining 'every animal of the field' as something other than themselves.

It seems as if the idea of the human could come into being only through the naming of the animal, or the non-human life, as that which it excludes.[15] What defines man, it seems, is that he is capable of naming that which is not part of himself: the non-human. It follows that 'language', by which Trench means not any particular tongue but the general *'power of naming'* characteristic of the whole of mankind, is here seen as the manifestation of a specific idea of the human.[16] More precisely, the use of language, or the ability to describe singular perceptions in general, reproducible terms, is taken to reveal the special nature of humans as privileged creatures made in the image of God.

It is this belief that the capacity to form words out of experiences is essentially founded on the creative wisdom of God which motivated the search for, and controversy about, the origins of language driving much of Victorian philology.[17] For there would have been no point in investigating the roots of language if it had not been assumed that language somehow exists 'as such', as an underlying system or structure, independent of the multiple ways in which it is actually used. As Tim Ingold has pointed out, if one believes that there is only a plurality of spoken tongues, but no one single language, then the ground for an enquiry into the origin of language is immediately removed.[18] For many representatives of what passed as 'comparative philology' or 'the science of language' in the nineteenth century, however, this belief in an ideal ground of language was still in place. Thus, even though language was regarded as a 'living' form of communication that changes and develops, its evolution was nevertheless taken to be governed by a specifically 'human genius', 'implanted' into man by God.[19] 'The idea of speech was innate, and the evolution of that idea may be traced in the growth and history of language,' as the liberal Anglican cleric Frederick W. Farrar puts it, one of the critics who, like Trench, was convinced that 'Thought and speech are inseparably connected'.[20] One upshot of this belief in an inherent *logos* of speech was what Farrar called 'a strong repugnance' at the suggestion that 'caprice or chance' may have had 'any considerable share in the origin of language'.[21] Language, then, is here seen as an instrument of logical thought, with each word functioning as an expression of 'human intelligence' rather than as an arbitrary compound of sounds.[22] Farrar concedes that it may often be hard, not to say impossible, to explicate the alleged rationale by which words are linked to the perception of specific referents. But he does not doubt, as he professes, 'that there must have been some reason in the nature of things, why certain impressions or feelings were connected with certain sounds'.[23]

Roots and Metaphors

One of the Victorian scientists of language who dedicated most of his writing and public lecturing to the project of uncovering this ideal reason taken to be at the bottom of the human capacity to speak is the German expatriate Friedrich Max Müller, a well-respected authority in the field of comparative philology. Yet, just as one may find traces of an idealist view of language in the predominantly process- and practice-based thought of Huxley and Lewes, so, conversely, the idealist concept of speech propagated by Müller can frequently be seen to drift into a non-idealist or pragmatist one. More precisely, while Müller seeks to demonstrate that there is an absolute *logos* at what he calls the 'root' of each word,[24] his actual writing intimates that the logic of language inheres in the multiple ways in which it is used, rather than dwelling in an ideal place outside of them. Thus, one only has to follow Müller's text for a few chapters in order to realise that the linguistic reason about which he speaks regularly seems to outgrow the roots in which it is supposed to be located, and to spread itself out across endless lists of examples and intricate networks of word formation. As I hope to show, this suggests that the logic by which Müller takes the invention and evolution of language to be governed is one that can only be exemplified in practice, through activities of speaking and writing, but that cannot be captured in a set of abstract ideas. In fact, Müller himself half-wittingly hints at this when he points out that the word *logos*, which he takes to comprise both speech and reason, refers 'originally' to a 'gathering' power, or to an ability to draw pieces together (*L* II, 63). '*Lógos* is derived from *légein*, which, like Latin *legere*, means, originally, to gather,' we are told in a way that is typical of Müller's style.

> Hence *Katálogos*, a catalogue, a gathering, a list; *collectio*, a collection. In Homer, *légein* is hardly ever used in the same sense of saying, speaking, or meaning, but always in the sense of gathering, or, more properly, of telling, for to *tell* is the German *Zählen*, and means originally to count, to cast up. *Lógos*, used in the sense of reason, meant originally, like the English *tale*, gathering; for reason 'though it penetrates into the depths of the sea and earth, elevates our thoughts as high as the stars, and leads us through the vast spaces and large rooms of this mighty fabric', is nothing more or less than the gathering up of the single by means of the general. (*L* II, 63)

This 'catalogue' assembles a collection of words, from 'the German *Zählen*' to 'the English *tale*', which are supposed to be parts of the same group. In this way, Müller's writing not only enacts the very process, namely 'the gathering up of the single by means of the general', that is allegedly contained in the term *lógos* and, indeed, in all the words derived from it; the passage also makes explicit that the 'reason' which Müller takes to be inherent in speech does not exist in an ideal, self-contained shape, but is constituted through activities of grouping or gathering: of connecting parts with wholes. In fact, every single word, as Müller argues, encapsulates a congregation of this kind; 'it represents the gathering of the single under the general' (*L* II, 64). While the term 'gathering' can refer both to a practice of drawing together and to its result, it is here primarily used in the active sense, as a synonym for 'to *tell*', 'to count, to cast up'. But this means that the reason which is supposed to be gathered up in each word ('*Lógos* used in the sense of word, means likewise a gathering', *L* II, 64) must be an effect of a process of meaning-making, rather than a cause that precedes it.

Yet, despite these intimations of a process-based view of linguistic reason, Müller is not expressly interested in words as results of formative activities. Rather, he views them as containers of what he calls 'a petrified philosophy' (*L* I, 363), a hidden logical system (to be uncovered by the scientist), the 'constituent elements' (*L*, I, 369) of which are the so-called 'roots'. On Müller's account, these roots are the 'ultimate facts' or 'simplest parts' of language (*L* II, 81; II, 80), from which the whole diversity of human speech has developed. More precisely, each root is taken to represent a general quality common to a multiplicity of things. 'The first thing really known is the general,' as he puts it. 'Man could not name a tree, or an animal, or a river, or any object whatever in which he took an interest, without discovering first some general quality that seemed at the time the most characteristic of the object to be named' (*L* II, 64). For example, the word '*rivus*, river', Müller claims, was formed 'from a root *ru* or *sru*, to run, because of its running water' (*L* I, 362). In this manner, all roots are taken to refer to such 'general qualities', which means that their significance is already at a remove from individual perception. For Müller, in short, the roots mark the boundary between mere noise and 'significant sound' (*L* II, 77) as well as between body and mind, 'the light within' (*L* I, 365) and the darkness without, or the 'animal experience' (*L* I, 364) of 'sensuous intuitions', and the intellectual world of signs and ideas.[25] Moreover, the presupposed existence of roots permits him to justify his view of the science of language as one of the physical sciences, for which reason he emphasises that these roots are not to be seen as products of human art, but of natural force. 'They exist, as Plato would say, by nature; though with Plato we should add that, when we say by nature, we mean by the hand of God' (*L* I, 370). Thus, for Müller, the 'true genesis of language' as well as the separation of man from 'the brute world' coincides with the institution of a large number of roots (*L* I, 365), an event which he imagines, similar to the biblical report, as singular and instantaneous: as the exhaustive outpouring of a 'creative faculty' which 'became extinct when its object was fulfilled' (*L* I, 371).

From a present-day perspective, this narrative about the sudden rise of linguistic origins may seem laborious and implausible. But it is fundamental to Müller's method, for it enables him to deduce the purported reason of language from a groundwork of allegedly natural elements. The purpose of this deductive procedure is to show that there is a rationale behind each word which can be discovered by tracing it to its root. In this way one may find, for instance, that the horse (Sanskrit *aśva)* was named after its swiftness ('from the root *aś*, to be sharp or swift', which also appears in the Latin *acus*, needle, as well as in the English *acrimony* and *acute*) (*L* II, 65). Likewise, a study of roots will yield the insight, to quote just a few more of Müller's examples, that wheat was so called because of its whiteness, or that the moon was first seen as 'the measurer', the sun as the 'the begetter', the earth as 'the ploughed' and the institution of the 'name' itself, being descended from the Sanskrit root *gnâ*, to know, as 'that by which we know a thing' (*L* II, 65; *L* I, 363, 365). Thus, the framing of words is presented as transparent and logical, governed by a communicative reason which, rather than being arbitrary, always hit upon the most 'useful' and easily comprehensible quality to define a perceived thing (*L* II, 65). The general object of these presentations is to convince the reader that speech is 'inseparable' from thought, a creed that Müller repeats in sundry variations. 'Words without thought are dead sounds; thoughts without words are nothing. To think is to speak low; to speak is to think aloud.' Or most simply: 'The word is the thought incarnate' (*L* I, 369).[26]

The point I wish to make, however, is that the kind of reason outlined by Müller's writing has an inbuilt tendency to run away with the very principles in which it is supposed to be contained. Far from being rooted in an ideal or absolute place, the thought or thinking that one is faced with in Müller's lectures is typically made to manifest itself through processes of making links and cross-references between seemingly different words: through the gathering up of catalogues. What is more, Müller expressly points out that the linguistic reason that he has in mind works not so much by discrimination and identification as by analogy and comparison. As he points out, it has more in common with 'wit', or 'the assemblage of ideas' through 'quickness and variety', than with 'judgement', or the careful separation of 'ideas wherein can be found the least difference' (*L* II, 66). More pointedly still, Müller suggests that the making up of 'pleasant pictures, and agreeable visions, in the fancy' played a more vital role in the invention and evolution of words than the avoidance of misleading affinities and kinships (*L* II, 66).

This emphasis on wit, on the quick and variable capacity to see one thing in terms of another, not only explains why Müller calls the creation of words man's 'first poetry' and finds that 'there is something more truly wonderful in a root than in all the lyrics of the world' (*L* II, 68; *L* I, 343); it also ties in with his interest in the use of metaphor, a way with words that he regards as 'one of the most powerful engines in the construction of human speech' (*L* II, 351). Only by paying attention to the function of metaphors, Müller argues, can one elucidate 'how any language could have progressed beyond the simplest rudiments' (*L* II, 351). Thus viewed, metaphor, defined as 'the transferring of a name from the object to which it properly belongs to other objects which strike the mind as in some way or other participating in the peculiarities of the first object', is not confined to a specifically poetic mode of speech (*L* II, 351). Rather, it is the vehicle through which the repertoire of human words has been increased to enable ever more fine-grained denotations. Crucially, however, Müller insists that the evolution of language powered by metaphor follows, like the instalment of roots, a natural course, or one that is comparable to the growth of a tree from its seed. Therefore, even though he regularly speaks of speech as a man-made achievement and of its first speakers as 'the ancient framers' of words, he professes himself to be convinced that the life of language cannot be substantially influenced by human art (*L* II, 376). He is therefore expressly not interested in metaphor as the 'conscious transference of a word from one object to another', achieved through the 'premeditated act of a poet' or any other individual.[27] Instead, he sees metaphor as a general motor force in what he thinks of as the natural development of language.

In sum, metaphor (for Müller) represents a tendency towards variation and transmutation to which all human speech is inevitably subjected. 'Man was driven to speak metaphorically, whether he liked it or not,' as he puts it in a related article, because otherwise man's expressive possibilities would have been 'too poor' 'for the ever increasing wants of his mind'.[28] In an attempt to illustrate this process by which the use of metaphor helped to broaden and enrich the repertoire of speech, Müller provides an example worth quoting at length. 'Suppose man had advanced as far as platting or weaving,' he suggests, 'it would be very natural that, after setting lines to catch birds, he should, when he had to describe his day's work, be reminded of the words for platting or weaving.'

> Weaving would thus take the sense of putting snares, and when a new word was wanted for setting snares – that is, for tricking, cheating, luring, inveigling a person by false words – nothing, again, was more natural than to take a word of a similar import, and to use, for instance, ὑφαίνειν, to weave, in the sense of plotting
> [. . .] This metaphor spread very widely and we may discover it even in our own word subtle, Lat. subtilis, which comes from subtexere, to weave beneath, like têla for texla.[29]

In this way, Müller seeks to reconstruct the ways in which language 'lived' and developed through the deployment of metaphors. Moreover, as his repeated use of the word 'natural' indicates, he does this in order to show that the 'growth' of language followed a logic of what he sees as reasonable thought. In his lectures Müller even adopts Darwin's term of *'natural selection'* to underpin the combination of the natural and the rational, as well as the unconscious and the conscious, that he takes to be integral to human speech (*L* I, 368 and generally). 'To weave', the reader is supposed to believe, was the natural selection of human wit when a term was wanted to describe the practice of setting lines to catch birds, just as it was natural that this new meaning of the word was later extended to refer to rhetorical techniques of plotting schemes and planning tricks. Yet, by acquainting his readers with the pathways on which verbal meaning was enabled, by means of metaphor, to travel freely through various locales, Müller's writing simultaneously emancipates the reason of language from its supposed roots and makes it move 'very widely' across an open-ended field. As a result, the wisdom or wit that Müller takes to be at the bottom of speech is made to appear mobile and decentred, capable of connecting all manner of seemingly different words, such as 'subtle' and 'to weave'.

Müller certainly tries very hard to justify the etymological relationships that he maps out as reasonable and evident, but the more studiously he works to follow the ramifications of metaphorical word-framing, the more his own language starts to perform the very processes that it attempts to reconstruct. As a result, his writing seems to create the metaphorical lines and interconnections with which he presents his readers as much as it finds them. It develops a life of its own, exemplifying a version of the very 'vitalism' of language that it seeks to propagate.[30] For example, one of Müller's etymological journeys supposed to map out the migration routes of linguistic meaning begins with the Sanskrit root *ark*, *arch* or *rich*, 'which means to be bright', but which, 'like most primitive verbs', he notes, is flexible enough to be used in the sense of '*to make bright*' (*L* II, 359). In addition, 'to make bright', Müller specifies, was also used in the wider sense of 'to cheer, to gladden, to celebrate, to glorify' which explains, he continues, why the root *ark*, 'by a very simple and intelligible process' (*L* II, 359), could become transformed into a new word, '*arkáh*', referring both to 'the sun' and to a 'hymn of praise' (*L* II, 360). As Müller describes it, this process of extending the root *ark* to make it designate both the sun and a cheerful song is an instance of a 'very natural' use of 'metaphor' (*L* II, 360). By contrast, another line in the development of speech, through which hymns of praise were somehow associated with the sun, is what Müller calls a case of 'mythology': an illogical or unreasonable transfer of ideas (*L* II, 360). But although Müller is keen to distinguish clearly between what he describes as the natural and the mythical use of metaphor, his own practice of following the trajectories of word-making exposes this distinction to be highly unstable and prone to collapse. A few lines later, for instance, he acquaints his readers with another offspring of the root *arch* or *rich*, namely '*ríkta*, in the sense of lighted up, or bright' (*L* II, 360), an attribute which came to be transferred onto *riksha*, meaning 'bear', as Müller reasons. '*Riksha*, in the sense of bright, has become the name of the bear, so called either from his bright eyes or from his brilliant tawny fur' (*L* II, 361). While this association of brightness and bears, albeit somewhat unusual, is still said to be a plausible transfer of qualities, it could easily become warped (Müller explains) when the characteristics of the bear came to be transposed, 'apparently without rhyme or reason', onto a constellation of bright stars (*árktos*, *ursa*). In this way, another myth was born, he concludes, which continues to live on whenever one speaks of the Arctic region (*L* II, 362).

It is not unlikely that many of Müller's original listeners would have lost track of his exact reasoning by that point in the lecture, and yet this does not necessarily mean that his claims appeared unconvincing or confused, as convoluted as they may be. For what results from this etymological study is a pattern in transformation which, like a constellation of stars, is both manifestly coherent and susceptible to changing into something else as soon as its components are construed differently: through a different medium, or from a different position.

One might say, coming back to James's term, that the assemblage of sun, stars, bear and hymn of praise that Müller draws together by making them all part of the root 'bright' forms a mosaic without a bedding, an emergent structure that remains open to be added to or recomposed. Concomitantly, the *logos*, or gathering power that Müller seeks to make evident by means of this structure, is a 'quick and variable' wisdom that is typically communicated and sustained through the use of metaphor. This means that in order to bring out what he sees as the logic of word formation, Müller's writing had to work by means of the very analogical constructions that it tried to examine. Arguably, the problem behind this predicament is that his science of language lacks a vantage point outside of the verbal material that it tries to scrutinise. The language that constitutes his science is subject to the same laws and tendencies as the language that it strives to elucidate. In short, the analysing medium is entangled with the analysed one, which explains why Müller's argument often seems to become part of the same processes of word formation that it attempts to expound, rather than remaining detached from them.[31]

This entanglement of discourse and theme is especially evident in the lecture on metaphor where Müller's argument is repeatedly sucked into the very 'stream of mythology' that it seeks to distinguish from the reasonable use of figurative speech (*L* II, 374). Typically, Müller begins with a root, such as 'GHAR, which, like *ark*, means to be bright and to make bright', only to spin more and more threads of meaning from it (*L* II, 369). In this case, for instance, he is led to discover offshoots of this root in records of certain horses which 'are called *vîtaprishtha*, with beautiful backs, and *ghritasnâh*, bathed in fat, glittering, bedewed' (*L* II, 369). Likewise, other branches of the root can be found, Müller tells his readers, in 'heat' or indeed in 'anything that is hot, the sun, the fire, warm milk, and even the kettle' (*L* II, 369). What is more, the texts of the Vedic poets are said to have it that the sun and the dawn are either themselves called horses or described as drawn by horses, which brings Müller's cataloguing to a preliminary conclusion. 'These horses,' he finds, 'are very naturally called *hári*, or *harít*, bright and brilliant' (*L* II, 370). Yet, my point is that, for Müller's listeners, what is 'very natural' (reasonable) and what is 'mythological' must have become rather difficult to tell apart by this point, no matter how evident the presented connections may appear. For, one effect of his explanations is that the bright horses, whether they refer to animals or the sun and the dawn, keep running away with the root from which they have sprung, as Müller himself inadvertently suggests after he has chronicled another addition to the paradigm. 'But who can keep the reins of language? The bright ones, the *Harits*, run away like horses, and very soon they who were originally themselves the dawn, or the rays of the Dawn, are recalled to be yoked as horses to the car of the Dawn' (*L* II, 370–1).

Language and Practice

What should have become clear, then, is that Müller's writing, as perhaps all etymology, has a tendency to be carried away with, and by means of, the same metaphorical language whose structures it attempts to map out.[32] Therefore, the only way of recognising the logic of what Müller says is to go along with the grain of his writing, to follow the intricate paths travelled by his text. As soon as one attempts to paraphrase this text in the form of an abstract theory or a set of linguistic (scientific) propositions, however, it will lose most of its persuasiveness and appeal; for much of the logic of what it says is closely tied up with the speaking (writing) activity through which it is conveyed. As a result, Müller's argument resists the attempt to be separated from the performance through which it is put forth. The reason of what he says refuses to be abstracted from the process of how it is said. Instead, it seems to be dependent on exemplification, on the practice of assembling catalogues which are gathered up to show the listener (reader) what he cannot be told in more abstract terms.

What this suggests is that the logic of Müller's lectures is inextricably entwined with the process of making it work. In fact, the sheer success of his public talks, occasionally attended by such well-known Victorians as J. S. Mill and Lord Tennyson,[33] seems to support his professed view of language as an organic form which cannot be arrested in a set of 'independent substantial' (or objective) facts. 'Language exists in man, it lives in being spoken,' as he says, 'it dies with each word that is pronounced, and is no longer heard. It is a mere accident that language should ever have been reduced to writing, and have been made the vehicle of a written literature' (*L* I, 47).

Yet, this dismissal of the written word as an accidental 'supplement' that 'breaks with' the 'Nature' of speech is no excuse,[34] as I hope to have shown, to ignore the printed version of Müller's lectures, as unconvincing and outdated as some of their contents may appear. It may rather serve as an incentive to read them as documents of a verbal activity that is animated by an essentially practice-based reason which refuses to be placed or captured, because it 'disappears into its own action, as though lost in what it does, without any mirror that re-presents it: it has no image of itself.'[35] One might say that what one can read by following Müller's writing is the becoming thought of language through rhetorical practice. With this practice-based conception in mind, it seems appropriate that Müller uses the word 'experiment', out of all others, in order to 'show that reason cannot become real without speech' (*L* II, 73). This suggests that, in practice, Müller knew, if only tenuously or unconsciously, that the reason made real by means of his speech is an experimental reason that is immersed in, and inseparable from, the activity of going through the verbal material he seeks to understand and expound. 'Let us take any word, for instance, *experiment*,' he writes.

> It is derived from *experior*. *Perior*, like Greek *perân*, would mean to go through. *Perītus* is a man who has gone through many things; *perīculum*, something to go through, a danger. *Experior* is to go through and come out (the Sanskrit *vyutpad*); hence *experience* and *experiment*. The Gothic *faran*, the English *to fare*, are the same words as *perân*; hence the German *Erfahrung*, experience, and *Gefahr*, periculum; *Wohlfahrt*, welfare, the Greek *euporía*. (*L* II, 73)

To learn by experience is to traverse a field of play in which risk and luck, disappointment and success, *Gefahr* and *Wohlfahrt* are still assembled, side by side, in one and the same space. Concomitantly, to enter this field means to become engaged in a practice of comparing and contrasting, sifting and sorting, whose outcome is yet unknown. The goal of Müller's text is to demonstrate that language is reason and reason is language, but my point is that in order to attain this goal, his writing had to pass through an extended site of word construction, an experimental field in which thought is still in the process of becoming speech.

Müller's *Lectures*, then, represent an activity of working through a language that functions both as its tool and as its subject-matter. His lectures speak from the inside of a medium in the formation of which they participate. As a result, Müller's writing is characterised by two mutually opposed tendencies. On the one hand, there is a clear and self-avowed attempt to take hold of language, to grasp the allegedly objective reason that ensures that it exists and persists as a self-contained system, clearly distinct from non-linguistic noise. On the other hand, there is a drift towards never-ending bifurcation and metonymic displacement that seems to be produced through the very endeavour to understand the logic of speech. The structure of what he says is continually overtaken by the process of saying it. Müller's writing, in other words, is made to run along with the life of the very language whose ideal grounds it seeks to locate in a set of roots. For instance, he holds that 'in the end, or rather in the beginning' of all language there is 'nothing but roots of the most general powers, meaning to go, to move, to run, to do' (*L* II, 67), which 'stand', as Müller puts it in his Darwin lectures, 'like barriers between the chaos and the kosmos of human speech'.[36] But at the same time, this emphasis on simplicity and reductive definition is counteracted by an enthusiasm for what he calls the 'poetical fiat', the process of metaphorical translation through which these general roots have been made to proliferate into a multiplicity of specific denominations (*L* II, 67). Hence his repeated presentation of lists such as the following:

> In Sanskrit, *sarit*, meaning *goer*, from *sar*, to go, became the name of river; *sara*, meaning the same, what runs or goes, was used for sap, but not for river. Thus *dru*, in Sanskrit, means to run, *dravat*, quick; but *drapsa* is restricted to the sense of a drop, *gutta*. The Latin *aevum*, meaning going, from *i*, to go, became the name of time, age; and its derivative *aeviternus*, or *aeternus*, was made to express eternity. Thus in French, *meubles* means literally anything that is moveable, but it became the name of chairs, tables, and wardrobes. (*L* II, 67)

Such catalogues can be seen to exemplify both the (vertical) attempt to gather parts into a whole, which is represented by metaphor, and the (horizontal) enumeration of parts instead of a whole, which is represented by metonymy. The lists simultaneously draw things together and take them apart, for they perform both an act of containment and comprehension and an act of spreading out and setting in motion. In this way, Müller's word-gatherings not only constitute an experimental field in which parts are made into wholes and wholes are split up into parts;[37] they also enact a practical reason that inhabits the fold between parts and wholes, integrating and disintegrating them. As the mobile verbs ('to go, to move, to run, to do') taken to be at the bottom of language suggest, this practical reason operates on variable premises which can be modified and adapted as one proceeds.[38] The reason Müller has in mind, whether he was aware of it or not, is rooted in action, for it shows itself in the skill of building ever more solid and specific referents (ideas), such as 'chairs, tables, and wardrobes' out of terms that signify flexible movements or mobile things, such as '*meubles*': 'literally anything that is moveable' (*L* II, 67).

To sum up, one can say that Müller's writing knows more than it seems to articulate. For it suggests that the thinking which makes man special is based on practical actions, on the attempt to interpret concepts as words and words as concepts, rather than on abstract ideas designated by linguistic roots. Implicitly, therefore, Müller's writing has much in common with the very scientists to whom he explicitly opposed himself – Charles Darwin and E. B. Tylor among them – because they questioned his axiomatic identification of thought with words. In line with the argument of these authors, as I will demonstrate in the remainder of this chapter, Müller's text shows, even though it does not say it, that thought begins with actions rather than with words.

This action-based view of thought is most concisely spelled out in a brief review article by Darwin's cousin Francis Galton which was written on the occasion of Müller's latest work. In this article Galton argues that there are in fact various instances in which people can be seen to be engaged in thoughtful activities that are manifestly not premised on the formation of words. The examples he provides include such activities as playing billiards, fencing, and scrambling 'in wild places',[39] all of which greatly exercise one's attention and judgement, even though they may well take place without the conception and expression of 'mental words'.[40] In fact, according to Galton, the framing of words would obstruct the nimble flow of these actions, not enhance it. 'There is no time in fencing for such a process.'[41] Thus, what Galton seeks to demonstrate is that there is a kind of practical thinking which is totally caught up in the physical processes through which it is acted out. For Galton, this practical intelligence shows itself in skilful movements which may be successfully performed regardless of whether or not their constituents can be named. As he argues, one may know how to 'pick one's way' across a 'broad torrent', jumping 'from stone to stone', even if one is 'mentally mute' during and after the accomplishment of this feat, incapable of saying exactly what one does or has done at each stage of one's acts.[42]

What Galton draws attention to, then, is the existence of a nonverbal reason, which operates 'upon quite another intellectual plane' as the use of words.[43] For him, the capacity to conceive of the world in clear and intelligent forms is not dependent on the ability to enunciate words. This case for the existence of a nonverbal reason became a key site of contention in the controversy between Müller and his opponents who often pointed to the example of deaf-mutes (then called 'the deaf and dumb'), arguing that, by Müller's logic, they would have to be regarded as incapable of abstract thought. Understandably, Müller refuses to accept this particular implication of his reasoning, claiming instead that 'the deaf and dumb certainly acquire general ideas' when they are instructed to do so (*L* II, 69–70). But he still insists that this was 'no objection' to his argument because it could be explained by the fact that deaf-mutes generally 'live in the society of other men', thus picking up 'something of their rational behaviour' too (*L* II, 70, 69). 'They are taught to think the thoughts of others, and if they cannot pronounce their words, they lay hold of these thoughts by other signs, and particularly by signs that appeal to their sense of sight' (*L* II, 70). In this way, Müller successfully reincludes deaf-mutes into the society of the speaking race, from which his argument seems to have excluded them. But at the same time he raises the question of why the natural seat of human reason should be exclusive to verbal communication if human thoughts can just as well be laid 'hold of by other signs'.

The Language of Gestures

One of the Victorian writers who did most to elucidate the relationship between verbal speech and such other modes of signification was the anthropologist E. B. Tylor who expressly regarded his own research as a critical complement to Müller's work. Like Müller's texts, much of Tylor's writing on language is driven by a fascination with all topics 'which lie close to the grand old problem', as he calls it, 'of the Origin of Language'.[44] But unlike Müller, Tylor does not locate this origin in the institution of roots, a construct which he rejects as too speculative. Instead, he turns his attention to other forms of human self-expression, namely the 'Gesture-Language and Picture-Writing'.[45] For both of these practices of signification, Tylor argues, seem to operate on an affiliation between signifiers and their referents that is far less arbitrary than it is in articulate speech. 'When a deaf-and-dumb child holds his two first fingers forked like a pair of legs, and makes them stand and walk upon the table, we want no teaching to show us what this means, nor why it is done' (*RE* 16). By contrast, as Tylor points out, the reason why humans have come to use the words 'stand' and 'go', rather than any others, to refer to these activities seems almost impossible to define: 'if we had been taught to say "stand" where we now say "go", and "go" where we now say "stand", it would be practically all the same to us' (*RE* 16). Tylor still professes himself convinced that there once was 'a sufficient reason' why these words have acquired the meanings they transmit. Yet, his point is that this reason is no longer evident to their users, since 'we have quite lost sight of the connection between word and idea' (*RE* 16). What Tylor shares with Müller, then, is a belief and interest in the reason informing linguistic signification, in the logic which ties seemingly arbitrary signifiers to the things they signify. What distinguishes him from his colleague, however, is that he does not search for this reason in the postulated existence of roots taken to embody the ultimate idea behind all speech. Rather, he claims that one can only hope to recover something of the lost connection between word and referent by studying how this connection is constructed in other types of meaning-making, such as drawing and gesturing, in which language is not, or not yet, verbal speech. To be sure, Tylor stresses that there is 'no proof' that these techniques represent an 'intermediate stage' in the history of language, which preceded man's communicating through words (*RE* 15). But his submission is that their investigation can nonetheless elucidate the practical logic of a language which otherwise appears to consist of nothing but arbitrary sounds.

Tylor's project, then, can be described as an attempt to restore the seemingly abstract system of words to the material world of experience out of which he believes it to have been framed. One offshoot of this approach is a comparatively advanced perspective on the signifying practices of people who are physically unable to utter and hear spoken words. Thus, whereas Müller views their mode of communication as a subordinate (or even deficient) version of verbal speech, which can convey no more than a vicarious image of what he takes to be the natural type of language, Tylor regards the gesture-language as a 'mother-tongue' in its own right, equal and related to, but not dependent on, the spoken word (*RE* 17). What is more, for Tylor, the gesture-language is a universal kind of communication which, to a large degree, transcends national, historical and cultural boundaries and could therefore, in its basic forms, be understood by everyone. It is, as he notes, 'the common property of all mankind' (*RE* 17), even though 'it is seldom cultivated and developed to so high a degree by those who have the use of speech, as by those who cannot speak, and must therefore have recourse to other modes of communication' (*RE* 17–18). His surmise, therefore, is that a study of how deaf-mutes make themselves understood will yield general insights into human sign-making that throw light on the special case of verbal language as well. More precisely, what fascinates Tylor about the use of gestures is that it makes visible the very transition from signifier to signified which has become invisible in most words. In this way, he argues, the gesture-language suggests a model of utterance as performance that has implications for all kinds of sign-based interaction.

Indeed, Tylor's point is that a study of communication among deaf-mutes allows one to follow the trajectories through which meaning comes into being: through which experience is translated into understandable signs. In order to make this point, Tylor presents his readers with a large amount of detailed information on the grammar of the gesture-language – partly acquired through his own field research in 'Deaf and Dumb Institutions' – which is supposed to show that gestures generally represent objects and ideas by way of enacting 'their most striking features' (*RE* 16, 15). He even draws on the theory of roots to demonstrate that the way the basic components of verbal language have been formed is 'thoroughly in harmony with the spirit of the gesture-language' (*RE* 63). Like gestures, he argues, roots generally refer to something by naming those of its qualities and activities that are perceived as outstanding. 'Thus, the horse is the *neigher*; stone is what *stands*, is *stable*; water is that which *waves*, *undulates*; the mouse is the *stealer*; an age is what *goes on*; the oar is what *makes to go*; the serpent is the *creeper*; and so on' (*RE* 63). As Tylor points out, it is by the very same logic that deaf-mutes frequently identify something by performing what it does, or by which properties it affects them. Thus, in the gesture-language, birds (he says) are what flies; fish what swims; plants what grows out of the earth; a man is represented by the action of taking off one's hat; a woman by putting a closed hand upon the breast; 'for "child" the right elbow is dandled upon the left hand' (*RE* 20). Tylor's purpose in enumerating these examples is to make explicit what, as we have seen, Müller had left implicit: that language, whether it is spoken or not, has its roots in experimental practices, rather than in abstract thoughts.

In sum, Tylor's contribution to the science of language is an attempt to replace the idealist or intellectualist model of language with a performance-based one. On his account, gestures, just as drawings, act out something about language that words hide. In this way, they show us what cannot in the same way be told: namely the activity through which things are made to speak (or made to signify) *as* meaningful and communicable thoughts. One might say that gestures, as Tylor sees them, draw out the vectors of experience by which things are translated into signs and signs are made to refer to things. He seeks to back up this perspective by presenting the reader with personal accounts by deaf-mutes, such as Friedrich Otto Kruse, whose writing is first quoted directly and then once again indirectly. For Tylor these accounts are instructive since they provide insights into what he calls 'the development of thought' (*RE* 68), the passages through which meaning travels from the material to the ideal, or from hand to head. As he puts it in his paraphrase of Kruse, what one can learn from a deaf-mute is

> how the qualities which make a distinction to him between one thing and another, become, when he imitates objects and actions in the air with hands, fingers, and gestures, suitable signs, which serve him as a means of fixing ideas in his mind, and recalling them to his memory, and that thus he makes himself signs, which, scanty and imperfect as they may be, yet serve to open a way for thought, and these thoughts and signs develope themselves further and further. (*RE* 68–9)

As this suggests, Tylor is interested in how deaf-mutes create ideal signs out of material things: how they 'open a way for thought' by converting their personal experience of 'objects and actions' into understandable figures of them, capable of being reproduced and refined. Again, he is more than aware that there is no sound evidence for an unbroken evolution in the history of language which has led directly from gestures and drawings to words. But he does avow that, to his mind, 'it seems more likely than not that there may be a similarity', as he carefully phrases it, 'between the process by which the human mind first uttered itself in speech, and that by which the same mind still utters itself in gestures' (*RE* 75).

Tylor concedes that words, unlike gestures, do not usually imitate the things to which they refer, but this does not stop him from expending considerable effort to corroborate his hypothesis of a kinship between these two instruments of human thought. To this end, he searches for traces of action in verbal speech, which could support the claim that words frequently function like gestures. For example, he identifies a number of what he calls 'concretisms, picture-words, gesture-words', such as: 'To *butter* bread, to *cudgel* a man, to *oil* machinery, to *pepper* a dish, and scores of such expressions' (*RE* 63). On his account, these words 'involve action and instrument in one word, and that word a substantive treated as the root or crude form of a verb' (*RE* 63). As a result, he seems to suggest, they work in the same way as gestures: they simultaneously represent actions which refer to things and things which are made to appear through actions. In short, they make actions like things and things like actions. Thus, one might say that such words as 'to pepper' or 'to cudgel' signify things in action, or objects in use.

For Tylor, these examples (as well as many other ones which he adduces to make the same point) lead to the conclusion that the very meaning of language contains vestiges of the material practice through which it is, and has always been, put to work. Words, as he sees them, could mean nothing without the activity of making one thing signify in terms of something else. Or as he puts it in *Primitive Culture*: 'Deep as language lies in our mental life, the direct comparison of object with object, and action with action, lies yet deeper' (*PC* I, 270).[46] On these grounds, language cannot be viewed as a product of nature, as something God-given that has always existed in a self-sufficient way. Rather, it has to be viewed as a repertoire of signs whose meaning is dependent on a practice of using it. This, moreover, is a practice which is comparable to, rather than essentially different from other arts such as cooking or baking. While one of the best-known expressions of this view can be found in Darwin's *Descent of Man*, where the author (with a nod to Horne Took) notes that 'language is an art, like brewing or baking', Tylor's argument amounts to much the same point.[47] Most emphatically, Tylor opposes the common notion, influentially propagated by Wilhelm von Humboldt, that language is an organism, at least (he specifies) so long as this notion is invoked in order to keep the capacity to speak 'apart from mere human arts and contrivances' (*PC* I, 214).

Instead, Tylor proposes to regard the use of language as one way of human meaning-making among others, comparable not only to 'hunting or fire-making' but also to painting and gesturing and the expression of affects through cries (*PC* I, 212). 'We must cease,' he argues,

> to measure the historical importance of emotional exclamations, of gesture-signs, and of picture-writing, by their comparative insignificance in modern civilized life, but must bring ourselves to associate the articulate words of the dictionary in one group with cries and gestures and pictures, as being all of them means of manifesting outwardly the inward workings of the mind. (*PC* I, 210–11)

By this account, words are not themselves thoughts. Rather, they are one means among others of engendering something – whether it be a sound, a sentence, a painting, a gesture, or a work of art – that is *like* thought. 'Indeed,' as Tylor puts this, 'the processes by which words have really come into existence may often enough remind us of the game of "What is my thought like?"' (*PC* I, 213). This implies that the meaning of words, just as that of gestures and pictures, is premised on the very analogical reason that Müller had called 'wit': on the 'quick and variable' capacity of construing and constructing similarities. Indeed, what Müller clearly shares with Tylor is an emphasis on the practices of making like, through which meaningful patterns come into being. As a result, both authors pay considerable attention to the function of metaphor as the medium and motor of these generative processes. However, one key difference between the two thinkers is that Müller limits the remit of metaphor to a self-contained realm of language ideally bounded by roots, whereas Tylor regards it as a kind of hub or turnstile by virtue of which different 'modes of existence' are connected.[48] As Tylor argues, since metaphor 'transfers ideas from hearing to seeing, from touching to thinking, from the concrete of one kind to the abstract of another', it can 'make almost anything in the world help to describe or suggest anything else' (*PC* I, 213). Thus conceived, metaphor, along with the 'imitative faculty' on which its use is premised (*PC* I, 194 and generally), is not confined to verbal language, but constitutes a passage through which language can be seen to pass into other, 'more simple and rude means of communication', such as painting and gesturing (*PC* I, 212).

Indeed, for Tylor, the unavoidable presence of (more or less) metaphorical constructions in almost all types of discourse, except perhaps for mathematics, is testament to the fact that language has not ideally been made for the expression of pure, self-contained thought. Instead, he takes it to prove 'that the language of civilized men is but the language of savages, more or less improved in structure, a good deal extended in vocabulary, made more precise in the dictionary definition of words' (*PC* II, 403). Accordingly, Tylor views the capacity to speak neither as an organic part of human nature nor as an embodiment of divine design, but as the outcome of a centuries-long career of makeshift and improvisation in which the formation of experience and imagination through the use of metaphor played a key role. 'The language by which a nation with highly developed art and knowledge and sentiment must express its thoughts on these subjects,' he notes 'is no apt machine devised for such special work, but an old barbaric engine added to and altered, patched and tinkered into some sort of capability' (*PC* I, 216–17). One might call this an experimentalist theory of language, since it foregrounds the practical work of skill as well as the temporal passage, or the learning process, through which experience is 'patched and tinkered into' meaningful forms.

Notes

1. Butler, *Life and Habit*, p. 87.
2. Ibid., p. 87.
3. See Richter, *Human Beasts*, pp. 17–61.
4. Huxley, 'Man's Place', pp. 155–6.
5. Ferguson, *Language*, p. 26.
6. Trench, *Study of Words*, p. 28.
7. Ibid., p. 20.
8. *Cambridge Bible*, Genesis 2: 19–20.
9. Trench, *Study of Words*, pp. 20–1.
10. Ibid., p. 20.
11. Ibid., p. 20.
12. Derrida, 'Animal', pp. 384–90.
13. Ibid., p. 386.
14. Trench, *Study of Words*, p. 21.
15. Cf. Agamben, *The Open*, pp. 12, 23–7.
16. Trench, *Study of Words*, p. 20.
17. As Harris ('Introduction', p. viii) notes, in the middle of the nineteenth century, 'the debate' on this question 'raged to such an extent that in 1866 the Societé de linguistique de Paris instituted a regulation refusing to accept any paper on that subject for presentation or discussion'.
18. Ingold, *Perception*, p. 392.
19. Farrar, *Essay*, p. 35.
20. Ibid., pp. 34, 40–1.
21. Ibid., p. 46.
22. Ibid., p. 3.
23. Ibid., p. 46.
24. Müller, *Lectures on the Science of Language*, 2 vols, 1861 and 1864, I, 7 and generally. All references to this edition (*L*) are given by volume and page number.
25. Müller, 'Mr Darwin's Philosophy. Third Lecture', p. 8. This is one of three additional lectures motivated by Darwin's remarks on language in *The Descent of Man*.
26. For the wider historical ramifications of this argument about language as a boundary between human reason and animal instinct see Radick, *The Simian Tongue*, pp. 15–49, 50–83.
27. Müller, 'Metaphor', pp. 621–2.
28. Ibid., p. 621.
29. Ibid., p. 621.
30. Abberley, *English Fiction*, p. 14. 'Language vitalism,' Abberley explains, 'assumed that language signified through a living inner essence that directed its growth through history' (p. 14). Two famous early exponents of this view were Jean-Jacques Rousseau and Johann Gottfried Herder (pp. 14–18).

31. There are no indications that Müller himself was trammelled by this situation, perhaps because he was so firmly convinced, as Dowling ('Victorian Oxford', p. 174) has suggested, of the natural co-operation of speech and reason that he regarded the danger of being misunderstood as a negligible risk.
32. As Willer, *Poetik*, shows, there has always been inherent in the very method ('Verfahren') of etymology a potential to irritate and disturb ('Verstörungspotential') the acknowledged meaning of words (p. 27).
33. Dowling, *Language*, p. 160.
34. Derrida, *Grammatology*, p. 151.
35. Certeau, *Practice*, p. 82.
36. Müller, 'Mr Darwin's Philosophy of Language. Second Lecture', p. 671.
37. A comparison of metaphor and experiment is undertaken in Specht, 'Experiment'. For the role of metaphor in science more generally see Harré and Martin, 'Metaphor'.
38. As Elkana has pointed out, this practical reason 'has always been with mankind', preceding and surrounding the theoretical or 'epistemic reason' like its shadowy and frequently unloved twin ('A Programmatic Attempt', p. 48).
39. Galton, 'Thought', p. 29.
40. Ibid., p. 28.
41. Ibid., p. 29.
42. Ibid., p. 29.
43. Ibid., p. 29.
44. Tylor, '[Review]', p. 407.
45. Tylor, *Researches*, pp. 14–54 and 83–106. This edition (*RE*) will henceforth be quoted in the text.
46. Tylor, *Primitive Culture*. All references to this edition (*PC*) are given by volume and page number.
47. Darwin, *Descent*, p. 108.
48. The term is borrowed from Latour, *An Inquiry*.

Chapter 6

William Morris's 'Work-Pleasure': Literature, Science and Fine Art

The Making of Fine Art

In Müller's lectures, as the preceding chapter has shown, language frequently appears as a self-regulative process that emancipates itself from its speakers and operates according to its own laws. His example may therefore be taken to show that, in the Victorian period, the very attempt to identify the roots of language with a structure of reasonable thought could often cause the medium of verbal communication to divide into a set of ideal signifiers on the one hand and a world of empirical referents on the other. While this division may not immediately have evoked the 'spectre of an autonomous language' or ushered in 'a linguistic crisis',[1] it certainly contributed to a refreshed awareness of the contingent (and hence fragile) connection between words and things. In fact, Edward Tylor's endeavours to reconcile the increasingly idealised meaning of words with the material practice of gesturing and drawing may already be seen as an attempt to (re)connect the specialised concept of 'language as thought' with a more general notion of 'meaning-making as practical work' that encompassed both verbal speech and various other ways of translating experience into signs. In this way, the use of language was reintegrated into the very meshwork of activities, out of which other philologists sought to abstract it by defining the realm of words as the epitome of a transcendental system of intelligent (and specifically human) thought.

Yet, such differences notwithstanding, what all nineteenth-century contributions to the discussion of the nature and organisation of human speech had in common was that they participated in the reconception of a medium, namely language, whose grounds and purposes were widely perceived to be in need of elucidation. The gradual rise of philology as a science was just as much implicated in this reconception of language as the emergence, often said to have occurred during roughly the same period, of a special sense of 'literature' as specifically 'imaginative' writing. Thus, according to Michel Foucault, the establishment of this narrow concept of 'literature' was a response, among other things, to what he calls the 'demotion of language to the mere status of an object'.[2] 'Literature,' thus conceived, 'is the contestation of philology' because it represents a way of working with language that deliberately refuses to make its meaning known in abstract terms.[3] When language became an object of research, as Foucault puts it, 'it was also reconstituting itself elsewhere, in an independent form, difficult of access, folded back upon the enigma of its own origin and existing wholly in reference to the pure act of writing'.[4]

More specifically, this reconstitution of language in the form of literature (sometimes written with a capital 'L') has often been associated with the historical discourse of Romanticism which is generally taken to be responsible for 'the fact that "literature"', as one eminently quotable phrase has it, 'meant one thing in 1780 – the whole array of educated genres from natural philosophy and history to poetry and drama – and something very different after 1820 (the restricted category of imaginary genres we know today)'.[5] Before the Romantic period, and for quite some time afterwards, it was the term 'poetry' in particular that came closest to the meaning later occupied by 'literature'.[6] Like literature in the 'restricted' sense of creative or imaginative text, poetry, which could, in principle, encompass both prose and verse,[7] had long been defined, in Philip Sidney's phrase, as an 'Arte' of 'making things either better than Nature bringeth forth, or, quite anewe'.[8] Similarly, in 1821, Percy B. Shelley referred to poetry as an 'exercise of the imagination' that 're-produces all that it represents', making 'familiar objects as if they were not familiar'.[9] Both of these famous descriptions of poetry include what came to be regarded as one of the defining qualities of literature in the strong sense, namely the capacity and licence to make the commonplace appear thought-provokingly strange or 'quite anew'. Crucially, however, neither of them limits the meaning of poetry to the mode of writing,[10] the rise of which is inseparable from the changing conception of literature. As Clifford Siskin has shown, one of the most profound social and cultural shifts taking place in the eighteenth and early nineteenth centuries was a massively growing 'proliferation of writing' that functioned as a 'technology' of boundary making.[11] The 'work' performed by this pervasive technology, Siskin argues, 'was to constitute new classification systems' that could serve as a basis for the disciplinary actions of professionals and specialists.[12]

Medical practice, for example, came to be increasingly regulated by being preserved in manuals and guidebooks that defined the behaviour deemed appropriate for expert doctors.[13] Likewise, the study of literature was more and more subordinated to educational schemes based on written 'standards of literacy' and 'chronologies of "great" works'.[14] As part of this process, any mode of what was considered to be specifically creative writing could find a 'disciplinary home' in the newly institutionalised domain of 'literature'.[15] By this account, the specialised category of literature, like many other social domains, came into being as a result of being 'written up – hierarchically up – as referring solely to special kinds of deeply imaginative writing', as Siskin puts it.[16] 'What we think of as Victorian professionalism', including professional authorship, 'had to be written up, word by word, before it became "real" and widespread.'[17]

One effect of this tendency towards the professionalisation of skills and the classification of subject areas fuelled by the proliferation of writing was a transformation of work itself which was redefined internally, by being more strictly divided into manual and intellectual labour, as well as externally, by being separated from art. At the same time, art, too, underwent a change in meaning by being reconceived as a specifically aesthetic practice: as fine art. In this way, art was not only supposed to be clearly separated from science, but also from the so-called mechanical arts, of which we would perhaps speak as applied sciences today. Because much of this work of constructing divisions and hierarchies was performed, as I said, in writing, this chapter has two goals. Firstly, I shall follow a small selection of the writing that participated in the setting-up of the boundaries that were supposed to define the aesthetic as a specific property of the fine arts, including literature or poetry in the narrow sense. Secondly, I shall try to reintegrate the idea of the fine arts into the net of work, or network, through which the sphere of the aesthetic remained entangled with a variety of technologies and skilful practices – including the use of experimental methods in the sciences – from which it was increasingly supposed to be kept apart.

In this way, I hope, among other things, to reactivate a broader and older notion of art as a craft of making, or as an activity that does not (yet) have the status of an (aesthetic) object or an accomplished (scientific) form. In the nineteenth century, as has been argued, this understanding of art as a practical 'exercise of skill', which was central to the self-conception of the arts and crafts movement, was more and more divorced from a supposedly more modern notion of art as 'fine art', as the embodiment of an aesthetic idea, or an idea of the aesthetic.[18] Concomitantly, the work of art was now often taken to refer primarily to a finished product, viewed in isolation from the productive process, the technical work, by way of which it was brought into being and put to meaningful use. As Raymond Williams has explained, the main reason for this separation of '(fine) art' from '(technical) work' may be found in an increasing industrialisation and economisation of traditional arts and crafts like weaving or engraving.[19] In Williams's account, these changes in the work environment gave rise to the need to define and protect a social niche in which the creative propensities of human agency could still be exercised independently from and unconstrained by the forces of market value and machine power. 'The fine arts' thus came to epitomise, at least in theory, a kind of counter-productivity, a free movement of the creative imagination in which the human capacities to make meaningful objects could be employed for their own sake, regardless of their economic purpose and practical use.[20] The result, Williams argues, was a division between art and labour as well as between aesthetic and financial value, and between the mass-produced commodity and the singular work. 'The artist is then distinct [. . .] not only from *scientist* and *technologist* – each of whom in earlier periods would have been called artist – but from *artisan* and *craftsman* and *skilled worker*, who are now *operatives* in terms of a specific definition and organization of work' as wage labour.[21]

What is more, this elevation of the artist to an emphatically fine artist – as well as the concomitant demotion of the artisan and craftsman to a mechanical operator – can be seen as 'symptomatic of a general tendency to distinguish intellectual from manual labour, along the common axis of a more fundamental series of oppositions between mind and body, creativity and repetition, and freedom and determination'.[22] An example of this tendency to map the specificity of the fine arts upon a more general distinction between rule-bound fabrication and inventive design can be found in the ninth edition of the *Encyclopaedia Britannica* which includes not only (as we have seen) an entry on 'Art', but also a separate and much longer one on 'Fine Arts'. These fine arts, namely painting, sculpture, music, poetry and (with reservations) architecture, are here defined as 'arts which exist independently of practical necessity or utility', with all of their other properties said to be 'implied in, or deducible from, this one fundamental character'.[23] More precisely, the fine arts are characterised as 'superfluous or optional' (*EB* 199), or as a set of occupations in which people engage not, or not only, because they must or ought, but because they like to do so – because it pleases them, as the author points out with a reference to Schiller's concept of play. 'Fine art is to mankind what play is to the individual, a free and arbitrary vent for energy which is not needed to be spent upon tasks concerned with the conservation, perpetuation, or protection of life' (*EB* 199).

As the article stresses, the making of a piece of fine art, being an open form of play, must therefore be seen as an activity that is not fully controlled by pre-determined 'rules' and 'ends' (*EB* 197). Instead, according to the *Encyclopaedia*, the '*performance*' of a work of fine art, although '*calling for premeditated skill*', is only '*capable of regulation up to a certain point, but, that point passed, has secrets beyond the reach and a freedom beyond the restraint of rules*' (*EB* 201). This means that the recipient of a work of art can 'account for, analyse, and, so to speak, tabulate the effects of' a piece of art only 'so far', the text has it, 'as rules, precepts, measurements, and other communicable laws or secrets can carry the artist' (*EB* 198). The point the *Encyclopaedia* seeks to make, then, is that both the production and the interpretation of fine art by definition involve secrets which resist elucidation. In fact, the article claims it to be nothing less than 'essential' to an art work to be partly premised on principles and goals which are inexplicable (*EB* 198). Why and for what purpose a piece of fine art is made as it is made can, on this account, never be quite spelled out. Rather, as forms of play – in contrast to forms of necessity and duty – all instances of fine art are said to retain an element of contingency, which makes them 'independent of utility', a term that is repeatedly highlighted in the marginal glosses of the text (*EB* 197). By this logic, the structure and appearance of works of fine art, the way they are composed, cannot be understood by recourse to predefined norms and functions alone. Instead, there is something singular about them (the author argues) by virtue of which they could, at least in part, just as well have been made otherwise or not at all.

No doubt, this argument that the special quality of fine art results from its ontological and functional non-necessity, from the secrecy of its ultimate motivation and purpose, is an equally thoughtful and influential one, parts of which are still often presupposed and reproduced today. This view is, however, premised on the assumption that the motivations and purposes of all other kinds of art and craft, from pottery to gardening and glassmaking, can be fully articulated in propositional terms. Thus, in order to keep the fine arts in their distinctive place, the *Encyclopaedia* article is at great pains to demonstrate that the work of gardeners, carpenters or builders is wholly governed by at least one 'useful end' which is taken to be, by definition, 'determinate' and 'prescribed' (*EB* 197). Strategically, this assumption is vital because it enables the author to conclude that the art of carpenters or gardeners has to be excluded from the domain of the fine arts, it being (said to be) mainly an instrument to attain a predefined end. 'To every end which is determinate and prescribed there must be one road which is the best. Skill in any useful art means knowing practically, by rules and the application of rules, the best road to the particular ends of that art' (*EB* 197). The point the article seeks to convey here is twofold: there is only one best road to reach a certain goal, and therefore this road can be defined in terms of a guidebook or a manual of rules that everyone may follow 'blindly', regardless of their inventive capacities. While this may sound logical, it reduces the 'skill' of the worker to a mere rule-following activity, an implementation of predefined sequences marking the most efficient path to a certain end. In this way, the 'useful' or 'serviceable' arts (*EB* 211) are supposed to be associated, if not equated, with the so-called 'mechanical arts', a group of practices in which the art of the worker can, in principle, be replaced by a machine (*EB* 198). One might therefore say that the *Encyclopaedia*'s attempt to define the specificity of the fine arts in opposition to a mode of useful work participates in the very economisation and mechanisation of traditional skills and crafts that, on Williams's account, had produced the need to delineate a social space for the free expression of individual creativity in the first place.

Yet, the sheer length and intellectual effort that the article requires to set up and justify the distinction between the serviceable and the fine arts suggests that in practice the relationship between these groups was still far more fluid than it was increasingly made out to be in theory. For example, the article is repeatedly compelled to draw attention to a wide range of 'dexterities and industries', from weaving to 'joiner's work', which are expressly said to be 'more than mere dexterities and industries because they add elements of beauty and pleasure to elements of serviceableness and use' (*EB* 201). To be sure, the author insists that in these intermediate cases of artwork it is always possible to distinguish 'the part which is beautiful or pleasurable from the part which is mechanical or merely useful' (*EB* 194). But at the same time he has to admit that such discrimination is 'often no easy task' (*EB* 201). As a result, the entry cannot help reincluding into the very process of defining the fine arts a panoply of so-called 'lesser or auxiliary arts', from 'pottery, glassmaking, goldsmith's work and jewellery' to 'eloquence' and 'gardening', that it seeks to exclude from the domain of the purely aesthetic, or 'the greater fine arts' (*EB* 201). What this suggests is that, at the time the ninth edition of the *Encylopaedia* appeared, 'fine art' was not yet a definite concept, firmly attached to a particular place on a well-ordered map of social sectors or systems. Rather, it still seems to have been mixed up among a variety of skills in the exercise of which usefulness and playfulness were often closely entwined.[24] 'Where are the Fine Arts to be found, and put under a scrutiny?', one puzzled contributor to *Blackwood's Edinburgh Magazine* asks in 1853, implying as much. 'There are conditions of art so contradictory, and all demanding supremacy, that I am at a loss where or how to look these real or allegorical personages, "The Fine Arts", in the face.'[25]

Art, Work, Pleasure

Of course, one social place 'where' one could try to look 'The Fine Arts' in the face were some of the newly founded art museums, especially the National Gallery in London which opened in 1838.[26] Yet, while the rise of the public museum certainly reinforces the argument that the domain of (fine) art became increasingly separated from, and purified of, the dirt and disorder of the (mechanical) workshop, there is evidence that this division did not remain unchallenged. For example, one influential expression of resistance against it is represented by the arts and crafts movement, a loose group of artisans and writers, which formed around a common interest in the so-called lesser or decorative arts, especially in the techniques of adorning and embellishing that often accompany the processes of making useful things. As John Ruskin and William Morris argued, these decorative practices can be taken to show that the values of serviceableness and pleasure have never been separate, but have always emerged from one and the same exercise of skill.[27] Ruskin, for example, in a lecture on 'The Relation of Art to Use', makes the case that 'the moment we make anything useful thoroughly, it is a law of nature that we shall be pleased with ourselves, and with the thing we have made; and become desirous therefore to adorn or complete it, in some dainty way, with finer art expressive of our pleasure'.[28] Likewise, Morris claims that the desire to be delighted by well-made patterns has always been part and parcel of the need to make useful things – an argument that he finds confirmed by the experience that decorative, playful, ornamental or otherwise non-necessary elements can be observed in almost all (not just in some) fields of human labour and life. 'To give people pleasure in the things they must perforce *use*, that is one great office of decoration; to give people pleasure in the things they must perforce *make*, that is the other use of it.'[29] On this view, the service-value of a product is enhanced if the activity of making and using it generates enjoyment. Work that does not give pleasure, Morris argues, is relatively useless while pleasure, conversely, can only be gained from works that are experienced as useful, or that are actively made to yield serviceable effects. For Morris, an artist is therefore no more than 'a workman who is determined that, whatever else happens, his work shall be excellent'.[30] Thus conceived, the work of all artists deserving that name will in some measure have decorative parts, 'the decoration of workmanship' being 'but the expression of man's pleasure in successful labour'.[31]

In sum, the point Morris seeks to make is that the values of pleasure (or beauty) and use are not extraneous to each other, but grow out of one and the same process of successfully producing work that is excellently, rather than just economically, adapted to its purpose. 'I beg you to remember,' as he puts this, 'that nothing can be a work of art which is not useful; that is to say, which does not minister to the body when well under command of the mind, or which does not amuse, soothe, or elevate the mind in a healthy state.'[32] According to Morris, much of the fripperies displayed in drawing-rooms and parlours can, by this definition, not be counted as works of art because they have long ceased to be useful and were instead allowed to fall into a condition of practical neglect. For him, such neglect is testament to nothing less than a widespread 'stupidity', one outcome of which is that 'the kitchen in a country farmhouse is most commonly a pleasant and homelike place, the parlour dreary and useless'.[33] What Morris clearly opposes, then, is a conception of art which segregates the work as product from the creative processes (of construction and interpretation) through which its meaning and value is made out.[34] This may explain why he preferred the work which is performed in the lively and pleasant, if messy and noisy, 'kitchen' over that which is exhibited in the clean and ordered, but dreary and (often largely) unused 'parlour'.

More specifically, Morris sees the work of art, both process and product, as a toggle between what he calls 'the mood of idleness' and 'the mood of energy', two complementary conditions which he associated with memory and hope respectively.[35] On his conception, this is the end of engaging in art work: 'the end proposed by a work of art is always to please the person whose senses are to be made conscious of it', as he argues in his essay on 'The Aims of Art':

> It was done *for* some one who was to be made happier by it; his idle or restful mood was to be amused by it, so that the vacancy which is the besetting evil of that mood might give place to pleased contemplation,

dreaming, or what you will; and by this means he would not so soon be driven into his workful or energetic mood: he would have more enjoyment, and better.[36]

As this quotation suggests, people engage in or with art work because it makes them happier. But at the same time the happiness elicited by such work seems to be, for Morris, a transitory experience, such that the state of pleased fulfilment or contemplation is likely, sooner or later, to become an incentive to produce or consume more of this work, so as to 'have more enjoyment, and better'. In fact, as Morris describes it, part of the delight of producing and consuming art issues precisely from the experience that the happiness it promises can never quite be attained. Rather, what motivates the continued production of art-work seems to be that human beings can always perform more and other activities than they must perform in order to stay alive, even though they do not have to do so. Morris therefore insists that the very existence of art is premised on the fact that human beings are, to some extent, free to cultivate and fulfil their physical needs in whatever fashion pleases them most, rather than in just the way that is dictated to them by some instinct or outside force. 'In other words, I believe that art cannot be the result of external compulsion,' as he puts this himself, 'the labour which goes to produce it is voluntary, and partly undertaken for the sake of the labour itself, partly for the sake of the hope of producing something which, when done, shall give pleasure to the user of it.'[37]

Like the *Encyclopaedia* article, then, Morris locates the defining feature of art in its non-necessity, in its being made out of a capacity – call it 'imagination' – which enables humans to take liberties, to play, if only to a tiny extent, with whatever circumstances or powers may exert their pressures on each individual act. Unlike the *Encyclopaedia*, however, he does not limit this play of the imagination to a special group called 'fine arts' which are supposedly 'independent of utility'. Instead, he promotes an inclusive notion of 'art' according to which artful practice is, by definition, never without use. One can therefore say that art, as Morris sees it, has many *possible* uses, the ever-fresh working-out of which generates pleasure. As Morris urges his readers, what should be understood clearly is that

> this production of art, and consequent pleasure in work, is not confined to the production of matters which are works of art only, like pictures, statues, and so forth, but has been and should be part of all labour in some form or other: so only will the claims of the mood of energy be satisfied.[38]

This conviction that 'sensuous pleasure' has been and should be 'always present in the handiwork of the deft workman when he is working successfully' explains Morris's fascination with medieval artisans who, for him, epitomise a way of working in which the maker and the made are lovingly related to each other in a kind of dynamic entanglement or embrace.[39] The increase in mass production, by contrast, has (according to Morris) divided the worker from his work, making him indifferent about it as a result. The upshot of this development, he argues, is a society in which wares are no longer treated 'as things to be handled, looked at – used, in short, but simply as counters in the great game of the world-market'.[40] Therefore, what, to Morris's mind, was most urgently needed was that the fine arts be realigned with the handicrafts, from which they had, to the detriment of both, been dissociated in recent years.[41] As Morris argues, 'the handicraftsman, left behind by the artist when the arts sundered, must come up with him, must work side by side with him',[42] so that art can become a truly popular occupation again, encompassing all possible expressions of skill. 'I do not want art for a few, any more than education for a few, or freedom for a few.'[43]

One of the most notable social and political implications of Morris's belief in the happiness-inducing power of craftsmanship is a social order which is primarily founded on the 'soft' practical reason of art, rather than on the 'hard' propositional logic of science.[44] This stands in stark contrast to a competing narrative according to which true social advancement must, to all intents and purposes, be built on the general and hard-headed wisdom of science, whereas the products of art, as wonderful and astonishing as they are, can only ever represent a relatively primitive way of cultivating the world. One typical instance of this last narrative is William Whewell's 1851 lecture on 'The General Bearing of the Great Exhibition on the Progress of Art and Science' which presents itself as a critical after-the-event evaluation of the World Fair display in the Crystal Palace. It makes for a good counterpoint to throw Morris's position into sharper relief.

On the face of it, Whewell is full of admiration for 'the innumerable treasures of skill and ingenuity, of magnificence and beauty' from such far-flung places as 'Sincapore and Ceylon, Celebes and Java, Mengatal and Palembang' which the world fair puts on show.[45] For him, these stunning manifestations of inventiveness and 'practical knowledge' (ranging from baskets and fishing nets to ploughs and silken ware) in even what he calls 'the works of the rudest tribes' are more than enough evidence to confirm his general theory 'that man is, by nature and universally, an artificer, an artisan, an artist'.[46] In fact, on this account, 'Art', which is here used in the broad sense of 'skilful practice', is, at least historically speaking, 'the mother of Science: the vigorous and comely mother of a daughter of far loftier and serener beauty'.[47] And yet, although Whewell is clearly enamoured by the 'natural' artistry to which he sees the opulence and splendour of the exotic spectacle at the Crystal Palace bear ample witness, he nonetheless insists that much of this spectacle still represents a stage of culture which from the point of view of an industrial nation like England – from the 'lofty summit of civilized and mechanically-aided skill' – can only be judged as inferior.[48] 'Surely our imagined superiority is not all imaginary; surely we really are more advanced than they, and this term "advanced" has a meaning; surely that mighty thought of a PROGRESS in the life of nations is not an empty dream; and surely our progress has carried us beyond them.'[49]

Although Whewell's conviction, stressed no fewer than four times, that Britain is 'surely' more advanced than all the nations which are still stuck in their state of natural artistry includes a suspicious amount of protesting, his reasons for this conviction are presented as if he had not the slightest doubts. Briefly, he credits the superior position of Britain to 'the vast and astonishing prevalence of machine-work in this country' which, he argues, has a simple 'meaning': it multiplies man's natural capacities to generate artworks, his 'art-energies', enabling 'millions of purchasers' to benefit from what comparatively few machine-operators have produced.[50] Therefore, the machine, for Whewell, is an instrument of public well-being, boosting wealth and social equality whereas 'uncivilised' art (as accomplished as it may be) is associated with a 'savage' condition of tyranny and inequality in which 'tens of thousands work for one', to quote his own words.

> There Art labours for the rich alone; here she works for the poor no less. There the multitude produce only to give splendour and grace to the despot or the warrior whose slaves they are, and whom they enrich; here the man who is powerful in the weapons of peace, capital and machinery, uses them to give comfort and enjoyment to the public, whose servant he is, and thus becomes rich while he enriches others with his goods.[51]

Whewell's story of social advancement from the 'natural' to the 'mechanical' production of artifacts even suggests that the 'most modern' arts existing in Britain are the ones in which the process of making goods is entirely grounded in the propositional knowledge embodied by science. In the case of manufacturing chemical products, for example, 'Art is the daughter of Science', rather than her mother, he claims, approvingly gesturing at 'the great chemical manufactories' which had sprung up in the north of England at the time. 'These arts never could have existed if there had not been a science of chemistry; and that, an exact and philosophical science.'[52]

News from Nowhere

To resume, whereas Morris sees the increasing 'prevalence of machine-work' as the result of a degeneration in the exercise of craftsmanship and skilful work, Whewell's account runs the other way around. For him, the machine is the motor of progress through art, since it harnesses the often magnificent but always 'rude' and uneducated capacities for producing useful and decorative works in the pursuit of a greater social good. Science, in this story, has to supply the exact, general knowledge, on which the machinery of industrial modernisation is supposed to turn. In Morris's account, by contrast, the practical and experiential wisdom of art ought to constitute the main foundation of a society that he has most extensively envisaged in his utopian pastoral *News from Nowhere*. In the city-garden of Morris's fictional England, which seems to be blessed with a kind of eternal sunshine, the very concept of art has been replaced by what Richard Hammond, an old and wise man, calls 'work-pleasure'.[53] More precisely, in the utopian society, to which Hammond introduces the reader-figure called Guest, this work-pleasure has not only 'become a necessary part of the labour of every man who produces' but is also presented as a kind of 'remedy' for the 'horrible burden of unnecessary production' imposed upon people by the so-called 'labour-saving machines' (*NW* 160, 124, 125). According to Hammond, these machines, far from saving people labour, made them 'waste' it on too many 'useless' commodities demanded by the voracious 'appetite of the World-Market' (*NW* 125). In Nowhere, this market has been abolished, which means that all that is produced is produced only because it is, in one way or another, needed for an end. 'Nothing *can* be made except for genuine use; therefore no inferior goods are made' (*NW* 127). Having been liberated from the pressure to make unnecessary commodities for an indefinite market that is beyond their control, Hammond explains, the members of the new society have gained 'time and resources enough to consider', and relish, their 'pleasure in making' things for themselves and their neighbours (*NW* 127). Therefore, what is made in Morris's fictional world is just as much made for the purpose that it is supposed to serve as it is made for the joy of making it matter. The process of creating things is an integral part of the products to which it gives rise, just as the activity of making things work is an integral part of the artefacts of which it makes use.

In *News from Nowhere*, this integration of processes and products, as well as means and ends, shows itself, for instance, in the 'line of very pretty houses, low and not large, standing back a little way from the river' that Guest, the narrator, observes (*NW* 48). To the eyes of Guest, these houses look not only 'comfortable' and beautifully adapted to their purpose, but also 'alive and sympathetic with the life of the dwellers in them' (*NW* 48). Like the other buildings in *News from Nowhere*, they are not accomplished objects, divided from the life of those who give meaning and value to their existence. Rather, they seem to be animated by the inhabitants whose activities make them into purposeful structures in the first place. The process of dwelling invigorates the building in, and by means of which it takes place while the building comes alive with the mode of dwelling that it enables. Quite in the spirit of Heidegger's famous essay, dwelling and building, thus viewed, are entwined with each other in a mutually sustaining way.[54] The novel's vision of an architecture that is expressive of 'generosity and an abundance of life' (*NW* 62) can therefore be seen to encapsulate the notion of a reconciliation of art and everyday life, or building and dwelling, doing and undergoing, that is at the centre of Morris's philosophy of work.

As Carolyn Lesjak has argued, for Morris, labour, reconceived as 'work-pleasure', has the capacity to serve as a tool to repair 'the broken link between art and daily life, between the intellectual and the decorative arts' as well as between products and their production, and even between 'the different parts of the body' and its various 'emotions'.[55] In agreement with this conviction, quite firmly held by Morris, about the synthesising power of artful work, the natives of Nowhere have almost forgotten that '"nature", as people used to call it' was once regarded 'as one thing, and mankind as another' (*NW* 200). In the world of Nowhere, the life of people seems to be so well suited to its environment that art itself (meaning work-pleasure) has become natural to them. 'Nature', 'as people used to call it' no longer exists as distinct from what they make of it by means of art. Or, in the words of Regenia Gagnier: 'Nature and culture are mutually influential, all the way down.'[56] By the same token, the 'neighbours' of Nowhere consider labour and leisure to be part and parcel of, rather than separate from each other whereas the foreign visitor from Morris's Victorian London remains continuously puzzled by this 'life of repose amidst of energy; of work which is pleasure and pleasure which is work', as one of the characters, Ellen, puts it (*NW* 222).

What is indeed most puzzling about the life in this world, not only for the narrator but also for the reader, who is made to see the strange world through Guest's late nineteenth-century eyes, is that it seems to represent a perfect balance of supply and demand, pleasure and use, the natural and the artificial (cultural) as well as exertion and rest. Here, everyone knows how much they need, and no one wants more than they need. There seems to be neither waste of energy nor excess of creative or destructive force. Instead, the social order appears to have attained a condition of almost static equilibrium and harmonious exchange, an 'epoch of rest', as the alternative title has it (*NW* 41), in which everything is settled and finished, all wishes having been fulfilled. As a result, such ideas as progress and ambition, along with 'a spirit of adventure' (*NW* 174) or competition and the very thought that the present state could be otherwise, seem to be either eliminated or relegated to outsider figures such as the 'grumbler' (*NW* 173). Yet, sceptical voices such as his are quickly silenced by the majority who believe that the world could never be, or have been, better than it currently is. In Nowhere, in short, society has reached what the text itself calls its 'second childhood' (*NW* 162), a mode of being in which, except for a couple of exceptions, nobody has any reason to call their present condition into doubt, or to be uncertain, apprehensive or curious about what the future might bring.

One way of coming to terms with *News from Nowhere*, therefore, is to describe it as an 'anti-novel' that deliberately refuses to be anything that could be characterised as Literature (with a capital 'l') or fine art.[57] In a world which, for the greatest part, knows neither conflict nor eventful change, 'there is no need for plot' or character development, as Patrick Brantlinger points out.[58] Therefore, he argues, Morris's text can hardly be compared with other Victorian novels that are built upon these elements.[59] More to the point, however, Morris's fiction may also be read as an experimental work that is not half as accomplished as the society that it seems to represent. In fact: '*Being some* chapters from a utopian romance,' as Lesjak quotes the novel's subtitle, 'the narrative is unfinished and fragmentary, an ongoing creation of a continuous present.'[60] Through Guest's attempts to make sense of an experience that is entirely new to him, Morris's writing, thus viewed, reincludes a strong element of curiosity and doubtfulness that is largely excluded from the world it describes. For most of the narrative, after all, Guest's first person narration enacts a mode of being uncertain about what he observes, of not quite knowing how it ought to be judged and whether it can be trusted at all. Hovering between two versions of the same place, as well as between the past and the future, he inhabits an ephemeral and transitional state, an experimental field in which experiences are still in flux and in which the unknown and ill-known is yet to be transformed into, or made to correspond with, what is already known. Read as an exploratory text, rather than as a political romance based on a pre-defined idea of which form it must take, Morris's writing appears much more adventurous and forward-looking, but also tentative and unresolved, than is suggested by the manifestly pre-industrial flavour of the happy and seemingly accomplished world it creates.[61] In fact, Morris was not even wholeheartedly opposed to technological innovation and the use of machines,[62] even though, on the whole, his integrative vision of a society based on work-pleasure certainly resisted the idea of a machine-powered modernisation based on a division of labour that created the need to preserve a special place for fine art, apart from all kinds of useful work.

Secrets of Art

To complete the picture, one should add that, as a kind of false compromise between the two positions represented by Whewell and Morris, the fine arts were sometimes woven into the technocratic progress narrative (embraced by Whewell), as Rachel Teukolsky has shown.[63] In this view, the fine arts were described as a direct upshot of cultural advancement, born out of an increased need of sensual sophistication that came with the prosperousness created by an economy based on industrial work.[64] The description of Henry Weekes, author of *The Prize Treatise on the Fine Arts Section of the Great Exhibition of 1851*, celebrated sculptor of portrait-busts and later Professor of Sculpture at the Royal Academy, is typical of this idea: 'As nations advance, labour and enterprise create wealth, and society becomes in consequence more artificial in its phases, employments more numerous and varied, customs and manners more costly and refined,' Weekes writes in his *Prize Treatise* on the Great Exhibition (1852) which he later reused in his *Lectures on Art*. 'By the wealth thus gained, man seeks to surround himself with luxuries of all kinds; every sense or feeling with which he is gifted must not only be gratified, but its power, as far as possible, increased.'[65] Advancing modernisation, by this logic, generates wealth, making customs and manners 'more costly and refined'. This, Weekes claims, leads to a growing demand for 'luxuries' by means of which the senses can be stimulated and educated. In this way, by being interpreted as a moral and aesthetic complement of material progress, the creation of fine art could be presented as if it were an integral component and, indeed, a necessary consequence of a market and machine-propelled economy. As Teukolsky notes, this view was well suited to 'the ideology' of the Great Exhibition, which placed its 'Fine Arts' exhibits in the midst of sections on 'Raw Materials and Produce', 'Machinery' and 'Manufacture' and thus 'wedded' the notion of the aesthetic 'with new technologies of mass-production'.[66] The 'hope' that drove this marriage of the mechanical and the aesthetic, she concludes, 'was that manufacturers would learn a lesson of taste from the styles of fine arts displayed at the Exhibition, taking these home to make their objects more beautiful, and hence, more marketable'.[67]

To sum up, what I hope to have suggested so far is that the multifaceted concept of 'art', despite all attempts to purify it, remained deeply entangled in a complex net of work in which literary, aesthetic, scientific, economic and mechanical activities and technologies were mixed up with each other, vying for precedence. As a result, the meaning of 'art', including 'fine art', could not (easily) be separated from the practical endeavours and technical means through which various expressions of skill were made into, and denominated *as*, works of art, or artful works. Instead, the concept of 'work of art', which, like 'building' or 'construction', can refer both to 'a process' and to 'its finished product',[68] might perhaps be more suitably conceived of as a 'com-position', a 'coming-together' of multiple ways of performing, applying, interpreting and evaluating the human exercise of craftsmanship and skill.[69] Thus conceived, the meaning, function and value of 'art' is essentially enmeshed with, and immersed in, practical works which can be carried out in various forms and to sundry effects. In this view, the essence of art is inherent, and thus partly hidden, in the activities of meaning-making through which it is modelled into different shapes. One general proposition that I would like to extract from this process-based conception of art-work is that the key point made by the *Encyclopaedia*, namely that the production and reception of 'fine art' involves 'secrets beyond the reach of and a freedom beyond the restraint of rules', could be extended to all sorts of artful practice, or 'work-pleasure', in Morris's and Ruskin's sense. This means that all ways of exercising skill can be taken to be premised, if only to a tiny degree, on a 'tacit' or fluid moment, a generative 'first-person' element of imagination and practical reason which escapes, to some degree, the propositional 'third-person' viewpoint defining 'science'. By virtue of this flexible moment, one and the same exercise of skill, whether it is dancing or writing, can assume multiple functions and forms.

One of the most ambitious Victorian attempts to develop a comprehensive theory of art revolving around this 'unconscious' component is E. S. Dallas's *The Gay Science*. It includes and modifies the concerns of both the *Encyclopaedia* and William Morris while simultaneously redefining the relationship between art and science in a way that is reminiscent of, but differs from Whewell's views. Most characteristically, everything that Dallas says proceeds from the premise that the ground and end of art is neither knowledge nor ignorance, but 'life ignorant of itself, unconscious life, pleasure'.[70] By associating 'pleasure' directly with 'unconscious life', Dallas not only creates a functional distinction between art and science, arguing 'that science is for knowledge, and that art is for pleasure' (*GS* I, 91); he also gives this assumption a specifically psychological twist by locating the source of this pleasure in a 'free, unconscious play of thought', taken to be synonymous with 'imagination', which is, he claims, 'but another name for that unconscious action of the mind which may be called the Hidden Soul' (*GS* I, 305, 312). Much of the first volume of Dallas's work is engaged in the collection and exposition of examples which are supposed to demonstrate that this hidden or unconscious part of the mind really exists, even though it cannot be fully grasped in the terms supplied by conscious thought. 'The thing to be firmly seized is, that we live in two concentric worlds of thought, – an inner ring, of which we are conscious, and which may be described as illuminated; an outer one, of which we are unconscious, and which may be described as in the dark' (*GS* I, 207). As Dallas points out, this 'dark' or 'unconscious' side of human life can, for instance, be seen at work in the performances of skilled artists who pursue several activities at the same time, co-ordinating them unconsciously or 'blindly'. One of his examples is an accomplished piano player who can read complicated notes while translating them into quick and well-co-ordinated movements of his fingers. 'See how many things he can do at once,' Dallas emphatically writes.

> With both hands he strikes fourfold chords – eight separate notes; he does this in perfect time; he lifts his foot from the pedal so as to give the sound with greater fulness; meanwhile his eye, fixed on the music-book, is reading one or two bars in advance of his hand; and to crown all, he is talking to a companion at his side. (*GS* I, 223)

As Dallas argues, what all such skilful exertions show is 'that many lines of action which when first attempted require to be carried on by distinct efforts of volition become through practice, mechanical, involuntary movements of which we are wholly unaware' (*GS* I, 223–4).

All further examples in *The Gay Science* amount to this same point: that thought, when in action, often works independently of conscious reflection, and that the imagination can 'remember, brood, search, poise, calculate, invent, digest' and co-ordinate our perceptions and sensations to make them fit for our purposes without our knowing about it (*GS* I, 227). Or, in Dallas's own, typically flowery words: that 'the mind keeps watch and ward for us when we slumber; that it spins long threads, weaves whole webs of thought for us when we reck not' (*GS* I, 227). In short, the mind as a whole, as Dallas conceives it, encompasses both the known and the unknown, mediating between them through bodily practice. The mind, he notes, 'may possess and be possessed by thoughts of which nevertheless it is ignorant' (*GS* I, 313). From this general observation about the 'unobserved traffic' (*GS* I, 207) between the conscious and the unconscious dimension of human actions, Dallas constructs a particular argument about the function of art. Art, he suggests, is a skilful practice whose office, unlike that of science, is to draw out the vast unknown dimension constituting the imaginative life. It can give shape and form to the hidden life by rendering it into manageable and readable, but not necessarily scientifically knowable terms or texts. As he puts it,

> while the object of science is to know and to make known, the object of art is to appropriate and to communicate the nameless grace, the ineffable secret of the know-not-what. If the object of art were to make known and to explain its ideas, it would no longer be art, but science. (*GS* I, 315–16)

While this sentence seems to set up a clear-cut opposition between art and science, claiming that it is not the business of art 'to make known', it also emphasises that art must still be capable of 'appropriating and communicating the unknown', of making it understandable in general forms. This means that the task of art is not just to revel in the unknown (then it might as well do nothing). Rather, art ought to translate the unknown into shapes that allow for it to be communicated, disseminated and interrogated further. Whereas the task of science is to eliminate secrets that have already been identified, one might paraphrase Dallas, the task of art is to identify these secrets and make them perceptible in the first place. In short, if science is supposed to represent secrecy in terms of actual knowledge, then art represents it in terms of virtual knowledge: as something that can be registered and discussed, but is still waiting to be fully cleared up. Or in his own terms: 'The essence of art is a secret, but it is an importunate secret that insists on being flaunted before us in visible and attractive disguises. It is a secret that demands to be seen and to be known' (*GS* II, 147). So, if art makes 'importunate' secrets visible and communicable while science makes them known, then art may be described as everything that is no longer or not yet science. Art, for Dallas, is preliminary to, and excessive of, but by no means opposed to science.

Dallas therefore insists that both art and science rely on one and the same medium, namely on what he calls 'fiction'. 'Fiction', in this sense, however, is not 'the reverse of truth', as he emphasises, but defines any kind of abstraction or 'general idea' (*GS* II, 209, 216). The abstract idea of 'man', by this token, is just as much a fiction as the idea of a triangle because neither of them can fully match the multiple particularities of the empirical world. 'Man' as such does not exist, or exists only in the abstract, but this does not mean that the idea of man represents a falsehood (*GS* II, 216). What art and science are here said to have in common, then, is that both employ the medium of fiction to translate personal perceptions into impersonal terms. Both represent forms of abstracting from experience. But what distinguishes them, on Dallas's conception, is that art is free to represent experience as something singular and unknown, or not yet known, whereas science, although exploring the unknown, has to represent the personal in terms of general concepts and systems that have already been established as known. Science has to justify all of its findings, even if they are completely new, in terms of an agreed logic. By contrast, art, not having to warrant its forms in this way, may represent the unknown as an experience of being puzzled, confused or faced with an obscurity that is yet to be cleared up. If art involves any kind of knowledge, then this can therefore, on Dallas's account, only be a practical knowledge of *how* to give form to the unknown, but not the propositional knowledge *that* this unknown works according to acknowledged laws.

One can summarise all this by saying that art typically appropriates and communicates the unknown in terms that never quite converge with the known, whereas science typically appropriates and communicates the unknown in a way that represents and justifies it as known. Consequently, science always operates from a vantage point, or with a yardstick, that can be explicated in terms of what is already known, whereas the vantage point of art will always remain partly unconscious (in Darwin's sense) or caught up in a process of becoming otherwise. As this indicates, Dallas's argument resonates not only with the *Encyclopaedia*'s claim that the specificity of fine (as opposed to mechanical) 'art' resides in the secrecy involved in its production and reception; it also ties in with Morris's view of art as a process of making excellent works that give pleasure. For the pleasure of art – that which makes art pleasing – is, according to Dallas (and here Morris would have concurred), that it offers a way for people to give form to their unconscious and imaginative life, to all that which refuses to be executed in mechanical sequences because it cannot quite be determined in terms of general propositions or rules. Yet, while art, according to Dallas, partakes of the unknown it is not opposed to the (propositionally) known. Rather, art represents the becoming known of the unknown. Art is a mode of experience in the process of taking abstract forms that can then be recognised and justified as science. Thus conceived, art is, by definition, at home in the experimental field, in the mode of 'work-pleasure', through which the unknown and the known as well as the personal and the general are translated into each other. In the medium of the experimental, one might say, all science is artful while all art is potentially science.

To be sure, one might argue that the difference between artists and scientists is often that their operations pursue different ends, as G. H. Lewes notes in a series of essays that correspond well with Dallas's approach. The scientist, Lewes argues, seeks to generalise and 'systematise the abstract *relations* of things', allowing the particular qualities of these things to 'drop out of sight'.[71] By contrast, the aim of the (fine) artist – in his case it is a poet – is to bring the empirical world 'into more vivid relief' and to enrich it with his personal vision.[72] And yet, Lewes adds: 'Imagination is obviously active in both,' for both the scientific 'discoverer and the poet are inventors'. Indeed: 'to imagine a good experiment is as difficult as to invent a good fable'.[73] Like Dallas, then, Lewes emphasises that scientific and artistic works emerge from, and contribute to the constitution of, a common ground while he simultaneously acknowledges the often divergent purposes that may derive from them. In a similar manner, the critic Edward Dowden alleges that a 'great poet' is 'deeply concerned about truth, and in his own fashion is a seeker for truth',[74] but even though this suggests a clear case for the continuity of poetic and scientific ways of knowing, Dowden also concedes that the truth that a poet seeks is 'not of the speculative kind. He has his own vision of life; but we shall discover this in his works not in views and opinions, so much as in the forms and colours and movement of life itself'.[75] The aim of the poet, thus viewed, is not to 'lift' his personal experience of life 'upwards' into a safe enclosure of impersonal theories and formulae, but to present this experience in the making, or as it takes shape. Like Dallas, Dowden therefore insists that a work of art 'rests not so much on any view of life (all views of life are unfortunately one-sided) as on a profound sympathy with life in certain individual forms' – a sympathy in which 'conscious activity and unconscious energy' are intermixed. In this way, the artwork 'comes forth full, not of speculation', he concludes, but 'of life, the open secret of art'.[76] Here, again, the motivation for engaging in artful work is not located in a predetermined position, but in a secret, the secret of a generative process, an ongoing life that has to be followed because it cannot be seized in steadfast terms.

Notes

1. Dowling, *Language*, pp. xii, xi.
2. Foucault, *Order of Things*, p. 323.
3. Ibid., p. 327.
4. Ibid., p. 327.
5. Klancher, 'Romanticism', p. 524.
6. Williams, *Keywords*, p. 186. Cf. the entries on 'Poetry' and 'Literature' in the *OED*.
7. 'The distinction between poets and prose writers is a vulgar error' (Shelley, 'Defence', p. 1236).
8. Sidney, *Defence*, pp. 87, 88.
9. Shelley, 'Defence', p. 1239.
10. Shelley at least distinguishes between a very broad meaning of 'poetry', which may encompass any kind of inventive action, and a narrow one which is confined to the use of language (though not to writing). See Baker, 'Poetry'.
11. Siskin, *Work of Writing*, p. 2.
12. Ibid., p. 20.
13. Ibid., p. 108.
14. Ibid., p. 116.
15. Ibid., p. 104. On the pre-history of literature in the modern sense see Berensmeyer, *Angles*.
16. Ibid., p. 6.
17. Ibid., p. 108.
18. Williams, *Keywords*, p. 42.
19. Ibid., p. 42.
20. Ibid., p. 42.
21. Ibid., p. 42.

22. Ingold, 'Beyond Art', p. 18.
23. Unsigned Article, 'Fine Arts', *Encyclopaedia Britannica*, vol. 9, p. 196. Note that the pertinent term is 'poetry' rather than 'literature', which indicates that the latter word was still used in a broader sense. There is, in fact, no general entry on 'literature' in this whole edition, although there are articles on 'English Literature' from the Anglo-Saxon Age to the French Revolution, and on some of its more traditional genres, namely 'Romance', 'Drama' 'Fable' and, again, 'Poetry' which is defined, in an 'absolute' sense, as *'the concrete and artistic expression of the human mind in emotional and rhythmical language'* (*Encyclopaedia Britannica*, vol. 19, p. 257). All references to the 'Fine Arts' article will be given in the text above (*EB*).
24. This corresponds with Klancher's observation (*Transfiguring*, pp. 17–18) that the '"upward" transfiguring' of the arts and sciences in the nineteenth century which aimed 'toward the autonomy of each substantive term' was frequently counteracted by a 'lateral movement' which made them appear 'rather as entangled, intermediated, confusing, contingent, messy, disorderly'.
25. Unsigned Article, 'The Fine Arts and Public Taste', p. 89.
26. See Black, *On Exhibit*.
27. For a more recent version of a similar argument see Staten, 'Wrong Turn'.
28. Ruskin, *Lectures on Art*, p. 95.
29. Morris, 'Lesser Arts', p. 5.
30. Ibid., p. 23.
31. Ibid., p. 23.
32. Ibid., p. 23.
33. Ibid., p. 24.
34. Cf. Freeman-Moir, 'Crafting Experience' and Petts, 'Good Work'.
35. Morris, 'Aims of Art', p. 81.
36. Ibid., p. 82.
37. Ibid., p. 83.
38. Ibid., p. 84.
39. Ibid., p. 84.
40. Morris, 'Art and its Producers', p. 348.
41. Morris, 'Lesser Arts', p. 14.
42. Ibid., p. 14.
43. Ibid., p. 26.
44. Cf. Macdonald, *William Morris*, pp. 101–50.
45. Whewell, 'General Bearing', p. 12.
46. Ibid., p. 12.
47. Ibid., p. 6.
48. Ibid., p. 13.
49. Ibid., p. 14.
50. Ibid., pp. 14–15, 7, 15.
51. Ibid., pp. 12, 15.
52. Ibid., pp. 21, 22.

53. Morris, *News from Nowhere*, pp. 43–228 (p. 160). This edition (*NW*) will be quoted above.
54. Heidegger, 'Building'. Heidegger tries to substantiate his claim that '[b]uilding is really dwelling' etymologically (p. 68), showing that the two words have been derived from the same source.
55. Lesjak, *Working Fictions*, p. 154.
56. Gagnier, 'Preface', p. xv.
57. Brantlinger, 'Socialist Anti-Novel'.
58. Ibid., p. 42.
59. Ibid., p. 42.
60. Lesjak, *Working Fictions*, p. 167.
61. Pinkney, in 'Versions of Ecotopia', traces a couple of uses of the word 'disappointed' in order to show that Morris's text itself 'suspects' that it can appear disappointing even to people who are in sympathy with its political cause (p. 98).
62. Lesjak, *Working Fictions*, p. 155.
63. Teukolsky, *Literate Eye*, pp. 67–71. I am indebted to Teukolsky for the reference to Weekes.
64. Ibid., pp. 69–70.
65. Weekes, *Lectures*, p. 13.
66. Teukolsky, *Literate Eye*, p. 70. For the wider significance of the Great Exhibition see Young, *Globalization*.
67. Teukolsky, *Literate Eye*, p. 70. As the catalogue of the exhibition explains, the section on 'Fine Arts' was specifically dedicated to those kinds 'of art which are, in a degree, connected with mechanical processes', such as 'working in metals, wood or marble'. It was, in other words, designed to provide a forum for 'those mechanical processes which are applicable to the arts, but which, notwithstanding this, still preserve their mechanical character, as printing in colour' (*Great Exhibition*, p. 819).
68. Dewey, *Art as Experience*, p. 53.
69. Massumi, 'Prelude', p. x.
70. Dallas, *Gay Science*, I, p. 90. This edition will be quoted in the text by volume and page number (*GS*).
71. Lewes, 'Principles of Success', p. 574.
72. Ibid., p. 574.
73. Ibid., pp. 574, 573.
74. Dowden, 'Scientific Movement', p. 86.
75. Dowden, 'Mr Tennyson', p. 194.
76. Ibid., p. 194.

Chapter 7

Robert Browning's Experiment: Composition and Communication in *The Ring and the Book*

Thinking in Difficulties

As the last chapter has shown, the place of Victorian art work could not be confined to the sphere of an aesthetic that was increasingly identified with the so-called 'fine arts'. The practice of making 'art' should rather be seen as a process that was continuously extended into an open field in which the distinction between play and work, creative invention and mechanical execution was still subject to controversy and had to be repeatedly drawn and negotiated afresh. This field of controversy and negotiation is best understood as a gathering of mobile relationships between the personal and the general, the imaginary and the mechanical, the material and the ideal as well as the aesthetic and the economic. As I hope to show in the next couple of chapters, the work of art, or rather the artful work, that is represented by much Victorian literature can therefore be seen as an activity of probing and redefining these unsettled relationships, or, in short, as 'literary experimentation'.[1]

One way of writing that has been identified as a 'central genre in a period rich with an extraordinary array of generic experimentation' is the dramatic monologue, especially the version made prominent by Robert Browning.[2] What makes this a 'central' genre of literary experimentalism is that it excessively foregrounds the collective processes of composition and interpretation through which meaningful forms are assembled and brought into shape. In fact, much of Browning's writing is so demonstratively displayed as open and incomplete, as work in the process of taking form, that the only way to read it is to actively participate in it. As a result, the meaning of the 'characters' that transmit Browning's monologues, as Herbert Tucker has argued, only arises from the 'ellipses and blank spaces'[3] – Wolfgang Iser would say the *Leerstellen* – between the literal words on the page and the figural sense that readers and writers work out of these words.[4] 'Character in the Browningesque dramatic monologue emerges as an interference effect between opposed yet mutually informative discourses', to use Tucker's words, 'between an historical, narrative, metonymic text and a symbolic, lyrical, metaphoric text that adjoins it and jockeys with it for authority.'[5] Paradoxically, this means that this kind of dramatic monologue is 'anything but monological'.[6] Rather, it is a prime instance of the Victorian 'double poem',[7] as it has been described by Isobel Armstrong. 'Epistemological and hermeneutic problems are built into its very form.'[8] No other work, perhaps, could serve better to flesh out, and add to, this argument than Robert Browning's *The Ring and the Book*, which has been described as a critique 'of the Romantic ideal of a whole, closed, poetic form',[9] and as one of the foremost instances of 'empiricism in literature'.[10] Deeply concerned with what Robert Langbaum has called 'the pursuit of experience in all its remotest extensions',[11] Browning's long poem certainly seems one of 'the most ambitious literary experiments in the period'.[12]

More specifically, *The Ring and the Book* is a series of twelve dramatic monologues by various voices, each of which offers a slightly different interpretation of the same Roman murder case.[13] This case is documented in a 'square old yellow Book' that Browning discovered, as the speaker of the introductory monologue describes in detail (*RB* I.33),[14] ''Mongst odds and ends of ravage' on a Florentine rummage stall (*RB* I.53). 'Here it is, this I toss and take again; / Small-quarto size, part print part manuscript: A book in shape, but, really, pure crude fact / Secreted from man's life' (*RB* I.84–7). As 'a book in shape', the 'quarto-sized' assemblage of paperwork from which the complex structure of *The Ring and the Book* has been constructed is both a reading device, a vehicle of meaning-making and piece of raw matter, 'pure crude fact'. It is, one might say, an 'epistemic thing', 'Secreted from man's life' that represents both the secrets of a particular episode in the life of man and the means through which these secrets may be explored. Drawing lines out of this thing, Browning's *Ring*-epic, with its various first-person witness accounts, can be seen as a cycle of attempts at interpreting, or working on, the secret that is embodied by the ramshackle collection of manuscripts, letters and legal papers (most of them in Latin) making up the yellow book.[15]

Yet, as the multi-voiced and plural-minded design of the *Ring*-epic suggests, this process of working ideal meaning out of a material book, as it is enacted by the different speakers of the *Ring*-epic, is not to be seen as one of passive consumption and re-presentation. Rather, the *Ring* that has been made out of the book represents a process of active variation and intervention that blatantly lacks anything like a final shape or a privileged point of view. Thus, the first speaker, who is usually taken to act the role of the poet, famously compares the activity of drawing the *Ring*-epic out of the information represented by the yellow book with the activity of crafting a ring, a piece of jewellery, from a block of gold. Just as an ingot may be of pure gold, this analogy suggests, so the yellow book may contain 'absolutely truth, / Fanciless fact' (*RB* I.143–4). But just as the ring out of the gold, so the truth has to be worked out of the book by means of an experimental activity that inevitably mixes itself up with this truth, contaminating its purity.[16] Yes, 'From the book', the 'lingot truth' was 'dug', 'Browning' notes in the first chapter (*RB* I.457–9). 'Yes; but from something else surpassing that, / Something of mine which, mixed up with the mass, / Made it bear hammer and be firm to file / Fancy with fact is just one fact the more' (*RB* I.461–4). Like the 'artificer', in other words, who 'mingles gold / With gold's alloy, and, duly tempering both, / Effects a manageable mass, then works' (*RB* I.18–21), so the reader-artist has to add something else to the material at hand in order to make any sense or use of it. But what exactly is 'this, the something else', the first speaker asks at one point. 'What's this [. . .] which proves good yet seems untrue?' (*RB* I.699–700).

> This that I mixed with truth, motions of mine
> That quickened, made the inertness malleolable
> O' the gold was not mine,–what's your name for this?
> Are means to the end, themselves in part the end?
> Is fiction which makes fact alive, fact too? (*RB* I.701–5)

As I wish to argue, this 'something else' refers to a skilful practice, to 'motions of mine', which draw out an impure field of experimentation between matter and meaning – or between the materials in the yellow book and Browning's *Ring* – in which the writing and reading of literature, as well as the making of truth or knowledge, take place. My overall point is that this artful practice, the activity of writing and reading, is an integral part of the published result that is known as *The Ring and the Book*, not something separate from it. That is to say that the process of working with the materials supplied by the yellow book does not simply precede the product that has come out of it. Rather, this process inheres in the very relations and distinctions that make up the pluralistic form of Browning's experimental work. As a consequence, the poem keeps returning upon itself, continually rereading and rewriting the indefinite source of its own existence, namely the forensic statements and details that are collected in the Old Yellow Book.[17] Thus, if an experiment is conceived, to repeat Mill's phrase, as a process of 'varying the circumstances' in relation to which something, such as the yellow book, is perceived, then Browning's work can be called experimental in more than 'just' a metaphorical sense. Yet, this does not mean that *The Ring* represents 'science' in the sense of 'justified true belief',[18] for its writing never claims to be more than an experiment, or to represent ideas that are more than 'experimental' as defined by Slinn. Instead, Browning's variations remain as inconclusive and preliminary as an experiment that is still being set up and tried out, as Henry James suggested in his engagement with the poem: 'all the while we are in presence not at all of an achieved form, but of a mere preparation for one, though on the hugest scale'.[19]

This experimental quality of *The Ring and the Book* is introduced at the end of the first book where Browning tinkers, in a characteristic way, with a potential metaphor for his exploratory poem. 'A novel country', he proposes, somewhat abruptly beginning a new paragraph.

> A novel country: I might make it mine
> By choosing which one aspect of the year
> Suited mood best, and putting solely that
> On panel somewhere in the House of Fame,
> Landscaping what I saved, not what I saw:
> —Might fix you, whether frost in goblin-time
> Startled the moon with his abrupt bright laugh,
> Or, August's hair afloat in filmy fire,
> She fell, arms wide, face foremost on the world,
> Swooned there and so singed out the strength of things.
> Thus were abolished Spring and Autumn both,
> The land dwarfed to one likeness of the land,
> Life cramped corpse-fashion. (*RB* I.1348–60)

As this suggests, to appropriate a 'novel country' ('make it mine') by representing it solely in the 'mood' of a particular season or 'aspect of the year', means to engage in a form of poetic monoculture ('Landscaping what I saved not what I saw'). While this method may help to reconcile the internal with the external, the text argues, it tends to 'dwarf' the experience of any 'land' to an artificial 'likeness' of it, smothering the 'strength of things'. Therefore, instead of appropriating what he sees, Browning's speaker summons the ghosts of the unifying imagination only to release them as 'dwarfs' and 'goblins' that 'startle' and 'laugh' at their own creations ('Moon', 'August') and then set them on 'fire', wreaking havoc on the very concept of a finished and accomplished form.

As is well known, the crabbed and coarse imagery of such passages led contemporary critics to condemn Browning's style as 'the very incarnation of discordant obscurity'.[20] These critics contended that Browning's verse ostentatiously refuses to subordinate its vocabulary, syntax and metrical pattern to anything like a recognisable idea or 'mood'.[21] Walter Bagehot famously called the resultant form 'grotesque', as distinct from 'ornate' and 'pure',[22] and thus provided a term that has since proved 'indispensable' to any discussion of Browning's technique.[23] According to Bagehot's definition, grotesque art 'takes the type, so to say, *in difficulties*. It gives a representation of it in its minimum development, amid the circumstances least favourable to it, just while it is struggling with obstacles, just where it is encumbered with incongruities'.[24] What makes this definition 'indispensable' to any engagement with Browning's work is that it sums up well its generative and experimental quality. In other words, the notion of the grotesque is apt to capture the intuition of many (not just nineteenth-century) readers that Browning's texts are not 'beautiful' in the traditional sense that takes this term to be defined by some form of 'concordia discors' or 'unity in multiplicity'. At the same time, the early critics' use of the term grotesque indicates that Browning's writing was frequently seen to represent types and categories 'in difficulties', or in the making, rather than in shapes that are (regarded as) established or already complete.

My point, then, is that the *Ring and the Book* may be seen to exemplify a concern with incipient and evolving conditions in which 'the type', whether it is a type of being or doing, is (still) at its most flexible and fertile, susceptible to the greatest number of possible interpretations, combinations, variations and (re)appropriations. For example, it is representative of the method of composition adopted in *The Ring and the Book* that the image of 'Life cramped corpse-fashion', which seems to conclude the scenario described in the quotation above, is immediately followed, in the same verse, by the hopeful exclamation 'Rather learn and love'. In this way, the imagery of destruction and death is made to blend almost seamlessly into a quite different mood. What is more, the writing even seems to reinvigorate partly the possibility of a synthesis that it had just abandoned, as the following lines suggest:

Life cramped corpse-fashion. Rather learn and love
Each facet-flash of the revolving year!—
Red, green and blue that whirl into a white,
The variance now, the eventual unity,
Which make the miracle. See it for yourselves,
This man's act, changeable because alive!
Action now shrouds, now shows the informing thought;
Man, like a glass ball with a spark a-top,
Out of the magic fire that lurks inside,
Shows one tint at a time to take the eye:
Which, let a finger touch the silent sleep,
Shifted a hair's-breadth shoots you dark for bright,
Suffuses bright with dark and baffles so
Your sentence absolute for shine or shade. (*RB* I.1360–73)

Commentaries on *The Ring and the Book* have established that there is little reason to believe that the poem ever attains anything like 'the eventual unity' intimated here, with 'Red, green and blue' all whirled 'into a white'.[25] In fact, in keeping with this insight, the invitation to 'See it for yourselves' seems to refer just as much to the 'miracle' of a final synthesis as to 'This man's act, changeable because alive'. This suggests that the formation of unity out of variety is premised on an unpredictable activity, a contingent performance, that remains open to yield multiple results. Indeed, if an 'Action now shrouds, now shows the informing thought', then neither action nor thought alone can be seen to motivate or explain the other. In this view, thought is rather exhibited in action while action, conversely, appears to be involved in a process of becoming thought. As the speaker indicates, this means that thought and action come together in a movement of form-taking, capable of assuming manifold meanings and shades. What is outlined here, then, is the form of a 'thought in the act',[26] continually changing its appearance, 'like a glass ball with a spark a-top', in relation to the position from which it is made out.

This kind of unsettled thinking in motion is precisely what Browning's writing performs, both in this passage and throughout the whole epic. In this way, it presents the reader with a kaleido-scopic display of aspects, 'one tint at a time', that combines and intermixes 'bright with dark and baffles so / Your sentence absolute for shine or shade'. In short, what the pluralistic, multifaceted form of the poem resists is any kind of logic that is premised on absolute hierarchies and clear-cut distinctions between dark and bright, shine and shade, good and bad. Instead, these categories are shown to be mixed up in processes of travelling towards, moving away from, or blurring into each other. This concern with processes and flexible arrangements, rather than definite structures and aggregate states is already indicated in the first monologue which contains a number of meditations on the experimental form that Browning's writing is about to draw out of the materials assembled in the Old Yellow Book. In one passage, for example, the speaker muses that it had been 'Writ down for very A B C of fact' that '"In the beginning God made heaven and earth"' (*RB* I.708-09), before he embarks on an attempt to draw a conclusion from this premise:

> From which, no matter with what lisp, I spell
> And speak you out a consequence—that man,
> Man,—as befits the made, the inferior thing,—
> Purposed, since made, to grow, not make in turn,
> Yet forced to try and make, else fail to grow,—
> Formed to rise, reach at, if not grasp and gain
> The good beyond him,—which attempt is growth,—
> Repeats God's process in man's due degree,
> Attaining man's proportionate result,—
> Creates, no, but resuscitates, perhaps.
> Inalienable, the arch-prerogative
> Which turns thought, act—conceives, expresses too! (*RB* I.710–21)

The 'consequence', stripped to its syntactical bone, which Browning draws from the supposition that 'God made heaven and earth' is the 'claim' (if that is what it is) 'that man creates, no, but resuscitates, perhaps'. Before it arrives at this tentative conclusion, however, the writing goes through a convoluted process which exemplifies the very mode of growth-by-trial that it describes. Thus, Browning's syntax enacts what it represents: it does not just execute a predefined design, as God might do, but unfolds slowly and incrementally, trying out formulations ('that man / Man—'), inserting qualifiers and dashes ('as befits the made, the inferior thing,— / Purposed, since made, to grow, not make in turn'), correcting itself ('Yet forced to try and make, else fail to grow') and starting anew in different terms ('Formed to rise, reach at, if not grasp and gain'). As the passage suggests, therefore, it is this attempt to 'reach at' something good and true, 'which attempt is growth', that is described here, not its result. The text is about man as an experimenter, a learner who can only repeat 'God's process in man's due degree', since he is incapable of knowing which option is the best without testing different ones first. 'Inalienable, the arch-prerogative / Which turns thought, act—conceives, expresses too!' For God, conception and expression may be one, but for man there is a difference between the two which is, in practice, turned into a field of experimentation and trial.

Letters and Actors

My purpose in quoting this passage is to make a point that applies to the whole poem: Browning's writing never seeks to conceal the processes through which its meaning takes shape in favour of a seemingly completed structure or story that can be abstracted from them. Instead, it makes these very processes readable as part of an experimental arrangement in which the reader is asked to participate as one actor among others. For each monologue represents both a version of the circumstances that make up the murder case and at least one way of interpreting them. A particularly intriguing example is the speech of Guido's rival, the priest Caponsacchi, whose character – on the basis of the historical documents in the yellow book – can be located at various points on a continuum between selfless rescuer and lustful lover of Pompilia, depending on which aspect of his relationship to the girl is emphasised.[27] In his monologue, Caponsacchi seeks to present the board of judges, including the reader, with his views on how he became acquainted with Pompilia and why he decided, or agreed, to elope with her and thus contributed to the circumstances which eventually made Guido kill his wife.

The beginning of this plea is fairly typical for the Browningesque dramatic monologue as characterised by Tucker, since it not only begins *in medias res*, but also addresses a group of listeners, among whom the reader is included. 'Answer you, Sirs? Do I understand aright?', Caponsacchi cries in the first verse. 'Have patience!' (*RB* VI.1–2). He then provides a description of the churned-up, turbulent circumstances in which he is made to speak. 'In this sudden smoke from hell,— / So things disguise themselves, —I cannot see / My own hand held thus broad before my face / And know it again' (*RB* VI.2–5). In this way, someone other is made to become a silent part of, or drawn into, Caponsacchi's opening, even though they never figure there in more specific terms. Moreover, his evocation of a 'sudden smoke from hell' making 'things disguise themselves' is not only a representation of the fictional situation in which Caponsacchi gives testimony. It can also be seen to refer to the indefinite ground or source of the dramatic monologue as a mode of speaking from within an environment whose full meaning is yet to be revealed. Thus immersed in an obscure context, Caponsacchi's character has no firm place outside of the process of talking through which he seeks to explain himself and his acts.[28] Who he is, and how his ethos is to be evaluated, must be inferred from the way he expresses himself, or makes himself appear, in words. He is, one might say, a figure of speech, wholly composed in and through his complicated speaking or rather (to be more precise) through the writing that conveys it.

At the outset Caponsacchi seems to present himself as a straightforward interpreter of the obscure tangle of actions and relations that led to Guido's killing of Pompilia and her parents: 'Well, then, let me, the hollow rock, condense / The voice o' the sea and wind, interpret you, / The mystery of this murder' (*RB* VI.72–4). But, as indicated by his self-characterisation as a 'hollow rock' resonating with the 'voices' of the surrounding world, it becomes more and more apparent that his interpretation of the case does not issue from anything that is identifiable with a predefined character or a single voice. Rather, what Caponsacchi's witness report gives evidence of is a 'major source of uncertainty about the origin' of the (linguistic) actions in which the priest participates.[29] Indeed, Caponsacchi's character can be said to embody this very uncertainty about who or what determines the causes and consequences of one's (speech) acts. He is not so much a self-sufficient agent and a reliable interpreter of his own actions as he is an 'actor-network' in Latour's sense: someone who is 'made to act' by a multiplicity of mediators that are shown to be inscribed into his operations, continually dislocating and diverting what he says and does.[30]

Indeed, if Caponsacchi's monologue is not primarily seen as a statement by a presupposed character, but as part of an experimental design arranged by an empirical author, then it can be read as an enquiry into the micro-level activities of taking notice and making signs through which the relationship between Pompilia and Caponsacchi was brought into being, maintained and eventually given what may be regarded as a specifically amorous dynamic and drift. In short, what Browning's writing enables the reader to do, one might say with reference to Latour, is 'to follow the veins, the conduits, the expectations, of relations and of prepositions – these major *providers of direction*'.[31] As Caponsacchi tells his listeners, one channel of connection between him and Pompilia began to be opened up on a night at the theatre, 'When I saw enter, stand, and seat herself / A lady, young, tall, beautiful, strange and sad' (*RB* VI.398–9). Deeply fascinated by, but not yet involved in a meaningful relationship with what he sees, Caponsacchi is reduced to a passive onlooker, riveted to the spot, until 'a brother Canon' (*RB* VI.396) interferes, setting an exchange of signifiers in train. 'I was still one stare,' Caponsacchi recalls,

> When—'Nay, I'll make her give you back your gaze'—
> Said Canon Conti; and at the word he tossed
> A paper-twist of comfits to her lap,

And dodged and in a trice was at my back
Nodding from over my shoulder. Then she turned,
Looked our way, smiled the beautiful sad strange smile. (*RB* VI.407–12)

Conti's act of tossing a 'paper twist of comfits' into Pompilia's lap functions as the invisible medium, hiding at the 'back', that both disrupts the indistinct gaze of Caponsacchi and simultaneously provides him with an opportunity to engage in a potentially significant way with the 'beautiful sad strange' object of this gaze. As a third instance between Caponsacchi and Pompilia, Conti thus acts as a translator, enabling Caponsacchi to convert his sensual experience of the 'beautiful sad strange smile' into a pattern of information that can be read. "T is my new cousin,' said he: / 'The fellow lurking there i' the black o' the box / Is Guido, the old scapegrace: she's his wife, / Married three years since' (*RB* VI.413–16). Here Conti supplies a background or context, 'The fellow lurking there i' the black o' the box', to the exposed figure or *gestalt* that dominates Caponsacchi's perception. This allows the fascinated priest to draw further inferences from what he sees as a 'sad strange smile', but it also engenders the possibility that the context itself comes to the fore, occupying the focus of attention. In this case, indeed, Guido, who had so far been relegated to the 'black' backdrop, soon reasserts his presence and disturbs the subtle process of interaction that had just started to unfold. 'Hallo, there's Guido, the black, mean and small,' Conti warns his companion. 'Bends his brows on us—please to bend your own / On the shapely nether limbs of Light-skirts there / By way of a diversion' (*RB* VI.427–30).

This scene illustrates not only that the '*The Ring and the Book*', as the writer G. K. Chesterton wrote in 1903, 'is the great epic of the enormous importance of small things,'[32] it also shows how these 'small things' – smiles, stares, winks, nods and comfits in twisted papers – function as vehicles, as enablers of communication and '*providers of direction*' in the processes through which meaningful relationships are engendered. Moreover, the encounter at the theatre draws attention to the space of translation and interaction between first-person perception and third-person communication in which Caponsacchi's whole speaking, along with the writing that represents it, takes place. Thus, the brief exchange of looks between the priest and the girl has made a difference between what Caponsacchi calls his 'limited world' and an outside that he does not yet know (*RB* VI.477). In this way, it has made him aware, as he points out, of a more general disconnection, a 'gap' between who he is and who he might be or become, "twixt what is, what should be' (*RB* VI.487).

As Caponsacchi's subsequent account suggests, the image of the sad Pompilia both marked this gap and offered a possible way for him to traverse it. 'One evening I was sitting in a muse,' he remembers,

> Over the opened 'Summa', darkened round
> By the mid-March twilight, thinking how my life
> Had shaken under me,—broke short indeed
> And showed the gap 'twixt what is, what should be,—
> And into what abysm the soul may slip,
> Leave aspiration here, achievement there,
> Lacking omnipotence to connect extremes—
> Thinking moreover . . . oh, thinking, if you like,
> How utterly dissociated was I
> A priest and celibate, from the sad strange wife
> Of Guido,—just as an instance to the point,
> Nought more,—how I had a whole store of strengths
> Eating into my heart, which craved employ,
> And she, perhaps, need of a finger's help,—
> And yet there was no way in the wide world
> To stretch out mine and so relieve myself,—
> How when the page o' the Summa preached its best,
> Her smile kept glowing out of it, as to mock
> The silence we could break by no one word, — (*RB* VI.483–503)

This is, among other things, a scene of interpretation in which the interpreter has lost belief in the authority of his text. Caponsacchi has become an unsettled, dislocated reader ('my life / Had shaken under me'), caught up in an emergent middle between 'achievement' and 'aspiration' that can no longer (and not yet) be defined as an intellectual position or hermeneutic stance. Consequently, the 'page o' the Summa', the epitome of an orthodox significance and absolute truth, no longer means to him what it 'preaches'. Instead, it turns into the medium of something (yet) unsaid, a sense of 'silence' or a silent sense that expresses itself in the thought of how 'utterly dissociated' he, 'a priest and a celibate', was from 'the sad strange wife / Of Guido'. In short, the text of the Summa refers not to a stable and transparent meaning but a meaning in crisis, caused by a crisis in meaning-making.

What this scene makes readable, then, is the thinking of a dissociation, or a dissociated thinking, graphically marked by the '. . .', which prevents the subject from connecting his thoughts in a meaningful way to an object. Suggestively, however, this very gap between self and other (or the reader and the read) is now filled, in the following lines, by the entrance of a medium, suddenly gliding into Caponsacchi's reading room in the figure of a messenger or go-between, a 'masked muffled mystery', as he describes it, who

'Laid lightly a letter on the opened book, / Then stood with folded arms and foot demure, / Pointing as if to mark the minutes' flight' (*RB* VI.506–9). In this way, the pages of the Summa are overlaid with another text which Caponsacchi finds to be, at least allegedly, from Pompilia. In it, she appears to inform Caponsacchi, as he reports, that she had love and 'a warm heart' (*RB* VI.512) to give to him in exchange for the comfits and the glances he had lately thrown at her, and that she therefore wanted him to come to a small balcony overhanging the street by her house. Yet, although this seems to be precisely what Caponsacchi, 'a priest and celibate', has secretly longed for – an opportunity to stretch out his finger and 'relieve' himself by making contact with Pompilia – he refuses to believe that this message means what it says. Instead, Caponsacchi turns into a suspicious reader, questioning the reliability of the medium, 'the masked muffled mystery', through which the letter has been delivered. '"And you?"—I asked: / "What may you be?"' (*RB* VI.520–1). The messenger replies that she was Guido's maid, but had been sent by Pompilia on this occasion, an answer that does not sound implausible per se. Nevertheless, Caponsacchi claims it to be 'transparent' that the letter has not actually been written by Pompilia but is part of a 'trick' designed by Guido (*RB* VI.537).

On the evidence of the Old Yellow Book, it may be instructive to note, Caponsacchi's sceptical way of interpreting the missive – his claim that the sending of the letter had been arranged by Guido – is neither refuted nor confirmed. For, even though the historical material includes a series of epistles which seem to have been exchanged between Caponsacchi and Pompilia, it raises doubts as to who actually wrote these letters. They may well have been forged by Guido, not least because the historical Pompilia, only fourteen at the time of her marriage, declared under oath that she could neither read nor write.[33] Yet, while it is certainly possible to read all the letters delivered to Caponsacchi as part of a counterfeit scheme invented by Guido, this scheme is by no means as 'transparent' as the fictional Caponsacchi says it is. Therefore, Caponsacchi's confidence in declining what appears to be a straightforward invitation is apt to come as a considerable surprise to the reader, especially because the priest, albeit anticipating questions ('what if the lady loved? / What if she wrote the letters?', *RB* VI.665–6), fails to elucidate the grounds on which he purports to know how to decode the dubious texts. Even more puzzlingly, Caponsacchi never explains why he not only replied to the (faked) letter but did so by means of a trick of his own. After all, it would have been comparatively easy to address the first epistle directly to Guido, if not to refuse answering it altogether, or even to take to task the alleged fraud in person. Instead, Caponsacchi seems to be intent on beating Guido at his own game, willingly accepting that this involves a kind of dissemblance on his part as well. What is more, he seems to derive considerable enjoyment from the prospect of turning Guido into a clumsy bear, unknowingly duped by him, the sly fox, as his own remarks imply. 'There's the reply which he shall turn and twist / At pleasure', he chuckles after having dispatched the first letter, 'snuff at till his brain grow drunk, / As the bear does when he finds a scented glove / That puzzles him,–a hand and yet no hand, / Of other perfume than his own foul paw!' (*RB* VI.543–7).

Such utterances suggest not only that Caponsacchi may not be quite as unlike his opponent as he has sometimes been taken to be.[34] Symptomatically, what the 'bear' finds on examination of what is given to him, is a variation of his own 'foul paw'. More importantly, the exchange of letters makes apparent how the actions and intentions defining Caponsacchi's personality are constituted in relation to, and in dialogue with, types of being and doing that seem to be other to, but may well be regarded as part of, his own.[35] In short, the writing of the letters makes readable how Caponsacchi's character comes to be composed. This means that in order to figure out the motives and purposes of Caponsacchi's behaviour, the reader has to follow the lines and passages in the course of which they take shape. In this way, it becomes apparent that the subject of Caponsacchi's monologue is not an identifiable, well-integrated agent, but a meshwork of voices and operations, all seeking to seize control of the meaning in the composing of which they partake. This is particularly evident in a scene that follows upon his eventual (and rather surprising) decision to give up on his resistance to see Pompilia by her window and to go to her place on the very same night.

This crucial scene is centred on a dialogue between Pompilia, bending down from her balcony, and Caponsacchi, looking up from the street. According to the testimonies in the yellow book, such an encounter, in one way or another, most certainly seems to have taken place in historical circumstances. Yet, as Browning's version brings out, what the historical record fails to capture is the work of the mediating agencies that influence the meaning of this dialogue within the murder case as a whole. 'You have sent me letters, Sir,' Pompilia (as paraphrased by Caponsacchi) begins, 'I have read none, I can neither read nor write; / But she you gave them to, a woman here, / One of the people in whose power I am, / Partly explained their sense, I think, to me' (*RB* VI.725–9). While this foregrounds the intervention of the medium, the messenger, who translated the writing presented to Pompilia into speech that she could understand, it leaves open who or what made the messenger talk as she did. All that seems evident from the subsequent lines is that she did not report to Pompilia what Caponsacchi, who claims his letters to have been phrased as more or less overt refusals of communication, actually wrote. As Pompilia points out (according to Caponsacchi's version), what the maid read out of or into the letters was:

> That you, a priest, can dare love me, a wife,
> Desire to live or die as I shall bid,
> (She makes me listen if I will or no)
> Because you saw my face a single time.
> It cannot be she says the thing you mean;
> Such wickedness were deadly to us both:
> But good true love would help me now so much–
> I tell myself, you may mean good and true.
> You offer me, I seem to understand,
> Because I am in poverty and starve,
> Much money, where one piece would save my life. (*RB* VI.731–41)

This passage exemplifies in a nutshell why Caponsacchi's speech is 'anything but monological', to repeat Tucker's line, for the simple question 'who says what to whom in which channel' can here no longer be answered in unequivocal terms. Instead, one reads a representation of Pompilia's voice as conveyed through Caponsacchi's speech, or of Caponsacchi's speech as delivered through Pompilia's voice. Moreover, what Pompilia, through Caponsacchi, says is itself a report of what was said to her by Guido's maid, who read from a letter alleged to be from Caponsacchi. In short, the meaning of the text, to whomever it may be ascribed, is passed through a string of transmitters which dislocate and transform it to such a degree that it is impossible to identify its source. As a result, Caponsacchi is temporarily turned into the addressee, 'you, a priest', of his own speech act, the seeming centre of which is occupied by Pompilia, 'me, a wife', telling the reader what she 'seemed to understand' from what the 'mistress-messenger' told her about the contents of the letter. It is as if Caponsacchi tried to face himself through a looking glass held up to him by Pompilia only to find that the perspective opened up in this way is itself refracted through a third one, that of the maid-messenger, whose motive and end is never revealed.

Therefore, the sense of the passage remains, for the most part, suspended indistinctly between different points of view, slipping and sliding into each other. For example, in the sentence 'But good true love would help me now so much– / I tell myself, you may mean good and true' the initial part ('good true love would help me now so much') can either be read as a report of what the maid read from the letter, or as an expression of Pompilia's wishful thinking. How one interprets it depends on whether 'I tell myself' is taken to belong to the first or to the second clause ('you may mean good and true'). This multiplication of what, on the face of it, seems to be the monologue of a single character, Caponsacchi, is apt to cast doubt on the very possibility of representing the process of communication as a transportation of meaning from one self-contained point or person to another. Tellingly, even the vision that Caponsacchi eventually presents as the solution to the whole letter case is expressly marked as the product of a 'passing glance', an elucidation in transition, during which the distinction between 'hell-smoke' and 'splendid moon', 'truth' and 'lie' appears as quickly as it may disappear (RB VI.922–7). What he eventually saw in this moment, Caponsacchi remembers, was that Guido 'not only forged the words for her / But words for me, made letters he called mine: / What I sent, he retained, gave these in place, / All by the mistress-messenger!' (*RB* VI.928–31). Yet, that it is indeed Guido who clandestinely sabotaged the whole exchange between Caponsacchi and Pompilia remains no more than one view among others. As Caponsacchi rightly points out, the whole communication between these two is performed 'by the mistress-messenger', the 'masked muffled mystery'. Whose meaning this messenger carries across to whom, however, is the 'open secret', to repeat Dowden's formulation, which is never fully divulged. Whatever meaning Caponsacchi, Pompilia or Guido dispatched or received may always have been intercepted, distorted, derailed, curtailed or otherwise altered in the process of being transmitted.

Wild Significance, Free Speech

By exposing this process of transmission while simultaneously leaving its motivation and purpose partly in the dark, Caponsacchi's text can be seen to exhibit, and play with, a more general issue that P. J. Keating has described as the 'experience' that 'immediate communication' is 'far less common' in Browning's poetry than it is in the texts of many of his contemporaries.[36] An early expression of this experience was the claim that Browning's writing deliberately obscures its meaning, making it difficult to comprehend, rather than clear. Today, this problem is hardly ever addressed explicitly, but it is most certainly the reason why the audience of works such as *The Ring and the Book* is sadly confined to a relatively small circle within the academic world. By contrast, for Browning's Victorian critics, most of whom took the artistic value and rank of his poetry to be anything but a settled issue, the obscurity of his writing was still a key issue for debate. Robert W. Buchanan (best known for his book on *The Fleshly School of Poetry*), for example, although a very favourable reviewer of *The Ring and the Book*, put his finger straight on the spot. 'Secretiveness' is the one 'prominent quality of Mr Browning's power', Buchanan writes in *The Athenaeum*, 'which so fascinates the few and so repels the many.'[37]

On Buchanan's account, this secretiveness typically expresses itself in labyrinthine forms of displacement and deferral which involve the reader in a game of hide and seek, with the author constantly laying out attractive baits for his readers only to set them on spurious tracks leading nowhere. To unsympathetic readers, Buchanan suggests, the secretive fashion of Browning's writing may therefore appear like a mere exercise in self-gratification, wilfully intended to lead the reader by the nose, so that the author can indulge himself in his wit. 'It involves the secretive chuckle and the secretive leer,' as he puts it, using the example of a sneaky bird. 'Mr Browning's manner reminds us of the magpie's manner, when, having secretly stolen a spoon or swallowed a jewel, the bird swaggers jauntily up and down, peering rakishly up, and chuckling to itself over its last successful feat of knowingness and *diablerie*.'[38] Buchanan's image of the magpie swaggering smugly up and down while secretly chuckling over his tricks captures what many of Browning's less favourable critics regarded as the major flaw of his works. To their mind, the quality that Buchanan called secretiveness represented no more than a glaring lack of thematic unity and formal coherence, a lack that was either interpreted as indicative of the author's solipsistic contempt for his readers' needs or, more frequently, as a symptom of his sheer incapacity to translate the particular into the general, or the parts into a whole.

Thus, according to the idealist George Santayana, Browning's work is the epitome of what he calls 'the poetry of barbarism', a mode of writing that he took as a 'verbal echo' of the 'general moral crisis and imaginative disintegration' of the latter part of the Victorian age.[39] When reading Browning, Santayana notes, 'we are in the presence of a barbaric genius, of a truncated imagination, of a thought and an art inchoate and ill-digested, of a volcanic eruption that tosses itself quite blindly and ineffectually into the sky'.[40] The

fact that Browning has chosen the dramatic monologue as his preferred genre is a symptom of precisely this 'inchoate and ill-digested'
make of his 'thought and art', Santayana argues, for what this preference testifies to is the poet's inability to separate his manner of
writing from the matter about which he wrote.[41] In this view, the
fault of Browning's imagination is that it is (still) personally involved
and entangled with the 'things' and characters that it creates, rather
than operating from an ideal vantage point outside of them. As a
result, Santayana complains, the poetic imagination keeps messing
around with disjointed particulars, adding ever fresh details to the
multifarious collection of curious personae, images and voices that
make up Browning's oeuvre, but appearing unable (or unwilling) to
integrate these details into a whole. 'He remained in the phenomenal
sphere: he was a lover of experience; the ideal did not exist for him.'[42]
Likewise, Alfred Austin, Browning's arch-enemey, diagnosed him as
'a mere analyst to the end of the chapter', a dilettante puzzle-freak
who enjoys 'pottering about among the brains and entrails of the
souls he has dissected' while being 'utterly unable to do anything
with them, except to call attention to the component parts he has
skilfully laid bare with his knife'.[43] Thus conceived, Browning's creative practice remains hopelessly embroiled, due to his 'indifference
to perfection',[44] in the 'dirty' realm of the incomplete and unresolved,
among the inchoate 'entrails' of meaning, the puzzling traces and
loose threads that have not yet been identified as integral pieces of a
compositional whole.

Such criticism, to be sure, is deeply prejudiced because it is predicated on a normative notion of beauty as material multiplicity in
ideal harmony with which many of Browning's twentieth-century
critics would have little truck. Still, most of the jaundiced judgements
of even his worst critics are based on observations that are essentially
correct. For not only has Browning's writing an evident penchant for
the formally and morally unsettled, displaced, unfinished and awry.
It also demands of its readers to participate in the work of weaving together what, on the face of it, seems to be no more than an
'ill-digested' assemblage of fragments and threads. As we have seen,
what is difficult about *The Ring and the Book* is that there is no
way of drawing on its meaning without allowing one's own reading
activity to be drawn into this meaning. '*The Ring and the Book*,' as
Vivienne J. Rundle notes, 'insists that the reader actively and continually participate in the process of judgement.'[45] This entails a reading
experience that, again, has been most poignantly expressed by Henry
James: 'Browning is "upon" us, straighter upon us always, somehow,

than anyone else of his race; and we thus recoil, we push our chair back, from the table he so tremendously spreads, just to see a little better what is on it.'[46]

To read Browning, then, means to be compelled to read from the inside of a structure in the making, rather than from a position above a finished product which only requires to be looked down upon as if it were an orderly spread table full of well-defined goods ready to be devoured. His texts have therefore repeatedly been associated with 'the aesthetics of postmodernism'.[47] But from a historicist point of view, the kaleidoscopic structure of *The Ring and the Book* may just as well be seen as an outcome of the methodological pluralism that is inherent in Victorian empiricism. After all, one central premise of empiricist epistemology, as we have seen, was that human beings – scientists included – can, as a rule, never stand outside of whatever they may want to examine, but only move in relation to it. Remember John Venn: There is no position without others that could be taken up instead.[48]

The Ring and the Book, I have argued, can be called experimental in more than a metaphorical sense since it lacks an authorial and authoritative speaker purporting to know the meaning of the epic's source material, the Old Yellow Book, any better than the multiple characters who are made to interpret it through their speeches. Instead, the voice of the poet, or the epic singer, which is most clearly recognisable in the first and the last book, is included as one among others in the thicket of gossip, guesses, suspicions, feints and accusations that is both constituted and represented by the polyphonic text of the epic. As Tucker has observed, Browning's authorial vision of the murder case, as it may be seen to be outlined in the first book ('I saw with my own eyes'; 'I saw the star stoop'; 'I saw the cheated couple find the cheat'; 'I saw them in the potency of fear', *RB* I.523, I.538, I.563, I.569), is so mixed up with the views of the epic's personae that it is made 'qualitatively indistinguishable' from them.[49] What is more, the poet, or the lyrical I, not only 'takes his stand' next to the figures he has enabled to speak, but explicitly asks his readers to add their own views and judgements to the tissue of perspectives and voices of, and by means of which, *The Ring and the Book* is composed (*RB* I.1364, I.825, I.695–7).[50] Consequently, the poem denies its readers an ideal vantage point on the basis of which they could realise its subject-matter in a conclusive form. It rather challenges them to work their own way through the 'Pleadings and counter-pleadings' that are spread out across its pages. 'Truth, nowhere, lies yet everywhere in these– / Not absolutely in a portion, yet / Evolvable from the whole', as Browning's Pope puts this, whose phrase exemplifies once more that in this epic 'nowhere' and 'everywhere' as well as 'truth' and 'lies' are so closely adjacent that each appears to be 'evolvable' into the other (*RB* X.229–31).

As explained, the objection some of Browning's early critics had against this method, and indeed against Browning's work in general, was that it assembled so many competing positions and perspectives that they cancelled each other out, leaving the reader with nothing substantial, no general idea or moral, to hold on to. Yet, it seems as if this risk of puzzling its audience by presenting them with nothing but a noisy, fuzzy clamour of multiple speech acts is one that Browning faced quite deliberately, as the final monologue indicates. Here, the poet's spokesperson asks the 'British Public' to 'learn one lesson hence / Of many which whatever lives should teach: / This lesson, that our human speech is naught, / Our human testimony false, our fame / And human estimation words and wind' (*RB* XII.836–40). As this suggests, to read *The Ring and the Book* for a single 'lesson' that can be isolated from its manifold discourse will most likely be frustrating. For Browning's art, his speaker goes on to say, is supposed to function as a medium of interpretation, rather than communication. This is to say that whatever 'truth' it may convey is one that can only be conveyed indirectly or 'obliquely', as the text has it in what are perhaps its most famous lines:

> How look a brother in the face and say
> 'Thy right is wrong, eyes hast thou yet art blind,
> Thine ears are stuffed and stopped, despite their length:
> And, oh, the foolishness thou countest faith!'
> Say this as silverly as tongue can troll–
> The anger of the man may be endured,
> The shrug, the disappointed eyes of him
> Are not so bad to bear–but here's the plague
> That all this trouble comes of telling truth,
> Which truth, by when it reaches him, looks false,
> Seems to be just the thing it would supplant,
> Nor recognizable by whom it left:
> While falsehood would have done the work of truth.
> But Art,–wherein man nowise speaks to men,
> Only to mankind,–Art may tell a truth
> Obliquely, do the thing shall breed the thought,
> Nor wrong the thought, missing the mediate word. (*RB* XII.845–61)

If the act of 'telling truth' is taken to carry an established piece of knowledge from one predefined position to another, the speaker

intimates, then this truth is bound to 'look false' as soon as its
destination is reached: 'Seems to be just the thing it would sup-
plant, / Nor recognizable by whom it left: / While falsehood would
have done the work of truth'. On this account, communication is
destined to take the form of a rhetorical contest between different
claims to truth, each seeking to prevail over the other ('"Thy right is
wrong, eyes hast thou yet art blind"'), even when it is performed 'as
silverly as tongue can troll'. By contrast, 'Art', as exemplified by the
writing of *The Ring and the Book*, is here said to represent a way
of speaking into the open, to an unspecific or universal audience
whose position remains indefinite ('wherein man nowise speaks to
men, / Only to mankind'). Yet, if a text is directed to everyone, as
it is said to be in this case, then no one can be persuaded of a particular truth. As a consequence, an utterance which reaches out to
the whole of mankind will have to remain suspended in the middle,
on the way to an addressee that is yet to be located in terms of a specific position or a point of view. In fact, in this instance, Browning's
writing partly performs the very mode of speaking 'obliquely'
to which it refers. For, by concluding on the verb 'miss', the text
makes ambiguous whether it means to say that art simply 'wants'
or incidentally 'fails to hit' the mediating term ('miss' can mean
both and more). It does not so much communicate a particular
thought as it hints at possible ones, creating a site of indeterminacy
and missing specificity on which various perspectives and readings
can come into play.

As the above passage suggests, *The Ring and the Book* as a whole
can accommodate so many voices and perspectives because it is not
close-knit and whole but rather 'loose-textured' and reminiscent 'of
something full of holes'.[51] It misses out on the mediating instance
that could hold its pieces together. Moreover, it seems precisely this
open-ended, loose-textured quality, the last speaker suggests, which
makes 'Art', as exemplified by *The Ring and the Book*, sufficiently
flexible to address not just a definite group of people, but something
as unspecific as 'mankind'. As a result, both the position from and
the position to which Browning's writing speaks remain as obscure
as the mind of man as described by the Pope. His vehicle to question
the human mind is 'a convex glass':

> Man's mind, what is it but a convex glass
> Wherein are gathered all the scattered points
> Picked out of the immensity of sky,
> To re-unite there, be our heaven for earth,
> Our known unknown, our God revealed to man?

Existent somewhere, somehow, as a whole;
Here, as a whole proportioned to our sense,–
There, (which is nowhere, speech must babble thus!)
In the absolute immensity, the whole
Appreciable solely by Thyself,–
Here, by the little mind of man, reduced
To littleness that suits his faculty,
In the degree appreciable too;
Between Thee and ourselves–nay even, again,
Below us, to the extreme of the minute,
Appreciable by how many and what diverse
Modes of the life Thou madest be! (*RB* X.1311–27)

Evidently, the 'mind' imagined here is essentially an assemblage or gathering ('Wherein are gathered all the scattered points'), a multifarious and heterogeneous medium which is 'always more than one'.[52] As a whole, such a mind can therefore not be grasped or represented in a single-minded form. At best, it can be referred to as 'our known unknown', or 'our heaven for earth', descriptions which reinforce the view of the mind as a composition of seemingly opposed parts. Even God, whom the Pope takes to embody the sense of wholeness that human beings lack, seems to exist only in a mode that is radically other to the human mind. In whatever way people may imagine what it means to be complete, they can only do so in a fashion that 'suits' their 'faculty', such that the whole of existence is 'by the little mind of man, reduced / To littleness'. In the meantime, the whole overseen by God is not 'Here' in the little world accessible to the human mind, but 'There (which is nowhere, speech must babble thus!)', in an 'absolute immensity' that cannot (yet) be defined or located in human terms.

Just as the inside of the human mind, according to the Pope, includes an unfathomable outside that is represented by God, so the position that could define *The Ring and the Book* as a whole is present in it only in terms of a palpable absence. *The Ring and the Book*, then, is like the Pope's 'mind', for if there is one position not included in it, or included only as a virtual reality 'existent somewhere, somehow', then it is the eternal or divine view which integrates all others. In Dallas's terms, one might perhaps say that this manifest absence, the virtual view of a whole, is the 'importunate secret' that Browning's writing insists on flaunting before the reader in a multiplicity of 'disguises'. Among these, the ceremonial robe of the Pope is given no more prominence than the blood-stained coat of Guido, or the chequered verbal vestments of the two garrulous lawyers (the prosecutor and defender of Guido respectively), each of whom enacts a particularly blatant method of what one of them calls 'circumstantially evolving facts' ('Thus circumstantially evolve we facts', *RB* VIII.139). Yet, whereas the Pope's speech has, until the present day, often been taken to represent the view of authority that comes closest to Browning's own, the advocates' utterances were, especially by the epic's Victorian critics, often blamed as exemplary of the text's flaws. More precisely, what many readers considered irritating about the lawyers' speeches was that they seemed to be deliberately 'adventitious', irrelevant, and in excess of whatever was considered to be the main subject of *The Ring and the Book*.[53] The critic William Sharp, for example, wished that Browning's work 'comprised but the Prologue, the Plea of Guido, "Caponsacchi", "Pompilia", "The Pope", and Guido's last Defence'.[54] All the other parts of the poem should have been cut out of the book, Sharp holds. 'Thus circumscribed, it seems to me rounded and complete, a great work of art void of the dross, the mere *débris* which the true artist discards.'[55] Again, such criticism is predicated on the assumption of a preconceived 'subject' or idea that defines what is to be seen as relevant and what as 'dross' and 'mere débris'. Yet, one may just as well argue, as G. K. Chesterton has done, that the 'essence' of *The Ring and the Book* is precisely the lack of a single subject – in the sense of both 'person' and 'theme' – that, by itself, is more important than all the other subjects that the poem equally contains.[56] Chesterton therefore places Browning's *Ring*-epic in the same line as the work of several other members of what he calls 'the modern movements'.[57] For Chesterton, all of these modern authors, among whom he includes Maeterlinck, Zola, Whitman, Gissing, Meredith and Shaw, 'ceased to believe certain things to be important and the rest to be unimportant'.[58] In their work, he argues, the distinction between what is and is not meaningful is no longer regulated by traditional orders and preconceived norms. Rather: 'Significance is to them a wild thing that may leap upon them from any hiding-place.'[59]

Evidently, this decentred and dislocated notion of significance according to which meaning could, in principle, be found anywhere corresponds well with an inquisitive and experimental attitude which is prepared to see sense in, and make sense of, any place and any thing, no matter how seemingly trivial it may appear. Moreover, this new uncertainty about the grounds and locations of significance must have been encouraged, and in turn sustained by, a secularised *Weltanschauung* according to which the very experience of being in the world could no longer be regarded as meaningful by itself.

As Chesterton argues, Browning's experimental epic is one of the
foremost products of this deregulated view – a view on which the
meaning of experience, as well as the experience of meaning, could
not be directly deduced from a transcendental design. One might
therefore say that *The Ring and the Book* explores not only the
insight, as propagated by empiricists such as Venn, 'that no man
ever lived upon this earth without possessing a point of view',[60] but
also the intimation that each of these multiple views might contain
something of interest, something that is worth enquiring into or
thinking about, if only to thoroughly reject it. Or, as Chesterton says
it, *The Ring and the Book* 'is the epic of free speech'.[61]

Indeed, if it is accepted 'that truth is so much larger and stranger
and more many-sided than we know of' and that one must therefore try 'at all costs to hear every one's account' of it,[62] then there
is no doubting the value of listening to the broadest possible range
of people and thoughts. Yet, whereas Chesterton considered it
Browning's main achievement that his writing 'has learnt to listen'
to the whole babble of voices in which it is immersed,[63] others (as
indicated) saw the polyphonic inclusiveness of his work as a serious want of discrimination and taste. Even Browning's friend Julia
Wedgwood found it gravely disconcerting that Browning's art gave
so much prominence to 'meanness and cruelty' that it threatened to
eclipse what she regarded as the 'luminous soul' that should have
been at the centre of his epic, namely the character of Pompilia.[64]
'One's memory seems filled by the despicable husband, the vulgar
parents, the brutal cutthroats, the pathetic child is jostled into a corner. I long for more space for her.'[65] In response, Browning defended
his work by emphasising that it was not predicated on a predefined
idea of what is supposed to be morally and aesthetically acceptable,
but on the experience of reading a historical record, from which various good ideas, or ideas of what is good, can be evolved.[66] As this
indicates, what divided Browning and Wedgwood, making their correspondence increasingly tetchy, was that they argued from different conceptions of what it means to make 'good' art – conceptions
which one might call empiricist (Browning) and idealist (Wedgwood)
respectively. Wedgwood believed that good works must follow from
morally and formally good ideas, with the ultimate measure of 'good-
ness' being defined, she thought, by the alleged perfection of God's
design.[67] Browning, by contrast, seemed convinced that good ideas
can just as well follow from works which appeared as manifestly bad
(in all respects) as many of the actions and speeches documented in
the yellow book. On this empiricist account, the absolute measure

of God's design is not here in the empirical world that is accessible to the human mind, but elsewhere, in God's reason, 'which is nowhere', to repeat the Pope's words. Thus conceived, the ideas of what it means for something to be 'good' or 'bad', 'right' or 'wrong', 'important' or 'unimportant' cannot be supposed to exist eternally in some abstract theoretical realm, but must be taken to be subject to practical experiences which may change.

For one thing, then, the Browning–Wedgwood correspondence can be taken to confirm that Browning's epic does not (manage or intend to) communicate well-defined ideas. Furthermore, the debate suggests a method for how *The Ring and the Book* should and should not be read. More precisely, what I want to argue is that the one reading not borne out by this work is a reading that, like Wedgwood's, attempts to find a subject in it that matches some preconceived ideal of formal, intellectual or moral completeness and propriety. Instead, the poem demands its readers to 'find the grain' of a pattern in formation 'and to follow its course while bending it to' an 'evolving purpose'.[68] The reader of *The Ring and the Book* has to become an experimenter, a craftsman (or craftswoman), willing to work with the threads and traces of an unsettled composition that (yet) lacks an idea or ground that could stabilise it or hold it together. In short, the poem challenges its addressees 'to *follow the materials*', as Ingold says.[69] Browning's poem may therefore be classified among a group of texts that Joshua Landy has described as 'formative fictions', as texts which 'will not do their work', unless readers creatively take part in them. Rather than transmitting knowledge of any kind, such texts, Landy argues, offer us opportunities to hone our reading skills and 'to fine-tune our mental capacities'.[70]

Fishing for Similarities

One way of demonstrating how Browning's formative fiction can be made to work in a productive way is to pursue one or more of the many analogies which suggest patterns of continuity across the different monologues.[71] Take the various instances in which aspects of the murder case are, in one way or another, described through images of catching fish. For example, in Book II, the account of Half-Rome, Violante Comparini, the self-proclaimed mother of Pompilia is depicted as a devious fisher-woman, casting about for a fresh catch. 'She who had caught one fish, could make that catch /

A bigger still, in angler's policy', Half-Rome argues, trying to make plausible his claim that Violante's insidious tactics are at the root of the whole affair which eventually led to the murder (*RB* II.270–1).

> So, with an angler's mercy for the bait,
> Her minnow was set wriggling on its barb
> And tossed to mid-stream; which means, this grown girl
> With the great eyes and bounty of black hair
> And first crisp youth that tempts a jaded taste,
> Was whisked i' the way of a certain man, who snapped. (*RB* II.272–7)

Here, the 'certain man, who snapped' refers to Guido who is assigned the part of a fish while Pompilia, 'this grown girl', is imagined as the bait or 'minnow' that Violante sets 'wriggling on its barb' and then tosses 'to mid-stream' in order to hook Guido into her scheme. This way of using the angler-simile makes Guido appear as the innocent victim who, though active himself ('snapped'), blindly falls prey to Violante's lust for status and wealth. Indeed, Half-Rome subsequently uses the same simile twice more in almost the same fashion, thus reinforcing his interpretation of the case, according to which the Comparini 'baited hook / With this poor gilded fly Pompilia-thing, / Then caught the fish, pulled Guido to the shore / And gutted him' (*RB* II.1355–8).

However, it is only when one comes across the angler-motif again in the monologue of Tertium Quid, that one begins to sense a network of related images that connects the individual accounts. Moreover, when the reader looks at the uses of the angler-simile more closely, she will notice that each of the speakers grafts the metaphor onto a slightly different context. Tertium, for instance, makes use of the fishing image in order to describe how the Comparini strove to 'wriggle themselves free' of their self-induced relationship with Guido (*RB* IV.707) as soon as they realised that he, though a nobleman, is not as rich as they expected him to be. 'They baited their own hook to catch a fish / With this poor worm, failed o' the prize, and then / Sought how to unbait tackle, let worm float / Or sink, amuse the monster while they 'scaped' (*RB* IV.708–11). Guido, in this interpretation of the triangulation is still the fish who is caught by means of a bait, here named as a 'poor worm', which refers to Pompilia. Yet, the Comparini no longer appear as successful fishermen, catching Guido to tie him into their design. They rather give the impression of trapped creatures themselves, accidentally caught up in an entanglement of their own making and now desperately trying to find a way of getting off the hook.

Guido himself, by contrast, specifically uses the fish metaphor to arouse pity for what he calls his 'stranded self, born fish with gill and fin / Fit for the deep sea, now left flap bare-backed / In slush and sand' (*RB* V.172–4). As he sees it, the Comparini 'hazarded awhile to hook' him with their 'wealth' (*RB* V.1401–2), but only to 'execute' a scheme that makes them 'gain all' and him 'lose all' (*RB* V.1399–400). The result, he claims, is that they 'Have caught the fish and find the bait entire' (*RB* V.1403). All the same, the Pope, who likewise 'relishes a sea-side simile' (*RB* IX.373), as one of the lawyers points out, is not convinced by this argument. To his mind, Guido remains an 'ambiguous fish' (*RB* X.486), who wears his nobility as strategically as the 'soldier-crab' her shell, stealing in and out of it as the occasion demands (*RB* X.510).

As one follows such subtle modifications of emphasis and transformations of meaning within what, on the face of it, looks like the same metaphor, the act of reading turns into a process of continuous recollection and rectification, in the course of which one assembles ever more fragments indicating an evolving design. Where one begins and how one proceeds to draw out this network of related images is not prescribed by the text. Readers can continue with the 'fishy' theme, which is anything but exhausted, or they can seek to work a pattern out of the abundance of bird figures which are distributed across *The Ring and the Book*. Or they may follow the image of Pompilia as 'worm', which they will then find to be turning into ever fresh shapes. In one description of a crucial encounter with Guido, for instance, Pompilia is no longer the passive victim at the mercy of others. 'No! Second misadventure, this worm turned, / I told you: would have slain him on the spot / With his own weapon, but they seized her hands / Leaving her tongue free, as it tolled the knell / Of Guido's hope so lively late' (*RB* III.1289–93). As it happens, Pompilia herself, in her own voice, justifies her changing from passive bait into active attacker or protester as a necessary act of defence against a malicious 'serpent towering and triumphant', as she puts it – 'then / Came all the strength back in a sudden swell, / I did for once see right, do right, give tongue / The adequate protest: for a worm must turn / If it would have its wrong observed by God' (*RB* VII.1588–93). But of course Guido has a rather different view of who was the malicious one, namely Pompilia: 'The worm which wormed its way from skin through flesh / To the bone and there lay biting, did its best,– / What, it goes on to scrape at the bone's self, / Will wind to inmost marrow and madden me?' (*RB* V.1485–8). In Guido's view, it is the sly motion of his wife, 'the writhings of the bargain', growing into an ever more poisonous worm, gnawing 'its way from skin through flesh', that is to be seen as the real 'serpent', not himself. 'A thousand gnats make up a serpent's sting, / And many sly soft stimulants to wrath / Compose a formidable wrong at last' (*RB* XI.890–2). This resonates with the account of Half-Rome for whom Guido's wife has been 'the snake Pompilia' all along who 'writhed transfixed through all her spires', tempting a fellow priest to escape with her (*RB* II.794–5). In fact, a little later, Half-Rome even goes so far as to claim that it is her 'Viper-like' quality which made Pompilia so 'difficult to slay' that she could live on for three more days after the murderous attack: 'Writhes still through every ring of her, poor wretch, / At the Hospital hard by' (*RB* II.1445–7) – like a worm, incidentally, that had been hacked to pieces. By contrast, The Other Half-Rome, another speaker, argues that Pompilia did not change until 'Guido turned the screw too much', provoking his wife to turn against him: 'she turned and made attack, / Claimed now divorce from bed and board' (*RB* III.1429, III.1431–2).

To conclude, by following these changes and twists of perspective one can both read and become part of a work in the process of taking form, a work whose contents keep rotating like a kaleidoscope, potentially altering their aspect with every turn of the page.[72] How – in what shape – the social relationship between Browning's people presents itself depends on how one links up the scattered fragments of meaning which are repeated across the individual accounts. To see Pompilia as a worm, for example, can mean to see her either as a device for the execution of Violante's 'angler-policy', or as a victim of Guido's lust, or as a poisonous insect (or even a snake) nettling Guido with so many little stings that he is eventually made to go berserk. All of these aspects are accrued and made to interact in the sequence of uses to which the image is put. Reading *The Ring and the Book* experimentally, then, can help to make apparent that its structure has less in common with that of a narrative poem telling a story than with that of an encyclopaedia in which hundreds of cross-references link up the individual accounts. Spinning a web of analogies, these cross-references form patterns of meaning that supplement, overlay and often counteract the way the monologues are syntactically arranged. Moreover, such a reading brings out how the very form of *The Ring and the Book* registers the experience of a world in transformation which can by definition only be grasped in an incomplete way. As Chesterton puts it in another snappy line of his: 'It is well sometimes to half understand a poem in the same manner that we half understand the world.'[73]

Notes

1. Slinn, 'Experimental Form', p. 47.
2. Pearsall, 'Dramatic Monologue', p. 67.
3. Tucker, 'Dramatic Monologue', p. 232.
4. Iser, *Der Akt*, pp. 284–314.
5. Tucker, 'Dramatic Monologue', p. 229.
6. Ibid., p. 231.
7. Armstrong, *Victorian Poetry*, p. 13 and generally.
8. Ibid., p. 13.
9. Niemann, 'Browning's Critique', p. 449. For Browning's general relationship to the Romantic tradition see Martens, *Browning*, esp. pp. 167–208.
10. Langbaum, *Poetry of Experience*, p. 105.
11. Ibid., p. 105.
12. Slinn, 'Experimental Form', p. 62.
13. One arrives at ten or eleven monologues respectively if one leaves out, or counts as one, the first and the last book, which are not spoken by one of the actors in the case, although the last one quotes the voices of two more contemporary witnesses.
14. Browning, *The Ring and the Book*. All quotations from this edition are given in the text by book and line numbers (*RB*).
15. On this aspect see Armstrong, 'Uses of Prolixity'.
16. As Wolfreys (*Literature*, p. 84) puts it, 'the "alloy" [. . .] is indispensable, crucial to the production of purity, so-called'.
17. Armstrong, 'Uses of Prolixity', p. 179.
18. Browning did have an interest in scientific knowledge, though, which is palpable in *The Ring and the Book*. Tate, *The Poet's Mind*, pp. 153–81, for instance, reads the poem as a 'psychological epic', which 'ties the movements of thought to the workings of the body' (p. 181).
19. James, 'The Novel', p. 393.
20. Austin, *The Poetry*, p. 64.
21. Ibid., p. 64.
22. Bagehot, 'Wordsworth, Tennyson, and Browning; or Pure, Ornate, and Grotesque Art'.
23. Armstrong, 'Browning and the "Grotesque Style"', p. 93.
24. Bagehot, 'Wordsworth, Tennyson, and Browning', p. 375.
25. Menaghan, 'Embodied Truth' and Slinn, 'Language and Truth', esp. p. 118. For a very different reading see Zietlow, 'The Ascending Concerns'. Zietlow argues that Browning's text 'calls for commitment to an uncompromising moral vision culminating in the imperative for self-sacrificing effort to save the good and blot out evil' (p. 194). According to Suzanne Bailey ('Somatic Wisdom'), the 'antithetical readings' elicited by Browning's text 'have a historical precedent in Victorian debates about the effects of the higher criticism' (p. 568).

26. Manning and Massumi, *Thought in the Act*.
27. Cf. especially the accounts by Pompilia and Caponsacchi in *The Old Yellow Book*, pp. 69–72 and pp. 73–6.
28. Cf. Tucker, 'Dramatic Monologue', p. 243.
29. Latour, *Reassembling*, p. 46.
30. Ibid., p. 217.
31. Latour, *An Inquiry*, p. 178.
32. Chesterton, *Robert Browning*, p. 163.
33. Cf. Cook, *Commentary*, pp. 290–4 (Appendix 5: 'The Monologues and the Depositions of Caponsacchi and Pompilia'); cf. also pp. 285–9 (Appendix 6: 'Could Pompilia Write?'). Although dated, most of Cook's commentary is still helpful.
34. Corrigan's historical research into additional documents about the murder case (*Curious Annals*, pp. xlii, 66–81), which had not been known to Browning, suggests that Caponsacchi's character might indeed have been less benign than it has often been taken to be; cf. Altick and Loucks, *Browning's Roman Murder Story*, pp. 53–56. Daniel Karlin, however, has provided an analysis of Caponsacchi's hatred for Guido (*Browning's Hatreds*, pp. 217–38) that agrees with my reading.
35. A similar claim is made by Buckler, *Poetry and Truth*, p. 141, who argues that there 'may be a significant portion of dishonesty and self-deception in Caponsacchi's monologue'.
36. Keating, 'Robert Browning', p. 328.
37. Buchanan, '[Unsigned Review]', p. 293.
38. Ibid., p. 293.
39. Santayana, *Interpretations*, p. 169.
40. Ibid., p. 189.
41. Ibid., p. 194.
42. Ibid., p. 198.
43. Austin, *The Poetry*, pp. 56–7.
44. Santayana, *Interpretations*, p. 189.
45. Rundle, 'Guido and the Reader', p. 104.
46. James, 'The Novel', p. 399.
47. Woolford, *Robert Browning*, p. 81.
48. See Chap. 1, pp. 42–3.
49. Tucker, *Epic*, p. 438.
50. Ibid., p. 438.
51. Armstrong, 'Uses of Prolixity', p. 179.
52. Manning, *Always More than One*, pp. 16–30.
53. Chesterton, *Robert Browning*, p. 160.
54. Sharp, *Life and Writings*, p. 127.
55. Ibid., p. 127.
56. Chesterton, *Robert Browning*, p. 163.
57. Ibid., p. 164.
58. Ibid., p. 165.

59. Ibid., p. 165.
60. Ibid., p. 171.
61. Ibid., p. 173.
62. Ibid., p. 174.
63. Ibid., p. 173.
64. Curle (ed.), *Robert Browning and Julia Wedgwood*, p. 154. For the background of this exchange see the introduction by Curle (pp. 5–19).
65. Ibid., p. 154.
66. Ibid., p. 159.
67. Ibid., p. 184: 'My longing is to see *his* work copied – I do not say exclusively; it could hardly be made evident to us apart from our own scrawls – but at all events that this be the main thing.'
68. Ingold, *Being Alive*, p. 211.
69. Ibid., p. 213.
70. Landy, *How to Do Things*, p. 13.
71. On the 'Drama of Metaphor' in the *The Ring and the Book* see also Altick and Loucks, *Browning's Roman Murder Story*, pp. 226–80. As they point out, many of the images, such as the lamb or the snake, which recur throughout Browning's epic are 'highly adaptable' precisely *because* they already carry with them a long and multifarious history of usages (p. 228).
72. One might also say that *The Ring and the Book* makes readable the transition from what Richard Shusterman calls 'understanding' to 'interpretation'; cf. Shusterman, *Pragmatist Aesthetics*, pp. 115–35. When we come across points of resemblance such as the ones between the worm and the serpent, we immediately *understand* that there is a connection between them, but in order to realise the meaning of this connection we have to start *interpreting* it.
73. Chesterton, *Robert Browning*, p. 158.

Chapter 8

The Making of Sensation Fiction

Braddon's 'Protracted Search'

One argument of the preceding chapter has been that *The Ring and the Book* represents an epic or large-scale version of what William James called 'a mosaic without a bedding', a mobile assemblage of positions and components that allow for various ways of association and (re)alignment while (yet) missing an overarching design to hold them in place. As a result, Browning's work offers the reader no opportunity to recognise it from without, as a (generic) form that is already known, or already whole. Instead, *The Ring and the Book* invites its readers to take part in the composition and evaluation of 'something else', an experimental form that transfers the tradition of the epic into 'a novel country' (as well as into the 'country' of the novel) to create a type of writing 'in difficulties', filled with 'obstacles' and 'encumbered with incongruities', to repeat Bagehot's phrase. For the reader, this form of writing 'in difficulties' is not least a writing that is difficult to comprehend in terms of general definitions or distinct ideas. It demands attention and intellectual exertion.

On the face of it, therefore, much of Browning's poetry seems to contrast sharply with the fast-paced eventfulness of sensation fiction which has often been taken to cater primarily to a need for short-lived entertainment and easily digestible consumption. Yet, while the immediate popularity of the 'Sensational School'[1] of fiction in the 1860s is certainly at odds with Browning's long poetic struggle for acknowledgement by the British public, both kinds of creative practice had in common that they were perceived as relatively unfamiliar and difficult to assign to predefined types. Like much of Browning's poetry, sensation fiction, as Janice M. Allan has pointed out, was viewed as a 'phenomenon that required reviewers to adjust their critical vocabulary and discursive practices'.[2] Of course, most of the elements of which sensation writing is made up could easily be recognised to have been derived from established genres, such as Gothic fiction, melodrama and domestic realism. Yet, the way these lines of tradition were adapted and rewoven yielded a gathering of pieces and threads that many critics perceived as puzzling or even threatening, since they could not (yet) capture it in predefined terms or assign it to a common place. What is more, even some of the key writers of the new genre themselves, Elizabeth Braddon in particular, seemed uncertain how to judge the literary phenomenon in the bringing about of which they had a major share. While Braddon, as her correspondence shows, was more than glad about the enormous economic success of her novelistic art, she remained doubtful whether it had sufficient aesthetic value to merit that success.[3]

In a letter to Edmund Yates, then editor of the journal *Temple Bar*, for instance, Braddon suggests that sensation fiction is mainly a stringing together of interchangeable ingredients that could be endlessly reshuffled and recycled, but never made into a form that is aesthetically self-sufficient or complete. Asked to supply another portion of what she calls the 'right-down sensational', she characterises it in terms of 'floppings at the end of chapters, and bits of paper hidden in secret drawers, bank-notes and title-deeds under the carpet, and a part of the body putrefying in the coal-scuttle',[4] before casually joking on the inherently fragmented nature of this kind of art:

> By the bye, what a splendid novel, *à la* Wilkie Collins, one might write on a protracted search for the missing members of a murdered man, dividing the tale not into *books* but *bits*! 'BIT THE FIRST: The leg in the gray stocking found at Deptford.' 'BIT THE SECOND: The white hand and the onyx ring with half an initial letter (unknown) and crest, skull with a coronet, found in an Alpine *crevasse*!'
>
> Seriously, though, you want a sensational fiction to commence in January, you tell me. I cannot promise you anything new, when, alas, I look round and find everything on this earth seems to have been done, and done, and done again! [. . .] I will give the kaleidoscope (which I cannot spell) another turn, and will do my very best with the old bits of glass and pins and rubbish [. . .] Any novel combination of the well-known figures is completely at your service, workmanship careful, delivery prompt.[5]

This indicates not only that the sensation novel was typically taken to be about a 'protracted' process of assembling dismembered pieces which are scattered across various, often far-flung places ('Deptford',

'Alpine *crevasse*'). The letter also makes explicit, if only half-seriously, that the form of publication that is best suited to this theme is not the single, seemingly completed 'book' brought out at once, but the open-ended series of multiple instalments or '*bits*', successively accumulated over a long stretch of time. Moreover, Braddon's wry, self-mocking attitude towards the very 'sensational' work for which she had become famous suggests that she was thoroughly aware that the contents of the tales she wrote were deeply entwined with the disjointed form in which they were made public and sold in the literary marketplace. In fact, there is a sense of ironic detachment in Braddon's epistle which intimates that the 'careful', promptly executed 'workmanship' that she had learned to 'deliver' appeared at times almost as questionable to herself as it did to many of her reviewers. 'Believe me I feel very little elated by the superficial success of my pair of Bigamy novels, & the hardest things the critics say of me never strike me as unjust,' she wrote to her friend and mentor, the novelist Edward Bulwer-Lytton, in 1863, shortly after *Lady Audley's Secret* and *Aurora Floyd* (her two bigamy novels) had both been published as books.[6] 'I know that I have *everything* to do yet; but it has been my good or bad fortune to be flung into a very rapid market, & to have everything printed & published almost before the ink with which it was written was dry.'[7]

As such statements suggest, in the 1860s, the writing of sensation fiction was above all an activity in 'rapid' motion, 'flung' into an equally mobile publishing industry that contributed as much to the production and reception of this new variety of work as sensation fiction, in turn, contributed to the formation of the literary market. Braddon's letters to Bulwer-Lytton convey a vivid self-portrait of an author at work, so deeply embroiled in an ongoing process that she could barely pause to reflect on, let alone arrest or change the direction of, the spectacular development in which she takes part. 'I know that my writing teems with errors, absurdities, contradictions, & inconsistancies [*sic*]; but I have never written a line that has not been written against time – sometimes with the printer waiting outside the door,' she notes in 1862, one month before the completion of *Aurora Floyd*.[8] From that point onwards, her novels followed upon each other so quickly that the termination of one seemed to blend almost seamlessly into the commencement of the next. 'I go on grinding & grinding until I feel as if there was nothing left in me but the stalest & most hacknied [*sic*] of ideas.'[9] Repeatedly, Braddon complains that her writing was so 'continuous' that she could hardly afford to make time to pick up and digest new ideas.[10] 'I have so little time for reading, & above all so very little quiet time that I am apt to begin a lot of books & never finish any of them – taking up any book I find in the room I happen to be in – and opening the volume anywhere.'[11]

She even describes herself as so thoroughly immersed in a creative practice of which she could neither see the beginning nor the end that the distinction between life and work had started to dissolve for her. 'Writing novels has become now a sort of second nature to me. I live for little else, & try to shut away all thought of trouble by plunging into pen & ink [*sic*].'[12] There could hardly be a better image than this of a writer 'plunging into pen and ink' to illustrate what it means to be inside 'the mangle of practice',[13] steeped in the work of composition that connects humans with non-humans and subjects with objects. More precisely, what Braddon seems to describe is the experience of participating in the construction of an emergent field of literary production that she cannot yet grasp or judge from a point of view outside of it. Her letters suggest that her writing was swept away by the very sensational process that it had itself helped to set in train. One point to be noted about these documents, therefore, is that Braddon's personal, close-up view of the literary affair in the creation of which her work was so deeply implicated is consonant with more general conceptions of the sensational as a mode of being that is, by definition, 'startling' and 'novel', or disquieting and ominous.[14] In all of these cases, whatever is sensational is, by virtue of being perceived to be so, still exceptional, obscure, or not fully understood. No matter how the sensational manifests itself, it is always tied to an intense experience of ignorance, thrill or surprise caused by a confrontation with something half hidden or yet unknown. It has the quality of an event.

While sensation fiction has become famous for engendering such events, fascinating masses of readers by the tantalising lure of excitement and shock, it has also been interpreted as itself a creative response to new kinds of nerve-racking affects induced by industrial modernity. According to Nicholas Daly, for instance, sensation fiction not only registers a transformation of sense perception brought about by rapid processes of industrialisation and technological advancement that many Victorians experienced as disconcerting. More to the point, it actively contributes to the very 'modernization of the senses' to which it seems to react,[15] bringing its readers 'up to speed' with an unsettling reorganisation of time and space.[16] The sensation novel, thus viewed, helped its readers to become accustomed to a world under stress, in which 'industrial technology', such as the railway, 'was becoming part of the fabric of everyday life', impinging not only on modes of consumption and communication, but also on read-ing habits and attention spans.[17] By simulating the upsetting condi-tions of industrial modernity, one might sum this up, sensation fiction enabled people to read, or come to terms with, their experience in a novel form that was itself stunning and unfamiliar enough to provide a model for it.[18]

Taking my cue from this account of sensation fiction as a mode of writing that was both a result of and a participant in processes of modernisation, I would like to add, along the lines of Braddon's letters, that it was also a genre that makes legible how it works out, and comes to assume, its role and function within an increasingly profit-driven culture of literary production in which it had yet to find its place. All that was evident when sensation fiction exploded onto the publishing scene was that it made an addition to it that was either embraced as refreshingly intriguing or rejected as a harmful violation of established codes. Beyond that, however, it was not quite clear, not even to the practitioners of the new 'school', what purpose it fulfilled, or was supposed to fulfil, in the society to the transforma-tion of which it contributed its share. If Braddon's own account is anything to go by, then it suggests that sensation fiction is not only a representation but also an expression of a 'protracted search'. It indi-cates that her writing is an activity that is, to some degree, uncertain about its status and goals, even if it is exciting and enthralling in its becoming. Braddon's letters, in short, make evident that there is a tendency towards self-investigation inherent in the sensational genre that might explain why many of its varieties often seem to 'read themselves being read', to borrow a phrase from Anna Maria Jones, whether intentionally or not.[19] Thus viewed, the extended quest for the secret that sensation novels so often represent in the stories they tell is a symptom of the quest for the knowledge that would capture their mode of operation and define what they are. Sensation fiction is a genre in search of itself.

Lady Audley's Secret

Suspended 'midway between romanticism and realism, Gothic "mys-teries" and modern mysteries, and popular and high culture forms', the sensation novel in the 1860s is both an inherently multifarious and a peculiarly indefinite kind.[20] The making of it participates in the simultaneous construction and observation of a novel site of literary communication and aesthetic experience, a space of potentiality and becoming that resembles the multi-layered and unfinished structure of Audley Court as it is described in *Lady Audley's Secret*. Suggestively, this 'noble place' is above all 'a house in which you incontinently lost yourself if ever you were so rash as to go about it alone' (*LAS* 8), as Braddon's text has it. It is

> a house in which no one room had any sympathy with another, every chamber running off at a tangent into an inner chamber, and through that down some narrow staircase leading to a door which, in its turn, led back into that very part of the house from which you thought yourself the farthest; a house that could never have been planned by any mortal architect, but must have been the handiwork of that good old builder – Time, who, adding a room one year, and knocking down a room another year, toppling over now a chimney coeval with the Plantagenets, and setting up one in the style of the Tudors; shaking down a bit of Saxon wall there, and allowing a Norman arch to stand here; throwing in a row of high narrow windows in the reign of Queen Anne, and joining on a dining room after the fashion of the time of Hanoverian George I to a refectory that had been standing since the Conquest, had contrived, in some eleven centuries, to run up such a mansion as was not elsewhere to be met with throughout the county of Essex. (*LAS* 8–9)

Like the new kind of literary work in the creation of which *Lady Audley's Secret* took a major part, Audley Court is an improvised edifice that has been assembled in an incremental or piecemeal fashion, rather than in consonance with a predesigned scheme ('a house that could never have been planned by any mortal architect'). The (provisional) result is a patchwork of period styles and traditions (Plantagenet, Tudor, Saxon, Norman, Queen Anne, George I), the organisation of which seems to be so idiosyncratic that it frustrates all attempts to be assimilated to a rational logic or plan. As the text indicates, this patched-up structure has never been completed, but always remained subject to be extended, rearranged and undone according to the whims and caprices of 'that good old builder – Time'. Time, thus viewed, is a creative agent that submits all seemingly finished and closed objects to a permanent drift of variation and change that exceeds any one human will.

In short, the construction of Audley Court, as it is described here, is a product that includes the process of its own (re)making, rather than excluding it. The activity that is (part of) the building continuously seems to make it surpass its status quo, extending, redesigning and repairing it again and again, and in all manner of incalculable ways ('adding [. . .] knocking down [. . .] toppling over [. . .] setting up [. . .] shaking down [. . .] allowing [. . .] to stand [. . .] throwing in [. . .] and joining on'). It follows that anyone who enters this labyrinthine site of construction must be prepared to risk losing themselves 'incontinently' in it, because its order cannot be contained in a fixed state or a map so as to be looked at from the outside. The only way to make sense of it, it seems, is to explore it from the inside, to follow its winding paths wherever they lead, even if that journey may unexpectedly end in places from which one had 'thought oneself the farthest'. In fact, the passage through Audley Court is like the passage of the sentence used to describe it. Its course is so involuted, with tangential connections, difficult traverses and unexpected turns ('running off at a tangent [. . .] down some narrow staircase [. . .] and back') that its exact layout and meaning is not easy to grasp as a whole. The text refers to an unsettled site that is just as much raised upon self-contained 'rooms' and apparent distinctions ('no one room had any sympathy with another') as it is raised upon potential relations and 'lines of flight' that make 'every chamber run off at a tangent'.[21]

Thus Audley Court, as it is depicted here, can not only be seen as a miniature model of the work that represents it, but also as a paradigm of the affected and suspended condition that has come to be defined as 'sensational'. The sensational, after all, exists, like the manor house, in a mode of latency and 'intensity', in a condition of 'incipient action and expression' that is replete with multiple, 'mutually exclusive pathways'.[22] As Braddon's letters indicate, however, sensation fiction may not only be seen as a way of creating these intense experiences, but also as an attempt to make readable sense of them. The genre is concerned with the movement towards structure, or with the process through which people make sense of an experience that, initially, presents itself as no more than a sensation or affect: an intense event. In *Lady Audley's Secret*, such a pattern-seeking movement begins to be enacted in the tenth chapter (entitled 'Missing') of the first volume where the reader finds Robert Audley, who had fallen asleep while he was fishing by the river with his friend George, awaking 'surprised to see the fishing-rod lying on the bank, the line trailing idly in the water', but his friend strangely, glaringly gone (*LAS* 82). While, before this incident, there have already been plenty of sinister forebodings and ominous traces of concealed meanings yet to be unveiled, it is not until George goes missing that the process of methodically investigating them is itself represented, or made legible, by the text. For what the 'Missing' chapter introduces is a rupture, a dissociation that, through the figure of Robert, makes itself felt as no more than an indefinite sensation of loss, the full meaning of which is yet to appear. The experience of a manifest lack releases both a feeling of pain and the desire to bring it under control by turning it into a story.

According to Alexander Bain, the medium that connects these two aspects of the mind–body complex, feeling and thought, and enables the one to be converted into the other, is the nervous system, a highly complex 'arrangement' that he compares to 'the course of a railway train' and 'a system of telegraph wires', two new technologies that co-emerged in the Victorian age. 'The various central masses are like so many stations where the train drops a certain number of passengers and takes up others in their stead, whilst some are carried through to the final terminus,' as Bain puts it. 'A system of telegraph wires might be formed to represent exactly what takes place in the brain.'[23] As this image suggests, the purpose of the nerves, in Bain's view, is not to engender '*impressions, influences, or stimuli*', but to transmit them from one 'central mass' or 'station' of the system to another.[24] 'The nerves,' as Bain says, 'originate nothing; they are exclusively a medium of communication; they have the carrying function.'[25]

Similarly, in *Lady Audley's Secret*, the railway and the 'telegraph wires' act as vehicles helping Robert to gather up the pieces of what he repeatedly calls 'the chain of circumstantial evidence' (*LAS* 257) that is supposed to reveal Lady Audley's secret scheme. Thus, from the moment when George and Robert are found seated 'in the first-class carriage of an express, whirling through the pretty open country towards Portsmouth' (*LAS* 42), the novel connects its places of meaning by means of a network of newspaper advertisements, letters, telegrams, timetables and, most prominently, railway-tracks. For example, when Robert travels down to Southampton for the first time to check if George's father-in-law knows anything about George's whereabouts, all he discovers is a 'twisted piece of paper', 'half burned', which turns out to be 'part of a telegraphic dispatch' (*LAS* 97). The contents of this paper, however, do not constitute a definite subject, but merely a set of fragments, whose purpose and origin remain obscure: ' alboys came to   last night, and left by the mail for London, on his way for Liverpool, whence he was to sail for Sydney' (*LAS* 97).

What is sketched out in this way is an emergent map of co-ordinates and communicative pathways indicating links of significance that have yet to be confirmed. We see the threads of connection before we know how to read them. Not unlike Bain's nervous system, one might say, the novel foregrounds the 'carrying function' of its channels while withholding, for as long as possible, the grounds and ends of the meaning that flows through them.[26] Along these channels, the story of *Lady Audley's Secret* unfolds through a dynamic interaction of concealment and revelation, secrecy and detection as well as affective motion and calculated exploration that takes the form of a competition between Robert and Lady Audley, two equally proficient navigators of the technologically structured spaces of the modern world. In fact, it seems as if, by means of this competition, the text represents, on the level of the story, the interplay between the two texts some critics say make up the structure of many novels with a detection plot.[27] The first text is the secret text written by the criminal who manipulates (obliterates, distorts) the marks and traces he cannot help imprinting on the empirical world when committing a crime. The second text is the one about the investigations carried out by a detective who has to find a way of recomposing the first text so as to make it readable *as* a crime.[28] Viewed in the light of this model, both the criminal, Lady Audley, and the detective, Robert, are creative authors of a story-text. Lady Audley invents, and tries to reaffirm, a tale that is supposed to make everyone believe that she really is the governess Lucy Graham, an innocent girl who was lucky enough to have been married by Sir Michael, thus becoming Lady Audley. Robert, by contrast, seeks to construct a counter-plot that proves Lady Audley to be someone other than she purports to be, namely Helen Talboys, née Maldon, who is married to his friend George and supposed to be dead. The production of the first text generates mysteries and makes the familiar appear strange, whereas the writing of the second text attempts to translate these puzzles into a logical pattern that resolves them.

While the authorial narrator, telling the story of Robert's investigations, enables us to read the second text, the first story, the one that has been invented by Lady Audley to conceal who she is and what she has done, is accessible only in the form of traces, innuendoes and half-concealed allusions. Building on Braddon's letters, what I wish to argue is that the representation of Robert's attempts to draw a coherent chain of causes and effects out of these traces inscribes into the story-world the 'protracted' process through which the novel's meaning comes to be composed. On this view, the fact that Robert is shown to become increasingly doubtful about the point and purpose of his enquiries reflects the uncertain function of the sensational work in the making of which he is made to take part. Like Braddon in her letters, Robert often seems to think of himself as being caught up in a development that controls him as much as he controls it. 'Am

I tied to a wheel, and must I go with its every revolution, let it take me where it will?', he asks himself repeatedly; 'Or can I sit down here to-night and say, I have done my duty to my missing friend; I have searched for him patiently, but I have searched in vain? Should I be justified in doing this?' (*LAS* 159).

One function of these reflections is of course to create suspense by protracting the process of investigation even further. But at the same time, they cannot help calling into question the very end of the actions that the novel's main character is made to perform by Braddon's text. '"Why do I go on with this?" he thought; "how piti-less I am, and how relentlessly I am carried on. It is not myself; it is the hand which is beckoning me further and further upon the dark road whose end I dare not dream of"' (*LAS* 174). It is almost as if the amateur detective were protesting against the remorseless way in which he is compelled to move towards a goal or end which will dis-illusion both him, who suspects that his friend is dead, and the reader of the novel, who is likely to notice that sensational events cease to be exciting as soon as they are cleared up. Even Braddon herself, as her letters show, was frequently disappointed about her work as soon she had completed and submitted it for publication.[29] Her writ-ing, in short, seems to be aware of the contingency of its perfor-mance, for there is a subtle irony in Robert's hesitant musings. They intimate that he participates in a search for meaning that may never arrive at a satisfying conclusion, or that may have no point unless it continues, whatever revelation may come at its end. 'If I *could* let the matter rest; if – if I could leave England for ever, and purposely fly from the possibility of ever coming across another clue to the secret, I would do it,' Robert tells Mr Maldon '– I would gladly, thankfully do it – but I *cannot*!' (*LAS* 174). Indeed, Robert cannot stop collect-ing further 'clues to the secret' because the writing, which carries him as much as he carries it, must maintain the mode of suspense and incipience, the mode of being on a quest, otherwise it would lose the very intensity that is the aesthetic and economic trademark of the sensational genre.

What these contemplations suggest, then, is that the writing of Braddon's novel continuously wondered whether it was on the right track. Suggestively, Braddon herself, like Robert, worried more than once about how remorselessly she was beckoned on by a power beyond herself, whether that was the market for 'serials, which force one into overstrained action in the desire to sustain the inter-est' or the 'inexorable printer's devil' who kept demanding '"more copy"'.[30] These worries indicate that there is a lingering sense of self-doubt inherent in the sensational imagination that finds expression in Robert's apprehensions about the reliability of his method. 'What if I am wrong after all?', he asks himself at a point when he has already pieced so many links together that he might rather be expected to believe himself right (*LAS* 252). 'What if this chain of evidence which I have constructed link by link is woven out of my own folly? What if this edifice of horror and suspicion is a mere collection of crochets – the nervous fancies of a hypochondriacal bachelor?' (*LAS* 252). While these questions can be taken for considerations of a fictional character, they can just as well be read as ironic anticipations of 'the worst things the critics said' about the kind of sensational storytelling that is exemplified by *Lady Audley's Secret*. After all, one accusation that was repeatedly advanced against sensation novels was that they were 'mere' 'edifices of horror and suspicion', as H. L. Mansel famously put it, fostering nothing but the same kind of 'nervous fancy' from which they originate.[31] On such a reading, sensation fiction, *Lady Audley's Secret* being Mansel's key example, is precisely what Robert suggests his inferences to be too: namely 'indications' of a 'morbid' and corrupt fantasy that both stimulates and supplies the 'cravings' of a 'diseased appetite' for thrilling revelations.[32]

My point is that attacks such as the one put forth by Mansel overlook that the writing of Braddon's novel itself includes a critical commentary on its own sensational form. The text not only reproduces its own storytelling activities in the medium of Robert's search. It also continuously reflects upon these activities, either by making Robert interrogate his own logic, or by confronting his detective work with other ways of viewing it, such as those of George's father Harcourt Talboys who 'sees no meaning in' what Robert views as a 'horrible mystery' (*LAS* 252). One of these self-reflexive passages occurs in the last chapter of volume two, in which Robert, cannily playing on his aunt's frail nerves, asks her to accompany him into the Lime Walk near Audley Court: 'You are nervous, my lady? [. . .] Let me be the physician to strike to the root of your malady' (*LAS* 263). Rather than trying to cure Lady Audley of her nervousness, Robert aims to 'strike' her with the story he has assembled so as to elicit an affective response from her that will make her confess to her secret deeds and prove his version of what happened to be true. 'Shall I tell you the story of my friend's disappearance as I read that story, my lady?' (*LAS* 264). In this way,

Robert does what writers of sensation fiction were generally said to do too: he tells a story that 'addresses itself primarily to the sympathetic nervous system' of the reader who here figures as Lucy.[33] At the same time, Braddon's writing foregrounds that one reader may well perceive a sensational story as exciting and shocking that another one finds improbable and overdone. Thus, whereas Robert presents Lady Audley (and the reader of the novel) with what he regards as the unveiling of a 'horrible secret', 'a conspiracy concocted by an artful women', 'the most detestable and despicable of her sex' (*LAS* 269, 266), Lucy's version of the same evidence sounds not half as melodramatic as that. For her, it is most 'likely' that George Talboys, having become 'eccentric and misanthropical' due to his wife's death, simply 'grew tired of the monotony of civilised life, and ran away to those savage gold-fields to find a distraction for his grief' (*LAS* 267). Robert, then, by engaging in a *hermeneutics of suspicion*, extracts a sensational conspiracy from the given circumstances whereas his aunt performs what one might call a 'reading for the obvious', or surface reading.[34]

In the end, Robert's text, critics have argued, seems to prevail, with his investigation restoring a social order that had become temporarily unsettled by his aunt's self-empowering tactics, her attempt to escape from the roles Victorian society conventionally assigned to middle-class women. This view, which turns Braddon's novel into a kind of detective fiction,[35] is premised on the assumption that Robert, along with the reader, comes to know Lady Audley's secret in the end. And yet, it is conspicuous that Lady Audley never actually confesses to the treacherous murder of which Robert accuses her, even when it seems already clear that his chain of evidence is sufficiently strong to convict her of it: 'When you say that I killed George Talboys, you say the truth. When you say that I murdered him treacherously and foully, you lie. I killed him because I AM MAD!' (*LAS* 340–1). On the face of it, this seems to be the revelation of the novel's ultimate enigma, Lady Audley's madness, beneath the ones that Robert has already cleared up; and yet it actually functions 'more as "cover-up" than disclosure'.[36] Arguably, if all one knows in the end is that Lady Audley killed her former spouse, or tried to do so, because she is insane, then that knowledge obfuscates her deed as much as it elucidates it. In fact, what kind of mental illness, if any, Lady Audley suffers from remains conspicuously dubious until the last page. While it is certainly possible to associate her condition, as several critics have done, with what the Victorian psychiatrist

James Cowles Prichard described as 'moral insanity',[37] the verdict of the one scientific authority in the text, the physician Dr Mosgrave, remains remarkably vague.[38] 'There is latent insanity! Insanity which might never appear; or which might only appear once or twice in a life-time' (*LAS* 372). And yet again: 'The lady is not mad; but she has the hereditary taint in her blood. She has the cunning of madness, with the prudence of intelligence. I will tell you what she is, Mr Audley. She is dangerous!' (*LAS* 372).

As this intimates, what makes Lady Audley dangerous is not that she is mad, which she is evidently not, but that she could *become* mad. Instead of identifying Lady Audley's actual illness in propositional terms, Mosgrave gestures at a virtual or 'latent' illness that she might be subject to. Likewise, he does not define what Lucy has done in the past; he certainly does not see 'adequate reason for believing that a murder had been committed by this woman' (*LAS* 372). Instead, he recommends preventing what she might do in the future. In short, the novel displaces Lady Audley's secret instead of resolving it. It is as if the text avoided passing judgement on Lady Audley's deed in any final, authoritative, socially sanctioned way. 'This Mr George Talboys has disappeared, but you have no evidence of his death,' Mosgrave tells Robert. 'If you could produce evidence of his death, you could produce no evidence against this lady, beyond the one fact that she had a powerful motive for getting rid of him' (*LAS* 372). Similarly, all the evidence that readers may have collected against Lady Audley is not sufficient to tell them whether she pushed George down the old well because she is mentally ill, or because she is an insidious criminal, or because a tangle of 'economic and class issues' drove her into a trap from which she could see no other way out.[39] All this remaining opaque, the very decision to send Lucy to an asylum seems to be, for all parties involved, no more than a convenient way of closing the whole affair without having to answer any more questions about it. The exact nature of Lady Audley's secret, in brief, remains ill-defined. 'Whatever secrets she may have will be secrets for ever!' (*LAS* 373).

Sensational Motion

Braddon's novel, to sum this up, does not end by revealing Lady Audley's secret, but by deferring it into a realm of the unknown beyond final decisions and authoritative judgements. In this way, it suggests that the driving principle of sensation fiction is not so much to clear up secrets as to make secrets proliferate. In order to maintain their suspended mode, sensation novels have to generate at least as many obscurities as they eliminate. For they do not (yet) have a principle or purpose outside of the process through which their effects are produced. While such novels may primarily seem to represent stories of detection, their motivation is a condition that has to remain essentially undetected, otherwise it would lose its sensational appeal. Thus, in *Lady Audley's Secret*, the subject-matter in question, whatever it is (Lucy's 'latent insanity'?), is not so much unlocked as it is arrested by force, shut up in a way that partly retains its secrecy. 'I sometimes fancy I am rather like one of those most unprofitable race horses that "shut up at the finish",' Braddon wrote to Bulwer-Lytton when talking about what she thought of as her incapacity to conclude her novels in a fashion that makes them rounded and whole.[40] Yet, what Braddon here thinks of as a deficiency, her tendency to conclude inconclusively, is arguably the defining principle of her writing.

After all, as a state of intensity, the sensational has to be thought of as essentially in motion. One might even say that sensation fiction anticipates in practice what William James's early essay 'What is an Emotion?' some twenty years later explicated in theory.[41] According to James, emotions (such as pity, fear, anger, or joy) are not so much conceptual states as feelings of '*bodily changes*' that '*follow directly the* PERCEPTION *of the exciting fact*'.[42] When someone sees a bear, to quote his most memorable example, they do not run because they are frightened. Rather, they are frightened because their body, upon noticing the 'exciting fact' of a bear, is set in motion, which may mean that they tremble or run. Mental emotion follows physical motion. On these premises, one can say that sensation fiction turns on the motional, rather than the emotional. It is a form of writing on the run, for it thrives on the experience that whatever is conclusive can, by definition, no longer be perceived as sensational, as an affective turmoil that has not yet been assigned to, or subsumed under, a particular mental state. The genre's concern is with motions not yet captured as emotions. Above all, then, sensation fiction is yet another attempt at giving form to the experience of being fundamentally unsettled or without firm ground, an experience which, as we saw, preoccupied many Victorians.

In Braddon's *Aurora Floyd*, the novel following immediately upon *Lady Audley's Secret*, the authorial narrator describes this characteristically incomplete experience in a paragraph that is worth quoting in full. 'What mortal ever was *quite* satisfied?', the narrator asks after one of the characters, Talbot Bulstrode, has just been dismissed 'for a while, moderately happy, and yet not quite satisfied'.[43]

> What mortal ever was *quite* satisfied in this world? It is a part of our earthly nature always to find something wanting, always to have a vague, dull, ignorant yearning which cannot be appeased. Sometimes, indeed, we are happy; but in our wildest happiness we are still unsatisfied, for it seems then as if the cup of joy were too full, and we grow cold with terror at the thought that, even because of its fulness, it may possibly be dashed to the ground. What a mistake this life would be, what a wild feverish dream, what an unfinished and imperfect story, if it were not a prelude to something better! Taken by itself, it is all trouble and confusion; but taking the future as the keynote of the present, how wondrously harmonious the whole becomes! How little does it signify that our joys here are not complete, our wishes not fulfilled, if the completion and the fulfilment are to come hereafter![44]

With its view of 'this life' as a prelude to 'something better' to come, this may sound like a vindication of Protestant eschatology, but it can also be regarded as yet another description of the sensational as an emergent condition in which 'trouble and confusion' are mixed up with the prospect of, and the desire for, resolution and 'harmony'. As a formal correlate of this incipient state, sensation fiction, I have tried to show, draws 'the future' into 'the present' and the virtual into the actual. A sensation novel such as *Aurora Floyd* can therefore, and indeed has been, regarded either as 'a wild feverish dream', 'an unfinished and imperfect story', or as the precursor of other, more consummate and complete types of text. Yet, what makes this kind of fiction sensational is, arguably, that it can be reduced to neither of these views, or includes them both.

On this conception, the writing of sensation fiction is a bridge towards the making and experiencing of the new. It 'operates as' what Louise Lee has called 'a fantasy of becoming',[45] similar to the one that Braddon describes in one of the most remarkable passages of her letters. 'I am terribly apt to take a disgust to the novel I am writing, & to devote all my thoughts to a novel I *mean* to write when free of present engagements,' she complains.[46]

> This unwritten novel always seems to me destined to become my magnum opus. *Je le couve*, as Michelet would say. I brood upon it night & day. I can *see* the scenes. I compose the dialogue, oh, such lovely, passionate outbreaks – I can never *write* anything half as good, for that

Archetype is a perfect eel in the matter of slipperiness. There he goes gliding through the turbid waters of the brain, such a beautiful shining rainbow-hued creature. You try to grasp him, and Lo he is gone. He has a rooted antipathy to pen & ink. Out walking in the dismal London streets, sitting in a railway carriage, reading other people's books, playing the piano, lying in bed, there he is always, my perpetual companion. I sit down to my desk, & hey presto, the creature is gone, not so much as a quarter of an inch of his silvery tail remains. If some new Dircks & Pepper would only invent an intellectual photographic apparatus – by means of which the Ghost of the Ideal could be siezed [*sic*] upon.[47]

What Braddon evokes here is a virtual or future work which continually comes to haunt her actual writing in the form of something wanting, of a palpable lack. The 'beautiful shining rainbow-hued creature' is a vision of what her actual writing could or should be but what it is not, or not yet. A 'perfect eel in the matter of slipperiness', the 'unwritten novel' Braddon means to write is always present in her work as a negative component, as something that escapes and eschews her 'pen & ink'. Braddon's writing, this suggests, is deeply informed by the 'Ghost' of what it might be and become. Her novels, she implies, follow the idea or spectre of what is missing in them, something that she can even imagine ('I can *see* the scenes. I compose the dialogue'), but that she has not yet learned to take hold of in written form.[48] This confirms, as suggested above, that Braddon's fiction represents an activity of aspiring towards a way of writing that is yet to be clearly defined. Her art, as she describes it, is of an electrifyingly impure, tentative, unconsummated kind, driven by a vague idea of 'something better' for which it is in search.

Collins's 'Mechanical Genius'

In summary, one can say that sensation fiction was the shorthand for a literary practice that extended the writing of novels into a relatively uncharted, but rapidly growing field. Both the creative composition and the critical evaluation of this new field were equally influenced by a rising demand for serial reading and by an opposing tendency to keep the very idea of literature away from what Mansel called the 'commercial atmosphere' of 'the manufactory and the shop'.[49] Thus, Braddon seemed still torn between a wholehearted espousal of this 'commercial atmosphere' and a lingering ambition, partly instilled by the encouragement of other novelists, to elevate 'the sensational' by a more refined 'art', 'something like excellence', as she called it, that would please not just a popular audience but also someone like Bulwer-Lytton.[50] While Braddon's papers remain vague about what exactly she means by 'something like excellence', they make sufficiently clear that it refers to a way of writing 'in which the story arises naturally out of the characters of the actors in it, as contrasted with a novel in which the actors are only marionettes, the slaves of the story'.[51] As this suggests, what Braddon had in mind is the notion of an organic form that conceals the artifice of its composing, making the unfolding of a story seem like the natural consequence of 'the characters of the actors' involved in it. Assessments such as this are therefore premised on, and reaffirm, a distinction between natural growth and artificial contrivance as well as between internal character and external characteristics. As we shall see, this distinction comes up again and again in the discussions about the emergence of the sensation novel.

Wilkie Collins, for example, was repeatedly accused of subordinating every part of his novels to the single goal of exciting and suspending the curiosity of his readers, or of making his 'audience uncomfortable without letting them know why', as one critic put it in a review of *Armadale*.[52] Observing 'a sort of unearthly and deadly look about the heroes and heroines' of Collins's 'narrative', this reviewer, too, uses the comparison with puppets to pinpoint what he considered the main flaw of Collins's text.[53] On his account, all the 'motions' of the characters in *Armadale* are such that they appear to be 'due, not to a natural process, but to the sheer force and energy of the author's will'.[54] 'They dodge each other up and down the stage after the manner of puppets at a puppet-show.'[55] This image of Collins's novels as spectacles of puppetry set up by a skilful engineer 'directing everything from behind the curtain' but giving his characters no leeway to act on their own was repeatedly used in the reviews of his novels.[56] It insinuates that his texts are not so much works of genuine imagination and deeply felt emotion as they are products of well-calculated plotting and technical know-how. While many critics, including Anthony Trollope, praised the mechanical skill with which Collins planned and executed his intrigues, they missed what they regarded as an element of 'natural' spontaneity and life in the way his characters were enabled to act.[57] One reviewer of *Armadale* even declared that most of the characters of this novel had been 'sacrificed to the story' they are made to carry forward: 'They are not characters, they are shadowy beings put in to answer the requirements of Mr Wilkie Collins's plot.'[58] Although this image of Collins as a mere 'carpenter of plot' lacking aesthetic responsiveness and versatility, survived until at least the second half of the twentieth century,[59] most later studies give a more nuanced account of his technique, sometimes even using the notion of 'experiment' to characterise it.[60]

As I wish to show, it is in fact quite justified to describe Collins's work as experimental because he repeatedly made, or was made to make his novel writing readable as a process in which the fictional characters actively participate alongside their author, rather than fully under his command. In *Armadale*, for example, there is one scene in which some of the protagonists are assembled in the house of Major Milroy, an 'extraordinary mechanical genius', who has been toiling on an unfinished 'model of the famous clock at Strasbourg', a well-known symbol for the argument from design, for eight years.[61] It being close to twelve o'clock, the major proposes to take the group to his 'workshop' in order to show them what the apparatus 'can do on the stroke of noon' (*A* 222). Having first explained to the group 'what the exhibition was to be, before the exhibition began' (*A* 223), the major draws attention to the likelihood that between the conception and the execution of the display a discrepancy might occur out of which incalculable incidents could arise. 'The machinery is a little complicated, and there are defects in it which I am ashamed to say I have not succeeded in remedying as I could wish. Sometimes the figures go all wrong, and sometimes they go all right' (*A* 224). The major, in other words, concedes that the figures involved in his 'little experiment' (*A* 222), might thwart their maker's design and start moving about in a way that he is unable to foresee or control.

As the narrator proceeds to detail, in the first part of the presentation everything still works as the major had described it, but a critical point is reached when the 'crowning exhibition' announces 'itself in a preliminary trembling of the sentry-boxes, and a sudden disappearance of the major at the back of the clock' (*A* 224) – a disappearance that indicates that the experimenter is both present and absent during the central part of his show.

> The performance began with the opening of the sentry-box on the right-hand side of the platform, as punctually as could be desired; the door on the other side, however, was less tractable – it remained obstinately closed. Unaware of this hitch in the proceedings, the corporal and his two privates appeared in their places in a state of perfect discipline, tottered out across the platform, all three trembling in every limb, dashed

themselves headlong against the closed door on the other side, and failed in producing the smallest impression on the immovable sentry presumed to be within. An intermittent clicking, as of the major's keys and tools at work, was heard in the machinery. The corporal and his two privates suddenly returned, backwards, across the platform, and shut themselves up with a bang inside their own door. Exactly at the same moment, the other door opened for the first time, and the provoking sentry appeared with the utmost deliberation at his post, waiting to be relieved. He was allowed to wait. Nothing happened in the other box but an occasional knocking inside the door, as if the corporal and his privates were impatient to be let out. The clicking of the major's tools was heard again among the machinery; the corporal and his party, suddenly restored to liberty, appeared in a violent hurry, and spun furiously across the platform. Quick as they were, however, the hitherto deliberate sentry on the other side, now perversely showed himself to be quicker still. He disappeared like lightning into his own premises, the door closed smartly after him, the corporal and his privates dashed themselves headlong against it for the second time, and the major appearing again round the corner of the clock, asked his audience innocently, 'if they would be good enough to tell him whether anything had gone wrong?' (*A* 224–5)

Unlike Paley's watch, which epitomises the result of a premeditated plan, the major's timepiece turns into the site of a spectacle that emancipates itself from the order it is supposed to enact, becoming subject to unexpected hitches and technical flaws.[62] As a result, the major himself does not appear as a sovereign creator who occupies a vantage point above his creation. Rather, he is presented as one actor among others, participating in the making of the work by means of his 'keys and tools' just as the figures participate in it by means of their movements and actions. Both the major's 'tools' and the figures they are meant to set in motion are 'mediators' in Latour's sense, that is, actors that 'transform, translate, distort, and modify the meaning or the elements they are supposed to carry'.[63] The artist, in short, is entangled with, rather than detached from his composition, for his work interferes with a contrivance whose components act just as much on him as he acts on them. Being thus enmeshed with his creation, it is no surprise that he does not see the outcome of his interventions 'among the machinery', but has to ask the audience 'whether anything had gone wrong'. What this goes to show is that he can influence the mechanical causes of the proceedings on the platform but wants control over, and insight into, the effects induced by his acts. The transition from the mechanical causes (the machinery and the 'tools and keys') to the experienced consequences (the movements of the puppets) seems to develop a life of its own, over the course of which neither the creator nor the audience of the spectacle has full command. No one knows, for example, whether the figures move as strangely as they do because of the major's interference or in spite of it. In fact, it is symptomatic that not only the actions of the figures on the platform spin strangely out of control, but also the reactions of the spectators who, as we are told, 'shouted with laughter' at the 'fantastic absurdity of the exhibition' (*A* 225).

As attentive readers of Collins's novels can hardly have failed to notice, the clock-display lends itself to be read as a model of Collins's own artwork, or rather of his art at work.[64] While it takes up the comparison of his characters with 'puppets at a puppet-show', it also modifies and reinterprets it. On the one hand, the goings-on on the clock's platform clearly resemble the events in Collins's novel, in which the characters, similar to the major's automata, frequently double-cross each other by all kinds of tricks and fakes, just as the 'provoking sentry' seems to outmanoeuvre the corporal and his privates. But on the other hand, the marionettes act conspicuously not like their creator wants them to act, suggesting that even puppet-shows can engender meanings and effects which exceed the intention and control of their maker, no matter how long and hard he may have tried to make his construction function as predictably as a mechanical clock.[65] In short, it seems as if Collins's writing here staged its own mode of operation as the performance of a 'little experiment' set up by a 'mechanical genius' who, despite his talent, is incapable of anticipating and controlling all the outcomes of his work.

There is, moreover, a wider point to be extracted from this episode: as a way of writing in search of its social and aesthetic function, both Collins's work and sensation fiction in general often included or played with the possibility of generating incalculable effects, of spinning out of control like the major's puppets and the delirious, convulsive responses that they induced. 'To write Sensation fiction, as to read it,' Daly points out, 'was to risk being carried away.'[66] The oxymoronic term 'mechanical genius' suggests, furthermore, that sensation novels such as Collins's *Armadale*, again like the major's 'little experiment', ostentatiously straddle the dividing line between the mechanical and the fine arts that critics and reviewers attempted to draw. What these works represented was a hybrid mode of writing: it could either be regarded as literature of the fine arts variety that smacked a little too much of puppetry and mechanical construction, or it could be viewed as literature of the mechanical (mass-produced) kind that aspired to, but had not yet reached, the status of fine art. One can therefore say that the controversy about sensation fiction is part of a wider discussion, some of which we have already examined, on the uses of writing literature and making (fine) art. John Ruskin, for example, bemoans in one of his Oxford lectures that too many of 'our neglected workmen' spent their 'original vivacity or genius' in making what he calls 'ridiculous toy[s]', one of which he encountered on a stroll through the Crystal Palace.[67] As he recalls:

> you dropped a penny into the chink of it, and immediately a little brass steam-engine in the middle started into nervously hurried action; some bell-ringers pulled strings at the bottom of a church steeple which had no top; two regiments of cavalry marched out from the sides, and manoeuvred in the middle; and two well-dressed persons in a kind of opera-box expressed their satisfaction by approving gestures.[68]

What worries Ruskin about this apparatus, which appears rather like the major's mechanical clock, is that it seems to have no purpose other than to make an entertaining show of the workman's dexterity. As Ruskin sees it, to make one's skill into a mere plaything, a medium of pure amusement, however meticulously it may be fabricated, is a useless activity; one that has no use outside of itself.

In a similar manner, sensation novels were often regarded as unhealthy toys, representing nothing but useless entertainment and 'nervously hurried action'. On a more positive view, however, these novels can also be seen as exploratory forms questioning the premises on which the distinction between mere amusement and useful work was typically maintained. What makes them experimental is that they toyed with the idea of engendering nothing but sensations of novelty and thrill. As I have argued, sensation fictions are ways of constructing and furnishing a generic niche that had by the 1860s not yet been located on the map of literary discourses and types. Even the audience at which the sensation novel was aimed was, to a considerable extent, an 'Unknown Public', as Collins called it in a famous essay, in which he expresses his intention not only to address this obscure public but 'to teach' it 'how to read'.[69] One might therefore say that his fictions spoke into a void, a vacuum that they tried to fill with new literary forms, appealing both to the established middle-class reader and to a 'reading public of three millions which lies right out of the pale of literary civilisation', as Collins puts it.[70] His novels emerged from within the established 'literary world' while simultaneously trying to move out of this world, towards a mass audience, 'the lost literary tribes', whose knowledge and tastes were yet to be reconciled with those of their reading peers.[71] The writing of his texts, like the performance of a scientific experiment, took place between the known and the unknown, but could not be assigned to either of these sides.

The Writing of *Armadale*

Perhaps none of Collins's texts is better suited to substantiate this argument than *Armadale*, a bulky series of 'books' which has been called 'a narrative about the very nature of narrative suspense'.[72] Rapidly pushing 'forward in an interminable quest for final form',[73] the writing of the novel also incorporates the delays, disruptions and time lags that are part of most inventive acts, often prolonging and complicating them. As I will argue, to read this novel means to follow the emergent composition of a story-world whose various 'thread[s]' (*A* 17) are shown to be woven by the very characters who participate in it. In one of the first scenes, for example, the German doctor at Wildbad asks the Scotchman Mr Neal whether he could perform a confidential writing task for his patient, Mr Armadale senior. Explaining to Mr Neal the reason for this request, the doctor then reports, 'in Mrs Armadale's own words', how she once eavesdropped upon her husband from behind the door (*A* 17):

> I heard him say to himself: *I shall not live to tell it: I must write it before I die.* I heard his pen scrape, scrape, scrape over the paper – I heard him groaning and sobbing as he wrote – I implored him for God's sake to let me in. The cruel pen went scrape, scrape, scrape; the cruel pen was all the answer he gave me. I waited at the door – hours – I don't know how long. On a sudden, the pen stopped; and I heard no more. I whispered through the keyhole softly; I said I was cold and weary with waiting; I said, Oh, my love, let me in! Not even the cruel pen answered me now: silence answered me. With all the strength of my miserable hands, I beat at the door. The servants came up and broke it in. We were too late; the harm was done. Over that fatal letter the stroke had struck him – over that fatal letter we found him, paralysed as you see him now. Those words which he wants you to write, are the words he would have written himself if the stroke had spared him till the morning. From that time to this, there has been a blank place left in the letter; and it is that blank place which he has just asked you to fill up. (*A* 17–18)

What is represented here is an act of writing that creates nothing but excitement, suspense and curiosity on the part of the reader, as well as physical hardship and health problems on the part of the author ('I heard him groaning and sobbing', 'Over that fatal letter the stroke had struck him'). The process of writing, rather than serving as a medium to tell a story or convey particular ideas, is exhibited as a purely material event, a practice of 'scraping' over paper. As a result, Mr Armadale's composition turns into a mere instrument, a painfully recalcitrant object void of reference and signification ('the cruel pen was all the answer he gave me'). All that his text communicates is a feeling of being tantalisingly denied the fulfilment for which one craves, or a sense of being made to wait for a revelation that is still to come ('Oh, my love, let me in!'). Tellingly, the scraping pen never engenders a meaningful whole, but at best a gaping hole, a 'blank place' that provokes the production of more text.

In sum, Mrs Armadale's overhearing of her husband's scribbling makes the writing of the novel readable as an activity that conceals at least as much as it seems to reveal. Like a reader of a sensation novel, Mrs Armadale seems to be deliberately kept on tenterhooks, excluded from the information she eagerly wants. As so often in sensation fiction, and particularly in *Armadale*, the activity of writing is here integrated into the written world of the story. As a consequence, this same story is exposed as a work in progress, a pattern in the making assembled by the very figures to whom it seems to refer. In this way, the characters of the novel are depicted as inhabitants of an unfinished construction in the setting-up of which they are themselves engaged. They act more like independent builders than like puppets on strings. As a reader, in turn, one reads about the tracing of a narrative thread that one can only come to see if one is willing to follow the movements and actions of the figures who contribute to its being composed. Thus, when the doctor has finished his task of telling Mrs Armadale's story, he transfers his office as mediator to Neal who first reads out Mr Armadale's text as far as it has already been written, before he fills in the missing lines upon the dictation of the dying man. It is as if the characters took turns in the drawing out of a design of which they know as little as the reader of the novel. As one subsequently learns, this activity comes to a preliminary end at the close of the first book when the dying Armadale reveals, and Neal writes down, that he once murdered a man whose son bears the same name as his own, Allan Armadale. While this revelation seems to conclude the first book, however, it simultaneously operates as a bridge towards future acts of rereading and rewriting Armadale's story under different circumstances and in different ways.

Thus, at the beginning of the second book, the first traces of the Armadale story soon recur in the memory of Reverend Brock, the tutor of the other Allan Armadale (the son of the murdered man), whom the reader is made to accompany on 'a journey through the past years of his own life' (*A* 53). Here, again, 'the progressive series' of events is told from the inside of the story that is made out of them (*A* 53). As Brock's memory unfolds, it first introduces the reader to (the rather mysterious) Ozias Midwinter, who is revealed to be Allan Armadale, junior, when he receives and peruses the letter read out and finished by Neal in the first book. After Brock, too, has read this epistle, Midwinter first acquaints him with 'the thread' of his biographical 'story' from his father's death until the present time, before the two men proceed to an extended 'consideration' of the late Armadale's confessional letter which effectively transforms the progress of the second book into a rereading of the first (*A* 97, 100). Spreading his father's text 'open before him' and Brock (*A* 100), Midwinter not only quotes the whole of his father's final verdict again ('Avoid the widow of the man I killed [. . .] avoid the man who bears the same name as your own', *A* 100); he also asks himself the kinds of questions that his author must have asked himself, too. 'What is it appointed me to do – now that I am breathing the same air, and living under the same roof with the son of the man whom my father killed – to perpetuate my father's crime by mortally injuring him? or to atone for my father's crime by giving him the devotion of my whole life?' (*A* 103). As in *Lady Audley's Secret*, such reflections both build up suspense and represent the process whereby the second book of Collins's novel takes form as a continuation and re-enactment of the first. Just as Midwinter wonders how he should relate to his father's superstitious warning, so Collins, too, had to decide how the contents of the letter were to be used in the further composition of a plot. When Brock, against Midwinter's wish to destroy and forget the document, insists on looking 'at it once more', it seems as if Collins's writing were scrutinising one of its key components, so as to see what else can be extracted from it (*A* 104).

> 'I view your father's superstition as you view it,' said the rector. 'But there is a warning given you here, which you will do well (for Allan's sake, and for your own sake,) not to neglect. The last link with the past will not be destroyed when you have burnt these pages. One of the actors in this story of treachery and murder is not yet dead. Read those words.'

He pushed the page across the table, with his finger on one sentence. Midwinter's agitation misled him. He mistook the indication, and read, 'Avoid the widow of the man I killed – if the widow still lives.' 'Not that sentence,' said the rector. 'The next.' Midwinter read it: 'Avoid the maid whose wicked hand smoothed the way to the marriage – if the maid is still in her service.' (*A* 104)

As this passage indicates, *Armadale* is a novel that insists that the reader look at its sentences closely and repeatedly. While this is the third time that one is presented with a warning about 'the maid' having had a 'wicked hand' in the affair that brought the late Armadale to kill his opponent, the reader has not yet had much occasion to consider this woman as a possible 'link' between the past life of the fathers and the present life of the sons. However, with Brock's explicit request to examine once again the sentence referring to her ('Read those words'), even less scrupulous readers can hardly avoid watching out for further traces of a 'wicked' female from now on. What one reads here, then, is how the characters make out the very plot pattern of which their own actions are parts. Thus viewed, Brock and Midwinter appear like fictions of Collins's readers who are similarly suspended over certain textual details to work out what they might (turn out to) mean.

Like readers of the novel, in sum, Brock and Midwinter are engaged in a process of trying to grasp the meaning of the words and signs to which they are exposed. Collins's story includes the activities of concatenating the details of which it is made up. It is evidently in progress. For example, when Brock remembers, and thereby reminds the reader, that he himself met the maid in question when she visited Mrs Armadale at her 'residence in Somersetshire, last year', Midwinter excitedly asks for more information (*A* 104). Thus he prompts Brock, along with the reader, to recall 'that she moved very gracefully, that she had a beautiful figure, and that she was a little over the middle height' (*A* 105). Last but not least, we are also reminded, as we have read earlier, 'that she wore a thick black veil, a black bonnet, a black silk dress, and a red Paisley shawl' (*A* 105). These details, in turn, bring to Midwinter's (as well as to our) mind a police report about a woman who threw herself from a river steamer – an incident which had already been mentioned in conjunction with a strange series of deaths in the Armadale family. '*That* woman,' too, Midwinter emphasises, as if he wanted to make the reader aware of another possible connection, 'wore a black veil, a black bonnet, a black silk gown, and a red Paisley shawl–' (*A* 105).

The point, once again, is that the process of composing and reading the story of *Armadale* is itself inscribed into it. In this way, the text of the novel manifestly offers us glimpses of its own extended genesis. It is instructive to note, for instance, that Collins did not mention the black silk gown and the red Paisley shawl when he originally wrote the scene in which Brock meets the veiled lady for the first time. As John Sutherland mentions in his notes (*A* 686), Collins added these accessories at the proof stage of the editing, which indicates that he only seized on their significance as his writing progressed. Like his characters and his readers, he does not seem to have known how to select and combine all the details of his plot-pattern until he actually began to build them into a coherent text. To be sure, Collins himself famously insisted that 'the great stages of the story, and the main features of the characters, invariably lie before me on my desk before I begin my book'.[74] But he also admitted that he left 'the minor details of incident, and the minuter touches of character' 'to suggest themselves to me at the time of writing for publication', as he revealed in an 1865 letter to a reader, using the example of *Armadale*.[75]

> *How* I shall lead you from one main event to the other – whether I shall dwell at length on certain details or pass them over rapidly – how I may yet develop my characters and make them clearer to you by new touches and traits – all this, I know no more than you do, till I take the pen in hand.[76]

In the case of *Armadale*, moreover, Collins was progressing much more slowly than usual, mainly due to frequent travelling and a continuous struggle with ill health.[77] These problems might supply one reason for why the activity of constructing a meaningful and coherent story has itself become such a prominent part of the fictional world which Collins's novel makes us imagine. Whether intentionally or unintentionally, the text repeatedly lays bare the artifice of its story. Both nineteenth- and twentieth-century readers have therefore often criticised that the novel seems to seek melodramatic effects too unabashedly. Braddon, for example, who followed the serial run of the text in the *Cornhill* magazine, found the first two numbers to be 'too openly & inartistically sensational'.[78] And after she had read the third number, her verdict sounded even more apodictic: 'Wilkie Collins *is* on the wrong track,' she averred. 'That women in the red Paisley shawl – the sudden & most inartistic deaths of a small family that need never have been born so far as the book is concerned strike me as unworthy the hand that so neatly put together that delicious puzzle "The Woman in White".'[79] What Braddon calls 'inartistic', however, is rather an 'excess of contrivance' which she takes Collins's technique to fail to conceal.[80] As she sees it, Collins is not artful enough (hence 'inartistic') to cover up the traces of his constructive work. More than a hundred years later Sue Lonoff made almost the same point: 'The mechanics of the plot are obtrusive, and while Collins is ingenious, he is also overzealous; he strains for effect, heaps ploy on ploy, supplies too many cues and warnings.'[81]

As indicated, such critiques are premised on the old assumption that well-made novels should, on the principle of *celare artem*, suppress the 'mechanics' of their storytelling, putting them at the service of an illusion of verisimilitude and 'real' life. My suggestion, by contrast, is to read *Armadale* not as a form of deficient realism but as an invitation to study the making of what we have come to see as sensational plots. For as long as Midwinter and Brock ponder over the manuscript of the letter, Collins's writing is effectively representing nothing but the search for an order of meaning on which the subsequent action of the characters can be built. The text delays and defers the telling of its sensational story in favour of showing the reader how it is brought into being. What readers are faced with here is an activity of meaning-making which, like their own, is caught up in a field between the 'gathering up' of 'facts' and the spinning of 'idle fancies' (*A* 106). We read about readers who are entangled in a web of clues and possible associations not yet or not quite knowing how to interpret them. To be sure, Midwinter does extract at least two pieces of 'positive' (*A* 106) information from his repeated examinations of the letter ('He began searching restlessly among the manuscript leaves scattered about the table, paused over one of the pages, and examined it attentively'; 'He searched among the papers once more, and stopped at another of the scattered pages', *A* 106), namely the present age of the woman in the red shawl and the name and history of the murder ship. But for the time being, these fragments of meaning are only presented to the reader as possible components for the future composition of a plot.

A 'text', D. C. Greetham has argued, is by definition 'an ambivalent place' because it consists of a material as well as of an ideal part, neither of which is reducible to the other: 'It is, on the one hand, a place of fixed, determinable, concrete signs, a material artefact, and yet, on the other, an ineffable location of immaterial concepts.'[82] What the above dialogue draws attention to are the activities of reading and writing that make material signifiers into immaterial concepts and that, conversely, translate abstract ideas into material inscriptions. By enabling us to read these 'discursive practices' as part of the emergent plot-pattern which we primarily seem to realise, Collins's text indicates that it is not a finished object with a meaningful story inside, but a work of writing and reading in the twofold sense: a work that is both 'produced and productive, generated and generative'.[83] As we have seen, Collins's 'characters' are repeatedly shown to operate on the threshold between the material and the ideal, the signs on the page and the patterns of meaning to which they refer. Making words matter as meaningful concepts, the figures of *Armadale* perform what one might call the '*intra-action*' through which discourse and story, signifiers and referents become separate in the first place.[84] More than once, the 'books' of Collins's novel are exposed as sites of constructive and interpretive activities, peopled by actors whose movements the reader is made to follow. Hence my point that these books do not only tell the sensational story of the two Armadales; they also show us how this story is being composed.

A crucial element in the process whereby the plot of *Armadale* comes together is the narrative of 'Allan Armadale's Dream', an embedded sequence of events which is carefully noted down by Midwinter according to Allan's first-person memory of what he saw while he was asleep on the 'fatal ship'. (This ship is one detail from the father's letter that has now come to matter in the story of the sons.) Altogether consisting of seventeen numbered events, Allan's dream narrative reads as follows:

1. The first event of which I was conscious, was the appearance of my father. He took me silently by the hand; and we found ourselves in the cabin of a ship.
2. Water rose slowly over us in the cabin; and I and my father sank through the water together.
3. An interval of oblivion followed; and then the sense came to me of being left alone in the darkness.
4. I waited.
5. The darkness opened, and showed me the vision – as in a picture – of a broad, lonely pool, surrounded by open ground. Above the farther margin of the pool, I saw the cloudless western sky, red with the light of sunset.
6. On the near margin of the pool, there stood the Shadow of a Woman.

7. It was the shadow only. No indication was visible to me by which I could identify it, or compare it with any living creature. The long robe showed me that it was the shadow of a woman, and showed me nothing more. [. . .]
10. Standing opposite to me at the window was the Shadow of a Man. [. . .] (*A* 141–2)

As the watery imagery of sinking and rising suggests, whatever these scenes refer to is made to float indefinitely in a state between the past and the future as well as between the material and the ideal.[85] Thus, even though the dreamy figures seem removed from the empirical world, they still propose themselves to be regarded as 'shadows' of it. Concomitantly, the represented events can either be viewed as (more or less imperfect) reproductions of past experiences or as outlines of future ones, just as they can equally be seen as descriptions of an actual (empirical, known) or of a possible (imaginary, unknown) world. The dream scenes, in short, exceed the familiar while simultaneously asking to be (re)included in it. In the ensuing discussion between Doctor Hawbury, Midwinter and Allan, these two tendencies of unsettling disruption and normalising reintegration are made to clash with and veer into each other. Whereas Hawbury verbosely and complacently seeks to explain the shadowy narrative by means of a 'rational theory' (*A* 150), according to which all of its components can be traced back to something Allan 'has said or thought, or seen or done, in the four-and-twenty hours, or less, which preceded his falling asleep' (*A* 144), Midwinter's silent refusal to accept the doctor's account speaks for the possibility that the dream might mean something altogether different, something not yet known.

As a result of this confrontation of an extended attempt to vindicate the rational with an unexplained belief in the supernatural, the last two books of the second volume ('The Shadow of the Past' and 'The Shadow of the Future') make the novel's familiar past fluctuate into its unknown future. Collins's text rewrites some of its preceding events in the form of a watery dream while almost simultaneously turning this same dream into a shadow of its further progress. One might say that Collins's writing at once reimagines its past and forecasts its future, showing its readers that it takes place between forward projection and feedback loops. In fact, the subsequent books, along with Collins's endnote, even seem to suggest that Hawbury's 'natural' or backward-looking reading of the dream is just as plausible as Midwinter's 'supernatural' or forward-looking account (*A* 678).

One reason why the readers of Collins's novel are invited 'to interpret' the dream 'as the bent of their own minds may incline them' (*A*
678) is that Collins's fiction, as we have seen, delegates much of its
interpretive work to its self-created characters, rather than leaving it
firmly in the hands of an authorial narrator. This form of composition resonates with the experimental theory of fiction that Collins
briefly sketched out in the 1860 Preface to *The Woman in White*.
Here Collins not only expressly describes his novel as an 'experiment'; he also specifies how it has been carried out: 'The story is
told throughout by the characters of the book. They are all placed
in different positions along the chain of events; and they all take the
chain up in turn, and carry it on to the end.'[86] Although *Armadale*,
unlike *The Woman in White* or *The Moonstone*, does have an authorial narrator, its story, as we have seen, is also predominantly made
out from within the very fictional environments that it creates and
to which it refers (Wildbad, Barbados, London, the Isle of Man,
Thorpe-Ambrose). As a result, the discursive practices of the characters seem to be related to the narrator in the same way as Major
Milroy is related to the actions of his puppets.

This authorial function of the characters becomes even more obvious when, at the beginning of the third book, two new actors, Lydia
Gwilt and Miss Oldershaw, are made to intervene in the Armadale
affair. Tellingly, they, too, announce their activities in writing, namely
as a series of letters they exchange on the subject of Lydia's past and
future relationship to the Armadale family. These letters – a narrative
device often used by Collins – not only serve to identify Lydia Gwilt
as the 'maid' with the 'wicked hand', the woman in the red Paisley
shawl, that had already been introduced earlier as a writer of dubious
missives. More importantly, they show us how she, helped by Mrs
Oldershaw, seeks to take control of the very action in which she had
so far only occurred as a minor, though ominous, figure with uncertain
goals. This 'plot-generating function'[87] of Miss Gwilt is highlighted by
the fact that both she and Oldershaw repeatedly describe their scheme
as an 'experiment', 'the Thorpe-Ambrose experiment' (*A* 161, 167),
which is supposed to begin with the interference of Lydia Gwilt in
'Major Milroy's household' (*A* 167) on the Norfolk estate inhabited
by Allan Armadale. Thus, as soon as Gwilt appears 'near the margin of
the pool' of Hurle Mere, 'fronting the sunset' and reinvoking the first
vision of Allan's dream (*A* 265), she varies the existing circumstances
considerably, exerting a kind of 'magnetic influence' (*A* 382) on most
of the other characters that causes them to react to her presence in
trouble-inducing ways. In the following pages, Gwilt increasingly

seizes control of the action, trying to execute a plot which compels the other characters to move according to her interests. Eventually (for the final third of the novel), she even turns into the very author of the text we read, with the whole story being told through the writing of her diary.

Ironically, Gwilt begins her diary both to 'compose' herself and to figure out her role in the 'story' of Allan and Midwinter which, she feels, has 'taken possession of me, never to leave me again' (*A* 424). This means that the subsequent paragraphs document not only how she becomes the criminal character that she is but also how she seeks to draw her own activities into a developing plot. Expressly described as an 'experiment', her diary both carries the story forward and represents an attempt to 'find my way through the difficulties at Thorpe-Ambrose that are still to come', as she puts it (*A* 424):

> Let me think. What *haunts* me, to begin with? The Names haunt me. I keep saying and saying to myself: Both alike! – Christian name and surname, both alike! [. . .]
>
> So there are two of them – I can't help thinking of it – both unmarried. The light-haired Armadale, who offers to the woman who can secure him, eight thousand a year while he lives; who leaves her twelve hundred a year when he dies; who must and shall marry me for those two golden reasons; and whom I hate and loathe as I never hated and loathed a man yet. And the dark-haired Armadale, who has a poor little income, which might perhaps pay his wife's milliner, if his wife was careful [. . .]
>
> And Allan the Fair doesn't know he has a namesake. And Allan the Dark has kept the secret from everybody but the Somersetshire clergyman (whose discretion he can depend on), and myself. And there are two Allan Armadales – two Allan Armadales – two Allan Armadales. There! three is a lucky number. Haunt me again, after that, if you can!
>
> What next? The murder in the timber-ship? No; the murder is a good reason why the dark Armadale, whose father committed it, should keep his secret from the fair Armadale, whose father was killed; but it doesn't concern *me* [. . .] What am I sure of that really concerns myself? [. . .]
>
> What does matter is, that Midwinter's belief in the Dream is Midwinter's only reason for trying to connect me with Allan Armadale, by associating me with Allan Armadale's father and mother [. . .] (*A* 425)

Nothing of what is spread out in this extended meditation is entirely new to the *Armadale* reader: the two Allan Armadales, the problem of names, the loss and regain of a family inheritance, the murder in the timber-ship, the dream, Midwinter's superstition, Gwilt's past as a dexterous writer. What is new, however, is Gwilt's attempt to transform herself into an active participant in the plot that has been made out of these details so far. By means of Gwilt's diary, Collins's text repeats the key components of its story while simultaneously making Gwilt reconfigure their relations according to a design which is yet to emerge in full. As a result, Collins's story is represented as a process of writing in search of a way to adapt itself to, and become rearranged by, a relatively new actor in it. Renegotiating the terms and conditions of the *Armadale* story, the passage draws attention to the mediating figure, the third instance ('There! three is a lucky number') of translation and composition, embodied by Gwilt, that is itself exhibited as immanent to the novel's plot. Inhabiting the construction site between story and discourse, signifier and signified, Gwilt (as her name suggests) embodies the slow and painful activity whereby the building blocks of Collins's work are gradually assembled and 'quilted' into a meaningful whole.

In a complicated and long-winded narrative such as *Armadale*, review passages like Gwilt's first diary entry were certainly necessary to remind the readers of the serial number, who could not just turn back the pages, of the main particulars and incidents of the story they had read so far. Yet they also gave Collins the opportunity to make his own activity of writing part of the events to which it refers. In this way, even the phases of exhaustion, flagging motivation and lack of imagination, of which Collins suffered more than usual while he was working on *Armadale*, could be built into the story without interrupting its progress. What is more, the chronicling of these 'creative setbacks' in Gwilt's diary even enabled Collins to use them as a means to create suspense.[88]

> I won't write any more. I hate writing! It doesn't relieve me – it makes me worse. I'm farther from being able to think of all that I *must* think of, than I was when I sat down. It is past midnight. To-morrow has come already – and here I am as helpless as the stupidest woman living! Bed is the only fit place for me. (*A* 426)

Again, the act of inventing and composing a text is here drawn into the very story that it conveys. In this way, the novel's meaning is shown to exist only by virtue of creative practices of which even the modes of waiting for inspiration and a revival of interest are integral parts. 'And here I am back again at my Diary, with nothing, absolutely nothing, to write about. Oh, the weary day! the weary day! Will nothing happen to excite me a little in this horrible place?'

(*A* 550). Such utterances can be interpreted both as expressions of a fictional character in the story and as representations of the 'weary', slow-going labour of bringing fictional characters and stories into the empirical world. They make Collins's writing legible as that of one of his characters.

Action in *The Moonstone*

This idea of having the main characters of a novel compose their own story finds its most famous expression in *The Moonstone*, in which the whole sequence of events is assembled from the inside of the fictional world, with all traces of authorial narration having been effaced entirely. As a consequence, neither the search for the lost diamond, which dominates most of *The Moonstone*, nor its representation is subordinated to, or policed by, a single-minded agency.[89] There is, to be sure, a memorable detective in the novel, namely Sergeant Cuff, a senior member of the police force, but even he ultimately turns out to be just one detective among others, not much better at solving the mystery than anyone else. According to D. A. Miller's influential interpretation, this 'dissemination of the detective-function' suggests that, in the world of *The Moonstone*, mutual surveillance is endemic to the conventions of social interaction, underpinning the codes of conduct to which everyone adheres.[90] Yet, while Miller's reading, like that of most critics, still takes *The Moonstone* to be 'a novel of detection',[91] another way of approaching Collins's work is to argue that it undermines the very premises on which the genre of detective fiction is now generally taken to rest. Crucially, detective novels are usually considered to be about the investigation and revelation of a crime, but even though there seems to be an obvious crime in *The Moonstone* at first, it becomes increasingly less obvious wherein it consists. First of all, it is more than questionable whether the Moonstone can be said to have been 'stolen' if neither of the persons who are most likely to be regarded as perpetrators of the 'theft', Franklin Blake and Godfrey Ablewhite, ever took it away by design. As far as the text allows one to understand, Blake removed the diamond unwittingly before placing it in the hands of Godfrey Ablewhite, who only decided to keep it when he realised that Blake had lost all knowledge of what he did the night before. Furthermore, the novel makes one wonder to what extent Ablewhite, to say nothing of Blake, can be held solely responsible for his acts when in fact many other agents, both human (Rosanna, Rachel, Dr Candy, Luker, the Indians, Betteredge) and non-human (alcohol, tobacco, opium, money) are directly or indirectly involved in the so-called theft.

As I wish to argue, therefore, the key question raised by *The Moonstone* is not 'whodunit' but 'who or what made them do (or not do) it'. The novel is not so much about a single (criminal) deed and its investigation as it is about the network of interlocking actors and factors in which human action is caught up and by means of which it comes to pass. As the decentred pattern of narration with its various writers and documents suggests, this 'network of mysteries and uncertainties' (*M* 92) surrounding the arrival and removal of the Moonstone seems to elude the attempt to grasp it from an authorial position outside of it. Instead, readers have to follow (some of) the actors that participate in its composition. The pluralised, many-voiced narration of the novel can therefore be seen as the formal correlate of what I regard as one of its key themes: the dislocation and diffusion of agency and responsibility. Again and again the novel casts doubt on the assumption that the source of human actions can be located in autonomous subjects or self-contained minds. In fact, as the prominent influence of drugs (alcohol, tobacco, opium) on the course of events indicates, Collins's text shrouds the origins of its story action in a hazy mist of uncertainty, showing that what someone does may spring from a multiplicity of motives, many of which may not even be part of their conscious intentions or thoughts.[92] The fact that Blake removed the diamond from Rachel's sitting room, for example, can, among other things, be attributed to: Colonel Herncastle's decision to bequeath the jewel to Rachel and his request to give it to her 'on her next birthday' (*M* 40); the presence of the Indians who are generally perceived as a threat; Murthwaite's claim (as pronounced during the dinner party) that these foreigners would seek to attain the gem 'with the ferocity of tigers' (*M* 72); Dr Candy's ambition to teach Blake a lesson; Blake's nervousness as well as his lack of sleep and nicotine; his dilettante statement that 'a course of medicine' was the same as 'a course of groping in the dark' and the ensuing dispute with Candy (*M* 69); his concern for Rachel; Rachel's declining Lady Verinder's offer to keep the diamond for her during the night; and of course the opium that Dr Candy administered to Blake with the help of Ablewhite, who was refused by Rachel and takes pleasure in the prospect of seeing Blake humiliated.

Yet, while all of these agents and activities may have had a necessary share in the disappearance of the jewel, neither of them is sufficient to explain what actually happened during the night in which the Moonstone was taken from its place. While the novel may seem to find (and punish) its culprit at the end, it also reveals Able-white's removal of the diamond from the house to be so mixed up in a meshwork of other actions that one wonders to what extent it can be called his own deed. At best, one could argue that Ablewhite *becomes* responsible, incrementally, for something that does not even begin as his own physical act. Although Collins claimed in his Preface that the writing of *The Moonstone* represented an attempt to 'trace the influence of character on circumstances', rather than 'of circumstances upon character' (*M* 'Preface'), his text actually shows the vectors that relate these two sides to run both ways. Characters such as Ablewhite, Blake and Rachel are just as much shaped by circumstances as they are shaping of them.

In sum, then, my argument is that *The Moonstone* is concerned with how actions are 'borrowed, distributed, suggested, influenced, dominated, betrayed, translated' in such a way that it seems almost impossible to ascribe them, as detective fiction is typically said to do, to self-contained subjects or characters with predefined (criminal) intentions and strategic goals.[93] Among other things, *The Moonstone* seems to explore the notion of an agency or subjectivity that is sus-pended between the inside and the outside of anyone's mind, rather than contained in and determined by either of these sides exclusively. 'My head,' as Betteredge puts this towards the end of his narra-tive, 'was by this time in such a condition, that I was not quite sure whether it was my own head, or Mr Franklin's' (*M* 173). As we have seen in Chapter 4, this ecological conception of self and intention was anything but foreign to Victorian psychology. In fact, it has even been argued that 'the distinctive aspect of Victorian mental science was' that it 'shifted attention away from what minds are to how they work in the world'.[94] One way of reading *The Moonstone* is to see it as a response to such a non-essentialist, 'Subjective-Objective' view of the psyche (*M* 42), according to which minds and selves are shaped through dynamic interactions with changeable environments. Thus, Franklin Blake's character is said to be susceptible to 'puzzling shifts and transformations' which are 'due to the effect on him of his foreign training' (*M* 42–3), as Betteredge speculates. There were, the headservant says about Blake, 'so many different sides to his charac-ter, all more or less jarring with each other, that he seemed to pass his life in a state of perpetual contradiction with himself' (*M* 43).

As the novel unfolds, Blake's 'state of perpetual contradiction' comes to matter most conspicuously in his double role as both appar-ent thief and notable detective. While Blake's return to Yorkshire about a year after the disappearance of the Moonstone is still motivated by his desire to clear up Rachel's ominous secret and lay his 'hand on the thief who took the Moonstone', his discovering the stained night gown, along with Rosanna's letter, changes the whole target of his enquiry in one fell swoop (*M* 307). Suddenly, the object of his search seems no longer (only) to be found outside of what he has taken to delineate his own self, but (also) inside it. For when Blake unearths the box with the nightgown from the quicksand, he unexpectedly finds himself to be both investigator and investigated, subject and object, not (yet) knowing how to separate the one from the other. Trying to come to terms with this puzzling condition, he embroils himself in a 'labyrinth of useless speculations', in which inside and outside, the material and the ideal, the fantastic and the real mingle and intersect (*M* 355). 'For the greater part of the night, I sat smoking, and building up theories, one more profoundly improbable than another' (*M* 355), he remembers.

> When I did get to sleep, my waking fancy pursued me in dreams. I rose the next morning, with Objective-Subjective and Subjective-Objective inextricably entangled together in my mind; and I began the day which was to witness my next effort at practical action of some kind, by doubting whether I had any sort of right (on purely philosophical grounds) to consider any sort of thing (the Diamond included) as existing at all. (*M* 355)

Blake's 'mind' reincludes the distinction between subject and object, self and other in the form of a chiasmus, an entanglement that is yet to be unravelled. This means that the subsequent investigation of possible motives for his act begins from a condition in which the conscious and the unconscious (or 'the waking' and 'the dreaming') part of his self are mutually included in, rather than distinct from, each other. What he faces is the task of drawing the other out of his self, or of making the unknown part of himself readable as an object that he and others can understand.[95]

Subsequently, Blake's exploration of what made him act as he appears to have done takes the form of a series of what he calls 'experiments in the art of enquiry' (*M* 357). This series culminates in the 'bold experiment', designed by Ezra Jennings, to make Blake 'steal the Diamond, unconsciously, for the second time, in the presence of witnesses whose testimony is beyond dispute' (*M* 384). On the story level, this experiment, as the reference to the 'testimony' of 'witnesses' indicates, operates (in Bernard's sense) as a mediator between the subjective and the objective, for it is supposed to convert a personal conviction – that Blake took the Diamond in a state of opium-induced trance – into a generally recognisable fact. On the level of form, moreover, Jennings's experiment re-presents one of the novel's past, though partly untold, episodes in the mode of a quasi-scientific work. In this way, Collins's writing makes itself readable as an artificial construction set up by an eccentric outsider of dubious authority who confesses to be dependent on the use of opium to maintain his apparently fragile health.

As so often in sensation fiction, there is a considerable degree of self-reflexive irony involved in this constellation, for Collins himself not only insinuated that pain and exhaustion forced him to dictate large stretches of *The Moonstone* from his bed. He even claimed later that the laudanum that he, like Jennings ('the physical suffering exhausts me', *M* 396–7), had to take to alleviate his aches drugged him so much that he could not recognise parts of the novel as having been written by himself.[96] While the first claim may at least have a kernel of truth in it, the second one has been unmasked as either an evident case of 'misremembering or a fib'.[97] Yet, no matter whether these assertions are true or false, the construction and execution of Jennings's experiment can certainly be read as a version of Collins's own act of designing and composing his text. After all, what one is presented with in the fictitious diary entries is how an episode of remarkably sensational events is being set up and acted out. In fact, Jennings's whole part, which follows upon Blake's, reads as if it was meant to represent how the central scene of *The Moonstone* – a variant of which we have already read earlier – is brought into existence as an experimental work overseen by an opium eater in urgent need of 'sympathy' and social recognition (*M* 393).

In short, by means of Jennings's diary, Collins's writing both looks back upon its own story and stages the process of its becoming increasingly exciting. The novel reimagines a part of itself in the form of a meticulously designed experiment, a 'medical enterprise' (*M* 404), while simultaneously drawing attention to the artful contrivance by which it creates its sensational effects. Thus both Betteredge and Bruff, the lawyer, view Jennings's work as a mere fabrication or spectacle, incapable of engendering the kind of proof that it is designed to yield. Betteredge even compares the experiment to 'a conjuring trick', 'a delusion and a snare', while Bruff, who insists on bringing some of his legal papers to the scene, finds it to be 'akin to the trickery of mesmerism, clairvoyance, and the like' (*M* 398, 401, 397). Ironically, the performance of the experiment, as it is then described in Jennings's diary, assumes a 'strong dramatic interest' indeed, making it highly similar to the kind of work in which it is contained (*M* 417). And although the witnesses are 'placed' behind the 'chintz curtains' attached to Blake's bed (*M* 417), they become increasingly drawn into the 'suspended interest' of the display (*M* 418), irrespective of how dispassionate and detached they purport to be.

Just as the laudanum acts on Franklin Blake, making his eyes gleam with 'the sublime intoxication of the opium' (*M* 419), then, so the progress of the experiment acts on its spectators, making them surrender to the spell of the events. '"For the Lord's sake, sir,"' Betteredge excitedly whispers to Jennings, '"tell us when it will begin to work"' (*M* 418). In this manner, the reactions of the spectators are made into an essential part of the proceedings watched by them. Jennings may tell us that he had 'utterly forgotten the two companions' of his 'night vigil', but in fact his diary text always keeps them in view (*M* 419). It seems just as much concerned with what is seen as with how it is seen. In Jennings's report, Bruff and Betteredge therefore appear as both subjects and objects, observers and observed:

> Looking towards them now, I saw the Law (as represented by Mr Bruff's papers) lying unheeded on the floor. Mr Bruff himself was looking eagerly through a crevice left in the imperfectly-drawn curtains of the bed. And Betteredge, oblivious of all respect for social distinctions, was peeping over Mr Bruff's shoulder. (*M* 419)

What the two characters have come to represent by this stage is no longer an adherence to impersonal principles and laws, but the 'breathless interest' that the experiment has aroused in all concerned in it (*M* 419), including Jennings himself, as his response to Blake's motions betrays: 'My heart throbbed fast; the pulses at my temples beat furiously [. . .] I was obliged to look away from him – or I should have lost my self-control' (*M* 420).

My point, then, is that Jennings's experiment operates on its viewers in the same way as Collins's fiction, and popular literature more generally, was (and is) often said to operate on its readers. Collins's story includes the process whereby it creates the 'disorienting and bewitching' effects that have earned sensation fiction the reputation of working on its readers 'like a dangerous drug'.[98] In fact, Jennings's experiment is just as much about the intoxicated condition of Franklin Blake as it is about the intoxicated condition of those who watch him, including the reader of Collins's book. In the experimental part, in short, Collins's novel makes legible how it performs its enthralling work. The text 'reads' itself 'being read', to come back to Jones's phrase, for the experiment in *The Moonstone* is a mock-version, complete with a 'mock Diamond' (*M* 422), of the text that represents it. At the same time, Collins's writing, by using a medical experiment as a model for its own performance, invites comparisons between literary fiction and scientific practice. It intertwines the literary and the scientific by depicting scientific work in the medium of literary fiction and literary fiction in the medium of scientific work. In fact, the integrative medium in which the literary and the scientific are brought together in *The Moonstone* is, crucially, a 'medical practice' (*M* 369) which, like sensation fiction, cannot (yet) claim the status of an acknowledged discourse.

What makes Jennings's method so contentious in the eyes of no-nonsense people like Betteredge and Bruff, after all, is that it is not unquestionably justified by a social system of thought that is widely accepted as reliable. Rather, Jennings's work seems to partake of heterogeneous arts and theories, such as mesmerism, physiology and (some kind of) medicine, the common basis of which remains as elusive as the history of his dubious person.[99] Jennings's experimental practice seems to offer a version of, or model for, Collins's literary activity precisely because it refuses to be assigned to an existing discipline or social place. It is not yet, or not quite, clear what kind of experiment it is that Collins's writing uses as a medium for its own performance. Rather, Collins's work, to take up a suggestion by Robert Mitchell, experiments with the very 'concept and practice of experimentation' in order to explore the functions and effects of its own mode of operation.[100] Collins's fiction does something sensational (startling, novel) while simultaneously trying to make it recognisable as an experimental practice, a mode of being in the making. It seeks to reinvent its own literary performance by means of a dubious medical art, trying to transform itself into something more and other than fiction used to be. 'Experimenting with experimentation is,' in Mitchell's words, 'an eccentric, excessive exercise, one that aims – if it can be said to "aim" at anything – only at facilitating new forms of thought and sensation.'[101]

It is this tendency towards the eccentric and excessive that is embodied by the hybrid figure of Ezra Jennings who, with his 'extraordinary parti-coloured hair' and 'the puzzling contradiction between his face and figure', is introduced as a figure of unresolved contrasts, looking 'old and young both together' (*M* 364). A 'gipsy' in appearance (*M* 364), Jennings is above all a rootless figure, whose function is to mediate between the familiar and the strange, the old and the new, but whose own position remains mobile and unfixed. Conspicuously, his book in progress is as incomplete and unsettled as the ambiguously 'intricate and delicate subject of the brain and the nervous system' with which it is concerned (*M* 369). Like this 'work' in progress which, on his own account, 'will probably never be finished' and 'certainly never be published' (*M* 369), Jennings's authority as a scientist remains as doubtful as the role of sensation fiction within the literary culture of the 1860s. For, like *The Moonstone*, the writing of sensation fiction in general may be viewed, as I hope to have shown, as the medium of a 'protracted search' for an unfixed object whose meaning and purpose is not quite clear, as dazzling and exciting as it may seem.

Notes

1. Austin, 'Our Novels'.
2. Allan, 'The Contemporary Response', p. 85.
3. Wolff, *Sensational Victorian*, pp. 148–87.
4. Yates, *His Recollections*, p. 172. Yates, who seems to be the only source of the letter, does not provide a specific context for it. He just quotes it as an example of Braddon's witty conversational style. According to Wolff, the epistle is 'probably' Braddon's 'letter of acceptance' to Yates on his offer to publish a novel in *Temple Bar*. This was to be *Sir Jasper's Tenant*, which 'began its run there in 1865' (*Sensational Victorian*, p. 137).
5. Yates, *His Recollections*, pp. 172–3.
6. Braddon, 'Devoted Disciple', p. 12.
7. Ibid., p. 12.
8. Ibid., p. 10.
9. Ibid., p. 14.
10. Ibid., p. 14.
11. Ibid., p. 30.
12. Ibid., p. 20. Cf. also Braddon, 'Devoted Disciple (concluded)', p. 135.
13. Pickering, *Mangle*, p. 1.
14. Flint, 'Sensation', p. 221.
15. Daly, *Literature, Technology and Modernity*, p. 34.
16. Ibid., pp. 3, 7.
17. Ibid., p. 5.
18. This corresponds with Dames's argument that there was a strand of Victorian 'physiological novel theory' that regarded the novel as 'a training ground for industrialized consciousness', rather than as 'a refuge from', or 'an antidote to' it (*Physiology*, pp. 3, 6).
19. Jones, *Problem Novels*, p. 6.

20. Brantlinger, 'What is Sensational', p. 3. On how *Lady Audley's Secret* re-engages conventions of the Gothic mode see also Tomaiuolo, *In Lady Audley's Shadow*, pp. 23–40. Subsequently, all references to Braddon, *Lady Audley's Secret (LAS)* are provided in the main text.
21. Deleuze and Guattari, *A Thousand Plateaus*, p. 3 and generally.
22. Massumi, *Parables*, p. 30.
23. Bain (1855), *The Senses and the Intellect*, pp. 30–1.
24. Ibid., p. 38.
25. Ibid., p. 38.
26. Cf. also Otis, *Networking*, esp. pp. 11–48 and Menke, *Telegraphic Realism*.
27. Todorov, *The Poetics of Prose*, pp. 42–52; Hühn, 'The Detective'.
28. Hühn, 'The Detective', p. 458. Cf. also Marcus, 'Detection', pp. 245–68.
29. About her novel *Eleanor's Victory* (1863), for instance, Braddon wrote: 'The story is not what I meant it to be, & I feel bitterly disappointed in it, in spite of the very great indulgence of some of my kind critics' (Braddon, 'Devoted Disciple', p. 17).
30. Braddon, 'Devoted Disciple', pp. 13, 27.
31. Mansel, 'Sensation Novels', p. 482.
32. Ibid., pp. 482–3.
33. Miller, *The Novel and the Police*, p. 146.
34. Attridge and Staten, 'Reading for the Obvious'.
35. Cf. Pallo, 'From Do-Nothing to Detective', p. 476; Tomaiuolo, *In Lady Audley's Shadow*, pp. 79–96.
36. Matus, 'Disclosure', p. 334.
37. Prichard, 'Forms of Insanity', p. 252.
38. Cf. Matus, 'Disclosure', p. 341; Tönnies, '"Serious" Science'.
39. Matus, 'Disclosure', p. 334.
40. Braddon, 'Devoted Disciple', p. 26.
41. 'Emotion' is not my concern here, but a short outline of the history of the term is provided by Dixon, 'Emotion'.
42. James, 'What is an Emotion?', p. 189.
43. Braddon, *Aurora Floyd*, p. 167.
44. Ibid., p. 167.
45. Lee, 'Lady Audley's Secret', p. 140.
46. Braddon, 'Devoted Disciple', p. 18.
47. Ibid., p. 18.
48. Cf. Wolfreys, *Victorian Hauntings*, pp. ix–xiv.
49. Mansel, 'Sensation Novels', p. 483.
50. Braddon, 'Devoted Disciple', pp. 14, 25. On the concomitant redefinitions of authorship see Deane, *The Making*, pp. 59–90.
51. Braddon, 'Devoted Disciple', p. 19.
52. Unsigned Review, *Saturday Review*, p. 151.
53. Ibid., p. 151.
54. Ibid., p. 151.
55. Ibid., p. 151.

56. Ibid., p. 151.
57. Trollope, *Autobiography*, p. 81.
58. Unsigned Review, *Spectator*, p. 150.
59. Pykett, *Authors in Context*, p. 220.
60. Lonoff, *Wilkie Collins*, p. 117; Bisla, *Wilkie Collins*, pp. 9–10.
61. Collins, *Armadale*, p. 177. All quotations referring to this edition (*A*) will be provided in the text.
62. See my comments on Paley's concept of design in Chapter 1; cf. also Zeitz and Thoms, 'Strasbourg Clock', p. 501.
63. Latour, *Reassembling*, p. 39.
64. This point is also made by Daly who refers to the same scene, though his reading of it is different. Showing that the passage couples the mechanical and the hysterical, he uses it to argue that sensation novels were sometimes ambivalent about the very subject of industrial modernity that they helped to form (*Literature, Technology and Modernity*, p. 50).
65. Latour, *Reassembling*, pp. 59–61, also uses the examples of puppets to illustrate his idea of acting as 'making do' (*faire faire*).
66. Daly, *Literature, Technology and Modernity*, p. 44.
67. Ruskin, *The Eagle's Nest*, p. 189.
68. Ibid., p. 190.
69. Collins, 'The Unknown Public', p. 222.
70. Ibid., p. 218.
71. Ibid., p. 218
72. Tondre, 'Interval', p. 595.
73. Zeitz and Thoms, 'Strasbourg Clock', p. 503.
74. Collins, *The Letters*, p. 259.
75. Ibid., p. 259.
76. Ibid., p. 259.
77. Cf. Lonoff, *Wilkie Collins*, pp. 33–6; Sutherland, 'Introduction' to *Armadale*, pp. xi–xii.
78. Braddon, 'Devoted Disciple', p. 30.
79. Ibid., p. 31.
80. Lonoff, *Wilkie Collins*, p. 120.
81. Ibid., pp. 120–1.
82. Greetham, *Theories*, p. 63.
83. Barad, *Meeting the Universe*, pp. 136, 137.
84. Ibid., p. 139.
85. Cf. Bourne Taylor, *In the Secret Theatre*, p. 160.
86. Collins, 'Preface', p. 644.
87. Maroni, 'Shadow', p. 60.
88. Tondre, 'Interval', p. 589.
89. Miller, *The Novel and the Police*, p. 42.
90. Ibid., p. 42.
91. Ibid. p. 37. See also Hutter, 'Dreams, Transformations'; Thomas, 'The Moonstone'. All references to Collins, *The Moonstone*, abbreviated as *M*, will be given in the main text.

92. See Zieger, 'Opium'.
93. Latour, *Reassembling*, p. 46.
94. Ryan, *Thinking*, p. 78.
95. As Bourne Taylor points out, *The Moonstone* is specifically a novel 'about the processes which underlie the invention of the past' ('Locating', p. 168). These processes presuppose what Nicholas Dames has, in his reading of the novel, called 'the amnesiac self' (*Amnesiac Selves*, p. 167).
96. Lonoff, *Wilkie Collins*, p. 171; cf. Sutherland, 'Introduction' to *The Moonstone*, p. xx.
97. Sutherland, 'A Note on the Composition', p. xxxvii.
98. Felski, *Uses of Literature*, p. 52.
99. Cf. Bourne Taylor, *In the Secret Theatre*, p. 183; Roberts, "'Shivering Sands'", pp. 175–6. On medicine and physiology in *The Moonstone* see also Talairach-Vielmas, *Wilkie Collins*, pp. 73–92.
100. Mitchell, *Experimental Life*, p. 34.
101. Ibid., p. 35.

Clothing Matter: Thomas Carlyle's *Sartor Resartus*

The Reader as Editor

The foregoing chapters have followed, as closely as possible, some of the ways and lines along which Victorian literature and science were brought into existence as various kinds of written text. As I have argued, what such seemingly different forms of writing as G. H. Lewes's and George Eliot's studies, Robert Browning's dramatic monologues, and the sensational fictions of M. E. Braddon and Wilkie Collins have in common is that they are expressive of experimental activities through which personal perception comes to matter in social forms. Moreover, almost all of the texts assembled here appear to be, in Thomas Carlyle's words, 'intensely self-conscious' about how they interpret and recreate the relationship between such concepts as the individual and the general, matter and thought, nature and culture, the human and the animal, science and art, or mechanical reproduction and original invention.[1] According to Carlyle, this intense self-consciousness is a hallmark of the very 'Society' in the continuous reassociation of which his works participated alongside that of multiple others.[2] 'Our whole relations to the Universe and to our fellow man have become an Inquiry, a Doubt,' he writes as early as 1831, 'all things must be probed into, the whole working of man's world be anatomically studied.'[3]

Shortly after he made this statement, Carlyle began to work on his own enquiry into 'all things', *Sartor Resartus*, which is not only about the philosophy of one Diogenes Teufelsdröckh, 'Professor of Things in General';[4] *Sartor Resartus* is also about the editorial activity of assembling the professor's life and ideas from an impenetrable jumble of printed text as well as from 'miscellaneous masses of Sheets, and oftener Shreds and Snips', written in a 'scarce-legible *cursiv-schrift*' (*SR* 60). As a result, *Sartor Resartus* is composed of both Teufelsdröckh's philosophical-biographical writing and of the demanding, often exasperating process of making it readable for an English audience, of bringing it into the public world. It presents the 'Life and Opinions' of a German professor in the process of being retailored according to the needs of an English readership (*SR* 10).

Carlyle's 'bold experiment in style and method' therefore offers an appropriate way of concluding this book.[5] In fact, *Sartor Resartus* can be read as both a performance of and a meditation on what the foregoing chapters were meant to examine: the means and works of dressing personal experiences in recognisable social forms. Take the depiction of the editor's 'efforts' to incorporate the 'imbroglio' of Teufelsdröckh's life, unhelpfully distributed across the heterogeneous contents of 'Six considerable PAPER-BAGS' (*SR* 61, 60), into his 'delineation' of the 'aqueous-chaotic Volume' supposedly containing 'the boundless, almost formless [. . .] Sea of Thought' that is the professor's philosophy (*SR* 61, 8). At the end of the first book, the editor is shown to 'sit' in the midst of various papers, trying to work out the meaning of the professor's 'unimaginable Documents' in '*cursiv-schrift*' while 'collating them with the almost equally unimaginable Volume, which stands in legible print' (*SR* 61). As Carlyle's text has it:

> Over such a universal medley of high and low, of hot, cold, moist and dry, is he here struggling (by union of like with like, which is Method) to build a firm Bridge for British travellers. Never perhaps since our first Bridge-builders, Sin and Death, built that stupendous Arch from Hellgate to the Earth, did any Pontifex, or Pontiff, undertake such a task as the present Editor. For in this Arch too, leading as we humbly presume, far otherwards than that grand primeval one, the materials are to be fished up from the weltering deep, and down from the simmering air, here one mass, there another, and cunningly cemented, while the elements boil beneath: nor is there any supernatural force to do it with; but simply the Diligence and feeble thinking Faculty of an English Editor, endeavouring to evolve printed Creation out of a German printed and written Chaos, wherein, as he shoots to and fro in it, gathering, clutching, piecing the Why to the far-distant Wherefore, his whole Faculty and Self are like to be swallowed up. (*SR* 61–2)

The 'English Editor' is here presented as a diligent, though overwhelmed, go-between, who, like all builders, writers and other craftspeople, inhabits a building site, a fluid field on the way towards a solid edifice. Mediating (shooting 'to and fro') between the empirical and the ideal ('the weltering deep' and 'the simmering air') as well as between causes and effects ('the Why' and 'the far-distant Wherefore'), he is 'struggling' to construct a bridge to help 'British travellers' escape the very 'German printed and written Chaos' that supplies him with the 'materials' for his work. More specifically, the editor participates in the making of a structure that is alleged to have been invented by someone else. It follows that the editor's form-giving work composes Teufelsdröckh's thinking as much as Teufelsdröckh's thinking composes the form of the editor's work. Hence the ever-present risk of his 'Faculty' becoming 'swallowed up' by the very subject-matter that he seeks to shape by means of it.

As this example indicates, *Sartor Resartus* is not only about the relationship between matter and form, the particular and the general as well as (British) empiricism and (German) idealism;[6] it also enacts the process of making a text in which these components become involved with each other. Thus, from the beginning, both the form of Carlyle's writing and its main theme, the philosophy of clothes, draw attention to the 'bridging' element of mediation and translation, the way of knowing, that the editor accuses 'Science' to have 'quite overlooked', even though its very existence depends upon it (*SR* 4). While almost all aspects of human life have been 'laid open' and 'scientifically decomposed' (*SR* 3, 4), as he points out at the beginning, the very medium or 'Tissue' in and through which all these revelatory activities take place has remained hidden from the public view (*SR* 4). In order to compensate for this deficiency, the editor sets out to present his English readership with Teufelsdröckh's all-encompassing theory of clothes.

The main tenet of this philosophy is that whatever seems to be bare or naked to the human eye is really the vestment of an ideal meaning that transcends experience. 'Matter,' thus conceived, 'is Spirit, the manifestation of Spirit', as the editor paraphrases Teufelsdröckh's argument in the chapter entitled 'Pure Reason', an undisguised reference to German transcendentalism. 'The thing Visible, nay the thing Imagined, the thing in any way conceived as Visible, what is it but a Garment, a Clothing of the higher, celestial Invisible?' (*SR* 52). In the next chapter, the editor has Teufelsdröckh make the same point by quoting him in his own words: 'All visible things are Emblems; what thou seest is not there on its own account; strictly taken, is not there at all: Matter exists only spiritually, and to represent some Idea, and *body* it forth' (*SR* 56). In short, 'the whole external Universe and what it holds is but Clothing; and the essence of all Science lies in the PHILOSOPHY OF CLOTHES' (*SR* 57–8).

Despite the unmistakable irony that pervades the editor's presentation of Teufelsdröckh's argument, most readers of *Sartor Resartus* have recognised this 'grand Proposition' that all physical matter is the cloth of an ideal reality, as the serious core of the book (*SR* 41). Moreover, critics generally hold that the founding assumption of Teufelsdröckh's philosophy corresponds to Carlyle's own belief that 'what matters' in the physical world is 'the spiritual reality' underlying it.[7] In fact, in a famous letter to his publisher, James Fraser, Carlyle himself claimed *Sartor Resartus* to have been 'put together in the fashion of a Didactic Novel',[8] suggesting that its 'little bits of Doctrine' amounted to 'a deep religious speculative-radicalism' that was 'firmly' held by himself.[9] It is crucial, however, that *Sartor Resartus* patently does not promulgate this belief in the unambiguous and straightforward manner with which Carlyle allegedly entertained it. Instead, Carlyle has decided to put forth his 'Doctrine' anonymously, through the cloudy and muddle-headed work of a fictitious German professor who, though 'a speculative Radical' like his inventor (*SR* 50), is hardly the best vehicle for moral instruction. Moreover, the message of his work is patched together by an unknown editor who not only struggles to make out its meaning, but who, more than once, confesses to have considerable doubts about the reliability and value of what he tries to make into a public shape. In one chapter, he characterises Teufelsdröckh's 'Work on Clothes' as 'a mixture of insight, inspiration, with dulness, double-vision, and even utter blindness' (*SR* 22). In the paper bags, he finds 'Nothing but innuendoes, figurative crotchets', but 'no clear logical Picture' (*SR* 141), and a little later, he even suspects that 'these Autobiographical Documents are partly a Mystification!' (*SR* 153).

As J. Hillis Miller has pointed out, one question raised by *Sartor Resartus*, therefore, is why Carlyle, if he meant to put forth a 'doctrine', tried to convey his views in such an extravagant, manifestly theatrical way. Would it not have been more conducive to his allegedly 'didactic' purpose, if he had expressed himself 'directly and plainly',[10] or used at least a single, more homogeneous and reliable voice to transmit his 'speculative radicalism'?[11] The reason these questions need to be asked is that the speculative truth that is expressed through Teufelsdröckh's clothes philosophy can indeed be found to remain essentially unchanged throughout the three books, even though it is decked out in ever more exuberant trappings, repeatedly questioned by a puzzled reader-editor, and made to appear through a dazzling multiplicity of images, contexts and examples. Thus the vision of 'Eternity' that Teufelsdröckh glimpses in Chapter 3, when he is looking down upon a 'living flood, pouring through' the 'streets' of Weissnichtwo, can already be found to contain his whole thought in a nutshell (*SR* 17). 'These are Apparitions: what else? Are they not Souls rendered visible; in Bodies, that took shape, and will lose it; melting into air?' (*SR* 17). On these grounds, George Levine once described *Sartor Resartus* as 'a giant elaboration of a basic insight into the spiritual nature of the material universe', or 'a series of elaborate reflections circling about a central position'.[12] And yet, the question remains why this position is scattered across a fragmented set of utterances, making reference to a chaotic score of details, topics, learned considerations and biographical episodes, rather than communicated to the reader directly, as more coherent whole.

Teufelsdröckh's Logic

One way of accounting for the excessively baroque or 'ornamental' style and structure of *Sartor Resartus* is to read the text as a 'self-consuming artefact', as Anne K. Mellor has argued, that deliberately irritates its readers, challenging them 'to discover the truth for themselves'.[13] Like the editor, Carlyle's readers are made to go through a painful process of conversion whereby they are supposed to learn, by themselves, that the reality, as they have become accustomed to perceive it, is not what it seems to be. Thus viewed, the figure of the editor performs the very work that Carlyle's writing wants its readers to perform as well. He exerts himself to come to terms with a text that does not fully satisfy him, as he admits, because it suffers from 'an almost total want of arrangement' and a highly uneven mode of expression (*SR* 26). Occasionally, it 'severs asunder the confusion' by 'cutting words' which hit the 'centre of the matter'; at other times, it seems to 'play truant for long pages', hiding its meaning behind 'the merest commonplaces' and heaps of redundant words (*SR* 23–4). Teufelsdröckh's style, too, is marred by 'rudeness, inequality' and impurity, as the editor adds, alternating bursts of 'consummate vigour' and 'true inspiration' with 'circumlocutions, repetitions' and 'touches even of pure doting jargon'. 'On the whole, Professor Teufelsdröckh is not a cultivated writer' (*SR* 24).

All of this could just as well be said about *Sartor Resartus* which, in all of these respects, is almost exactly like the text that it purports to edit and bring out. Crucially, however, Carlyle's book has a twofold structure that denies it the total certainty on which Teufelsdröckh's *Die Kleider* seems to be based. This means that *Sartor Resartus* continually interrogates its own form and content. It includes within itself both a fictional version of itself and a suggestion for how it ought to be read. More precisely, the editor's commentary indicates that Teufelsdröckh's work, as well as, by implication, the one containing it, should not be viewed as the representation of a logical argument that can be spelled out in general terms of neatly concatenated premises and consequences. 'Our Professor's method is not, in any case, that of common school Logic, where the truths all stand in a row, each holding by the skirts of the other,' as the editor puts it (*SR* 41). Rather, the professor's method was 'at best that of practical Reason, proceeding by large Intuition over whole systematic groups and kingdoms' (*SR* 41). According to the editor, this paradoxically infuses Teufelsdröckh's philosophy with 'a noble complexity', giving it the form of 'a mighty maze', as well as with 'a certain ignoble complexity' that 'we must call mere confusion' (*SR* 41–2).

On this view, the general logic of Teufelsdröckh's thought cannot be abstracted from the singular writing practice through which it is enacted. It has a logic of its own. Hence the editor's need to learn more about the biography of his author,[14] about the personal life, by which his method of thinking and working appears to be informed.

> For it seems as if the demonstration lay much in the Author's individuality; as if it were not Argument that had taught him, but Experience. At present it is only in local glimpses, and by significant fragments, picked often at wide enough intervals from the original Volume, and carefully collated, that we can hope to impart some outline or foreshadow of this Doctrine. (*SR* 42)

These assessments can, again, be applied to both Teufelsdröckh's writing and to Carlyle's fiction of publishing it. If *Sartor Resartus* is a didactic novel trying to convince its readers of the essentially spiritual nature of the material world, then the method by which Carlyle demonstrates this thesis seems to 'lay' more 'in the Author's individuality' than in some general school logic. Carlyle's argument, like Teufelsdröckh's, can be caught 'only in local glimpses and by significant fragments', in 'little bits', assembled from a fictitious (or non-existent) 'original' of which *Sartor Resartus* purports to be an edition or review. As a result, all that one can expect from Carlyle's (as much as from Teufelsdröckh's) work is 'some outline or foreshadow' of a 'Doctrine' that has not (yet) been elaborated in terms of a full-fledged demonstration based on generally acknowledged principles of rational thought. 'No firm arch, overspanning the Impassable with paved highway, could the Editor construct,' he admits at the end of his endeavours, but only 'some zigzag series of rafts floating tumultuously thereon' (*SR* 203–4).

In sum, *Sartor Resartus* can be described as the fantasy of a chaotic philosophical vision in the process of being made into a coherent argument. It is a fiction of being in the middle of a work in progress, or on the way towards a knowledge that is yet to become apparent in its true form. 'Up to this hour we have never fully satisfied ourselves,' the editor notes in his attempt to capture the 'singular attraction' of Teufelsdröckh's style, 'whether it is a tone and hum of real Humour, which we reckon among the very highest qualities of genius, or some remote echo of mere Insanity and Inanity, which doubtless ranks below the very lowest' (*SR* 24–5). According to Teufelsdröckh himself, the medium in which the highest and the lowest, along with 'revelation' and 'concealment' or 'the Infinite' and 'the Finite', are brought together is 'the wondrous agency of *Symbols*' (*SR* 166).[15] Yet, while the professor repeatedly praises the capacity of symbols, especially those of religion and fine art, to act as vehicles of 'Eternity' and 'the Godlike', he also points out that their meaning, like that of all material forms, is subject to time and the changing evaluations that come with it (*SR* 169). 'Our whole terrestrial being is based on Time, and built of Time; it is wholly a Movement, a Time-impulse; Time is the author of it, the material of it' (*SR* 99). The terrestrial being of humans, their very practice of living in and working by means of an earthly world, inevitably draws all visions of unconditional truth into the current of time, the 'Time-impulse' that varies and multiplies them, showing them to be historically contingent.

On the one hand, *Sartor Resartus* is an attempt to escape the fleetingness and changeability inscribed into all human constructions, including the 'Axioms, and Categories, and Systems, and Aphorisms' that Teufelsdröckh denounces as mere wrappings: 'Words, words. High Air-castles are cunningly built of Words, the Words well bedded also in good Logic-mortar; wherein, however, no Knowledge will come to lodge' (*SR* 43). On the other hand, the labyrinthine excesses of its 'piebald, entangled, hyper-metaphorical style of writing' repeatedly (*SR* 221), even in this very passage, exhibit themselves as yet another 'Air castle' in which 'no Knowledge will come to lodge' for any longer than a transient period of time. These two aspects – the belief in ideal or metaphysical knowledge and the acknowledgement of material contingency and change – are never reconciled in *Sartor Resartus*. They remain in tension until the very end, which is why the book has, with equal justification, either been famously loathed for the 'clotted heap of nonsense' that it produces,[16] or celebrated for the sense of metaphysical wonder that it reveals, at least in glimpses, to be hidden amongst it. *Sartor Resartus*, as Jerome McGann put it, 'is transcendental Dog's-meat'.[17] In fact, the divine and the profane components of the book are not only condensed in the very name of Diogenes Teufelsdröckh, which translates as God-begotten Devil's dung. They also constantly wrestle with each other in his gospel.

What is more, Carlyle reinforced the tension between the wonderful and the nonsensical by adding to the 1838 book edition of *Sartor Resartus* a series of 'Testimonies of Authors' which provide a panoply of conflicting responses to the text. One of the most favourable among them is Ralph Waldo Emerson's preface to the American edition which draws attention to the text's 'masquerade' of 'quaint and burlesque style', 'the gay costume in which the Author delights to dress his thoughts' while simultaneously claiming that 'no book has been published for many years, written in a more sincere style of idiomatic English'.[18] In short: 'Under all his gaiety the Writer has an earnest meaning, and discovers an insight into the manifold wants and tendencies of human nature.'[19] This indicates that the hilarious spectacle of *Sartor Resartus* and its seemingly 'earnest meaning' were not always seen as mutually exclusive, even though their odd intermixture certainly disturbed many readers. As McGann has suggested, what makes *Sartor Resartus* an experiment in writing is that it seems, quite deliberately, to test out the formal possibilities engendered by popular magazines such as *Fraser's* and *Blackwood's*.[20] 'This has struck me much of late years in considering *Blackwood* and *Fraser*,' Carlyle wrote in a letter to J. S. Mill, 'both these are furnished as it were with a kind of theatrical costume, with orchestra and stage-lights, and thereby alone have a wonderful advantage; perhaps almost their only advantage.'[21] According to Carlyle, then, the advantage of these magazines was that they provided him with a stage to present his philosophy as a frivolous masquerade: in a manifestly theatrical manner. Yet, the travesty of *Sartor Resartus* was not primarily meant to create a sense of illusion, or to conceal true beliefs behind a fictional mask. Rather, *Sartor Resartus* makes a show of its writing, so as to exhibit it as a staged performance while simultaneously inviting the reader to work out, along with the editor, what it might really mean.

Thus viewed, the fictional form of Carlyle's text exemplifies, in an exaggerated manner, Teufelsdröckh's central claim 'that all Forms are but Clothes, and temporary' (*SR* 248).[22] If Carlyle had transmitted his meaning 'directly and plainly', he would no longer have been transparently true to the insight 'that all Symbols are properly Clothes; that all Forms whereby Spirit manifests itself to Sense, whether outwardly or in the imagination, are Clothes' (*SR* 205). In order to act in consonance with this philosophy, Carlyle had to make it unmistakeably clear that he was speaking in metaphors, or in a form 'which, in one way or another, discounts itself in its act of being proffered.'[23] The bridge that the editor pretends to have been building out of Teufelsdröckh's prints and scribbles can therefore neither be finished nor represent the last word on the theme of clothes. Like all human constructions, it remains subject to being altered, amended and replaced according to changeable fashions. 'New labourers will arrive; new Bridges will be built: nay, may not your own poor rope-and-raft Bridge, in your passings and repassings, be mended in many a point, till it grow quite firm, passable even for the halt?' (*SR* 204). As the question mark indicates, *Sartor Resartus*, as it stands, remains in question, or in the mode of the experimental. It testifies to an experience in the making, or a process of becoming, in which knowledge and ignorance, false beliefs and foreshadows of truth have not quite or not yet been set apart.

Literature, Science, Knowledge

Being a form in transition, *Sartor Resartus* has often been said to constitute a 'passage' between Romanticism and Victorianism,[24] but it also touches upon a central concern in the historical study of literature and science. More specifically, both the form and the content of *Sartor Resartus* foreground the relationship between the belief in context-independent truths and the contingent ways and means through which they have to be represented and communicated. Thus Carlyle's book raises an issue that is worth being briefly discussed in closing this book. Similar to capitalised Literature or Art, which occasionally were (and sometimes still are) said to represent trans-historical (and trans-cultural) insights into the human condition, science is often taken to have the task of discovering timeless facts and objective laws about the natural or material world. On this view, the kinds of truth created or represented by both literature and science, even though they may be radically different, are credited with at least a relative mode of what is usually called *autonomy*.[25] This means that the knowledge produced by works of both literature and science is, by virtue of the autonomy ascribed to them, raised above social, political, ideological, technological, linguistic, material or other constraints. In contrast to this view, research in the cultural history of literature and science has usually been premised on the assumption that all knowledge, no matter of what kind, is deeply embedded in the changeable historical tissues by means of which it comes to be woven and rewoven. The making of both science and literature is therefore now usually taken to be 'significantly informed by the linguistic, social and cultural contexts' through which it is mediated and brought forth.[26] Thus conceived, neither literature nor science can be entirely isolated from the historical discourses, the cultural cloth or 'texture',[27] that enables and shapes them. This historicist approach has not only made it easier to compare the creating of literature and science both of which can, on such a view, be said to be made, at least to some extent, out of the same cultural material. More importantly, it has considerably broadened the concept of knowledge which could no longer be confined to, and ordered by means of, allegedly autonomous ideas such as Science, Literature or Art. Instead, it has become free to travel widely across seemingly separate modes of cultural activity, such that it can, within a 'given period', be 'found not only in demonstrations', but also 'in fiction, reflexion, narrative accounts, institutional regulations, and political decisions'.[28]

Such an inclusive notion of knowledge has inspired much productive work because it has enabled researchers to follow the migration and transformation of theorems and ideas through the various kinds of writing in which they were found to be clothed.[29] But it has also provoked a considerable amount of criticism by more analytically minded scholars eager to put the concept of knowledge back into the ideal, clearly demarcated places and boxes in which they took it to belong.[30] There is no doubt that this criticism is justified to some extent, especially in its plea that one recognise differences between science writing and literary fiction, instead of glossing them over. Yet, to draw attention to that which distinguishes works of science and literary fiction is not necessarily to reinstate an unbridgeable gulf between them or even to revive the antagonistic talk of the 'two cultures'. Little is gained, if one simply replaces a single, overly

broad conception of knowledge with various different, overly narrow ones. There is no point, for instance, in simply denying literary
fictions the capacity to know anything 'properly', on the presumption that knowledge 'proper' belongs to the realm of scientific or
philosophical as opposed to literary ideas. Indeed, to claim that all
stories and poems can hope to represent are opinions and points
of view, as one critic has suggested, is to toss out the baby with the
bath water.[31] This claim not only contradicts the old and widespread
intuition that works of poetry and literary fiction are capable of
being, in an impersonal sense, true to experiences, or of revealing
'something about the way things are'.[32] Such narrowly analytical
arguments also have to presuppose a clear-cut distinction between
the individual and the general that risks conjuring up once more 'the
reductive alignment of science with rational objectivity and literature with subjective fancy that was a characterization of the debate
on the two cultures'.[33]

To avoid both an antagonistic opposition and an indifferent identification of literature and science, my approach in this book has
been to study texts as ways of knowing, rather than as structures of
knowledge. On such a conception, most of the writings analysed in
this book do not necessarily have to be regarded as either representative of science or productive of an art that is entirely different from
science. Instead of assigning textual works to narrowly predefined
kinds, such as 'science' and 'literature', and then studying the traffic
between them, what I have tried to do is to examine how writing
becomes what it is, as well as how it inscribes itself into, or contributes to the construction of, certain categories or types. Viewed epistemologically, such domains as 'science' and 'literature' may exist in
distinction from or opposition to each other, but viewed ontologically, as I hope to have suggested, they become with, and often grow
into each other, issuing from within the same world.

To read texts as ways of knowing, then, means to read them
as forms in the making or as makings of form. It means, in short,
to allow for the possibility that writing, both fictional and non-
fictional, can be an experimental mode, a practice of trying things
out, in which, as in *Sartor Resartus*, sense and nonsense, the
known and the unknown, the scientific and the artful and even
inspiring insights and inane phrases are (still) entangled with or
jostle against each other. As we have seen, what a text like *Sartor
Resartus* expresses is a knowledge that is constantly in the process
of becoming confused and a confusion that is constantly trying to
become knowledge. Like most of the other texts brought together

in this book, Carlyle's novel exemplifies an experimental reason that includes, and quite recklessly plays with, that which exceeds its grasp. As an epistemological attitude, this experimental reason corresponded, ontologically speaking, to a world in motion that was increasingly perceived to run ahead of whatever institutional, theoretical, or conceptual framework people attempted to impose upon it. Much Victorian writing follows an evolving reality that it never quite manages to contain in any of its various shapes.

Notes

1. Carlyle, 'Characteristics', p. 366.
2. Ibid., p. 366.
3. Ibid., p. 366.
4. Carlyle, *Sartor Resartus*, p. 14. All further references to this edition (*SR*) will be given in the text.
5. McGann, 'Innovation', p. 289.
6. On the cross-cultural and world literary aspect of the text see Lüdeke, 'Contingencies' and Iser, 'Cross-Cultural Discourse'.
7. Levine, *The Boundaries*, p. 38.
8. Carlyle, *Sartor Resartus*, Appendix I, p. 227.
9. Ibid., p. 228.
10. Hillis Miller, '"Hieroglyphical Truth"', p. 3.
11. Ibid., p. 5.
12. Levine, *The Boundaries*, p. 68.
13. Mellor, *English Romantic Irony*, p. 131. Mellor quotes Stanley Fish who coined the term 'self-consuming artefact'.
14. Zwierlein, *Der physiologische Bildungsroman*, pp. 53–90 analyses *Sartor Resartus* as a physiological bildungsroman while Linda H. Peterson, *Victorian Autobiography*, pp. 31–59, focuses on how Carlyle re-engages the genre of autobiography.
15. On the symbol see Kohns, *Die Verrücktheit*, pp. 298–309 and Hillis Miller, '"Hieroglyphical Truth"', pp. 8–14.
16. Carlyle, *Sartor Resartus*, Appendix V, p. 237.
17. McGann, 'Innovation', p. 290.
18. Carlyle, *Sartor Resartus*, Appendix V, p. 241.
19. Ibid., p. 241.
20. McGann, 'Innovation', p. 292.
21. Carlyle, 'To John Stuart Mill'.
22. This quotation is from the summary Carlyle added to the 1838 book edition. It belongs to Book III, Chapter 9.
23. Hillis Miller, '"Hieroglyphical Truth"', p. 7.
24. Haney, 'Shadow-Hunting', p. 307.

25. Klancher, *Transfiguring*, p. 17.
26. Dawson, 'Literature and Science', p. 303.
27. For a theory of this concept see Reinfandt, 'Texture'.
28. Foucault, *Archaeology*, pp. 191, 183–4.
29. The general approach is well represented by Vogl, 'Für eine Poetologie'; Vogl, ed. *Poetologien des Wissens*; Klausnitzer, *Literatur und Wissen*, pp. 148–59. A critical response can be found in Stiening, 'Am "Ungrund"'. For the specifically Victorian context see Rauch, *Useful Knowledge*.
30. A polemic view is offered by Livingston, *Literary Knowledge*; for a systematic approach see Danneberg and Spoerhase, 'Wissen in Literatur'.
31. Köppe, 'Vom Wissen'.
32. Felski, *Uses of Literature*, p. 77. See also Wood, *Literature*, pp. 1–12 and Scholz, *Phantasmatic Knowledge*, pp. 161–2.
33. Willis, *Vision*, p. 231.

Bibliography

Abberley, Will, *English Fiction and the Evolution of Language*, Cambridge: Cambridge University Press, 2015.

Agamben, Giorgio, *The Open: Man and Animal*, trans. Kevin Attell, Stanford: Stanford University Press, 2004.

Allan, Janice M., 'The Contemporary Response to Sensation Fiction', in Andrew Mangham (ed.), *The Cambridge Companion to Sensation Fiction*, Cambridge: Cambridge University Press, 2013, pp. 85–98.

Allen, Grant, 'The Origin of Cultivation', *Fortnightly Review*, May (1894), 576–92.

Allen, Kristie M., 'Habit in George Eliot's *The Mill on the Floss*', SEL 50.4 (2010), 831–52.

Altick, Richard D. and James F. Loucks, *Browning's Roman Murder Story: A Reading of* The Ring and the Book, Chicago: The University of Chicago Press, 1968.

Amigoni, David, *Colonies, Cults and Evolution: Literature, Science and Culture in Nineteenth-Century Writing*, Cambridge: Cambridge University Press, 2007.

Anger, Suzy, 'George Eliot and Philosophy', in George Levine (ed.), *The Cambridge Companion to George Eliot*, Cambridge: Cambridge University Press, 2001, pp. 76–97.

Armstrong, Isobel, 'Browning and the "Grotesque Style"', in Isobel Armstrong (ed.), *The Major Victorian Poets*, London: Routledge, 1969, pp. 93–124.

Armstrong, Isobel, '*The Ring and the Book*: The Uses of Prolixity', in Isobel Armstrong (ed.), *The Major Victorian Poets*, London: Routledge: 1969, pp. 177–98.

Armstrong, Isobel, *Victorian Poetry: Poetry, Poetics, Politics*, London: Routledge, 1993.

Armstrong, Isobel, *Victorian Glassworlds: Glass Culture and the Imagination 1830–1880*, Oxford: Oxford University Press, 2008.

Arnold, Matthew, 'Literature and Science' [1882], in R. H. Super (ed.), *The Complete Works of Matthew Arnold*, vol. 10, Ann Arbor: University of Michigan Press, 1974, pp. 53–73.

Ashton, Rosemary, *G.H. Lewes: A Life*, Oxford: Clarendon Press, 1991.

Attridge, Derek and Henry Staten, 'Reading for the Obvious in Poetry: A Conversation', *World Picture* 2 (2008), 1–16.

Austin, Alfred, 'Our Novels: The Sensational School', *Temple Bar* 29 (1870), 410–24.

Austin, Alfred, *The Poetry of the Period*, repr. from *Temple Bar* (June 1869), London: Richard Bentley, 1870.

Bacon, Francis, *The Major Works*, ed. Brian Vickers, Oxford: Oxford University Press, 1996.

Bagehot, Walter, 'Wordsworth, Tennyson, and Browning; or Pure, Ornate, and Grotesque Art in English Poetry (1864)', in Richard Holt Hutton (ed.), *Literary Studies by the Late Walter Bagehot*, vol. 2, 2 vols, 4th edn, London: Longmans, Green, and Co., 1891, pp. 338–90.

Bailey, Suzanne, 'Somatic Wisdom: Refiguring Bodies in *The Ring and the Book*', *Victorian Studies* 41.4 (1998), 567–91.

Bain, Alexander, *The Senses and the Intellect*, London: Parker, 1855.

Bain, Alexander, *The Senses and the Intellect*, 3rd edn, London: Longmans, Green and Co, 1868.

Baker, John Ross, 'Poetry and Language in Shelley's Defence of Poetry', *The Journal of Aesthetics and Art Criticism* 39.4 (1981), 437–49.

Baker, William, 'Preface', in George Eliot, *The Spanish Gypsy*, ed. Antonie Gerard van den Broek, London: Pickering & Chatto, 2008, pp. ix-xxv.

Balaguer, Mark, 'Mill and the Philosophy of Mathematics: Physicalism and Fictionalism', in Antis Loizides (ed.), *Mill's A System of Logic: Critical Appraisals*, London: Routledge, 2014, pp. 83–100.

Barad, Karen, *Meeting the Universe Halfway: Quantum Physics and the Entanglement of Matter and Meaning*, Durham, NC: Duke University Press, 2007.

Barthes, Roland, 'From Science to Literature' [1967], in Roland Barthes, *The Rustle of Language*, trans. Richard Howard, Berkeley: University of California Press, 1989, pp. 3–10.

Barthes, Roland, 'From Work to Text' [1971], in Roland Barthes, *Image, Music, Text: Essays*, ed. Stephen Heath, New York: Hill and Wang, 2007, pp. 155–64.

Beer, Gillian, *Darwin's Plots: Evolutionary Narrative in Darwin, George Eliot and Nineteenth-Century Fiction*, Cambridge: Cambridge University Press, 1983.

Beer, Gillian, 'Has Nature a Future?', in Elinor S. Shaffer (ed.), *The Third Culture: Literature and Science*, New York: de Gruyter, 1998, pp. 15–27.

Bender, John, 'Novel Knowledge: Judgement, Experience, Experiment', in Yota Batsaki, Subha Mukherji and Jan-Melissa Schramm (eds), *Fictions of Knowledge: Fact, Evidence, Doubt*, Basingstoke: Palgrave, 2012, pp. 131–51.

Bennett, Andrew, *Ignorance: Literature and Agnoiology*, Manchester: Manchester University Press, 2009.

Bennett, Andrew, 'Wordsworth's Poetic Ignorance', in Alexander Regier and Stephan Uhlig (eds), *Wordsworth's Poetic Theory*, London: Palgrave, 2010, pp. 19–35.

Berensmeyer, Ingo, *Angles of Contingency: Literarische Kultur im England des 17. Jahrhunderts*, Tübingen: Niemeyer, 2007.

Bernard, Claude, *Experimental Medicine* [1865], trans. Henry Copley Greene [1927], London: Transaction Publishers, 1999.

Bertram, Georg W., 'Praktiken als Basis der Sprache und des Geistes', in Jens Kertscher und Dieter Mersch (eds), *Performativität und Praxis*, München: Fink, 2003, pp. 211–27.

Bhaskar, Roy, *A Realist Theory of Science*, 2nd edn, London: Verso, 2008.

Bibby, Cyril, *T. H. Huxley: Scientist, Humanist, and Educator*, London: Watt, 1959.

Birch, Dinah, 'Education', in Kate Flint (ed.), *The Cambridge History of Victorian Literature*, Cambridge: Cambridge University Press, 2012, pp. 331–49.

Bisla, Sundeep, *Wilkie Collins and Copyright: Artistic Ownership in the Age of the Borderless Word*, Columbus: Ohio State University Press, 2013.

Black, Barbara J., *On Exhibit: Victorians and their Museums*, Charlottesville: The University of Virginia Press, 2000.

Bode, Christoph, 'Theorietheorie als Praxis: Überlegungen zu einer Figur der Unhintergehbarkeit, oder: Über eine Theorie-Praxis-Asymmetrie', in Mario Grizelj and Oliver Jahraus (eds), *Theorietheorie: Wider die Theoriemüdigkeit in den Geisteswissenschaften*, München: Wilhelm Fink, 2011, pp. 79–94.

Böhm-Schnitker, Nadine and Philipp Erchinger, 'Scientific Cultures in the Nineteenth Century: Introduction', in Silvia Mergenthal and Reingard M. Nischik (eds), *Anglistentag 2013 Konstanz: Proceedings*, Trier: WVT, 2014, pp. 1–7.

Bourdieu, Pierre, *The Logic of Practice*, Cambridge: Polity Press, 1990.

Bourne Taylor, Jenny, *In the Secret Theatre of Home: Wilkie Collins, Sensation Narrative, and Nineteenth-Century Psychology*, London: Routledge, 1988.

Bourne Taylor, Jenny, 'Obscure Recesses: Locating the Victorian Unconscious', in J. B. Bullen (ed.), *Writing and Victorianism*, London: Longman, 1997, pp. 137–79.

Bourne Taylor, Jenny, 'The Later Novels', in Jenny Bourne Taylor (ed.), *The Cambridge Companion to Wilkie Collins*, Cambridge: Cambridge University Press, 2006, pp. 79–96.

Braddon, Mary E., 'Devoted Disciple: The Letters of Mary Elizabeth Braddon to Sir Edward Bulwer-Lytton 1862–1873', ed. Robert Lee Wolff, *Harvard Library Bulletin* 22.1 (1974), 5–35.

Braddon, Mary E., 'Devoted Disciple: The Letters of Mary Elizabeth Braddon to Sir Edward Bulwer-Lytton 1862–1873 (concluded)', ed. Robert Lee Wolff, *Harvard Library Bulletin* 22.2 (1974), 129–61.

Braddon, Mary Elizabeth, *Lady Audley's Secret*, ed. Jenny Bourne Taylor, London: Penguin, 1998.

Braddon, Mary Elizabeth, *Aurora Floyd*, ed. P. D. Edwards, Oxford: Oxford University Press, 2008.

Brantlinger, Patrick, '*News from Nowhere*: Morris's Socialist Anti-Novel', *Victorian Studies* 19.1 (1975), 35–49.

Brantlinger, Patrick, 'What is Sensational about the Sensation Novel?', *Nineteenth-Century Fiction* 37.1 (1982), 1–28.

Brontë, Emily, *Wuthering Heights*, ed. Richard J. Dunn, 4th edn, New York: Norton, 2003.

Brown, Daniel, *The Poetry of Victorian Scientists: Style, Science, and Nonsense*, Cambridge: Cambridge University Press, 2013.

Browning, Robert, *The Ring and the Book*, ed. Thomas J. Collins and Richard D. Altick, Peterborough: Broadview, 2001.

Browning, Robert, *Robert Browning's Poetry*, ed. James F. Loucks and Andrew M. Stauffer, 2nd edn, New York: Norton, 2007.

Browning, Robert and Julia Wedgewood, *Robert Browning and Julia Wedgwood: A Broken Friendship as Revealed in their Letters*, ed. Richard Curle, London: Murray & Cape, 1937.

Buchanan, Robert, '[Unsigned Review] in *The Athenaeum* 1868 (December)', in Boyd Litzinger and Donald Smalley (eds), *Robert Browning: The Critical Heritage*, London: Routledge & Kegan Paul, 1970, pp. 293–6.

Buckland, Adelene, *Novel Science: Fiction and the Invention of Nineteenth-Century Geology*, Chicago: The University of Chicago Press, 2013.

Buckler, William E., *Poetry and Truth in Robert Browning's* The Ring and the Book, New York: New York University Press, 1985.

Bulwer-Lytton, Edward, *England and the English*, vol. 2, London: Richard Bentley, 1833.

Butler, Samuel, *Life and Habit* [1878], The Shrewsbury Edition, vol. 4, New York: AMS, 1968.

Butler, Samuel, *Unconscious Memory* [1880], The Shrewsbury Edition, vol. 6, New York: AMS, 1968.

Campbell, Matthew, *Rhythm and Will in Victorian Poetry*, Cambridge: Cambridge University Press, 2004.

Capelle, Birgit, *Time in American and East Asian Thinking: A Comparative Study of Temporality in American Transcendentalism, Pragmatism and (Zen) Buddhist Thought*, Heidelberg: Winter, 2011.

Carlyle, Thomas, 'Characteristics', *The Edinburgh Review* 54 (Dec. 1831), 351–83.

Carlyle, Thomas, *Heroes, Hero Worship, and the Heroic in History*, London: Chapman and Hall, 1840.

Carlyle, Thomas, *Sartor Resartus*, ed. Kerry McSweeney and Peter Sabor, Oxford: Oxford University Press, 2008.

Carlyle, Thomas, 'To John Stuart Mill, 20 January 1834', in Thomas Carlyle, *The Collected Letters*, vol. 7, pp. 69–74, *The Carlyle Letters Online*, ed. Brent E. Kinser, Durham, NC: Duke University Press, 2007–16, www.carlyleletters.org.

Certeau, Michel de, *The Practice of Everyday Life*, trans. Stephen Rendall, Berkeley: University of California Press, 1984.

Chambers's Encyclopaedia: A Dictionary of Universal Knowledge, new edition, vol. 9, London: William & Robert Chambers, 1904.

Chesterton, G. K., *Robert Browning*, London: Macmillan & Co., 1903.

Chesterton, G. K., *The Victorian Age in Literature*, London: Williams and Norgate, 1914.

Coleridge, Samuel Taylor, *Biographia Literaria*, ed. James Engell and W. Jackson Bate, vol. 1, Princeton: Princeton University Press, 1983.

Collins, Wilkie, 'The Unknown Public', *Household Words* XVIII (August 1858), 217–22.

Collins, Wilkie, 'Preface [1860]', in Wilkie Collins, *The Woman in White*, ed. John Sutherland, Oxford: Oxford University Press, 1996, pp. 644–6.

Collins, Wilkie, *Heart and Science: A Story of the Present Time*, ed. Steve Farmer, Peterborough: Broadview, 1996.

Collins, Wilkie, *The Moonstone*, ed. John Sutherland, Oxford: Oxford University Press, 1999.

Collins, Wilkie, *The Letters*, ed. William Baker and William M. Clarke, vol. 1: 1838–1865, London: Macmillan, 1999.

Collins, Wilkie, *Armadale*, ed. John Sutherland, London: Penguin, 2004.

Connor, Steven, 'A Short Stirring to Meekness', in Carolyn Birdsall, Maria Boletski, Itay Sapir and Pieter Verstraete (eds), *Inside Knowledge: (Un) Doing Ways of Knowing in the Humanities*, Newcastle: Cambridge Scholars Publishing, 2009, pp. 193–208.

Cook, A. K., *A Commentary upon Browning's* The Ring and the Book, London: Oxford University Press, 1920.

Corrigan, Beatrice, *Curious Annals: New Documents Relating to Browning's Roman Murder Story*, Toronto: University of Toronto Press, 1956.

Culler, Jonathan, *Structuralist Poetics: Structuralism, Linguistics, and the Study of Literature*, London: Routledge & Kegan Paul, 1975.

Cunningham, Valentine, *Victorian Poetry Now: Poets, Poems, Poetics*, Chichester: Wiley Blackwell, 2011.

Curle, Richard (ed.), *Robert Browning and Julia Wedgwood: A Broken Friendship as Revealed in their Letters*, London: Murray & Cape, 1937.

Dale, Peter Allan, 'George Henry Lewes' Scientific Aesthetic: Restructuring the Ideology of the Symbol', in George Levine (ed.), *One Culture: Essays in Science and Literature*, Madison: The University of Wisconsin Press, 1987, pp. 92–113.

Dallas, E. S., *The Gay Science*, 2 vols, London: Chapman and Hall, 1866. Reprint, Bristol: Thoemmes Press, 1999.

Daly, Nicholas, *Literature, Technology and Modernity 1860–2000*, Cambridge: Cambridge University Press, 2004.

Dames, Nicholas, *Amnesiac Selves: Nostalgia, Forgetting, and British Fiction, 1810–1870*, Oxford: Oxford University Press, 2001.

Dames, Nicholas, *The Physiology of the Novel: Reading, Neural Science, and the Form of Victorian Fiction*, Oxford: Oxford University Press, 2007.

Danneberg, Lutz and Carlos Spoerhase, 'Wissen in Literatur als Herausforderung einer Pragmatik von Wissenszuschreibungen: sechs Problemfelder, sechs Fragen und zwölf Thesen', in Tilmann Köppe (ed.), *Literatur und Wissen: theoretisch-methodische Zugänge*, Berlin: de Gruyter, 2011, pp. 29–76.

Darwin, Charles, *The Variation of Plants and Animals under Domestication*, 2 vols, London: John Murray, 1868.

Darwin, Charles. *On the Origin of Species. A Facsimile of the First Edition*, ed. Ernst Mayr, Cambridge, MA: Harvard University Press, 1964.

Darwin, Charles, *The Descent of Man and Selection in Relation to Sex*, ed. James Moore and Adrian Desmond, London: Penguin, 2004.

Daston, Lorraine and Peter Galison, 'The Image of Objectivity', *Representations* 40 (1992), 81–128.

Daston, Lorraine and Peter Galison, *Objectivity*, Brooklyn: Zone Books, 2007.

Davis, Philip, *The Victorians* (The Oxford English Literary History, vol. 8: 1830–80), Oxford: Oxford University Press, 2002.

Dawson, Gowan, 'Literature and Science under the Microscope', *Journal of Victorian Culture* 11.2 (2006), 301–15.

Deane, Bradley, *The Making of the Victorian Novelist: Anxieties of Authorship in the Mass Market*, London: Routledge, 2003.

Deleuze, Gilles, *Difference and Repetition* [1968], trans. Paul Patton, London: Continuum, 2004.

Deleuze, Gilles and Félix Guattari, *A Thousand Plateaus: Capitalism and Schizophrenia*, trans. Brian Massumi, London: Bloomsbury, 2013.

Derrida, Jacques, *Of Grammatology*, trans. Gayatri Chakravorty Spivak, Baltimore: The Johns Hopkins University Press, 1976.

Derrida, Jacques, '"Genesis and Structure", and Phenomenology', in Jacques Derrida, *Writing and Difference*, trans. Alan Bass, London and New York, 1978, pp. 193–211.

Derrida, Jacques, 'Signature, Context, Event', in Jacques Derrida, *Margins of Philosophy*, trans. Alan Bass, Chicago: The University of Chicago Press, 1982, pp. 307–30.

Derrida, Jacques, 'The Animal That Therefore I Am (More to Follow)', trans. David Wills, *Critical Inquiry* 28.2 (2002), 369–418.

Desmond, Adrian, *Huxley: The Devil's Disciple*, London: Michael Joseph, 1994.

Dewey, John, 'The Experimental Theory of Knowledge' [1906], in John Dewey, *The Influence of Darwin on Philosophy and Other Essays in Contemporary Thought*, New York: Henry Holt and Company, 1910, pp. 77–111.

Dewey, John, 'The Need for a Recovery of Philosophy', in *Creative Intelligence: Essays in the Pragmatic Attitude*, New York: Henry Holt and Company, 1917, pp. 3–69.

Dewey, John, *Experience and Nature* [1925], rev. edn, London: George Allen & Unwin, 1929.

Dewey, John, *Art as Experience*, New York: Perigee, 2005.

Dickens, Charles, *Hard Times*, Ware: Wordsworth Editions, 1995.

Dixon, Thomas, '"Emotion": The History of a Keyword in Crisis', *Emotion Review* 4 (2012), 338–44.

Dowden, Edward, 'Mr Tennyson and Mr Browning', in Edward Dowden, *Studies in Literature 1789–1877*, 4th edn, London: Kegan Paul, Trench & Co., 1887, pp. 191–239.

Dowden, Edward, 'The Scientific Movement in Literature', in Edward Dowden, *Studies in Literature 1789–1877*, 4th edn, London: Kegan Paul, Trench & Co., 1887, pp. 85–121.

Dowling, Linda, 'Victorian Oxford and the Science of Language', *PMLA* 97.2 (1982), 160–78.

Dowling, Linda, *Language and Decadence in the Victorian Fin de Siècle*, Princeton: Princeton University Press, 1986.

Duncan, Ian, 'George Eliot's Science Fiction', *Representations* 125 (2014), 15–39.

Eliot, George, *Selections from George Eliot's Letters*, ed. Gordon S. Haight, New Haven, CT: Yale University Press, 1985.

Eliot, George, 'The Ilfracombe Journal', in George Eliot, *Selected Essays, Poems and Other Writings*, ed. A. S. Byatt and Nicholas Warren, London: Penguin, 1990, pp. 214–36.

Eliot, George, 'The Natural History of German Life', in George Eliot, *Selected Essays*, ed. A. S. Byatt and N. Warren, London: Penguin, 1990, pp. 107–39.

Eliot, George, *Middlemarch*, ed. David Caroll, Oxford: Oxford University Press, 1996.

Eliot, George, *The Mill on the Floss*, ed. Gordon S. Haight, Oxford: Oxford University Press, 1996.

Eliot, George, *The Spanish Gypsy*, ed. Antonie Gerard van den Broek, London: Pickering & Chatto, 2008.

Elkana, Yehuda, 'A Programmatic Attempt at an Anthropology of Knowledge', in Everett Mendelsohn and Yehuda Elkana (eds), *Sciences and Cultures*, Dordrecht and Boston, MA: Reidel, 1981, pp. 1–76.

Ellegård, Alvar, *Darwin and the General Reader: The Reception of Darwin's Theory of Evolution in the British Periodical Press, 1859–1872*, Chicago: Chicago University Press, 1990.

Erchinger, Philipp, 'Nature, Culture and Art as Practice in Victorian Writing', *Literature Compass* 9.11 (2012), 786–800.

Erchinger, Philipp, 'Reading Experience: William James and Robert Browning', *Journal of Literary Theory* 11.2 (2017), 162–82.

Ermarth, Elizabeth, 'Maggie Tulliver's Long Suicide', *SEL* 14 (1974), 587–601.

Ermarth, Elizabeth Deeds, *George Eliot*, Boston, MA: Twayne, 1985.

Ernst, Christoph und Heike Paul (eds), *Präsenz und implizites Wissen: Zur Interdependenz zweier Schlüsselbegriffe der Kultur- und Sozialwissenschaften*, Bielefeld: transcript, 2013.

Farrar, Frederic W., *An Essay on the Origin of Language, Based on Modern Researches, and Especially on the Works of M. Renan*, London: John Murray, 1860.

Felski, Rita, *Uses of Literature*, Oxford: Blackwell, 2008.

Felski, Rita, 'Context Stinks!', *New Literary History* 42.4 (Autumn 2011), 573–91.

Ferguson, Christine, *Language, Science and Popular Fiction in the Victorian Fin-de-Siècle: The Brutal Tongue*, London: Ashgate, 2006.

Fleishman, Avrom, *George Eliot's Intellectual Life*, Cambridge: Cambridge University Press, 2010.

Flint, Kate, 'Sensation', in Kate Flint (ed.), *The Cambridge History of Victorian Literature*, Cambridge: Cambridge University Press, 2012, pp. 220–42.

Foucault, Michel, *The Archaeology of Knowledge*, trans. A. M. Sheridan Smith, New York: Pantheon, 1972.

Foucault, Michel, *The Order of Things: An Archaeology of the Human Sciences*, London: Routledge, 2002.

Fraiman, Susan, 'The Mill on the Floss, the Critics, and the Bildungsroman', *PMLA* 108.1 (1993), 136–50.

Frederickson, Kathleen, *The Ploy of Instinct: Victorian Sciences of Nature and Sexuality in Liberal Governance*, New York: Fordham University Press, 2014.

Freeman-Moir, John, 'Crafting Experience: William Morris, John Dewey, and Utopia', *Utopian Studies* 22.2 (2011), 203–31.

French, Richard, *Antivivisection and Medical Science in Victorian Society*, Princeton: Princeton University Press, 1987.

Gagnier, Regenia, 'Preface', in Rosie Miles and Philippa Bennett (eds), *William Morris in the Twenty-First Century*, Oxford: Lang, 2010, pp. xv–xix.

Gagnier, Regenia, 'Twenty-First-Century and Victorian Ecosystems: Nature and Culture in the Developmental Niche', *Victorian Review* 36.2 (2010), 15–20.

Galton, Francis, 'Thought Without Words', *Nature* 12 (May 1887), 28–9.

Gamper, Michael, 'Einleitung', in Michael Gamper (ed.), *Experiment und Literatur: Themen, Methoden, Theorien*, Göttingen: Wallstein, 2010, pp. 9–14.

Gamper, Michael, '"Experimentierkunst" – Geschichte, Themen, Methoden, Theorien', in Stefanie Kreuzer (ed.), *Experimente in den Künsten: Transmediale Erkundungen in Literatur, Theater, Film, Musik und bildender Kunst*, Bielefeld: transcript, 2012, pp. 19–48.

Garratt, Peter, *Victorian Empiricism: Self, Knowledge, and Reality in Ruskin, Bain, Lewes, Spencer, and George Eliot*, Madison: Fairleigh Dickinson University Press, 2010.

Gillespie, Neal C., 'Divine Design and the Industrial Revolution: William Paley's Abortive Reform of Natural Theology', *Isis* 81.2 (1990), 214–29.

Goethe, Johann Wolfgang, 'Der Versuch als Vermittler', in Johann Wolfgang Goethe, *Werke*, ed. Friedmar Apel et al., vol. 6, Frankfurt am Main: Insel, 1998, pp. 380–9.

Goldstein, Amanda Jo, *Sweet Science: Romantic Materialism and the New Logics of Life*, Chicago: University of Chicago Press, 2017.

Gooding, David, '"Magnetic Curves" and the Magnetic Field: Experimentation and Representation in the History of a Theory', in David Gooding, Trevor Pinch and Simon Schaffer (eds), *The Uses of Experiment: Studies in the Natural Sciences*, Cambridge: Cambridge University Press, 1989, pp. 183–224.

Gooding, David, *Experiment and the Making of Meaning: Human Agency in Scientific Observation and Experiment*, Dordrecht: Kluwer, 1990.

Gooding, David, 'Mapping Experiment as a Learning Process: How the First Electromagnetic Motor Was Invented', *Science, Technology, and Human Values* 15.2 (1990), 165–201.

Gooding, David, 'Putting Agency Back into Experiment', in Andrew Pickering (ed.), *Science as Practice and Culture*, Chicago: The University of Chicago Press, 1992, pp. 65–112.

Gooding, David, 'Envisioning Explanations: The Art in Science', in Bernard Frischer and Anastasia Dakouri-Hild (eds), *Beyond Illustration: 2D and 3D Digital Technologies as Tools for Discovery in Archaeology*, Oxford: Archaeopress, 2008, pp. 1–20.

Gosse, Philip Henry, *The Romance of Natural History*, London: James Nisbet, 1860.

Great Exhibition, 1851: Official Illustrated and Descriptive Catalogue of the Great Exhibition, 1851, London: Spicer Brothers, 1851.

Greetham, D. C., *Theories of the Text*, Oxford: Oxford University Press, 1999.

Haney, Janice L., 'Shadow-Hunting: Romantic Irony, *Sartor Resartus* and Victorian Romanticism', *Studies in Romanticism* 17.3 (1978), 307–33.

Harré, Rom and Janet Martin, 'Metaphor in Science', in David S. Miall (ed.), *Metaphor: Problems and Perspectives*, Brighton: The Harvester Press, 1982, pp. 89–105.

Harris, Mark (ed.), *Ways of Knowing: New Approaches in the Anthropology of Knowledge and Learning*, New York: Berghahn, 2007.

Harris, Roy, 'Introduction', in Roy Harris (ed.), *The Origin of Language*, Bristol: Thoemmes Press, 1996, pp. vii–xii.

Heidegger, Martin, 'Building Dwelling Thinking', in Joanne Morra and Marquard Smith (eds), *Visual Culture: Critical Concepts in Media and Cultural Studies*, vol. 3, London: Routledge, 2006, pp. 66–76.

Herbert, Christopher, *Victorian Relativity: Radical Thought and Scientific Discovery*, Chicago: The University of Chicago Press, 2001.

Heringman, Noah, *Romantic Rocks: Aesthetic Geology*, Ithaca: Cornell University Press, 2004.

Herrnstein Smith, Barbara, *Scandalous Knowledge: Science, Truth and the Human*, Edinburgh: Edinburgh University Press, 2006.

[Herschel, John], '[Review of William Whewell's] *The Philosophy of the Inductive Sciences*', *Quarterly Review* 68.135 (June 1841), 177–238.

Herschel, John, *Preliminary Discourse on the Study of Natural Philosophy* [1830], new edition, London: Longman, 1851.

Hillis Miller, J., 'The Two Rhetorics: George Eliot's Bestiary', in G. Douglas Atkins and Michael L. Johnson (eds), *Writing and Reading Differently: Deconstruction and the Teaching of Composition and Literature*, Lawrence: University Press of Kansas, 1985, pp. 101–14.

Hillis Miller, J., '"Hieroglyphical Truth" in *Sartor Resartus*: Carlyle and the Language of Parable', in John Clubbe and Jerome Meckier (eds), *Victorian Perspectives: Six Essays*, Basingstoke: Macmillan, 1989, pp. 1–20.

Hillis Miller, J., 'A Conclusion in which Almost Nothing is Concluded: Middlemarch's "Finale"', in Karen Chase (ed.), *Middlemarch in the Twenty-First Century*, Oxford: Oxford University Press, 2006, pp. 133–56.

Holmes, John, 'Poetry on Pre-Raphaelite Principles: Science, Nature, and Knowledge in William Michael Rossetti's "Fancies at Leisure" and "Mrs Holmes Grey"', *Victorian Poetry* 53.1 (2015), 15–39.

Hopkins, William, 'Physical Theories of the Phenomena of Life. Part II', *Fraser's Magazine* 62.367 (July 1860), 74–90.

Hühn, Peter, 'The Detective as Reader: Narrativity and Reading Concepts in Detective Fiction', *Modern Fiction Studies* 33.3 (1987), 451–66.

Hume, David, *An Enquiry Concerning Human Understanding*, ed. Tom L. Beauchamp, Oxford: Oxford University Press, 1999.

Hutter, Albert D., 'Dreams, Transformations, and Literature: The Implications of Detective Fiction', *Victorian Studies* 19.2 (1975), 181–209.

Huxley, Thomas Henry, 'On the Advisableness of Improving Natural Knowledge' [1866], in Thomas Henry Huxley, *Collected Essays*, vol. 1, London: Macmillan, 1893, pp. 18–41.

Huxley, Thomas Henry, 'Man's Place in Nature' [1863], in Thomas Henry Huxley, *Collected Essays*, vol. 7, London: Macmillan, 1895, pp. 1–208.

Huxley, Thomas Henry, 'Possibilities and Impossibilities' [1891], in Thomas Henry Huxley, *Collected Essays*, vol. 5, London: Macmillan, 1895, pp. 192–208.

Huxley, Thomas Henry, 'Scientific and Pseudo-Scientific Realism' [1887], in Thomas Henry Huxley, *Collected Essays*, vol. 5, London: Macmillan, 1895, pp. 59–125.

Huxley, Thomas Henry, 'Six Lectures to Working Men "On Our Knowledge of the Causes of the Phenomena of Organic Nature"' [1863], in Thomas Henry Huxley, *Collected Essays*, vol. 2, London: Macmillan, 1902, pp. 303–475.

Huxley, Thomas Henry, 'Science and Morals' [1886], in Thomas Henry Huxley, *Collected Essays*, vol. 4, London: Macmillan, 1903, pp. 117–46.

Huxley, Thomas Henry, 'On the Educational Value of the Natural History Sciences' [1854], in Thomas Henry Huxley, *Collected Essays*, vol. 3, London: Macmillan, 1905, pp. 38–65.

Huxley, Thomas Henry, 'A Liberal Education; and Where to Find It' [1868], in Thomas Henry Huxley, *Collected Essays*, vol. 3, London: Macmillan, 1905, pp. 76–110.

Huxley, Thomas Henry, 'Scientific Education: Notes of an After Dinner Speech' [1869], in Thomas Henry Huxley, *Collected Essays*, vol. 3, London: Macmillan, 1905, pp. 111–33.

Huxley, Thomas Henry, 'On the Study of Biology' [1876], in Thomas Henry Huxley, *Collected Essays*, vol. 3, London: Macmillan, 1905, pp. 262–93.

Huxley, Thomas Henry, 'Science and Culture' [1880], in Thomas Henry Huxley, *Collected Essays*, vol. 3, London: Macmillan, 1905, pp. 134–59.

Huxley, Thomas Henry, 'On Science and Art in Relation to Education' [1882], in Thomas Henry Huxley, *Collected Essays*, vol. 3, London: Macmillan, 1905, pp. 160–88.

Ingold, Tim, *Perception of the Environment: Essays on Dwelling, Livelihood and Skill*, London: Routledge, 2000.

Ingold, Tim, 'Beyond Art and Technology: The Anthropology of Skill', in Michael B. Schiffer (ed.), *Anthropological Perspectives on Technology*, Albuquerque: University of New Mexico Press, 2001, pp. 17–32.

Ingold, Tim, *Being Alive: Essays on Movement, Knowledge, and Description*, London: Routledge, 2011.

Ingold, Tim, *Making*, London: Routledge, 2013.

Ingold, Tim, *The Life of Lines*, London: Routledge, 2015.

Iser, Wolfgang, *Der Akt des Lesens*, München: Fink, 1976.

Iser, Wolfgang, 'The Emergence of a Cross-Cultural Discourse: Thomas Carlyle's *Sartor Resartus*', in Sanford Budick and Wolfgang Iser (eds), *The Translatability of Cultures: Figurations of the Space Between*, Stanford: Stanford University Press, 1996, pp. 245–64.

James, Henry, 'The Novel in *The Ring and the Book*' [1912], in Henry James, *Notes on Novelists with Some Other Notes*, New York: Charles Scribner's Sons, 1914, pp. 385–411.

James, William, 'What is an Emotion?', *Mind* 9.34 (1884), 188–205.

James, William, *The Meaning of Truth*, New York: Longmans, Green, and Co., 1909.

James, William, *Radical Empiricism*, in William James, *The Writings of William James*, ed. John McDermott, Chicago: 1977, pp. 134–310.

James, William, *The Principles of Psychology* [1890], ed. Frederick Burkhardt, 3 vols, Cambridge, MA: Harvard University Press, 1981.

James, William, *Pragmatism*, New York: Dover Publications, 1995.

[Jardine, William], '[Review of Darwin's] On the Origin of Species', *Edinburgh New Philosophical Journal* 11 (1860), 280–9.

Jay, Martin, *Songs of Experience: Modern American and European Variations on a Universal Theme*, Berkeley: University of California Press, 2005.

Jevons, Stanley W., 'John Stuart Mill's Philosophy Tested', *Contemporary Review* 31 (Dec. 1877), 167–82.

Johnson, Steven, *Where Good Ideas Come From: The Seven Patterns of Innovation*, London: Penguin, 2010.

Jones, Anna Maria, *Problem Novels: Victorian Fiction Theorizes the Sensational Self*, Columbus: Ohio State University Press, 2007.

Kambartel, Friedrich, 'Erfahrung', in Joachim Ritter, Karlfried Gründer and Gottfried Gabriel (eds), *Historisches Wörterbuch der Philosophie*, vol. 2, Basel: Schwabe, pp. 609–17.

Kant, Immanuel, *Critique of Judgement*, trans. J. H. Bernard, New York: Hafner Press, 1951.

Kant, Immanuel, *Kritik der Urteilskraft*, ed. Heiner F. Klemme, Hamburg: Meiner, 2001.

Karlin, Daniel, *Browning's Hatreds*, Oxford: Oxford University Press, 1993.

Keating, P. J., 'Robert Browning: A Reader's Guide', in Isobel Armstrong (ed.), *Robert Browning*, London: Bell, 1974, pp. 299–328.

Klancher, Jon, 'Romanticism and its Publics: A Forum – Introduction', *Studies in Romanticism* 33.4 (1994), 523–5.

Klancher, Jon, *Transfiguring the Arts and Sciences: Knowledge and Cultural Institutions in the Romantic Age*, Cambridge: Cambridge University Press, 2013.

Klausnitzer, Ralf, *Literatur und Wissen: Zugänge – Modelle – Analysen*, Berlin: de Gruyter, 2008.

Kogge, Werner, 'Erschriebene Denkräume: Grammatologie in der Perspektive einer Philosophie der Praxis', in Gernot Grube, Werner Kogge, and Sybille Krämer, *Schrift: Kulturtechnik zwischen Auge, Hand und Maschine*, München: Fink, 2005, pp. 137–69.

Kogge, Werner, 'Empeirìa: Vom Verlust der Erfahrungshaltigkeit des Wissens und vom Versuch, sie als "implizites Wissen" wiederzugewinnen', in Jens Loenhoff (ed.), *Implizites Wissen: Epistemologische und handlungstheoretische Perspektiven*, Weilerswist: Velbrück Wissenschaft, 2012, pp. 31–48.

Kohns, Oliver, *Die Verrücktheit des Sinns: Wahnsinn und Zeichen bei Kant, E. T. A. Hoffmann und Thomas Carlyle*, Bielefeld: transcript, 2007.

Köppe, Tilmann, 'Vom Wissen *in* Literatur', *Zeitschrift für Germanistik* 17.3 (2007), 398–410.

Koschorke, Albrecht, *Wahrheit und Erfindung: Grundzüge einer Allgemeinen Erzähltheorie*, Frankfurt am Main: Fischer, 2012.

Krasner, James, '"Where no man praised": The Retreat from Fame in George Eliot's *The Spanish Gypsy*', *Victorian Poetry* 32.1 (1994), 55–74.

Kurnick, David, 'Unspeakable George Eliot', *Victorian Literature and Culture* 38 (2010), 489–509.

Landy, Joshua, *How to Do Things with Fictions*, Oxford: Oxford University Press, 2012.

Langbaum, Robert, *The Poetry of Experience: The Dramatic Monologue in Modern Literary Tradition* [1957], New York: Norton, 1963.

Latour, Bruno, *Science in Action: How to Follow Scientists and Engineers through Society*, Cambridge, MA: Harvard University Press, 1987.

Latour, Bruno, 'Drawing Things Together', in Michael Lynch and Steve Woolgar (eds), *Representation in Scientific Practice*, Cambridge, MA: MIT Press, 1990, pp. 19–68.

Latour, Bruno, 'One More Turn After the Social Turn . . .', in Mario Biagioli (ed.), *The Science Studies Reader*, London: Routledge, 1999, pp. 276–89.

Latour, Bruno, *Pandora's Hope: Essays on the Reality of Science Studies*, Cambridge, MA: Harvard University Press, 1999.

Latour, Bruno, *Reassembling the Social: An Introduction to Actor-Network Theory*, Oxford: Oxford University Press, 2005.

Latour, Bruno, 'A Text-Book Case Revisited – Knowledge as a Mode of Existence', in Edward J. Hackett et al. (eds), *The Handbook of Science and Technology Studies*, Cambridge, MA: The MIT Press, 2008, pp. 83–112.

Latour, Bruno, *An Inquiry into Modes of Existence: An Anthropology of the Moderns*, trans. Catherine Porter, Cambridge, MA: Harvard University Press, 2013.

Latour, Bruno and Steve Woolgar, *Laboratory Life: The Construction of Scientific Facts,* Princeton: Princeton University Press, 1979.

Laudan, Larry, 'William Whewell on the Consilience of Inductions', *The Monist* 55.3 (1971), 368–91.

Lee, Louise, 'Lady Audley's Secret: How *Does* She Do It? Sensation Fiction's Technologically Minded Villainesses', in Pamela K. Gilbert (ed.), *A Companion to Sensation Fiction*, Chichester: Wiley-Blackwell, 2011, pp. 134–46.

Lesjak, Carolyn, *Working Fictions: A Genealogy of the Victorian Novel*, Durham, NC: Duke University Press, 2006.

Levine, George, *The Boundaries of Fiction: Carlyle, Macaulay, Newman*, Princeton: Princeton University Press, 1968.

Levine, George, *Dying to Know: Scientific Epistemology and Narrative in Victorian England*, Chicago: The University of Chicago Press, 2002.

Levine, George, *Realism, Ethics and Secularism: Essays on Victorian Literature and Science*, Cambridge: Cambridge University Press, 2008.

Lewes, George Henry, 'Sea-Side Studies', *Blackwood's Edinburgh Magazine* 80.490 (August 1856), 184–97.

Lewes, George Henry, 'Sea-Side Studies', *Blackwood's Edinburgh Magazine* 80.491 (Sept. 1856), 312–25.

Lewes, George Henry, 'Sea-Side Studies', *Blackwood's Edinburgh Magazine* 80.492 (Oct. 1856), 472–85.

Lewes, George Henry, 'New Sea-Side Studies', *Blackwood's Edinburgh Magazine* 81.500 (June 1857), 669–85.

Lewes, George Henry, 'New Sea-Side Studies', *Blackwood's Edinburgh Magazine* 82.501 (July 1857), 1–17.

Lewes, George Henry, 'New Sea-Side Studies', *Blackwood's Edinburgh Magazine* 82.502 (August 1857), 222–40.

Lewes, George Henry, 'New Sea-Side Studies', *Blackwood's Edinburgh Magazine* 82.503 (Sept. 1857), 345–57.

Lewes, George Henry, 'New Sea-Side Studies', *Blackwood's Edinburgh Magazine* 82.504 (Oct. 1857), 410–23.

Lewes, George Henry, *Sea-Side Studies at Ilfracombe, Tenby, the Scilly Isles & Jersey*, Edinburgh: Blackwood and Son, 1858.

Lewes, George Henry, *Studies in Animal Life*, London: Smith and Elder, 1862.

Lewes, George Henry, 'The Principles of Success in Literature: Chapter III', *Fortnightly Review* 1 (July 1865), 572–89.

Lewes, George Henry, *Problems of Life and Mind, First Series*, 2 vols, Boston, MA: James R. Osgood and Company, 1874/1875.

Lewes, George Henry, *Problems of Life and Mind, Third Series*, 2 vols, London: Trübner & Co., 1879.

Lightman, Bernard, Victorian *Popularizers of Science: Designing Nature for New Audiences*, Chicago: The University of Chicago Press, 2007.

Lightman, Bernard, 'Science and Culture', in Francis O'Gorman (ed.), *The Cambridge Companion to Victorian Culture*, Cambridge: Cambridge University Press, 2010.

Livingston, Paisley, *Literary Knowledge: Humanistic Inquiry and the Philosophy of Science*, Ithaca: Cornell University Press, 1988.

Lobsien, Eckhard, *Zeit der Imagination: Das Imaginäre (in) der englischen Romantik*, Heidelberg: Winter, 2008.

Lonoff, Sue, *Wilkie Collins and his Victorian Readers: A Study in the Rhetoric of Authorship*, New York: AMS Press, 1982.

Lüdeke, Roger, 'Contingencies of Comparison: The Impossible Coordinates of a World Literature System', *European Journal of English Studies* 13.1 (2009), 43–60.

Lüdeke, Roger, 'Die Gesellschaft der Literatur: Ästhetische Interaktion und gesellschaftliche Praxis in Bram Stokers *Dracula*', *Jahrbuch der Heinrich Heine Universität Düsseldorf* 2008/2009 (2010), 361–82.

Lüdeke, Roger, 'The Eigensinn of Literary Things: Reading Social Practice with Robinson Crusoe', in Birgit Neumann (ed.), *Präsenz und Evidenz fremder Dinge im Europa des 18. Jahrhunderts*, Göttingen: Wallstein, 2015, pp. 377–94.

Lukács, George, *The Theory of the Novel: A Historico-Philosophical Essay on the Forms of Great Epic Literature* [1920], trans. Anna Bostock, Cambridge, MA: The MIT Press, 1971.

Maag, Georg, 'Erfahrung', in Karlheinz Barck et al. (eds), *Ästhetische Grundbegriffe*, vol. 2, Stuttgart: Metzler, 2001, pp. 260–74.

Macdonald, Bradley J., *William Morris and the Aesthetic Constitution of Politics*, Lanham, MD: Lexington, 1999.

Mann, Karen, 'George Eliot's Language of Nature: Production and Consumption', *ELH* 48.1 (1981), 190–216.

Manning, Erin, *Always More than One: Individuation's Dance*, Durham, NC: Duke University Press, 2013.

Manning, Erin and Brian Massumi, *Thought in the Act: Passages in the Ecology of Experience*, Minneapolis: University of Minnesota Press, 2014.

Mansel, H. L., 'Sensation Novels', *The Quarterly Review* (April 1863), 481–514.

Marcus, Laura, 'Detection and Literary Fiction', in Martin Priestman (ed.), *The Cambridge Companion to Crime Fiction*, Cambridge: Cambridge University Press, 2006, pp. 245–68.

Maroni, Francesco, '"A Shadow on the Wall": Armadale and Lydia Gwilt's Narcisisstic Text', in Mariaconcetta Costantini (ed.), *Armadale: Wilkie Collins and the Dark Threads of Life*, Rome: Aracne, 2009, pp. 51–68.

Martens, Britta, *Browning, Victorian Poetics and the Romantic Legacy*, Farnham: Ashgate, 2011.

Mason, Michael, 'Browning and the Dramatic Monologue', in Isobel Armstrong (ed.), *Writers and their Background: Robert Browning*, London: G. Bell & Sons, 1974, pp. 231–66.

Masschelein, Jan, 'E-ducating the Gaze: The Idea of a Poor Pedagogy', *Ethics and Education* 5.1 (2010), 43–53.

Masschelein, Jan, 'Experimentum Scholae: The World Once More . . . But Not (Yet) Finished', *Studies in Philosophy & Education* 30 (2011), 529–35.

Massumi, Brian, *Parables for the Virtual: Movement, Affect, Sensation*, Durham, NC: Duke University Press, 2002.

Massumi, Brian, 'Prelude', in Erin Manning, *Always More than One: Individuation's Dance*. Durham, NC: Duke University Press, 2013, pp. ix–xxiii.

Massumi, Brian, 'Envisioning the Virtual', in Mark Grimshaw (ed.), *The Oxford Handbook of Virtuality*, Oxford: Oxford University Press, 2014, pp. 55–70.

Matus, Jill L., 'Disclosure as "Cover-Up": The Discourse of Madness in *Lady Audley's Secret*', *University of Toronto Quarterly* 62.3 (1993), 334–55.

McGann, Jerome, 'Innovation and Experiment', in Kate Flint (ed.), *The Cambridge History of Victorian Literature*, Cambridge: Cambridge University Press, 2012, pp. 288–310.

Mecke, Klaus, 'Zahl und Erzählung: Metaphern in Erkenntnisprozessen der Physik', in Klaus Mecke und Aura Heydenreich (eds), *Quarks and Letters: Naturwissenschaften in der Literatur und Kultur der Gegenwart*, Berlin: de Gruyter, 2015, pp. 31–84.

Mellor, Anne K., *English Romantic Irony*, Cambridge, MA: Harvard University Press, 1980.

Menaghan, John M., 'Embodied Truth: *The Ring and the Book* Reconsidered', *University of Toronto Quarterly* 52 (1983), 263–76.

Menke, Richard, 'Fiction as Vivisection: G. H. Lewes and George Eliot', *ELH* 67.2 (2000), 617–53.

Menke, Richard, *Telegraphic Realism: Victorian Fiction and Other Information Systems*, Stanford: Stanford University Press, 2008.

Merrill, Lynn L., *The Romance of Victorian Natural History*, New York and Oxford: Oxford University Press, 1989.

Merriman, Peter, 'Unpicking Time-Space: Towards New Apprehensions of Movement-Space', in Ingo Berensmeyer and Christoph Ehland (eds), *Perspectives on Mobility*, Amsterdam: Rodopi, 2013, pp. 177–92.

Middeke, Martin, *Die Kunst der gelebten Zeit: Studien zur Phänomenologie literarischer Subjektivität im Roman des ausgehenden neunzehnten Jahrhunderts*, Würzburg: Königshausen & Neumann, 2004.

Mill, John Stuart, *An Examination of Sir William Hamilton's Philosophy and of the Principal Philosophical Questions Discussed in his Writings*, 2nd edn, London: Longmans, Green and Co., 1865.

Mill, John Stuart, *A System of Logic, Ratiocinative and Inductive, Being a Connected View of the Principles of Evidence, and the Methods of Scientific Investigation*, 2 vols, 8th edn, London: Longmans, Green, Reader, and Dyer, 1872.

Mill, John Stuart, 'Nature', in John Stuart Mill, *Collected Works*, vol. 10, ed. J. M. Robert, London: Routledge & Kegan Paul; Toronto: University of Toronto Press, 1969, pp. 373–402.

Miller, D. A., *The Novel and the Police*, Berkeley: University of California Press, 1988.

Millgram, Elijah, 'John Stuart Mill, Determinism, and the Problem of Induction', *Australasian Journal of Philosophy* 87.2 (2009), 183–99.

Millgram, Elijah, 'Mill's and Whewell's Competing Visions of Logic', in Antis Loizides (ed.), *Mill's* A System of Logic: *Critical Appraisals*, London: Routledge, 2014, 101–21.

Mitchell, Robert, *Experimental Life: Vitalism in Romantic Science & Literature*, Baltimore: Johns Hopkins University Press, 2013.

Morley, John, *On Compromise*, London: Chapman and Hall, 1874.

Morris, William, 'The Lesser Arts' [1877], in *The Collected Works of William Morris*, vol. 22, London: Longmans, Green and Company, 1914, pp. 3–27.

Morris, William, 'The Aims of Art' [1886], in *The Collected Works of William Morris*, vol. 23, London: Longmans, Green and Company, 1914, pp. 81–97.

Morris, William, 'Art and its Producers' [1888], in *The Collected Works of William Morris*, vol. 22, London: Longmans, Green and Company, 1914, pp. 342–55.

Morris William, *News from Nowhere and Other Writings*, ed. Clive Wilmer, London: Penguin, 1993.

Müller, Friedrich Max, *Lectures on the Science of Language*, vol. 1, London: Longman, Green, Longman & Roberts, 1861.

Müller, Friedrich Max, *Lectures on the Science of Language*, vol. 2, London: Longman, Green, Longman, Roberts, & Green, 1864.

Müller, Friedrich Max, 'Lectures on Mr Darwin's Philosophy of Language. Second Lecture', *Fraser's Magazine* 7.42 (June 1873), 659–78.

Müller, Friedrich Max, 'Lectures on Mr Darwin's Philosophy of Language. Third Lecture', *Fraser's Magazine* 8.43 (July 1873), 1–24.

Müller, Friedrich Max, 'Metaphor as a Mode of Abstraction', *Fortnightly Review* 40:239 (Nov. 1886), 617–32.

Nasim, Omar, *Drawing by Hand: Sketching the Nebulae in the Nineteenth Century*, Chicago: The University of Chicago Press, 2013.

Neumann, Birgit, 'Kulturelles Wissen und Literatur', in Marion Gymnich, Birgit Neumann and Ansgar Nünning (eds), *Kulturelles Wissen und Intertextualität: Theoriekonzeptionen und Fallstudien zur Kontextualisierung von Literatur*, Trier: Wissenschaftlicher Verlag, 2006, pp. 29–51.

Newton, K. M., *Modernizing George Eliot: The Writer as Artist, Intellectual, Proto-Modernist, Cultural Critic*, London: Bloomsbury Academic, 2011.

Niemann, Michelle, 'Browning's Critique of Organic Form in *The Ring and the Book*', *Victorian Poetry* 52.3 (2014), 445–64.

Nord, Deborah Epstein, 'Marks of Race: Gypsy Figures and Eccentric Femininity in Nineteenth-Century Women's Writing', *Victorian Studies* 41.2 (1998), 189–210.

Nord, Deborah Epstein, *Gypsies and the British Imagination, 1807–1930*, New York: Columbia University Press, 2006.

Norris, Christopher, *Against Relativism: Philosophy of Science, Deconstruction and Critical Theory*, Oxford: Blackwell, 1997.

O'Connor, Ralph, *The Earth on Show: Fossils and the Poetics of Popular Science, 1802–1856*, Chicago: The University of Chicago Press, 2007.

O'Connor, Ralph, 'From the Epic of Earth History to the Evolutionary Epic in Nineteenth-Century Britain', *Journal of Victorian Culture* 14.2 (2009), 207–23.

O'Toole, Sean, *Habit in the English Novel: Lived Environments, Practices of the Self*, Basingstoke: Palgrave, 2013.

OED Online, Oxford University Press, Web.

Otis, Laura, *Organic Memory: History and the Body in the Late Nineteenth and Early Twentieth Centuries*, Lincoln: University of Nebraska Press, 1994.

Otis, Laura, *Networking: Communicating with Bodies and Machines in the Nineteenth Century*, Ann Arbor: The University of Michigan Press, 2001.

Paley, William, *Natural Theology, or Evidence of the Existence and Attributes of the Deity, Collected from the Appearances of Nature* [1802], ed. Matthew D. Eddy and David Knight, Oxford: Oxford University Press, 2006.

Pallo, Vicky A., 'From Do-Nothing to Detective: The Transformation of Robert Audley in *Lady Audley's Secret*', *The Journal of Popular Culture* 39.3 (2006), 466–78.

Paradis, James G. (ed.), *Samuel Butler – Victorian against the Grain: A Critical Overview*, Toronto: University of Toronto Press, 2007.

Paris, Bernard J., *Experiments in Life: George Eliot's Quest for Values*, Detroit: Wayne State University Press, 1965.

Pearsall, Cornelia D. J., 'The Dramatic Monologue', in Joseph Bristow (ed.), *The Cambridge Companion to Victorian Poetry*, Cambridge: Cambridge University Press, 2000, pp. 67–88.

Pearson, Karl, *The Grammar of Science* [1892], reprint: Bristol: Thoemmes Press, 1991.

Peterson, Linda H., *Victorian Autobiography: The Tradition of Self-Interpretation*, New Haven, CT: Yale University Press, 1986.

Petts, Jeffrey, 'Good Work and Aesthetic Education: William Morris, the Arts and Crafts Movement, and Beyond', *Journal of Aesthetic Education* 42.1 (2008), 30–45.

Pickering, Andrew, 'Living in the Material World: On Realism and Experimental Practice', in David Gooding, Trevor Pinch and Simon Schaffer (eds), *The Uses of Experiment: Studies in the Natural Sciences*, Cambridge: Cambridge University Press, 1989, pp. 275–97.

Pickering, Andrew, *The Mangle of Practice: Time, Agency and Science*, Chicago: The University of Chicago Press, 1995.

Pickering, Andrew, *The Cybernetic Brain: Sketches of Another Future*, Chicago: The University of Chicago Press, 2010.

Pickstone, John V., *Ways of Knowing: A New History of Science, Technology and Medicine*, Chicago: The University of Chicago Press, 2000.

Pinkney, Tony, 'Versions of Ecotopia in *News from Nowhere*', in Rosie Miles and Philippa Bennett (eds), *William Morris in the Twenty-First Century*, Oxford: Lang, 2010, pp. 93–106.

Plunkett, John, Ana Parejo Vadillo and Regenia Gagnier, 'Introduction', in John Plunkett, Ana Parejo Vadillo and Regenia Gagnier (eds), *Victorian Literature: A Sourcebook*, Basingstoke: Palgrave, 2012, pp. 1–12.

Polanyi, Michael, *Personal Knowledge: Towards a Post-Critical Philosophy*, London: Routledge & Kegan Paul, 1958.

Polanyi, Michael, *The Tacit Dimension*, Chicago: The University of Chicago Press, 1966.

Porter, Theodore M., 'The Fate of Scientific Naturalism: From Public Sphere to Professional Exclusivity', in Gowan Dawson and Bernard Lightman (eds), *Victorian Scientific Naturalism: Community, Identity, Continuity*, Chicago: The University of Chicago Press, 2014, pp. 265–87.

Prichard, James Cowles, 'Forms of Insanity', in Jenny Bourne Taylor and Sally Shuttleworth (eds), *An Anthology of Psychological Texts 1830–1890*, Oxford: Oxford University Press, 1998, pp. 251–6.

Pykett, Lyn, *Authors in Context: Wilkie Collins*, Oxford: Oxford University Press, 2005.

Radick, Gregory, *The Simian Tongue: The Long Debate about Animal Language*, Chicago: The University of Chicago Press, 2007.

Rauch, Alan, *Useful Knowledge: The Victorians, Morality and the March of Intellect*, Durham, NC: Duke University Press, 2001.

Reckwitz, Andreas, 'Grundelemente einer Theorie sozialer Praktiken', in Andreas Reckwitz, *Unscharfe Grenzen: Perspektiven der Kultursoziologie*, Bielefeld: transcript, 2008, pp. 97–130.

Reinfandt, Christoph, 'Texture as a Key Term in Literary and Cultural Studies', in Rüdiger Kunow and Stephan Mussil (eds), *Text or Context: Reflections on Literary and Cultural Criticism*, Würzburg: Königshausen & Neumann, 2013, pp. 7–21.

Reynolds, David, *The Realms of Verse 1830–1870: English Poetry in a Time of Nation Building*, Oxford: Oxford University Press, 2001.

Rheinberger, Hans-Jörg, *Toward a History of Epistemic Things: Synthesizing Proteins in the Test Tube*, Stanford: Stanford University Press, 1997.

Rheinberger, Hans-Jörg, 'Experimental Systems: Historiality, Narration, Deconstruction', in Mario Biagioli (ed.), *The Science Studies Reader*, New York: Routledge, 1999, pp. 417–29.

Rheinberger, Hans-Jörg and Peter McLaughlin, 'Darwin's Experimental Natural History', *Journal of the History of Biology* 17.3 (1984), 345–68.

Richter, Virginia, *Human Beasts in Western Fiction 1859–1939*, Basingstoke: Palgrave, 2011.

Richter, Virginia, 'Anschauung des Unsichtbaren: Rhetoriken des Nichtwissens im Umfeld des Darwinismus', in Michael Bies and Michael Gamper (eds), *Literatur und Nichtwissen: Historische Konstellationen in Literatur und Wissenschaft, 1750–1930*, Berlin: diaphanes, 2012, pp. 359–77.

Roberts, Lewis, 'The "Shivering Sands" of Reality: Narration and Knowledge in Wilkie Collins' *The Moonstone*', *Victorian Review* 23.2 (1997), 168–83.

Roth, Robert J., *British Empiricism and American Pragmatism: New Directions and Neglected Arguments*, New York: Fordham University Press University Press, 1993.

Rouse, Joseph, 'Understanding Scientific Practices: Cultural Studies of Science as a Philosophical Program', in Mario Biagioli (ed.), *The Science Studies Reader*, London: Routledge, 1999, pp. 442–56.

Rouse, Joseph, 'Practice Theory', in Stephen Turner and Mark Risjord (eds), *Handbook of the Philosophy of Science*, vol. 15, Amsterdam: Elsevier, 2006, pp. 499–540.

Rundle, Vivienne J., '"Will You Let Them Murder Me?": Guido and the Reader in *The Ring and the Book*', *Victorian Poetry* 27.3/4 (1989: Autumn/Winter), 99–114.

Ruskin, John, *Lectures on Art* [1870], in John Ruskin, *The Works*, ed. E. T. Cook and Alexander Wedderburn, vol. 20, London: George Allen, 1905, pp. 4–179.

Ruskin, John, *The Eagle's Nest: Ten Lectures on the Relation of Natural Science to Art* [1872], in John Ruskin, *The Works*, ed. E. T. Cook and Alexander Wedderburn, vol. 22, London: George Allen, 1906, pp. 114–287.

Ryan, Judith, *The Vanishing Subject: Early Psychology and Literary Modernism*, Chicago: The University of Chicago Press, 1991.

Ryan, Vanessa L., *Thinking Without Thinking in the Victorian Novel*, Baltimore: The Johns Hopkins University Press, 2012.

Rylance, Rick, *Victorian Psychology and British Culture 1850–1880*, Oxford: Oxford University Press, 2000.

Ryle, Gilbert, 'Knowing How and Knowing That', in Gilbert Ryle, *Collected Papers*, vol. 2, London: Hutchinson, 1971, pp. 212–26.

Santayana, George, *Interpretations of Poetry and Religion*, New York: Charles Scribner's Sons, 1900.

Schatzki, Theodore R., 'Praxistheorie als flache Ontologie', in Hilmar Schäfer (ed.), *Praxistheorie: Ein soziologisches Forschungsprogramm*, Bielefeld: transcript, 2016, pp. 29–44.

Schatzki, Theodore R., Karin Knorr Cetina and Eike von Savitzky (eds), *The Practice Turn in Contemporary Theory*, London: Routledge, 2001.

Scholz, Susanne, *Phantasmatic Knowledge: Visions of the Human and the Scientific Gaze in English Literature, 1880–1930*, Heidelberg: Winter, 2013.

Schulz, Dieter, 'Wandern und Methode: Thoreaus Walking im Lichte Emersons und Gadamers', in Astrid Böger, Georg Schiller and Nicole Schröder (eds), *Dialoge zwischen Amerika und Europa: Transatlantische Perspektiven in Philosophie, Literatur, Kunst und Musik*, Tübingen: Francke, 2007, pp. 107–29.

Sennett, Richard, *The Craftsman*, London: Penguin, 2009.

Serres, Michel, *Genesis*, trans. Geneviève James and James Nielson, Ann Arbor: University of Michigan Press, 1995.

Sharp, William, *Life and Writings of Robert Browning*, London: Walter Scott, 1897.

Shelley, Mary, *Frankenstein*, ed. J. Paul Hunter, 2nd edn, New York: Norton, 2012.

Shelley, Percy B., 'A Defence of Poetry', in Duncan Wu (ed.), *Romanticism: An Anthology*, 4th edn, Oxford: Wiley-Blackwell, 2012, pp. 1233–47.

Showalter, Elaine, *A Literature of Their Own: British Women Novelists from Brontë to Lessing*, Princeton: Princeton University Press, 1977.

Shusterman, Richard, *Pragmatist Aesthetics: Living Beauty, Rethinking Art*, 2nd edn, Lanham, MD: Rowman & Littlefield Publishers, 2000.

Shuttleworth, Sally, *George Eliot and Nineteenth-Century Science: The Make-Believe of a Beginning*, Cambridge: Cambridge University Press, 1984.

Sidney, Sir Philip, *Defence of Poesie, Astrophil and Stella and Other Writings*, ed. Elizabeth Porges-Watson, London: Everyman, 1997.

Siskin, Clifford, *The Work of Writing: Literature and Social Change in Britain, 1700–1830*, Baltimore: The Johns Hopkins University Press, 1998.

Sleigh, Charlotte, *Literature and Science*, Basingstoke: Palgrave, 2011.

Slinn, E. Warwick, 'Language and Truth in *The Ring and the Book*', *Victorian Poetry* 27.3–4 (1989), 115–33.

Slinn, E. Warwick, 'Experimental Form in Victorian Poetry', in Joseph Bristow (ed.), *The Cambridge Companion to Victorian Poetry*, Cambridge: Cambridge University Press, 2000, pp. 46–66.

Small, Helen, *The Value of the Humanities*, Oxford: Oxford University Press, 2012.

Smiles, Samuel, *Self-Help: With Illustrations of Character, Conduct, and Perseverance*, ed. Peter W. Sinemma, Oxford: Oxford University Press, 2002.

Snow, C. P., *The Two Cultures and the Scientific Revolution*, The Rede Lecture 1959, New York: Cambridge University Press, 1961.

Snyder, Laura J., 'Discoverer's Induction', *Philosophy of Science* 64.4 (1997), 580–604.

Snyder, Laura, *Reforming Philosophy: A Victorian Debate on Science and Society*, Chicago: The University of Chicago Press, 2006.

Specht, Benjamin, 'Experiment und Metapher: Zur Tropologie der Wissenschaft', in Michael Gamper (ed.), *Experiment und Literatur: Themen, Methoden, Theorien*, Göttingen: Wallstein, 2010, pp. 252–77.

Spencer, Herbert, *First Principles* [1855], 2nd edn, London: Williams and Norgate, 1867.

Spencer, Herbert, *Principles of Psychology* [1857], vol. 1, 3rd edn, New York: D. Appleton, 1910.

Stachowiak, Herbert (ed.), *Der Aufstieg des pragmatischen Denkens im 19. und 20. Jahrhundert*, Hamburg: Meiner, 1987.

Stanley, Matthew, 'Where Naturalism and Theism Met: The Uniformity of Nature', in Gowan Dawson and Bernard Lightman (eds), *Victorian Scientific Naturalism: Community, Identity, Continuity*, Chicago: The University of Chicago Press, 2014, pp. 242–62.

Staten, Henry, 'The Wrong Turn of Aesthetics', in Jane Elliott and Derek Attridge (eds), *Theory after Theory*, London: Routledge, 2011, pp. 223–36.

Staten, Henry, *Spirit Becomes Matter: The Brontës, George Eliot, Nietzsche*, Edinburgh: Edinburgh University Press, 2014.

Stiening, Gideon, 'Am "Ungrund" oder: Was sind und zu welchem Ende studiert man Poetologien des Wissens?', *KulturPoetik* 7.2 (2007), 234–48.

Stott, Rebecca, 'Darwin's Barnacles: Mid-Century Victorian Natural History and the Marine Grotesque', in Roger Luckhurst and Josephine McDonagh (eds), *Transactions and Encounters*, Manchester: Manchester University Press, 2002, pp. 151–81.

Sutherland, John, 'A Note on the Composition', in Wilkie Collins, *The Moonstone*, ed. John Sutherland, Oxford: Oxford University Press, 1999, pp. xxx–xxxix.

Sutherland, John, 'Introduction', in Wilkie Collins, *The Moonstone*, ed. John Sutherland, Oxford: Oxford University Press, 1999, pp. vii–xxix.

Sutherland, John, 'Introduction', in Wilkie Collins, *Armadale*, ed. John Sutherland, London: Penguin, 2004, pp. vii–xxxv.

Symonds, John Addington, 'Culture: Its Meaning and Its Uses', *The Key of Blue and Other Prose Essays* [1892], London: Elkin Mathews & John Lane, 1893, pp. 195–216.

Talairach-Vielmas, Laurence, *Wilkie Collins, Medicine and the Gothic*, Cardiff: University of Wales Press, 2009.

Tate, Gregory, *The Poet's Mind: The Psychology of Victorian Poetry*, Oxford: Oxford University Press, 2012.

Teukolsky, Rachel, *The Literate Eye: Victorian Art Writing and Modernist Aesthetics*, Oxford: Oxford University Press, 2009.

The Cambridge Annotated Study Bible, new rev. standard version, ed. Howard Clark Kee, Cambridge: Cambridge University Press, 1993.

The Old Yellow Book: *Source of Browning's* The Ring and the Book*, in Complete Photo-Reproduction with Translation, Essay, and Notes*, ed. Charles W. Hodell, Washington, DC: Carnegie Institution, 1908.

Thomas, Ronald R., 'The Moonstone, Detective Fiction and Forensic Science', in Jenny Bourne Taylor (ed.), *The Cambridge Companion to Wilkie Collins*, Cambridge: Cambridge University Press, 2006, pp. 65–78.

Todorov, Tzvetan, *The Poetics of Prose*, trans. Richard Howard, Ithaca: Cornell University Press, 1977.

Tomaiuolo, Saverio, *In Lady Audley's Shadow: Mary Elizabeth Braddon and Victorian Literary Genres*, Edinburgh: Edinburgh University Press, 2010.

Tondre, Michael, 'The Interval of Expectation: Delay, Delusion, and the Psychology of Suspense in *Armadale*', *ELH* 78.3 (2011), 585–608.

Tönnies, Merle, '"Serious" Science vs "Light" Entertainment? Femininity Concepts in Nineteenth-Century British Medical Discourse and Popular Fiction', in Anne-Julia Zwierlein (ed.), *Unmapped Countries: Biological Visions in Nineteenth-Century Literature and Culture*, London: Anthem Press, 2005, pp. 183–92.

Trench, Richard Chenevix, *On the Study of Words: Lectures Addressed (Originally) to the Pupils at the Diocesan Training-School Winchester*, 9th edn, enl. and revd, London: John W. Parker & Son, 1859.

Trollope, Anthony, *An Autobiography*, vol. 2, Edinburgh: William Blackwood and Sons, 1883.

Tucker, Herbert F., 'Dramatic Monologue and the Overhearing of Lyric', in Chaviva Hošek and Patricia Barker (eds), *Lyric Poetry: Beyond New Criticism*, Ithaca: Cornell University Press, 1985, pp. 226–43.

Tucker, Herbert F., *Epic: Britain's Heroic Muse 1790–1910*, Oxford: Oxford University Press, 2008.

Turner, Frank M., 'The Victorian Conflict between Science and Religion: A Professional Dimension', *Isis* 69.3 (1978), 356–76.

Tylor, Edward B., *Researches into the Early History of Mankind and the Development of Civilization*, London: John Murray, 1865.

Tylor, Edward B., '[Review of] Lectures on the Science of Language [. . .] by Max Müller', *Quarterly Review* 119:238 (April 1866), 394–435.

Tylor, Edward B., *Primitive Culture: Researches into the Development of Mythology, Philosophy, Religion, Art, and Custom*, 2 vols, London: John Murray, 1871.

Tylor, Edward B., *Anthropology: An Introduction to the Study of Man and Civilization*, London: Macmillan, 1881.

Unsigned Article, 'The Fine Arts and Public Taste in 1853', *Blackwood's Edinburgh Magazine* 74.453 (1853), 89–104.

Unsigned Article, 'Art', in *The Encyclopaedia Britannica: A Dictionary of Arts, Sciences, and General Literature*, vol. 2, 9th edn, Edinburgh: Black, 1875, pp. 636–9.

Unsigned Article, 'Fine Arts', in *The Encyclopaedia Britannica: A Dictionary of Arts, Sciences, and General Literature*, vol. 9, 9th edn, Edinburgh: Black, 1879, pp. 194–215.

Unsigned Article, 'Poetry', in *The Encyclopaedia Britannica: A Dictionary of Arts, Sciences, and General Literature*, vol. 19, 9th. edn, Edinburgh: Black, 1885, pp. 256–73.

Unsigned Review, 'Mr Darwin's Recent Inductions', *Eclectic Review* 14 (April 1868), 345–62.

Unsigned Review, *Spectator* xxxix [9 June 1866], in Norman Page (ed.), *Wilkie Collins: The Critical Heritage*, London: Routledge & Kegan Paul, 1974, pp. 149–50.

Unsigned Review, *Saturday Review* xxi [16 June 1866], in Norman Page (ed.), *Wilkie Collins: The Critical Heritage*, London: Routledge & Kegan Paul, 1974, pp. 151–5.

Vanderbeke, Dirk, *Theoretische Welten und Literarische Transformationen: Die Naturwissenschaften im Spiegel der 'science studies' und der Literatur des ausgehenden 20. Jahrhunderts*, Tübingen: Niemeyer, 2004.

Venn, John, *The Principles of Empirical or Inductive Logic*, London: Macmillan & Co., 1889.

Vogl, Joseph, 'Für eine Poetologie des Wissens', in Karl Richter, Jörg Schönert and Michael Titzmann (eds), *Die Literatur und die Wissenschaften 1770–1930*, Stuttgart: M&P, 1997, pp. 107–27.

Vogl, Joseph (ed.), *Poetologien des Wissens um 1800*, München: Fink, 1999.

Watt Smith, Tiffany, *On Flinching: Theatricality and Scientific Looking from Darwin to Shell Shock*, Oxford: Oxford University Press, 2014.

Weekes, Sir Henry, *Lectures on Art: Delivered at the Royal Academy London, with a Short Sketch of the Author's Life*, London: Bickers and Son, 1880.

Whewell, William, *The Philosophy of the Inductive Sciences: Founded on their History, a New Edition, with Correction and Additions*, 2 vols, London: W. Parker, West Strand, 1847.

Whewell, William, 'The General Bearing of the Great Exhibition on the Progress of Art and Science', in *Lectures on the Results of the Exhibition: Delivered before the Society of Arts, Manufactures, and Commerce*, London: David Bogue, 1852, pp. 3–25.

Whewell, William, *On the Philosophy of Discovery: Chapters Historical and Critical*, London: John W. Parker & Son, 1860.

White, Paul, *Thomas Huxley: Making the Man of Science*, Cambridge: Cambridge University Press, 2003.

White, Paul, 'Ministers of Culture: Arnold, Huxley and Liberal Anglican Reform of Learning', *History of Science* 43 (2005), 115–38.

White, Paul, 'The Experimental Animal in Victorian Britain', in Lorraine Daston and Greg Mitman (eds), *Thinking with Animals: New Perspectives on Anthropomorphism*, New York: Columbia University Press, 2005, pp. 59–82.

Willer, Stefan, *Poetik der Etymologie: Texturen sprachlichen Wissens in der Romantik*, Berlin: Akademie Verlag, 2003.

Williams, Raymond, *Culture and Society 1780–1950*, Harmondsworth: Penguin, 1963.

Williams, Raymond, *Keywords: A Vocabulary of Culture and Society*, London: Fontana Press, 1988.

Willis, Martin, *Vision, Science and Literature, 1870–1920*, London: Pickering & Chatto, 2011.

Wise, M. Norton and Crosbie Smith, 'Work and Waste: Political Economy and Natural Philosophy in Nineteenth-Century Britain (II)', *History of Science* 27.4 (1989), 391–449.

Wolff, Robert Lee, *Sensational Victorian: The Life and Fiction of Mary Elizabeth Braddon*, New York: Garland, 1979.

Wolfreys, Julian, *Victorian Hauntings: Spectrality, Gothic, the Uncanny and Literature*, Basingstoke: Palgrave, 2002.

Wolfreys, Julian, *Literature, in Theory: Tropes, Subjectivities, Responses, and Responsibilities*, London: Continuum, 2010.

Wood, Michael, *Literature and the Taste of Knowledge*, Cambridge: Cambridge University Press, 2005.

Woolford, John, *Robert Browning*, Tavistock: Northcote House Publishers, 2007.

Wordsworth, William, 'Preface' [1800/1802], in William Wordsworth and S. T. Coleridge, *Lyrical Ballads 1798*, ed. W. J. B. Owen, Oxford: Oxford University Press, 1967, pp. 153–79.

Wordsworth, William, *Selected Poetry*, ed. Stephen Gill and Duncan Wu, Oxford: Oxford University Press, 1997.

Yates, Edmund, *His Recollections and Experiences*, vol. 2, London: Richard Bentley and Son, 1884.

Yeo, Richard R., *Defining Science: William Whewell, Natural Knowledge, and Public Debate in Early Victorian Britain*, Cambridge: Cambridge University Press, 1993.

Young, Paul, *Globalization and the Great Exhibition: The Victorian New World Order*, Basingstoke: Palgrave Macmillan, 2009.

Zeitz, Lisa M. and Peter Thoms, 'Collins's Use of the Strasbourg Clock in *Armadale*', *Nineteenth-Century Literature* 45.4 (1991), 495–503.

Zieger, Susan, 'Opium, Alcohol, and Tobacco: The Substances of Memory in *The Moonstone*', in Pamela K. Gilbert (ed.), *A Companion to Sensation Fiction*, Chichester: Wiley-Blackwell, 2011, pp. 208–19.

Zietlow, Paul, 'The Ascending Concerns of *The Ring and the Book*: Reality, Moral Vision, and Salvation', *Studies in Philology* 84.2 (1987), 194–218.

Zola, Emile, 'The Experimental Novel' [1879], in Gerhard Stilz and Bernhard Greiner (eds), *Naturalismus in England 1880–1920: Texte zur Forschung*, Darmstadt: Wissenschaftliche Buchgesellschaft, 1983, pp. 53–69.

Zwierlein, Anne-Julia, *Der physiologische Bildungsroman im 19. Jahrhundert: Selbstformung, Leistungsethik und organischer Wandel in Naturwissenschaft und Literatur*, Heidelberg: Winter, 2009.

Index

mind (*cont.*)
  Tylor and, 158
  Venn and, 43
  Victorian ideas of, 11, 250
  Whewell and, 34–5, 37, 42
  see also reason; thought
Mitchell, Robert, 5, 254
model-making, 4, 5, 233–4
modernism, 11, 207
Moonstone, The (Collins)
  characters as active participants,
    248, 249, 253
  experimentation, 251–5
  exploration of agency, 249–50
  psychological confusion, 250–1
  reader participation, 253–4
  subverting detective fiction, 248–9
  writing process, 252, 255
morality
  Browning and, 201, 202, 204,
    208–9, 213n
  Collins and, 77, 78
  Eliot and, 95, 98–9, 100, 101,
    102–3, 106n, 128–9, 137n
  Huxley and, 59
  Lewes and, 140
  Mill and, 31, 47
  scientific, 48
Morris, William, 169–70, 172, 179
  'The Aims of Art', 170–1
  News from Nowhere, 174–7, 185n
  see also work-pleasure
mosaic analogy, 111, 112, 150, 216
Müller, Friedrich Max
  analogy and comparison, 147
  and Darwin, 148, 161n
  deaf-mutes, communication, 154–5
  dependence of reason on language,
    152, 162n
  language as self-regulatory, 163
  language as tool and subject-matter,
    10–11, 150–1, 152–3
  logos, 144–5, 150
  metaphor, 147–9
  roots, 145–6
  on science, 49, 50
  and Tylor, 155, 156
  word-gathering, 144–5, 146–7,
    149–50, 153
  and writing, 151
museums, 17, 169
music, 20, 57, 58, 120, 166, 179

naming, 93, 141–3, 145
natural history *see Sea-Side Studies*
  (Lewes)
natural selection, 8, 25, 27, 45n
  linguistic, 148
nature (non-human)
  art and, 28, 40, 164
  culture and, 12, 55, 73n, 175–6
  as experimenter, 11, 39–40, 41
  God-created, 21–2, 23
  laws of, 64–5
  science and, 2, 4, 65, 105n
  as teacher, 58–60, 62, 63
necessity, 33, 34, 167, 171
nervous system, 223, 227, 255
niche-building, 55, 94–5, 101, 166,
  236
Nord, Deborah E., 124
Norris, Christopher, *Against
  Relativism*, 16n

object
  Allen and, 55
  art as, 165–6, 175, 178
  Bernard and, 52
  Braddon and, 219, 221
  Collins and, 238, 243, 250, 251–2,
    253, 255
  Eliot and, 126–7
  James and, 131
  Lewes and, 80, 82, 83, 86, 110–11,
    114–15
  literature and, 164
  Mill and, 30–1
  Müller and, 145–6, 147
  Paley and, 22, 24
  of science, 61
  vs subject, 6–7, 12
  and subject, 48–9, 130
  traceable, 6
  Tylor and, 157, 158–9
  Whewell and, 34, 35, 43
objectivity
  Butler and, 129–30
  and established knowledge, 2
  impartial, 70, 77
  Müller and, 151, 152
  scientific, 268, 269
observation
  Allen and, 54–5, 56
  Bernard and, 101
  Browning and, 10